The Journal of a Victorian lady

Louisa Thomas of Hollingbourne

Edited by Helen Allinson

Synjon Books 2011

Synjon Books
5 Homestead View, Borden,
Sittingbourne, Kent. ME9 8JQ

ISBN 978 0 904373 14 1

Contents

Acknowledgements

The journals which form the basis of this book belong to Bryan Gipps the great great grandson of Louisa Thomas the diarist. His generosity in allowing me to borrow the precious journals enabled the book to be written.

Thanks are due to my husband, Barry, who took all of the photographs which are not otherwise acknowledged. My parents, John and Dorothea Teague, have given me encouragement throughout the project and read every word more than once. Both they and Barry have proof read the text. My brother, Tony Teague, has kindly spent hours formatting the book.

Introduction

Louisa Thomas kept a diary for eighty years, from the age of sixteen to the age of ninety-five. It is most unusual for the diaries of one person to cover such a long span, in her case from 1826 to 1905, from the age of stage coach travel to the age of the motor car. The volumes contain a complete record of the life of a privileged, wealthy woman of the time. Once she was married Louisa rarely omitted a day in her journals. The focus is personal, yet she had a keen interest in politics and national events and social changes impinge. Louisa was not an introspective diarist who pondered her own thoughts and feelings, rather she recorded daily doings, so her character emerges only slowly as we read and we get to know her immediate family and their joys and sorrows. She was extremely discreet; her journals would not have caused trouble if read by a curious servant. At times this makes them tantalising to read and we wish she had written more. However her purpose in writing was as an aid to memory for herself when looking back.

She purchased small, hard-covered, many-paged notebooks and wrote in the dates herself. Her handwriting is always legible, large and flowing. Twenty-six volumes of Louisa's journals are still in existence, treasured by her descendants.

A few of the journals today

This book was started in October 2009 when I began to borrow the volumes to transcribe. That took a year and resulted in a 500 page document on my computer. The text of the diaries has been reduced here to a little less than half the original length. I have shortened innumerable entries and left out many completely. My aim was both to allow Louisa's voice speak and to let the narrative flow. For decades every entry began with a note of letters received and letters written. These have been omitted, but it is noteworthy that the writing of letters was an important daily task for Louisa. I have also omitted most references to the weather as being of little interest. Louisa's journals are short on punctuation, almost in note form at times, but after all she was writing only for herself.

The diaries have never been published before. I learned of them when researching my book on the history of Hollingbourne[1] during the 1990s, when the late Bryan Gipps[2] loaned me a volume. He had already compiled a pamphlet published by Hollingbourne church entitled 'Hollingbourne and the Thomas family'. This contains a number of short extracts. It is certain that the diaries deserve a wide readership.

A page of one of the journals showing Louisa's clear handwriting

[1]   'Hollingbourne a Kentish parish'

[2]   The father of Bryan Gipps who loaned me the journals.

Family Tree

Louisa's family

Richard Thomas (1792-1881) m Louisa deVisme (1810-1911)
(changed to her mother's maiden name, born Goldsmid)

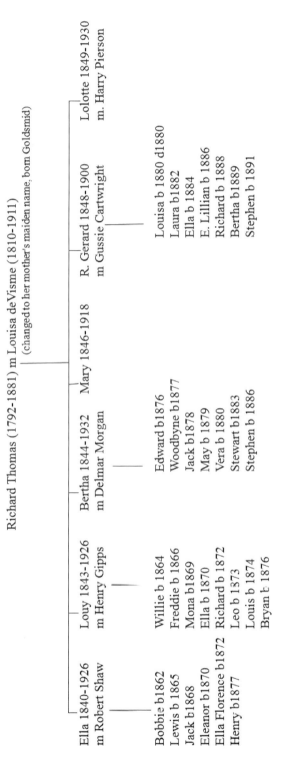

Ella 1840-1926 m Robert Shaw	Louy 1843-1926 m Henry Gipps	Bertha 1844-1932 m Delmar Morgan	Mary 1846-1918	R. Gerard 1848-1900 m Gussie Cartwright	Lolotte 1849-1930 m. Harry Pierson
Bobbie b1862	Willie b 1864	Edward b1876		Louisa b 1880 d1880	
Lewis b 1865	Freddie b 1866	Woodbyne b1877		Laura b1882	
Jack b1868	Mona b1869	Jack b1878		Ella b 1884	
Eleanor b1870	Ella b 1870	May b 1879		E. Lillian b 1886	
Ella Florence b1872	Richard b 1872	Vera b 1880		Richard b 1888	
Henry b1877	Leo b 1873	Stewart b1883		Bertha b1889	
	Louis b 1874	Stephen b 1886		Stephen b 1891	
	Bryan b 1876				

These are not necessarily given names but names used in the journals for example Bertha's daughter Woodbyne was christened Bertha.

1826-1829: A cosmopolitan youth

Louisa Thomas was born Louisa Goldsmid to a wealthy family in Dorking in 1810. Her parents, though both English, were of very different descent. Her mother Louisa de Visme had Huguenot origins whilst her father John Goldsmid was Jewish. John's father was Benjamin Goldsmid a banker who became powerful during the Napoleonic Wars through loaning money to the government. Tragically both he and his brother over-reached themselves in business were declared bankrupt, became depressed and committed suicide. Benjamin's widow converted to Christianity and she and her children were baptised. Jews were almost second-class citizens in England for much of the early 19th century, unable for instance before the 1850s to hold public office unless they converted.

Louisa's earliest memories were of living at the mansion her grandfather Phillip de Visme leased for a decade in Notting Hill. The house was then called Notting Hill House but later renamed Aubrey House. When Louisa was a child the mansion stood in the countryside.

We can glean a little about Louisa's childhood from her journals. She refers on several occasions to being brought up as 'one of seven'. She had only two siblings however and the other four children were maternal cousins. These were the children of her mother's sister Harriette de Visme and her husband barrister Edward Goulburn, (the Uncle Go of the journals). Harriette died young in 1823 and the four children were sent to live with their Aunt Louisa, (our diarist's mother). The two daughters, Harriet and Susan died young in the 1830s. The sons were named Edward and Freddy. Edward, although eight years younger, remained close to his cousin Louisa all his life.

Young Louisa spent much of her late childhood and early adulthood in Paris with her parents and siblings. Brother Louis was a year younger than she and sister Amelia, (Milly in the diaries), was four years younger.

In Paris the family moved in the highest social circles. Sir Sidney Smith, a wealthy ex naval officer, who had found fame during the Napoleonic Wars was one of their friends.

8

Notting Hill House drawn by Louisa's mother Louisa Goldsmid. (Courtesy of the Royal Borough of Kensington and Chelsea)

In 1826 when she was sixteen, Louisa started to write her first journal in a slim, soft-back notebook. She had not yet made her debut at the French court and was still being educated at home. Her cousins had returned to live with their father when he remarried.

Louisa was educated to a very high standard in languages and in literature. She could read and write German, French and Italian. To broaden her general knowledge she read subjects from Encyclopaedia Britannica. The expected social graces of singing, playing the piano and dancing needed to be

9

practised. Louisa had terrific energy and loved to dance. She was not very musical and we do not hear of requests for her to entertain with a song. When relaxing she played shuttlecock or chess with Milly. Mama and Papa often dined out or went to the theatre, Grandmama Goldsmid called every week.

The journal begins:
Rue St George 4 Paris, **November 26th 1826**.
I have often represented to myself the satisfaction derived from a journal. I do not mean by this the pleasure of writing |it but the pleasure of returning to it when written – for as it often happens that the most agreeable events of our lives are forgotten – whilst those which we would rather have banished from our minds are ready at all times to present themselves to our recollection. I have therefore resolved to write all that befalls me with the greatest exactness'.
Went to Lord Granville's (*the British Ambassador*) chapel, heard a good sermon. Baron de Mielle, a savant; called he writes for several periodicals. Read prayers at home in afternoon. Wrote to Aunt Ella. Endeavoured to form a drama on the history of Job, but did not succeed.
27th Worked, repeated to Mama a page of Shakespeare's 'King Lear' & the same quantity of Voltaire, a stanza of Orlando's Furioso, a portion of German grammar, read a chapter of Campe's Robinson Crusoe. After luncheon visited with Mama. After dinner read chapter of Gibbon's "Decline & Fall of Roman Empire".
December 12th Read German. Out in carriage with Mama & Louis, began to learn Arabic with Papa.
16th Walked to the Tuileries with Mama, read the Bible, read Gibbon, practised for the dancing mistress.
19th Louis set off for London. After luncheon out in the carriage with Milly & Grandmama, we proceeded to the Louvre to view the curiosities that have lately been sent from Pompeii, not yet to be seen.
27th Practised dancing. Out in carriage with Grandmama who bought us each a pink silk gown.
31st Sunday. After the service I was confirmed by Bishop Luscombe *(the Embassy chaplain)* with four others. In evening charades.
1827 January 1st Went to the Grand Couvert Du Roi. (*one of the ante chambers at Versailles*) We had a delightful view of

the royal family. The Dauphin has a very foolish countenance, ladies loaded with feathers & diamonds, court ladies in magnificent dresses dazzling with light. Music & singing.

10th Read the Bible & my lessons, played at battledore & shuttlecock. Went in the carriage with Mama to pay visits, took Papa to the Bourse & brought him home. Played chess after dinner.

11th Sir Sidney Smith brought us bonbons.

There is then a gap in the journals, with the second volume starting some months later in 1828. Louisa has made her debut and attends social events.

1828 July 24th In confusion on account of preparations for journey to Dieppe.

27th Arose 4.30, breakfasted, set out for Dieppe at 6, slept at Vernon.

28th Slept at Rouen, visited the cathedral. Magnificent.

August 4th Bathed for first time since arrived, very agreeable. The tent for undressing pitched on the shore, the conducteur carries one out into the sea. This method not half so convenient as the English bathing machine. Papa set off for Paris.

September 13th Expedition to a chateau with friends, several carriages, a nine hour outing.

19th At 6 entered steam packet *(with Papa)* at 8 to bed. At 5 in morning at Brighton. Delightful passage. Went & found Uncle Gerard & Ella both in bed at their hotel.[3]

21st Travelled with Gerard & Ella as far as Horley where slept in a very clean inn.

22nd Set out 11, in London by ½ past 1. Ella's house at St Andrews Place delightful, the streets of London appear spacious deserts after those of Paris.

24th Went with Papa to see *(John)* Martin's picture of the 'Destruction of Ninevah', quite magnificent. Ella was good enough to buy a gown for Milly & myself. Went to Kensington & the new ride round Hyde Park which is beautiful.

October 2nd To our old house in Dorset Square to fetch away the things we need in Paris.

3rd To Drury Lane theatre to see 'The Man of the World.'

4th Packed & took leave of E & G, drank tea at Chatham.

5th At 5 in morning arrived in Dover, breakfasted York Hotel. At 7.30 on to steam packet to Calais, then on to Boulogne

---

[3]   Uncle Gerard de Visme was Mama's brother & Ella was his wife.

hotel. Mr Harry Goldsmid called & begged us to take tea at his house where saw Mammy Steele our old nurse. Travelled all night.

6th Paris, exhausted, all our party returned from Dieppe.

7th Arranged the house which was in confusion. Grandmama dined here.

November 5th It is reported that yesterday placards were put up in the street announcing that if the price of bread be not diminished His Majesty shall be guillotined.

10th Dined at Grandmama's[4] to keep Papa's 40th birthday.

21st Read German. We were introduced to Madame de Genlis, *(a famous French writer)* all alone, one maid, 84 in complete possession of faculties, still writing.

December 2nd Louis left for England, we miss him very much.

5th To a little dance, very agreeable, but Papa would take me away at 11.30 in spite of all I could say or do.

11th We held a ball which succeeded very well, danced till 1.30.

1829 January 7th To Duc d'Orleans reception it was brilliant.

8th Mr Trafford's ball, we arrived first at 8.30, our two male servants there all day assisting, orchestra delightful, rooms wonderfully arranged, stayed till 3.30 ball over by 4.

February 5th The grand ball at Monsieur de Vallarino's. Over 2500 people present, 500 came unasked, the rooms too crowded to move.

---

[4]   Jessie Goldsmid

1835-1838: A spinster in Brighton

There is now a gap in the journals until 1835. Perhaps Louisa wrote journals during these years and destroyed them later in life. The missing years must have been painful ones for we know from later references in the journals that it was during 1829 that her father left the family never to be seen by his wife and children again. Although John Goldsmid had deserted them there was no rift with other Goldsmid relatives. Dear Uncle Albert, Papa's brother, and his wife Caroline remained close.[5]

Mama moved with Louisa, Louis and Milly to Brighton. They remained wealthy, and completely socially acceptable to those near the top of the social pyramid. Nevertheless life inevitably lost some of its glittering promise for a while. Louisa, Louis and Milly changed their surname by deed poll to de Visme.

It was also during 1829 that the four Goulburn cousins returned to live again with their Aunt Louisa and three cousins on the untimely death of their step-mother Esther Chetwynd.[6]

Time was passing and most of Louisa's contemporaries were married by the age of 25. We can sense her anxiety on this point in her Valentine's Day entry for 1835 and also see her enjoyment of the company of good-looking, intelligent men. She was far from being a beauty herself, but was bright, lively and interested in others. Importantly, any prospective husband could be certain of a large dowry.

Brighton during the 1830s was a place of style and distinction with crowds of visitors. The town had long been favoured by royalty, the Royal Pavilion had been remodelled, England's elite came for the sea air, sea bathing and to be seen.

The town had experienced a great building boom during the 1820s and early 1830s when Kemp Town and Brunswick Town were erected. Silwood Place, built in 1833, where Louisa, her siblings and Mama lived was part of this boom; a close of fine houses whose architecture can still be admired today.

---

[5]   Uncle Albert Goldsmid was a colonel who had fought at Waterloo.

[6]   'The Goulburn Norwich Diaries' ed N Henderson.

Silwood Place today

Beside Silwood Place stood Silwood House a grand residence which had been erected in 1827. It was designed for Sir David Scott a wealthy director of the East India Company, His son Sibbald and daughter Ellen became life-long friends of Louisa and Milly. Neighbours in Silwood Place included Horace Smith and his family. Horace was a well known novelist and humorist and Louisa formed an enduring friendship with his daughters Rosalind and Eliza. After Horace Smith's death in 1849 they continued his tradition of hosting literary and artistic parties. The Smith's parties were attended by such luminaries as the Rev. Sydney Smith, Dr Gideon Mantell the geologist and the actor Charles Kean.

Louisa and her friends saw a good deal of Kean for a while. Then in his twenties he was becoming a favourite with fashionable society. His famous father, the actor Edmund Kean, had cut him off, but by 1838 Charles became a brilliant success in London. When Louisa knew him he was establishing himself in the provinces and appearing at Brighton's Theatre Royal.

The elite of Brighton mingled at many social occasions in the town. Balls and concerts were held at the Old Ship Hotel with its Assembly Rooms and card room.

Brighton's beautiful suspension Chain Pier was put up in 1823 and this enabled the town to improve as a seaport by providing better landing and embarkation facilities for the rapidly increasing passenger traffic between England and France. No longer did passengers have to be carried the last few yards to shore. Steam vessels then began to sail from Brighton to Dieppe.

For centuries the only church in Brighton had been St Nicholas', where Louisa was later to marry. By the 1830s the town had outgrown the little church and several new ones had been built. St Peter's, constructed of a dazzling white stone, went up in the 1820s and here the Rev. Henry Wagner was the incumbent for over forty years. He had a large personal fortune and a great devotion to his many parishioners. Five other churches were built using Wagner's own money and public subscription. Louisa's brother Louis had been ordained and appointed curate to the Rev. Wagner. Louisa, Milly and their mother attended the church every Sunday morning and afternoon, Louisa often commenting on the sermons in her journal. As was then the convention she refers to all the clergymen in the journals as 'Mr' not 'Rev'.

It was through her brother that Louisa became involved in helping for a while at the church school and in a 'District.' The parish was divided into districts and a pair of ladies collected for the poor within it and also visited needy cases. This did not awaken a hidden vocation in Louisa. However after she married, though she was never involved in this kind of formal voluntary work again, she helped the poor of Hollingbourne for the rest of her life.

Oriental Place today.

It was during this period that Louis' mental health began to give cause for concern and he was obliged to give up his theological studies at Oxford, and ceased to work as a curate.

Louisa always loved art. She was a good amateur artist who was asked to do portraits for friends, and above all she loved to go and look at great paintings. Whilst in Brighton she got to know the Irish artist William Mulready who gave her some tips on her technique.

It was also at this time that the Duppa family became close and lasting friends. It was they who brought about Louisa's marriage, for it was on a visit to the Duppa's family home in Hollingbourne, Kent that they introduced Louisa to Richard Thomas her future husband. There were in all eleven Duppa siblings, a lively, musical, high-spirited group who did much to enliven Louisa's early years in the village.

1835 February 10th Today reached a quarter of a century! 25 years have passed over my head. In the evening went to while away the dreary lonely hours of Lady Lachampton.

11th Called on Mrs Wykeham, at her request promised to give her a few instructions in German.

14th Valentine's Day, made by us the spinsters' day. Milly & I dined at Miss Greathed's with two Miss Palmers. Where shall we all be next Valentine's Day?

15th Mr Yard preached at the old church in the morning, Louis in the afternoon.

16th Dined, Louis & I, at Sir Gregory & Lady Way's.

17th A morning at Mr Mantell's museum with Mr Rickards, afterwards walked with him to Kemp Town. He dined with us.

18th A long visit of two hours, from Sir William & Major Hutchinson the father is a terrifying knight of the old school – but a very agreeable old man, he brought us some of his poetry. His son a very pleasing soldier, and very good looking.

19th A soiree at home, invited 100 people & 40 came, the night was most stormy.

20th The Miss Dennisons & Miss Greathed accompanied us to the Chain Pier to see Captain Norton's experiment. He has invented a shell to set on fire ammunition wagons which he wishes to bring into general use in the army, but which is opposed by the veterans of the engineers, he has laboured 15 years to perfect it. Sir William Hutchinson & son met us at the pier when fuse fired off to satisfaction of all. In the evening to a regular sitting party at Lady Carr's.

22nd Louis preached at the old church, his sermon very much approved.

23rd Miss Greathed, the Palmers, Louis & I set off for the County Hospital, I was rather afraid of entering at first, not from fear of infection, but from dread of seeing something horrible. However I took courage, & the sight was rather a satisfactory one, great cleanliness & comfort for the patients.

24th A party to Mr Mantell's museum, each visit it improves on one. Then to Captain Marryat's house which is to be sold tomorrow.

25th Louis, Mama & I went to Captain Marryat's sale & bid for two cups in the form of lotuses, got for 10 shillings but the possessions of Peter Simple were not to be had for nothing.[7]

March 10th Taught at the National School from 10-12, as the schoolmistress is ill.

11th Again to the school, the Miss Dennisons assisted us & Louis. Reading Johnson's 'Tour of the Hebrides.'

12th School again, Mr Wagner taught with us. Gave Mrs Wykeham a lesson in German. Walked with Louis & vicar to the parish houses of which there are five. The first we saw was inhabited on the ground floor by Stuart McKenzie, first cousin to a Scotch peer & related to many of the noble families of Scotland- his wife lay in bed and his daughter, a very pretty interesting looking person, was standing by the fire. He has reduced himself to his present poverty & wretchedness by drinking & has been both town crier and schoolmaster but failed in both employments from the same cause. The second storey was inhabited by a family of the name of Gunn - I never saw a picture of more abject misery than the whole room presented – a wretched mattress on the floor – a few broken chairs & scarcely a spark of fire in a most cheerless grate - Mrs Gunn was hollow eyed & weak with absolute starvation & her child pallid & dirty – her husband is a shrimper & during the stormy weather has not been able to ply his trade, so that they had literally nothing to eat. Mr Wagner gave both her & Mackenzie a Sunday dinner.

16th Went to the school where Louis, & the Dennisons were assisting. Traversed the whole of Brighton & entered every shop in search of a cotton gown to suit us- & after much perseverance succeeded.

19th The school, two walks, a soiree at Horace Smith's, very agreeable, the ventriloquist Mr Love performed, admirable but

---

[7]   'Peter Simple' was a popular seafaring novel by Captain Frederick Marryat.

not over refined, & tedious. He carried on a conversation with five people at once.

April 16th Drank tea, Milly & I, at the Scott's where discussed church with the vicar, Valentines & education with Sibbald Scott, & flowers & magisterial business with Sir David.

18th Drank tea this evening with the three elder Miss Percivals, a stately room in a house in Brunswick Terrace, chairs, tables and sofas immovable from their weight, not a book or sign of occupation visible.

23rd Left Brighton for London *(with Mama)* proceeded to St Andrews Place, where found Uncle Gerard very ill & very much reduced.[8]

24th Edward & Freddy *(Goulburn)* called on us & then we went to the Pantheon a mixture of statue & picture gallery & bazaar. *(on the south side of Oxford Street)*

27th Walked with Edward in the park. Dined at Uncle Go's.[9]

May 5th Went with the boys to the Zoological Gardens where much amused with the quarrels of the bears and monkeys for the distributed buns.

6th Went to the exhibition where Turner's paintings of Hastings etc & Landseer's 'Highland Drovers'. A letter from my Father.

19th Left St Andrews Place, Uncle much better. Coach departed from the Elephant & Castle at 4.30, arrived Brighton 9.30 where we found Milly & Louis.

November 2nd Miss Dennison called to commit her District to our keeping.

3rd Went round the District to receive the money, found the most industrious people generally the least charitable.

20th Dined at Silwood, a large dinner party & a large soiree, plenty of gentlemen.

23rd Aunt Ella arrived. Drank tea at Lady Chetwynd's.

December 9th To a ball at Lady Scott's, a very pleasant ball.

20th Uncle Go, Edward & Freddy spent the day with us.

25th Drank tea at Uncle Go's, a family party –the Chetwynd's[10] & ourselves.

---

8   St Andrews Place where Aunt Ella & Unce Gerard lived was a stylish address on the south east corner of Regents Park, built by John Nash between 1826-28.

9   Uncle Go was Edward Goulburn (1787-1868). He began a career in the army & then when his satirical verses led to him being sued for libel, resigned his commission & trained in the law. He was called to the bar rising to be a serjeant-at-law.

10   Uncle Go's mother was Hon. Susannah Chetwynd daughter of Viscount Chetwynd. When his first wife died he married in 1825 his cousin the Hon. Esther

29th To the 4th Dragoons ball at the Old Ship, beautifully arranged in every respect.

1836 January 8th To a Christmas party at Silwood, games & country dances.

2nd To a little party at Admiral Tomlinson's. Danced.

August 21st (*There is a gap of a few months between one journal & next.*) Mama left us for St Leonards to see Louis.

24th A letter from Mama with a very bad account of Louis.

26th Called on the Duppas, saw a great many beautiful drawings by Edward Duppa.[11]

28th I felt sadly harassed. Uncle Go & Freddy appeared, they have come for two months.

31st A letter from Mama begging Uncle Go to go to St Leonards.

September 1st Committee at National School.

2nd Shopping with Freddy. Louis returned from St Leonards with Uncle Go looking & talking much better. Wrote to Mama who is still very nervous.

4th Louis, I am thankful, is certainly better, happier in mind & tranquil.

5th Louis took his departure for Oxford.

7th At 11 o'clock came Miss Fanny Duppa to drive us to the country in her little pony chaise. We went to Admiral Tomlinson's place & found the young ladies & their brother John at home, had luncheon with them, saw their garden, golden pheasants & returned to dinner. To our great surprise found that Mama had returned in our absence & Freddy & Miss Duppa dined with us.

8th Uncle Go came in, walked out with him, & took places to view Kean in Hamlet.

9th Dined at Uncle Go's where met Kean, & Mr Hogg M.P. for Beverley, I sat between Kean & Uncle Go. A very agreeable day.

15th Kean kindly wrote to beg we would accept the King's Box at the theatre this evening to see him in 'King Lear'- refused as we were engaged to take tea at the Duppa's.

18th Called on Duppas, shopping with Milly. The Tomlinsons drank tea here & accompanied us to see Kean in 'Richard',

---

Chetwynd.

[11]   (Bryan) Edward Duppa was a talented artist who occasionally showed paintings at the Royal Academy.

which he did better than ever. The fullest house ever seen in Brighton.

October 3rd To a soiree dansante where danced three times with Mr Forbes & quadrilles with Frank W. Martyn.

6th Drank tea at the Horace Smith's. Bought a dark mousseline de laine *(woollen muslin)* gown.

8th Church. Uncle Go & the boys came & read 'Pilgrims Progress' & looked over some old letters, a melancholy occupation.

11th Called on Mary Duppa who accompanied us to Mrs Jones' where I danced.

18th Freddy left Brighton for Cambridge to begin his university career, he was very unhappy. Yesterday Kean called & sat with us an hour.

19th A soiree at the Horace Smith's, singing & dancing, the room shook terribly. Kean was in great spirits. Mary Duppa accompanied us. Our old acquaintances Ellen & Emily Thomson called on us, they have not grown up good looking.

21st Drank tea at the Smith's where met Kean, wish I could recollect one half of the amusing anecdotes told by Horace Smith & Kean between whom I sat.

25th In the evening went to see Kean in his 'Edward Mortimer' which he acted magnificently & looked very well, melancholy & interesting.

26th Drank tea at the Duppa's to meet Mulready the artist, an agreeable but very sentimental person. Played at 'Why, When & Where'.

28th Went with Duppas to a lecture by Dr Mantell on corals, interesting but I had heard most of it before. He had some splendid specimens. Spent the day with Duppas, saw their magnificent diamonds.

31st Called on Kate, the vicar accompanied us. A little soiree at home consisting of Chetwynds, Miss Halifax, Duppas, Mrs Mostyn, Mr Kean etc & played at 'Why When & Where'. Poor Kean looking quite out of sorts. He took leave of us as he quits Brighton the day after tomorrow.

November 1st In the evening the Miss Duppas went with us to see Kean in 'Othello'. He acted beautifully, I hope he may succeed in London.

4th Dr Mantell's lecture on the nervous system, his last in Brighton. Went home with Miss Duppa & dined with her, after which Mulready began my portrait.

8th Sat to Mulready, his likeness of me said to be very successful. All the Duppas sat drawing me, talked with them, & in the evening drank tea at the Struth's.

10th Dined on goose at the Duppa's. Only Mulready there. He looked over my drawings & said they were better than he expected them to be.

14th To the Duppa's, walked out with Mary, bought some blue satin bonnets.

17th Called on the Duppas. Edward Duppa arrived, showed me some of his paintings, walked with us to hear the band in Brunswick Square & then into the country. A soiree at the Duppa's.

19th Church, drank tea at the Duppa's, some good advice from Mulready, he wishes I would tell more of what I think.

27th Out shopping with Mama. Edward Duppa called & discussed poor Louis.

December 18th Louis home looking ill. Small party at the Horace Smith's, plenty of music, the Miss Duppas with their brother Frank took us & brought us back.

22nd Mr Scott came in to beg artificial flowers to prepare for the gala tonight. The hairdresser called to curl our heads all over for the Batchelors' Ball, where we appeared as ladies of the court of Louis XIV, dressed after a picture of La Valliere. First went to Lady Carhampton's[12] & Miss Gladwin's to show ourselves. At the first house met Mrs Martyn dressed in some Italian costume, all over red & gold, Mr Scott in Nelson's uniform, & Mr Martyn as a Tyrolean with high crowned hat & jacket of green & gold. The ball was brilliant, Miss Bonham was well dressed as a Turk or Albanian with a scarlet veil & a crescent on her forehead. Mr Derby was a mameluke *(a slave in a Muslim country)* making low salams to everyone who passed down the room. The supper table very striking to look down the tables and see the inhabitants of every country there assembled – home by 3 – some of the people however stayed until 6.

23rd Did not go to church in the morning not being well but went in afternoon.

26th Drank tea at the Rooper's & acted charades with George & Edward Rooper & John Tomlinson, 'Innocence' & 'Bondage' & then danced with Mr Moore & Edward Rooper.

---

12   Lady Carhampton was the widow of Viscount Carhampton.

28th Drank tea at Lady Carhampton's, played at Commerce & won a shilling-Miss Campion taught me a lace stitch.

29th Dined at Mr Gregory Way's.[13] Went to Mr Moore's in the evening, talked to Mr Rooper & Mulready who gave me some more good advice.

1837 February 22nd Played at Vingt et Un, danced with Sibbald Scott & Mr Bethune. A panel of glass in Mrs Steen's door broken during our revelry.

23rd A long walk with Mama, began Ellen Scott's portrait, Sibbald came in dressed as a woman.

24th Another letter from Louis, satisfactory as he likes his new abode. Drank tea at Lady Carhampton's. Rather a large party for an invalid. Played at Avocat.

March 7th Began to read prophet Jonah in Bible. Went to a musical party. I had a rather agreeable coterie in a corner with Horace Smith, Miss Smith, Dr Clay etc

12th The first day of our District – Miss Patching a very simple nice person, daughter to the Quaker coal merchant, came round & saw all the poor people with us. Drank tea at Mrs Walpole's, plenty of singing.

15th Miss Scott changed her name for Maxwell. A bridal breakfast of 50. Went to the ball at Silwood in the evening, danced with F. Wykeham Martin etc, went into supper with Mr Bates & ate wedding cake to the health of the nouveaux maries who are gone to St Leonards. A most pleasant evening.

19th Went half round our district, but could not finish for want of *(visiting)* cards. Want of work the general complaint.

20th A soiree at home & a petit souper in the dining room about 60 people, danced.

23rd Mr Scott sat to me for his portrait, went out with Milly on a shawl hunt. In the evening a party at Duppa's. Danced.

24th A better letter from Louis, Mammy Steele died last week. *(her old nurse)*

26th A soiree at Mrs Mostyn's,[14] abundance of card playing but mostly for love. Commerce, Lotto & two whist tables. Got through our district more easily this morning.

27th A young soiree at Mrs Jordan's, dancing reels, cotillion & charade acting.

---

13   Sir Gregory Way (1776-1844), army officer who distinguished himself in the Peninsular War.

14   Mrs Cecilia Mostyn lived in Silwood Place & became a close friend..

29th Mrs Mostyn called us in to a little dejeuner & after we accompanied her to Mr Frederick Taylor's he is an artist in watercolour, principally Scottish scenery.

30th Sibbald & Ellen Scott & Mrs Perry came to sit to me for their portraits.

April 2nd Went our district circuit, drank tea at Mrs Steer's, whist & commerce.

3rd Paid for & wore our new white shawls, much approved.

18th Worked at our caps for the ball this evening, black lace & velvet & pink ribbons & roses. Dined with the Duppas at 2. At 10 went to the ball. Charlotte Duppa as a Spaniard & Fanny with a Scotch cap & scarf. Mrs Walpole had done the best she could for a fancy ball in a small house. Young ladies as the seasons, children as the months, the floor chalked, walls hung with flowers. Miss Smith in white & silver. Danced with Mr Mantell in moustaches with a ribbon of the legion of honour. An amusing evening, home at 3.

22nd Church. Drank tea with Duppas saw Edward Duppa magnetise the two Miss Gorgons. Never believed animal magnetism before but their stupefaction was so great, their heads rolled & they gave such unmeaning smiles that my faith was taken by force.

26th Consecration of the new church, soiree at the vicarage, a dinner part of 40, only eight of whom were ladies.

May 12th Unfavourable letter from poor dear Louis.

22nd Walked with Mary Duppa & her Godfrey to Hove. Mr Godfrey sat for his picture.

June 4th Our District. Poor Mrs Redpath the Scotch woman who had been burnt has returned. She is miserably poor, past threescore and ten & far from every relation she has in the world.

14th Drank tea at Lady Carhampton's discussed railroads & mines with Horace Smith.

17th A very bad letter from Louis, so Oxford is given up.

21st Mama left us to see Louis. Went to a pic-nic at Shoreham, the Swiss cottage very pretty but the weather & the people cold. Boating on the lake, dinner in the concert room. Danced Roger de Coverly with Horace Smith.

28th The Coronation. *(of Queen Victoria)* An ox roasted whole on the Steine, 50 bathing women & many thousands of children dined on the Steine & pier. The plum pudding nine feet in circumference. We went to the Hove school with the Roopers, saw Coronation medals given to the children. Mr

Rooper gave an exhortation then repaired to a field near the sea where 200 children dined on roast beef, mutton & plum pudding & we with Mama & others waited upon them while the gentlemen carved. Mama returned yesterday, Louis much the same.

July 19th Mama & I drove over to Lewes, arrived at Meriams a very rural place, a cottage in a farmyard surrounded by field & wood, geese, turkeys, dogs & ducks.

22nd Went to Hadlow Down Chapel, a little building commanding one of the most beautiful prospects I ever saw. The chapel itself plain in the extreme but elegant. Mr Edwards is the clergyman & indefatigable among a very ignorant people.

30th Mrs Morgan Thomas took me to Uckfield where met the Maidstone coach which conveyed me safe & sound to the place of my destination. My fellow passengers two ladies & an elderly farmer as far as Tonbridge where the farmer got out - & the old gentleman & I pursued our journey alone till a fearful storm came on & then a soul took shelter within too, one flash of lightning darted down to the south like a long white shaft of flame. Found the Hollingbourne party were all well *(at Hollingbourne House)* except for Mr Duppa. A warm welcome, Edward at home

31st A walk in the garden & fruit eating & a walk in the evening over the fields & hills with Ellen, Charlotte & Fanny. A lovely evening larks soaring & singing & hay smelling sweetly.

August 1st Began a sketch of the house, the cows rushed into the garden & frightened me. Edward painting a picture of all his sisters. Went with Mary in the pony carriage to Mrs Wheeler's a widow lady at Otterden Park, a fine old house of Henry VIII & Elizabeth's reigns. Plenty of portraits said to be by Vandyke & Sir Peter Lely & one really beautiful one of Charles 1 by Vandyke. Mr Goodyer the vicar & his two daughters & Mr Marjoribanks dined there. Danced all the evening with the latter.

3rd Drove with Mary to Pett the seat of Mr G. Sayer who received us & then appeared his colossal sister & a Mrs Cage. Walked in the garden.

4th Began a sketch of Charles I, dined at 3 after receiving great kindness from Mrs Wheeler & her mother Mrs Tattersall. Miss Tattersall is strange & not quite sane, returned to Hollingbourne.

Hollingbourne House (Drawn by Margaret Parsons)

8th Mary & I in the pony phaeton & Fanny & Ellen on horseback went to Chilston the seat of Mr Douglas, an old, solid, square house, the deer grazing in the park & the flower gardens beautiful. From thence to Leeds Castle to call on Mrs

C. Martin, a completely feudal dwelling. *(Leeds Castle had been restored by the Wykeham-Martin family in 1822 and was a few minutes walk from Louisa's home.)* A very cheerful dinner party. Danced with Henry Duppa & Mr Attice.

9th Walked to Hucking on a farming expedition with Henry Duppa.

11th Walked to the village with Harriet & Ellen called on an old lady Mrs Disternell, the village very picturesque.

12th Went to church. Old Mr Hasted[15] read prayers & preached rather indistinctly. The church is a very old <u>clean</u> building with many curious monuments.

13th Drove to Maidstone with Fanny Duppa. Greeted on our way into the shrubbery on our return by the whole party who met us singing.

14th Mr Radcliffe dined here & Mr Thomas. After dinner walked out over the hills & far away.

15th Mr Thomas called & dined here, yesterday out sketching in morning with Henry Duppa & strained my knee so that could not walk much today.[16]

16th Very lamc, only walked in the garden with Henry Duppa & ate cherries, dined at the Douglas's. Mr Douglas a fine looking man & very pleasing, Mrs D very good natured. Almost met with an accident coming home from the darkness of the night the wheels of the carriage got tangled in Mr...

It is frustrating that here the diary ends as the rest of the page is torn out & the rest of the book is empty. The next journal begins four months later on Louisa's wedding day. The initial mentions of Mr Thomas do not hint at the breakneck speed of their courtship and engagement.

---

[15] Rev Edwad Hasted (1760-1865) rector of Hollingbourne, son of the historian of Kent.

[16] Thomas family legend has it that when Richard Thomas saw Louisa at church he was so struck with her that he offered to forego repayment of money he had lent to Duppa, for the privilege of an introduction. Certainly the Duppas were in financial difficulties.

1838-1839: Marriage and the Grand Tour

In December 1837 at the age of 27, Louisa married Richard Thomas in Brighton. Louisa was quite a catch for she brought Richard a dowry of £10,000.[17] At 44 Richard was 17 years older and socially not such a great catch. He was a Kentish squire of ability but not nobility, minor gentry though very important in his own parish. He had inherited Eyhorne House in Hollingbourne from his childless uncle in 1833. This uncle was a Welsh squire and magistrate who had been High Sheriff for Carmarthen, and had bought Eyhorne House in 1789. He had then settled there letting out his Welsh property and beginning the long association of the Thomas family with Hollingbourne. Financially, and in terms of status, Louisa married a little below her, however Richard's less wealthy and less socially well-connected background had the merit of being solidly British, tied to the soil.

Richard himself was a successful gentleman farmer, energetic and athletic as demonstrated by his mountain climbing exploits whilst on the honeymoon. His true interests were masked from Louisa during their courtship and Grand Tour when he was at his most anxious to please her and they were far from home and routine. In truth he was happiest farming, shooting, and playing cricket. Time would prove that he preferred not to travel nor did he share Louisa's hankering after art exhibitions, museums and literature. Nevertheless he dearly loved her and was prepared for her to make changes.

Louisa embarked upon wedded life well provided for. Upside down at the back of her journal are some accounts headed 'For trousseau £100'. It reads:

'Long cloth, muslin, flannel & diaper, tape & binding, embroidered collars, pocket kerchief & lace, lace, shawl, stockings, mousseline de laine, chequered muslin, brooch, gloves, lace for night caps, buckle, boots, purse, cap, prayer book, toothbrush & combs, thimble, scissors, travelling case, apron, stays, boa & cuffs, poplin, velvet, pins, white gloves, sealing wax, embroidery cotton. total £62.'

---

[17]   The value of this in today's money is £441,000. There are numerous ways of calculating the value of money in the past. I have used the National Archives currency converter.

St Nicholas church Brighton where Louisa and Richard were married.

The material such as the chequered muslin (cotton) and the mousseline de laine (fine light woollen fabric) would be made up into dresses by a dressmaker. Nightdresses too would have been prettily stitched by the dressmaker. The trousseau included a good deal of haberdashery for finishing and accessories. Mama had not stinted on the trousseau and this was apart from the money spent on the wedding dress.

Louisa had obviously visited Richard's home Eyhorne House during her stay in Hollingbourne but she was not to take up the reins as mistress of the house until many months had passed.

After the wedding Louisa and Richard were in no hurry to set off on their honeymoon tour of Europe and a week went by in Hastings with congratulatory visits from friends and family. Brother Louis was not well enough to attend the wedding but Louisa and Richard visited him at Warbleton where he was being looked after by a clergyman.

The honeymoon tour followed very much the path of grand tours which had begun in the seventeenth century as a rite of passage for young English noblemen and had become customary for the opulent middle class. A good deal of money and time were essentials. This trend together with widespread rail development ended the Grand Tour. An interest in art, architecture and culture were expected and Louisa certainly had those.

Richard and Louisa's tour lasted a full six months, the first ten weeks of which were passed in Paris. There followed a fortnight journeying south through France to Italy. In Italy they lingered for over two months. Half of June was spent in Switzerland and the tour finished with a week in Germany.

There are occasional mentions of homesickness in the journal but it is apparent that married life got off to a happy start. Louisa recorded an evening of natural misgivings days after the wedding. She was after all entrusting herself completely to this man whom she had known but a short time and leaving behind the close daily companionship she enjoyed with Mama and sister Milly.

When you hold in your hands two of the journals which at first glance appear identical it becomes clear that Louisa was in love with Richard. One is the volume which she took on the Grand Tour and the other is the carefully copied and slightly amended version which she made for him the following year. Hours and hours of copying were required.

In the front of the copy, a real labour of love, is the following verse:

'Go to my husband little book
Folly & fault I know are thine
Yet bid him on thee kindly look
For sake of her who traced each line

Thou'llt speak to him of long passed hours
When first he was not all alone
Thou'llt tell of sunshine & of showers
As where on earth are they not known?

But be the pages bright or dim
Chequered with thought of joy or woe
Say that the brightness came from him
He dried the tear, not made it flow

And should he weary of his vow
His feelings e'er grow cold & stern
Thou, little book, wilt show him how
He loved – and bid that love return.'

Not a good poem but certainly a loving one and Richard must have been touched to receive the gift.

About two thirds of this particular journal is reproduced here. Louisa and Richard embarked from Dover with their carriage accompanied by Louisa's young maid Mary.[18]

1838 December 27th Exchanged my name of de Visme for that I now bear & my maiden status for a married one - God grant that it may be for the happiness & good of my husband & myself. The service was performed in the parish church of St Nicholas, Brighton by the Rev. Henry Wagner. Uncle Go, Uncle Albert, Milly & Charles Duppa being present - I never was so much impressed with anything as with the solemnity of the promise took upon ourselves before God & man. Returned home to Silwood Place – the bells ringing merrily

---

[18]   This was very likely Mary Cover the only maid in Louisa's service when the 1841 census was taken. She must have been a bright and capable girl.

both here & at Hollingbourne – breakfast- an immense cake – a painful parting. A carriage at four & a most prosperous journey at Hastings & along the coast, the white cliffs of Albion, Martello towers, Pevensey Castle, bright moonlight succeeding a cloudless day & arrived at the Marina Hotel about 5 o'clock.

Louisa drawn by Edward Duppa in 1838 and copied by Penny Johnstone

28th Visits from my cousins Edward & Freddy Goulburn. Walked to St Leonards, something like Brunswick Terrace Brighton. Hastings a picturesque irregular town with an ancient castle.
29th Uncle Go, Mary & Fanny Duppa each called on us. Richard gave me that indispensable appendage to a lady & a journey - a dressing case of rosewood inlaid with mother of

pearl. Drank tea at Lady Chetwynd's, only Uncle Go & the Hulls there. Harry Duppa came in unexpectedly in the evening.

30th Harry Duppa breakfasted with us, Mary Duppa then called & then Edward & Freddy. Read prayers with Richard & some essays.

31st Harry Duppa again breakfasted with us, called on his sisters who are staying with their aunt, & on the Hulls[19] & then started for Warbleton to see Louis whom we found rather better & very warm in the welcome he gave us, but he has still the nervous shutting his eyes & breathing. Mr Burgess, a cheerful, pleasing young clergyman resides in the house with him.

1839 January 1st What a change to me the beginning of this year from the beginning of the last, a change in life, & thoughts, habits, feelings, a complete & entire change. Took leave of the Duppas & Hastings & set out for Dover passed through a beautiful countryside till we reached Romney Marsh, the ancient archway at Winchelsea very fine, Martello towers in abundance, Dymchurch Wall an embankment thrown up to protect the Marsh from the encroachment of the sea. All this & more we saw, till night forbade. Reached Dover about 8 & took up our quarters at the Ship Hotel our windows overlooking the harbour. Sailors so unquiet half the night I could hardly sleep, piers, a harbour, steam packets, a castle, & an illuminated clock.

3rd On board a French steamer for Calais, my husband as happy & at ease as the most veteran heart of oak, I ill in the carriage & Mary worse on deck. Reached Calais in 2½ hours. Underwent the questioning at the Douane & Mary was led to a private room where she was closely searched by two women. Dined & slept at the hotel. I felt almost melancholy at being on foreign strand, & beginning life as it seemed again, & many foolish groundless fears took possession of my mind, too foolish to record.

4th Started for Boulogne reached it & the Hotel du Nord, dined at the table d'hote, walked a little about the town. Everyone we met seemed English.

On 5th stayed night at Abbeville and on 7th at Beauvais.

---

[19]   Mrs Jane Hull was Aunt Ella's sister.

8th Left Beauvais, as we rolled along in our comfortable easy carriage, the booted postillion cracking his whip with no slight energy. Arrived in Paris, went to the Hotel de Bristol.

11th Removed to the Hotel Mirabeau, walked in the Tuileries, to the Madeleine. The Miss Halifaxes under the same roof with ourselves. Richard & I called on them after dinner.

14th Went to the little chapel or rather room where Mr Sayer preached. There is something very wretched in a French Sunday the people are all employed in their usual daily calling.

15th Went out shopping with Richard, astonished at the changes in Paris. Called on the Halifaxes, went shopping & bought a black velvet gown and ordered a black satin cloak. Went with Dr & Mrs McLaughlin to the Italian opera now at the Theatre de l'Odeon, choruses beautiful.

17th Called on Monsieur Jullien, found him in his high room. He was as kind as usual & gave us tickets for the Societe d'Emulation. In the evening thither we went, the room was full, two or three savants presided at table where the pieces of prose & poetry were read, after which came the music, Mr Dubois played beautifully on the violin. Like most of the rising generation of Frenchmen his hair was long & flowing & his beard pointed.

18th Called on the Halifaxes, went to the Louvre with them, had not time for more than the long gallery.

20th To the Episcopal Chapel & heard Bishop Luscombe preach one of his tedious sermons. Walked in the Tuileries. The Miss Halifaxes dined with us.

21st Passed a great deal of the day with Mrs McLaughlin arranging our fancy dresses for Mrs Latham's ball tomorrow, mine will be of the time of Louis XVII again, hers Spanish.

22nd Miss Halifax went with us to the ball. The dresses were good but not half the people costumed. Talked to Sir Sidney Smith who has become very old & decrepit.

23rd A letter from home, Louis is with Mama & Milly. He left Warbleton unknown to Mr Meeke & walked to Lewes, a distance of 17 miles, & from there made his way in the mail to Brighton. They have had to go through a great deal of fear & anxiety on his account. He is now safe at home.

28th Out shopping with Richard, to the ball given in the Rue de Richelieu for the pensioners of the Civil List, numerous people, the rooms were a blaze of light. The diamonds splendid & the coiffeur more varied than ever. Almost crushed to death.

February 4th To a concert, I wrote to <u>Brighton</u> I must not say <u>Home</u>.

10th Went to Mr Sayer's chapel. The streets crowded on account of the expected appearance in this quarter of the Boeuf Gras.

12th Called on Mrs MacLaughlin who gave me a little blue rosary. The Boeuf Gras made his appearance at last-preceded by a fat Leicestershire sheep - & followed by his usual train of butchers in various disguises - gods & goddesses, Cherokee Indians etc & on each side two figures on horses enveloped in what seemed to be white sheets. The poor beast doomed to a perambulation of the streets of the city during three days, after which to be slaughtered & portioned out to the pre-eminent among the citizens, not excepting Louis Philippe himself.

13th Being the first day of Lent went to church, Richard treated himself to some cigars & I myself to a Venetian bag of beads & a black satin gown. The unfortunate Boeuf Gras died in the night from fatigue & another was obliged to be brought forward for Tuesday's promenade.

14th Went with the Halifaxes to the Diorama where first saw the valley of Goldau in Switzerland smiling & calm, then the dark storm came on. Everything was hidden from view, the fall of the mountain takes place & we next beheld the valley as it seemed by moonlight after the rain & then it was restored to its first serenity. The view of the valley was very beautiful but the storm unnatural. Then we were summoned to the inauguration of the Temple of Soloman the courts of which were first empty then filled with people. The temple was lighted up & then was a sound of distant music. On the whole the exhibition did not satisfy our expectations.

17th To church & afterwards to the Hotel de Cluny, formerly the Abbaye de Cluny. It is now in the possession of Monsieur de Sommerard & there he has placed & arranged his immense collection of curiosities, particularly old wood carving, porcelain, armour, looking glasses, tapestries etc.[20] The Halifaxes as usual partook of the apology for roast beef that is the never failing fare at the Sunday table d'hote.

---

[20]   The Hotel de Cluny is now the Musee National du Moyen Age

21st Called on Mrs Burkett & saw her fat, fair, good-tempered baby, dined with them at the Rocher de Cancale, a most Epicurian repast. I felt completely satiated with the sight & smell of all these dainties, & Richard said that it out-dinnered all the dinners he had ever eaten.

26th To the Luxembourg - first went through the picture gallery, all of the modern French school, but I feel almost bewildered among the number & variety of pictures we see. We then visited the House of Peers, saw their salles de conference, de comites, & the King's especial hall & chair of state. From there we proceeded to the rooms of Marie de Medici; her chapel in which are original pictures of the Last Supper, her bedroom, the ceilings painted by Rubens. This room is one of the most beautiful things I have seen while in France.

27th Sir Sidney Smith dined with us at the table d'hote. The old seaman was more communicative than usual upon Acre, & Jaffa, & as full of projects & plans & all sorts of chimeras as in his younger days. Sir Sidney told us that Napoleon was the greatest scoundrel that ever existed.[21]

March 1st At seven o'clock went to the Grand Opera where first saw the first act of Victor Hugo's 'Esmeralda' & then the ballet of 'The Gipsy' – everyone is raving of the said ballet, but I am more than ever persuaded that a ballet is a very stupid thing or that I am a person of no taste.

2nd To the Mint, saw furnaces heated 'nine times red hot', bars of metal, weighing machines, certifying machines, coining machines, stamping machines - & human beings who looked anything but human beings so black & grim. From thence took our way to the Pantheon, the Halifaxes accompanied us. At ½ past 8 went to a ball.

5th Out shopping bought a black mantilla & a green silk gown with pink flowers.

6th To the Louvre, the pictures far too many to be inspected & the greater number bad to excess, what Milly would call 'super-hideous'. The crowds of people & pictures were too great to see much.

7th To the Jardin des Plantes, almost frozen, to the Museum of Natural History, the stuffed animals appeared in a decaying state, very much moth eaten. The Miss Halifaxes dined with

---

[21]   Sir Sidney Smith was 75 in 1839 & died the following year. He had successfully commanded the Siege of Acre against the French in 1799.

us it being their last evening. Richard, in putting on a new pair of boots continued to sprain his back & was very poorly in consequence.

9th Saw the Halifaxes depart & envied them their return to their own land & home. Richard in bed all day. Walked with Mrs Macloughlin.

10th Sunday, read prayers at home with Richard as he was not able to go to church. Walked to the Rue de Richelieu alone, much frightened as to the crossings, carriages rushed whistling by me till I felt so dizzy & distracted that I scarcely knew how I arrived in safety at the Hotel de Castile. I fortunately found Mrs Burkett at home, she then conveyed me to the Rue de Rivoli to call on Mrs Kerr. Reports of a prophecy that the English in Paris are to be massacred on the 14th of next month. Some say <u>all,</u> some restrict the bloodshed to 15,000.

11th Sat for my portrait to Mrs Hemmings from 12 till 4 - cold & tired.

13th Sat all day to Mrs Hemmings. Every time that the drums beat in Paris I dread that a revolution has broken out or the predicted massacre begun, & my portrait painter's apartment being close to a sort of barrack, I was in constant terror the whole day. Mr Jullien dined with us.

14th Sat for an hour to Mrs Hemmings after which accompanied Mr & Mrs Burkett by the rail road to St Germains. Very glad when our 14 miles in ½ an hour was at an end, especially the gloom of the tunnel.

15th After breakfast Mr Burkett put four horses to his carriage & drove us to Versailles. The Palace unfortunately closed, but saw the library, where is a curious book representing in a most detailed manner a fete given by Louis XIV. We then proceeded to the Orangerie.

16th Mr & Mrs Burkett accompanied us to Versailles, the sunshine & the country though leafless, looked very beautiful. Hares were suddenly about in all directions in the park. The chateau at Versailles magnificent, the rooms & the pictures & the statues infinite, the pictures are for the most part large & bad.

18th Returned to Paris by the rail road. Our new courier Louis Vahod awaiting us with a letter from Mr Jullien containing introductions to his friends in the different towns through which we shall pass on our at length decided tour.

20th Set out at 9 o'clock for Fontainebleau, reached the Hotel de la Ville de Lyons at 4 & forthwith proceeded with all the energy of 'fresh' travellers to see the castle, a large mass of heavy ancient building. We saw room after room of gilding & tapestry. The chamber de travail of the king is the room where Napoleon signed his abdication & the table still stands there, on which he forfeited France.

Then a night at Losne, a night at Moulins a night at Rouannes.

24th Our beds last night clean, everything else dirty in the extreme. The descent of Mont Tarare very fine, a magnificent road wound round the mountain. Just after we reached Tarare the Alps became visible. I was quite awed in beholding for the first time, as ages past beheld them, these ancient barriers covered with eternal snow. Reached Lyons, our sitting room is much gilt & adorned with paintings.

26th Rose a little past 4 & left Lyons at 6 by the steam-boat to Avignon. We passed Orange & Montelimar & sat in the carriage on deck almost the whole voyage.

27th To the Convent des Celestins in mistake for the ruins of the church of Cordeliers to search for Laura's tomb.[22] We hired a carriage & we wended our way to Vaucluse, reached the classic ground, saw the poet's fountain. Nothing can be conceived more beautiful & picturesque than this vale. On our return to Avignon stopped at the Palace of the Popes & saw the interior of the cathedral.

28th To the church of the Cordeliers of which are scarcely any remains, a stone has been placed over the tomb of Laura by Mr Kelsall an English man. The stone is surrounded by cypress trees & on it is a Latin inscription. We took our way to Nimes where we arrived in time to see the amphitheatre a splendid building.

29th Left the Hotel de Luxembourg at Nimes. The very disagreeable thing there, to which we shall be often compelled to submit, is that the service of the bedroom is entirely in the hands of men. Slept at Aix.

30th Left Aix for Marseilles, that town which I had all my life long been longing to behold; that place of ceaseless variety & traffic where all the nations of all the world may be surveyed at once without further trouble or travel. We had the first view of the deep blue Mediterranean.

---

[22]   The muse of the poet Petrarch.

April 1st Left Marseilles, with which town I must confess myself disappointed, & reached Toulon in 4 hours. A dirty sea port, slept at Le Luc, a poor but clean inn.

2nd Quitted Luc, passed through a land of figs, olives & cork trees reached the Pont du Var. At the French custom house at one end of the bridge received a third of the deposit made for our carriage at Calais. After crossing the stream, the boundary line of the two countries, we reached Nice & took up our quarters.

4th *A night at San Remo.*

5th Quitted San Remo, the road wending the Maritime Alps. At Oneglia a tall gay postillion, not unimportant in his own opinion, attired in a black velvet coat, peaked hat, & high boots drove the pair of horses nearest to the carriage. One of the horses was very restive & we were obliged to get out & walk. The road lay at the edge of a precipice so that the least jerk might have been fatal to us & all our belongings. The horse began to rear & had to be taken back. We walking, the carriage advancing with three horses, we were within an inch of being precipitated from the rock & as to the descent we were all obliged to walk down the steep winding road & the coach began each turning almost perpendicularly. Louis the courier threatened to lodge a complaint with the authorities against the gay postillion for his carelessness in driving & allowing to be driven, such undisciplined horses. We slept at Finale.

6th Arrived at Genoa, rooms like those in a palace, painted in fresco.

7th To the English church. After dinner Signor Charles Alberti, the banker to whom Monsieur Jullien had given us a letter of introduction, called. He is a plain dark little man, he spoke of his old instructor with great affection. He promised us his box at the opera tomorrow.

8th To the Palazzo Ducale, & then to a velvet shop where Richard bought two waistcoats & I enough for a bonnet. To the theatre with Mr Alberti.

11th At the cathedral mass was being performed in the chapel of St John the Baptist where his relics are enclosed in a shrine of gold.

12th After dinner bid adieu to Genoa & went on board the 'Maria Antionetta', a medley of all nations, English, French, Italians, Russians & priests.

13th I slept all last night in a very comfortable little cabin all to myself, almost all the other apartments were occupied by threes & fours & fives who had never been thrown together before. Breakfasted at Leghorn (*Livorno*), Thomson's Hotel. Went to Pisa, 14 miles, saw the Campo Santo & the cathedral, returned to Leghorn got into the little boat which takes us to the packet. Madame de Rosel brought with her from Leghorn a large grasshopper which she confined in a box, when it was not enduring the more severe torture of being swung about for the amusement of herself & her friends by a string attached to its leg.

14th While Madame de Rosel was on shore Richard ended at once the life & suffering of the unfortunate grasshopper by pressing its head, then shutting it up in the box again. Left all as he found it. Vehement however were the lamentations & shrieks of the lady on her return & discovery of the fate of her victim.

15th In the bay of Naples, all the hotels full, so we slept on board.

16th A cabin is not the most comfortable situation in the world & to make it more than usually disagreeable the noise of caulking the deck began before six o'clock & was so violent & protracted that without affectation it amounted in my opinion to actual suffering. I felt so wretched & overpowered that I sat down on my bed & burst into tears, not a little to my husband's astonishment. Richard went to his bankers, Rothschild, for permission to disembark the carriage which was at last obtained. Then we had to wait on board while Louis & Mary went with the carriage to the custom house, & on board we remained from 12 till near 5 pacing the deck & at length took our dinner with the Captain & his party. Louis appeared with the announcement that our own carriage was safely locked up, & that a carriage of the country was awaiting us. Left Naples for Castellaman where we slept.

17th Devoured by mistake at breakfast the roast fowl that was intended for our luncheon at Pompeii so obliged to content ourselves after the fatigues of visiting the ancient site with hard-boiled eggs. Many little lizards were darting in & out every part of the ruins. Only 50 men are employed to make excavations & not the half of it is disentombed. We saw the Forum with the beautiful temples round it. Richard brought away a piece of stucco, another of pottery & two or three other relics. I expected to have purloined some antique vase or lamp as some more fortunate pilgrims have done before, but there was nothing of the sort to be discovered so I returned as I went empty handed. The poor people about brought us oranges & wine. They seem as prone to beg & cheat as the rest of the Italian world. Slept at Salerno.

Richard drawn by Louisa

19th We reached Herculaneum. Our guide lighted small wax tapers & we began the descent to the amphitheatre & the excavations, these vaults so cold dark & lonely formerly all light & life. Richard added to his store of relics some fragments of marble from this entombed city. Reached our lodgings in Naples.

23rd We proceeded to Lake Avernus, with a ruined temple. We were admitted to the grotto of the Sybil, a completely dark passage leading to the baths. I remained above in darkness & smoke while Richard, on the back of the guide, descended into the baths. We visited Nero's hot baths in a steaming cave.

24th At 11 set out attended by courier & Mary for Vesuvius in a carriage of the country which, being left at Zevina, we all mounted mules & reached the Hermitage. We proceeded on our mules for another ½ hour & then dismounted. I was carried in a chair on the shoulders of six men up the last mile of the mountain. Mr Thomas & Louis & Mary walked up the ascent over masses of lava. There were two other gentleman pulled up by the guides with straps of leather girded round them. The ascent of Vesuvius is awful. At four miles distance from the crater the lava which was thrown out during the last eruption on the 2nd January of this present year was in some places still so hot that it was impossible to hold it. The crater is three miles in circumference & about 200 feet deep.

We sat down & had our luncheon on the side of the crater from eggs roasted during eight minutes by its hidden fires & then made our descent as well as we could, till we reached our mules, which with the exception of my falling off, carried us without accident to the Hermitage. Reached Naples about 8 o' clock. On the way back we passed a funeral. The priests were as usual walking before the bier & chanting. On the bier lay the deceased in his everyday cap & clothes with no pall covering beyond being strewn with flowers. The more I see of foreign parts, the more I love my own country.

25th Shopping at the tempting shops of coral, cameos & lava. Richard purchased two coral necklaces, one for Milly & three cameos, one for a brooch for Wifey.

May 1st Left Naples. We stopped for the night at Mola di Gaeta.

On 3rd arrived in Rome.

5th To St Peters, the mass of marble pillars are of stupendous size. The black statue of St Peter was approached by many while we were present & the toe kissed with great reverence while a short prayer was uttered. To my mind more like a dark idol & blind worshippers than anything I have yet seen.

7th Drove to the Forum & the Colosseum now used as a religious edifice to preserve it from demolition. To the church of San Gregorio on Monte Celio, from thence to the ruins of the Palace of the Caesars. Little now remains & it stands in a market garden. We had some trouble to reach it through the narrow paths almost overgrown with brambles & artichokes. To the church of Santa Martina her relics are preserved in a shrine in a dark, damp, subterranean chapel. The shrine is bronze gilt & inlaid with lapis lazuli & amethysts.

9th Ascension Day. A grand ceremony took place in the magnificent church of San Giovanni in Laterano at which the Pope officiated. His Holiness appeared preceded by the Cardinals in their gorgeous scarlet & white robes. The Pope was habited in a white & gold mantle his golden mitre on his head & a massive glittering ring. We had a good place to see him give the benediction to the multitude. The solemn words said & two papers inscribed with plenary indulgence for future & past sins to those happy enough to obtain them were thrown & the scramble for them began. After dinner drove to the gardens of the Villa Borghese till it was dark enough for the fireflies to come forth. I saw them darting about & sparkling among the thick trees. These gardens have cooling fountains & ruined temples.

13th To the museum of the Vatican, the collection of sculpture is magnificent. Miss MacKenzie told me that after seeing the Apollo Belvedere 'I should never look on any male creature again' & certainly no form or expression can be conceived more entirely faultless than that imparted to this statue.

17th Started for Florence, we slept at Civita Castellana.

18th Reached Terai to see the Cascade of Velino from above, which is the easiest. A little while before reaching it we heard the distant fall of waters & saw the foam ascending like a cloud of white smoke from amid the surrounding hills & then all at once it burst upon our view, as it rushed thundering down the rocks. We were thoroughly wet through with the expedition for we had a short distance to walk from the carriage to the waterfall. Slept at Spoleto which we did not reach till ½ past 9. The latter part of our journey lay among lonely hills. Knowing the reputation for robbers of this part of the country I did not feel quite happy in being out after dark.

19th Today we reached Perugia. No view can be conceived more beautiful in extent & colouring than the country which lay outspread before us as we mounted the steep hill on which the town is situated. The luxuriant vines hung from the trees & blue mountains glistening with snow lay in the distance. Our hotel was the Grand Hotel de l'Europe & had it not been for the animated attack made on me by countless fleas during the whole night all would have been well. As it was I had not one undisturbed hour of rest.

20th On our road to Passignano. At 12 we breakfasted at the little inn on the shores of the blue lake of Passignano. Our landlady's daughter & the maid were two dark-eyed, dark-haired girls, very obliging, & gave us a very good breakfast on roasted eel from the lake, fried carp & roasted mutton chops. I gave them a few English needles & a little thread which very much pleased them. Slept the night at Arezzo, our beds were clean & peaceful. *On 22nd arrived in Florence.*

23rd Music under our windows during the whole of last night at intervals. Went to Pejani's alabaster shop, made several acquisitions in that line, but no bargains, then to the Duomo. *On 28th arrived in Bologna.*

29th Took a carriage & went to see the cathedral & the church of St Petronio where Charles V was crowned. To the public cemetery where we walked through room after room of tombs of monuments from the 13th century to the present time. Left Bologna. *On 31st arrived in Venice.*

June 1st Embarked on a gondola attended by a laquais de place to see all the sights of Venice.23 1st the bead manufactory & all the various processes of drawing out, cutting, setting & rounding the glass till it is fitted for the bead mosaic for which Venice is so famed. 2nd The church of St John & St Paul which contains monuments & pictures infinite. 3rd The manufacture of gold chains. 4th Rowed down the grand canal & viewed all the splendid palaces, 5th San Giorgio Maggiore very fine, 6th Santa Maria dei Frari where rests Canova beneath a large & splendid monument of his own work & which he intended for Titian. After dinner rowed out in our gondola on the lagunes.

2nd Richard poorly, so read prayers to him instead of attending church. At 2 o'clock went to see the pigeons fed in the Piazza de San Marco. Some whimsical old lady left in her will a certain sum to be thus expended daily at a certain hour which bequest is strictly adhered to. Saw the Ducal palace, had a thorough examination of St Marks.

5th En route for Verona. Arrived, breakfasted, hired a laquais de place & set out sight-seeing, our first object the tombs of the Scalieri. To the tomb of Juliet. It is the common saying at Verona that the bodies of Shakespeare's lovers have been removed to England. Saw the balcony & visited two churches. From Verona we made our way to Brescia where we slept. A storm came on & the lightning was incessant. I was frightened as usual. *On 6th stayed night in Milan.*

---

23   Laquais de place is an obsolete term for a manservant temporarily hired in a foreign city.

7th A letter from Mama, Milly & Aunt Ella. They will meet us on the Rhine!!! Went with Richard to the Duomo a gorgeous mass of minarets, pinnacles, statues, & fretwork. Drove to the churches.

8th A day of toil. Ascended by means of 25 centimes & a winding staircase of almost endless length to the top of the Duomo & looked down upon its forest of minarets. We were told that 5000 statues already decorated the cathedral & that 10,000 more are to be put up. At ½ past 8 took our places at the Scala & would have remained for the 2nd act had not the ballet, intervened. I thought the Scala very rich & beautiful.

10th Left Baveno at a little before seven deceived by Richard into thinking it ½ past eight. Began our route over the Simplon. Of all Napoleon's wonderful works this road appears to me the best. After passing in safety through all the wildness & wonders of the mountains & gloomy rocks, we had attained at eventide the village of the Simplon encircled by snowy peaks as if winter had returned. The inn was very clean & comfortable & we had a capital dinner. Two large dogs of St Bernard kept us company during the repast & our little snug beds were as white as the mountains' driven snow.

11th Houses of refuge were erected at intervals on the mountain here. Arrived at the hospice or monastery of the Simplon, where reside constantly four monks of the order of St Bernard. We were served by one of the monks, raisins, cheese, figs, nuts and wine through an opening in the wall. He then showed us over the monastery, the summer rooms, the winter rooms lined with wood & the chapel where we left our little alms, the only way in which travellers repay them for hospitality received. We then began to descend, several beds of snow lying by the roadside. Richard made a snow ball & threw it into the carriage & this in the middle of June. Next year we shall not believe that this adventurous journey had been real. We reached Sierre where we slept at an excellent inn, very rural but the fare & beds very good. The Simplon abounds with wild flowers we gathered two sorts of <u>intensely blue</u> gentians, the other plants I did not know.

12th Lake Geneva. At the Castle of Chillon we dismounted, crossed the drawbridge attended by a chattering female guide & descended by the grand rooms to the execution room where is still the window from which bodies were thrown into the water, to the dungeon of Bonnivard. In this cold abode there are several compartments, & on the column are carved the names of Byron, Dumas, Cooper etc. Bonnivard was released after eight years imprisonment, six chained to the pillar in his cell. Lord Byron lived five days within the castle walls. Halting for the hours of darkness at Vevey, Richard out of humour with the toothache & I with hunger.

13th stayed night at Lausanne & 14th at Geneva.

15th Richard & the courier hurried off to the junction of the Arne & Rhone not far from hence. He had read glowing descriptions of the meeting & was therefore disappointed. Mary & I went out shopping. Dinner party of 40 at the table d'hote, nearly all English.

17th Hot & dusty on our way to St Martin, reached there & instantly hired a charabanc for Chamonix where we arrived after four hours of shaking & jolting. It is a kind of movable armchair on wheels, no springs & holding three instead of one. In this machine we were dragged by two horses up & down precipices, which till proved the contrary by experience, one would have thought neither bones nor wheels could have born & remained entire. Mont Blanc repaid us with the brightest glances. It was a splendid view but still Mont Blanc, or as Mary called it Saint Blanc, did not impress us with its gigantic size. We at last came in sight of the glacier of Bossons.

18th Mr Thomas up at four in the morning & on his way to the Montanveil & the Mer de Glace. Malgre persuasions I remained at home & made a little sketch of the valley &, what is rarely the case on these occasions, did not regret my absence from the petrified sea. The weather was intensely hot & the path is one of extreme difficulty. Richard not only heard but saw the avalanches fall & his expedition was performed with, I believe, unexampled celerity. The courier considered it such an extraordinary feat that he begged it might be recorded in the travellers' book. This however we did not do. Again embarked on our char-a-banc & again reached St Martin where we dined & slept.

19th at Geneva, 20th at Lausanne, 21st arrived Freibourg.

22nd Left Freibourg for Berne. On our arrival at the Hotel du Faucon breakfasted, made our toilettes & walked out of the town to see the review of the little soldiers of Thun, Berne & Brienne who here assemble once a year from their different schools to go through their military manoeuvres. Richard's nephew arrived from Hofwyl.

24th Drawn by three horses we began our journey to Hofwyl & reached the celebrated establishment. We were received by Mr Emile de Fellenberg[24] who showed us his various arrangements; gymnastics, carpenters workshops, painting room etc. I sketched the house while Mr Thomas visited the agricultural department. We dined at the little hotel in the village, four of us, Frank Duppa being added to our party.[25] Little Richard gave me three boxes & his uncle a desk of his own manufacture.

25th My cousin Monsieur de Bondely called on us & we accompanied him to see his wife. They reside just outside the gates of the town in what was formerly a convent. He is a serious, gentle person, she very lively. They asked us to drink tea with them & we asked them to dine with us. Mr de Bondely took us out driving round Berne. The mountains in the distance, high & clear. Drank tea with Madame de Bondely, the repast was served in a portico overlooking the river & the surrounding hills. The three little children played while we were regaled in a most primitive but very agreeable manner. The next destination was to the ramparts, where we sauntered & ate ices.

26th At nine left Berne, received two letters, one from Uncle Albert, the other a very disappointing one from Mama & Milly who will not meet us on the Rhine. Luncheon at the inn & then embarked in the Thun steamboat on the Lake of Thun for Interlaken. It is really a beautiful place, the number of hotels or 'pensions' is quite wonderful. They are almost entirely supported by the English travellers.

27th On our way to Lauterbrunnen where we breakfasted, rocks steep & rugged, rushing torrents. The mountains here are not so gigantic but far more beautiful than at Chamounix. Halted for the night in Grindelwold, just opposite to the upper & lower glaciers & immediately on our arrival started off for the latter. It was within ½ an hour walk. The mere roughnesses of a distant view, increasing in size as we approached, & growing at last to pyramids & pinnacles of ice, & a small blue cavity becoming a spacious archway of crystal,

---

[24]   De Fellenberg was an experimental educationalist whose school included a farm where the boys were taught practical skills as well as religious teaching, reading and arithmetic.

[25]   Frank Duppa was himself an education reformer. He was impressed by Fellenberg's ideas & had taken his youngest brother George to be educated there.

through which foamed an impetuous torrent. While Mr Thomas & Richard went to the upper glacier, I walked in the little garden. The two Richards soon effected their pilgrimage.

30th Madame de Bondely called & sat with me some time, we then walked together to the ramparts & the platform. The more I see of the Swiss the more I like the manners of this simple people. I was very sorry so soon to loose my newly known cousins. Took little Richard some way towards Hofwyl & then continued our route to Solothurn where we slept.

July 1st Left Solothurn, reached Basle. Summoned from our beds by the bell of the steam packet at ¼ to 4.

2nd To embark. The vessel was a small one & on board was the enormous Count Demidoff & his handsome, young, but very large Countess. He is only 38 & so corpulent that he literally got wedged in the cabin door & could neither move backwards nor forwards. After some difficulty he extricated himself. At Strasbourg exchanged our small boat for a larger one. The shores of the Rhine extremely flat. Reached Mannheim thoroughly weary, the carriage a long time coming on shore & we awaiting it most anxiously at the hotel, till ½ past 11 when it arrived.

4th & 5th on board the packet for Cologne.6th & 7th travelling by boat to Rotterdam.

8th I took my first walk in Rotterdam. The people all look money-making & prosperous, & the town is a matter of fact, happy Venice, intersected with canals on the banks of which are flourishing trees, & on the water vessels innumerable. The houses are like the palaces of Venice too, a little out of the perpendicular from the sinking of the soil. Richard tried to obtain some tulip roots.

9th On board the 'Batavier' & homeward bound, our last voyage I hope for some time to come. I suffered more from heat & discomfort than from illness having taken the precaution of lying down the whole time in our little close cabin on deck, but the heat of the day was nothing when compared to that of the night, though I went regularly to bed, & disencumbered myself of all supernumary clothes. I lay in the lower berth, & the steaming heat issued just upon me from a crevice in the walls till I felt as if in Nero's hot baths near Naples without the freedom from impurity. All the night we kept the cabin door open, & constantly did I protrude my head there-from, to try to intake a little fresh air, but the atmosphere was so imbued with smoke, oil & blackness, the very effort was vain, & I passed a sleepless wretched night, thinking however by way of consolation that every stroke of the paddles & every billow we cleft brought us nearer home.

10th Rose betimes, paced the encumbered deck, breakfasted, thought the vessel slow, felt weak & weary, watched the paddles, marvelled at the mighty ships upon the tranquil water, & the oppressive thickness of the air as we approached London. Saw the colossal new steam packet 'The British Queen' as she lay amid a forest of masts & at last reached the Tower Stairs with all the dread of custom-house superintendence before our eyes. Who should be the first person we met but Mr Radcliffe & afterwards on our road to the bank, Mr Read the clergyman? Money matters being arranged we returned to the Custom-House, all our own goods & chattels landed, & the examination most favourably passed by means of five shillings to the examiner. The courier's account paid & we on our journey to Hollingbourne by three o'clock. Reached Eyhorne House my future home at eight. The servants amazed as they had had no intimation of our return. The village bells soon ringing, & ourselves soon seated at our own tea table beneath our own roof & on our own ground. Were we happy or not?

1840-1849: The Country life

Now began a new and lasting phase of life for Louisa as the wife of a country squire. Hollingbourne lies in a beautiful Kentish landscape with the steep North Downs above, and rolling farmland below. It is a large parish with the two separate settlements of Upper Street and Eyhorne Street within it.

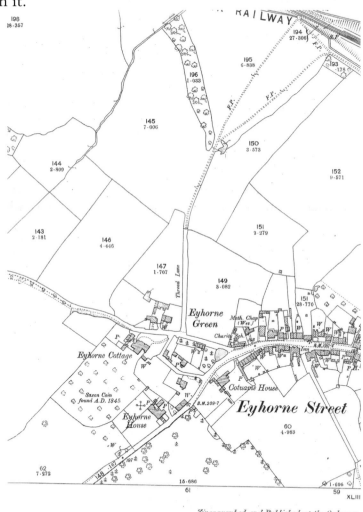

The 1897 Ordnance Survey map showing Eyhorne Street and Eyhorne House

Louisa had never lived in the countryside before. In spite of having an eye for the beauties of nature, city-life, and London in particular, always remained Louisa's first love and her sociable, out-going temperament was better suited to the buzz and variety of cosmopolitan living. In 1840 she commented on the monotony of the life she was then leading compared to her earlier years.

Events moved at a slow pace in the country and it took time to establish a circle of firm friends. She did however have the advantage of already being close to the numerous Duppa family. Over the next decade she saw one or other of the Duppa siblings every week. They had long lived at the top of the very steep Hollingbourne Hill in Hollingbourne House above the Upper Village whilst Richard and Louisa lived down in Eyhorne Street with the Ashford-Maidstone road nearby. Their home, Eyhorne House, was a fine Georgian building built in 1779.

Within the parish the Thomas family had respect and influence; they were consulted on all matters regarding the church and school. Poor people knew they could come for advice and help. Both Richard and Louisa occasionally lent money to those whom they considered deserving of help.

Richard was no longer the attentive constant companion of the honeymoon months but was occupied with his farming and shooting, usually being absent all day. He also took frequent overnight journeys to London which seem to have been a combination of business and seeing his brother Thomas. He had his own long-established bachelor life.

He was a systematic, organised man who kept factual notes and accounts over many years showing that he supervised his farms closely, deciding when to buy and sell stock, when to sow and reap and when to take on more hands. He noted when peas were drilled, when hop poles were sold, and when rent was paid. He kept sheep, and some cattle too and often noted the births of calves. Woodland was cropped to produce not only hop poles but stakes and hurdles.

With the enormous help of Louisa's large dowry Richard could hardly have failed to prosper, and his account books record additional land and properties purchased.[26] In 1839 he bought the blacksmith's forge and five cottages in Upper Street for £550.

---

[26]   Also in the possession of Bryan Gipps.

Eyhorne House, Hollingbourne

Two years earlier he had bought a wood in Hollingbourne as well as the Kings Head Inn with land in the Upper Village. That same year he bought Elnothington House close to

Eyhorne House for over £1000. This was purchased as being suitable to let out to people of means.

Louisa's journals of this decade show her initially settling into a routine, taking charge of the household, adding to her collection of books, stitching embroidery, writing letters every day, reading, taking daily walks, playing the piano and calling on friends and acquaintances. This daily round was punctuated by regular stays with Mama and Milly in Brighton and visits to London staying with beloved Aunt Ella who had no children of her own, and seeing the uncles, aunts and cousins. Friends and relatives came to stay in Hollingbourne too, which was a great pleasure. Louisa had relatives who were moneyed, intellectual and distinguished in their fields. Richard did not. She loved to go to large gatherings where there was a chance to dance the night away. The birth of her children in no way altered this.

Six children were born, all during the 1840s. For the first birth Milly came to stay a month beforehand and stayed on for two more afterwards. When the children were small Louisa was not much involved in their daily care as was normal for her time and class, but she became close to all of them when they grew up. As soon as they were old enough she read with them progressing to teaching Latin, Italian and French. She taught them to paint and draw. A governess was appointed in 1848 when Ella, the eldest, was eight years old. Once Ella was born there were five live-in servants and in addition they always employed a coachman and a gardener living in neighbouring cottages.

The relationship between Louisa and Richard was soon permanently tarnished by the revelation of the existence of his illegitimate son which he did not confess to Louisa until sometime after they were married. Matters were made far worse by the fact that he had passed off young Richard to Louisa on their honeymoon as his nephew. Young Richard had been born to Mary Victualler in Hollingbourne in 1823 when Richard was 31. Why he did not marry her is unknown. Mary was his cousin and he had gone abroad with her and the child in 1834, settling them into life there.[27] It is not known when Mary died.

Such matters were immensely difficult to discuss at this period when a well brought up woman would have considered

---

[27]   Gipps B, 'Hollingbourne & the Thomas Family', 1991.

the whole business distasteful and shameful. No doubt Richard feared that Louisa might turn him down if he told her the facts before they were married. When, months later, young Richard was staying with them, Richard did tell her the truth. Louisa's distress must have been great but none of this is included in her journal. She considered it as far too private a matter to put into writing. After their first wedding anniversary subsequent ones are recorded without comment and there are no affectionate references to Richard indeed he is often 'Mr Thomas'. This contrasts strongly with the diaries of Louisa's cousin Edward Goulburn who referred to his wife Julia as 'dear Ju' and always bought her anniversary presents.

Within a couple of years of Louisa's arrival in Hollingbourne the officers of the Cavalry Depot in nearby Maidstone and their wives became an important part of the Thomas's or at least Louisa's, social life. Maidstone had long been a town with a barracks for what later became the Royal West Kent Regiment. The officers who became friends were all part of the cavalry establishment; such men came from well-off families.

This decade of the 1840s is the one where we see the family change their method of travel on their journeys to Brighton or London, from coach and horses to the railway. The first trip they took to London by rail was in 1841 when staying at Brighton. Their first rail journey to Brighton came in 1843 when the South Eastern Railway opened a line from Reigate to Paddock Wood. So it was possible to change at Reigate for the Brighton line. Maidstone's first station opened in 1844 and so the capital came into easy reach which was a great blessing for Louisa.

Louisa resumed the writing of her journal five months after her arrival in Holllingbourne at the end of the Grand Tour.

1839 December 5th Bade farewell to Brighton & all its gaieties at nine o'clock this morning after remaining nearly five weeks under Mama's hospitable roof. 'Posted' as far as Tonbridge where found our own horses waiting for us, who brought us to Hollingbourne. The little drawing room with its blazing fire looking very cheerful. Regaled ourselves on tea & beef steaks & tried the new pianoforte which is a delightful one, interior & exterior both to be admired.

6th Charles, Mary & Ellen Duppa called, their elder brother's health does not improve. The new china makes our house very gay. Busy the whole morning with setting the house in order & washing the said china.

Leeds Castle as it was during Louisa's time in Hollingbourne. Copyright Leeds Castle Foundation

7th My husband started at nine on a shooting expedition & myself on a sunny walk beyond Park Gate & along the high path beneath the trees overlooking Leeds Castle. Richard appeared at tea time with eight rabbits a pheasant & a brace of partridges.

8th Looked over the books we purchased at the auction at Tunbridge Wells. Most of them religious. Went to afternoon church, Mr Hasted almost inaudible & singing too audible as usual, saw the Duppas.

10th Arranged the books newly bound, began a pilgrimage to Hollingbourne Hill but it thawed & rained so compelled to return. Richard had a day's shooting.

12th My husband was with me nearly the whole day, it being too rainy to go out.

17th Richard drove me up the Hollingbourne Hill & we called on the Duppas; then proceeded to the Dollings. *(Rev. Robert Dolling was vicar of the nearby village of Wormshill)* Returned to Hollingbourne House to collect Mary Duppa who dined & slept chez nous.

22nd Wrote tickets for a Christmas Dinner to 28 poor families. Too rainy to go to church so read prayers with Richard. Harry Duppa dined here. *(Even before Louisa married Richard he had established a tradition of giving tickets to poor families for a Christmas dinner provided by himself. This Louisa continued her whole life.)*

23rd Went to the charity school & heard the children read a chapter in the testament & looked at their work.[28] Richard drove me up The Hill, called on the Duppas, on to Sharsted we reached the mansion of Mrs Faunce & her two sons. It is a spacious old house, most inaccessibly situated. *(Sharsted Court home of the Faunce family in Newnham. It is an ancient manor house.)*

24th In the evening came the singers of Christmas carols & the ringers of hand-bells, which have a pretty, cheerful, simple sound, & in the morning we had been early greeted by the warlike achievements of the Seven Champions, boys being dressed up to personate the sainted heroes & performing various feats in imitation of their knightly prowess.[29]

25th Richard went to church but I could not for the rain. In the afternoon the weather cleared so we took a sunny but very wet walk east along the road. I longed for the hard, paved ways of Brighton. At ½ past 4 called for Mrs Disternell & conveyed her up The Hill to dine at Mr Duppa's. Roast beef, holly & cheerfulness in abundance. Little Ellen sang & Charlotte played the harp.

26th The Bearsted Band played under our window after tea.

---

[28]   This very year 1839, William Horton a Hollingbourne shopkeeper had left the parish money for a school to be built in Eyhorne Street for the education of poor children. Richard was one of the trustees.

[29]   In some parts of Kent the mummers were known as the Seven Champions, they always spoke in rhyming couplets.

27th The first anniversary of our marriage, I only hope that the coming year may bring as little of sorrow as the last. Christmas carols again this evening & bells ringing both now & in the morning on account of the said anniversary.

28th Had a few household affairs to transact on account of our little dinner party. Mary & Charlotte Duppa made their appearance early, Richard came in from shooting. Dinner very well served & champagne excellent. Guests remained till past 12. Mary Duppa gave me a little bag of her own workmanship.

30th Richard drove me to see his woods & cottages at Coxheath. The woods are wild & beautiful, the cottages small & so situated that they cannot be converted into dwelling houses.

1840 January 1st Mary Duppa called & Mrs Disternell, & in the afternoon Charlotte & Emma Duppa & Mr & Mrs Dolling.

2nd Richard drove me to Maidstone where I did shopping. Stephen *(the groom)* chose to go up The Hill on Tom in our absence & on his road home the horse threw him over his head & instead of rushing away, stayed & danced upon him.

3rd Mary Duppa dined with us & Harry drank tea here. Yesterday Stephen gave warning alleging Mrs Tully's temper as the reason.*(Mrs Tully was the cook)*

4th Worked rather more than usual. (*This means embroidery*)

6th Started at 10 o'clock for town by the 'Tally Ho' coach, Richard outside. My companions inside were a very talkative right-thinking intelligent old lady of 73 – who took snuff & kept up an incessant conversation with the clergyman of Tenterden & his son who sat opposite, discussing religious books, writers, opinions & times. Reached London at ½ past 2. Aunt Ella in very good spirits.

7th Talked with Aunt Ella the whole morning, viewed the three old family portraits now mine, called on Kate. *(Uncle Go's third wife)* Bought a collar & a mousseline de laine gown. Tidings of poor Frank Duppa's death which happened on Sunday.[30]

8th Dined at Uncle Go's. Edward very well & very agreeable.

9th Walked with Richard to Park Street where found Uncle Go & Edward. Kate soon appeared. Edward walked with me to St Andrews Place.

10th Edward called & then Aunt Ella & I called on Kate to say goodbye & took Uncle Go to his chambers in Serjeant's Inn,

---

30   Baldwin Francis Duppa, known as Frank, education reformer, the eldest of the 11 Duppa siblings died aged 39, leaving a widow & six children.

thence proceeded to Howell & James'. Short gipsy cloaks the grande mode & all the dresses flounced. Penny post began.

11th Edward dined with us yesterday & made himself very agreeable. Richard was at Woolwich the whole day. Took leave today of Aunt Ella & left town.

14th Little Richard arrived from Hofwyl, so not much done beyond writing my foreign journal, working & talking.

15th Heard little Richard read the history of England, worked & played chess.

16th Drove to Maidstone & having concluded my affairs there, drove home again & read 'Corinne' & worked. Dined at six after which both Richards were so sleepy that I was left to my own music & meditations.

22nd Little Richard went early to Rochester & I began husband's portrait, no easy matter, read, played chess. What a monotonous life I am now leading & particularly so when compared with what I have led. Household settled again by a reconciliation between Stephen & Mrs Tully.

27th Alabaster arrived from Florence. The pleasure of unpacking, but in spite of tow, sawdust, paper, patience, care & dexterity the right up-lifted hand of Immortal Hebe had been severed from the fair arm. The other objects safe.

28th Amused myself for at least two hours by arranging the alabaster where it might be seen to the most advantage. Heard Richard's lessons.

29th Mrs Tully & her accounts. Reading. Husband went out shooting, a hare, a couple of rabbits, five brace of partridges & a brace of pheasants.

February 1st Little Richard en route to Brighton this morning. Mr Radcliffe called immediately after breakfast in his scarlet hunting coat.

6th Much frightened in the night by noises in the house & dogs barking, which proved to be nothing more or less than some ferocious animal intent upon the poor sheep, & Mrs Tully opening the window & creeping out to drive them away. In the morning one of the flock was found to be very much torn & two slightly injured, besides which three timid creatures had, from fear, taken refuge in the mill pond. Johnson & George were out all day in pursuit of the offender. Richard at Chatham.

7th Stephen & Johnson to sit up all night to watch the fold.

9th Mary, Fanny, Charlotte & Ellen Duppa all called on me. Regaled them with apples & gingerbread & the sight of the newly arrived portraits & alabaster.

10th The little Queen's marriage. Bells ringing in consequence. Felt very poorly & able to do nothing but work & go to bed early.

11th Drove up The Hill, called on the Dollings, Mrs Dolling gave me some very good advice.*(Re imminent birth of first baby no doubt)* Brought Mary Duppa home to dine & sleep.

13th To Maidstone & made many purchases; all sorts of muslin.

14th Fanny Duppa & Ellen called, & then Mrs Dolling. Ordered the carriage & trotted off to Maidstone to fetch Milly. Richard gone to preside at a farmer's dinner & Milly & I sat together till ½ past 10 talking over past times.

16th Fanny & Ellen Duppa called, drove to church not feeling very strong. Last night received a present of a pale green silk gown from Richard which I intend for Milly's wedding day.

17th Dispatched to Brighton little Richard's box & some elderberry wine & rabbits to Mama. Fox hounds & hunters in sight skirting Combe Wood the dark figures distinctly outlined upon the light sky & 'View Halloo!' audible.

25th Paid a pottering visit to Miss Hasted whom we found with old Mr Hasted, looking the portraiture of invalidism & gloom.

27th The architect came to see our house to see if the projected alterations & improvements are feasible, in which I rejoice to say he finds no difficulty.

28th Made arrangement for the dinner party which went off very well, though political discussion ran very high & Edward Duppa, being the only radical, was exposed to all the vehemence of a complete body of Conservatives.

March 1st Walked to morning service but there was none, Mr Hasted being too poorly. Read prayers. Fanny, Ellen & Charlotte Duppa called.

3rd Letter from Mama pressing Richard to go to Brighton instantly on account of Louis' state.[31] The horse was saddled immediately & he departed. The architect brought the plans for our house which seem to me to be very well executed. Milly & I talked over our work the whole evening.

---

[31]   Mama needed Richard's help & advice as the nearest male relative whom she could rely upon.

5th A letter from my husband with very bad news of poor Louis, but saying that Mama bears all her trials better than could have been expected. Drove to Maidstone with Milly & made purchases.

6th Richard arrived from Brighton. All is over & arranged as quietly as possible & Louis I rejoice to say under medical restraint & treatment. God grant that it may be for his benefit! I am sure that it will be for Mama's advantage & happiness. *(Louis was to spend the rest of his life in private asylums.)*

17th At half past 2 o'clock in the morning my little daughter was born.

April 29th *(Next entry)* Many a day has flown since I last took pen in hand & days & hours seem now fleeting on with a little being. The fifth week of her existence she was Christened by the name of Ella de Visme. Her godmothers Mama & Aunt Ella & her godfather my cousin Edward. The whole business & pleasure & end of her life seems to be at present eating, sleeping & crying. Mama has been staying here a fortnight & is gone, Milly too is gone after a stay of nearly three months. Little Richard is with us.

May 2nd Heard Richard's lessons, visited Miss Ella in her lofty room.

5th Mama writes of some means of employment that she hopes to have obtained for little Richard. Milly's letter is enclosed in one of the new envelopes.[32]

13th Edward Duppa dined here & talked as much nonsense as ever.

21st Mrs Dolling called, upon which I exhibited my little daughter, that is to say I took her upstairs to the nursery & the baby show. She considered Miss Ella looking very strong & healthy.

22nd To Maidstone & brought home Mama who is pale & bilious & still very weak.

28th Richard went to see poor Louis, a distance of 30 miles.

29th A large bough, almost an oak tree at our door this morning & just as we came down to breakfast Johnson appeared with an immense garland to be born in procession by the Benefit Club, it being their 'gaudy day'. Fireworks

---

[32] Previously letters were sent as a folded sheet sealed with wax.

ended the festivities.[33] Mr Thomas returned from Ticehurst where he saw Louis who is gradually becoming worse.[34]

30th Mr Thomas played at cricket at Chatham & did not return till the evening.

July 24th Mr Whatman, *(Dr Whatman of Maidstone)* called & vaccinated little Ella for the third time, the first & second both proving unsuccessful.

25th Worked hard in the garden, thought that I should never complete the pruning one rose tree.

29th Drove to Maidstone with Mama, Fanny & Ellen Duppa, did a great deal of shopping & bill paying, our friends dined with us.

August 19th To Maidstone for Miss Ella's fifth vaccination.[35]

20th Wrote letters for Richard, selected rules for the school here, Mrs Disternell drank tea here.[36]

31st Mr Whatman called. After dinner drove to Frinningham House *(Bearsted)* to call on Mrs H. Duppa. She looked very pretty, delicate & interesting. *(Henry Duppa aged 35 had recently married)*

September 5th Little Richard took his departure for London & Woolwich.

8th Uncle Go & Kate arrived about 6 o'clock the former in high spirits.

9th Took a potter with Uncle Go as far as the church & Manor House. At ½ past 9 went to the Duppas' ball, the supper beautifully arranged but a great want of people & animation. Home at four.

10th Later than usual. Took Uncle Go & Kate round our territories with which much pleased & then a drive to Coxheath & the Farleighs with their luxuriant hop grounds & orchards. Home by Maidstone stopping on our way to see the *(Bishop's)* Palace.

---

33   29th May was Oak Apple Day which celebrated the restoration of the monarchy in 1660. In Hollingbourne this special day had been chosen as the village benefit club feast day.

34   Ticehurst House near Wadhurst was opened in 1792 by Dr Samuel Newington as a sanctuary for those with mental illness. Dr Newington did not approve of restraint. Treatment was kindly with plenty of treats in a beautiful mansion and grounds. Patients came from affluent families.

35   Vaccination was a term coined by Edward Jenner in 1798 to describe his new process of protection against smallpox through inoculation with cowpox.

36   Mrs Disternell was an elderly widow in reduced circumstances. Sometimes called Dis in the diaries.

16th *(Cousin)* Freddy arrived, much grown, it is more than a year since I have seen him.

17th Mama & Milly left us after a sejour of so long a duration that I had almost forgotten it was not their home. Sauntered a little about Maidstone with Freddy & then took him up The Hill where we had luncheon with the Duppas.

26th Drove to Sittingbourne to call on Mrs Hassells.

28th Drove to Chatham to see the launch of the 'London' man of war 92 guns. It was a wonderful & splendid sight, the glory & power of England & the extent of human genius & invention. The ponderous mass glided down, at first slowly, & then with amazing velocity into the water where we went to view it calmly floating.

October 7th A very sad accident happened to James Radcliffe out shooting, his gun went off & nearly carried off his fingers.

8th The two Richards returned. Mr Radcliffe very poorly. A bad account of Louis whom the two Richards visited in their way from Brighton.

10th Called at Hollingbourne & saw poor Mr Radcliffe looking wretchedly with his hand bound up & clad in a dressing gown, seeming scarcely able to speak. Called on the Dollings & saw the additions to their house.

16th At dinner we were joined by Charles Duppa who laughed & sang almost more than usual.

17th Called on Mr & Miss Hasted, found then both at home wearing on together their melancholy existence in their melancholy room. What a contrast to the sunshine of the Duppas.

19th Went to the school with Emily Struth, heard the children read. Presently in walked Miss Phene, *(the teacher),* looking black as thunder cloud.

20th Edward & Charles Duppa called. Yesterday Ella cut her first tooth after sundry unintelligible screams.

24th Charles Duppa called. Drove up The Hill & on our way met the Duppas who invited us there in the evening. Emily S. & I went & met the regular family party. A most pleasant evening, an abundance of vocal & instrumental music.

30th Last night the house was attacked by thieves & plundered of much that was valuable, my watch, seals, chain, charms, Richards seals, coats, hat, cloak, game, Neopolitan paper knife, silver knife, candlesticks, thimbles, scissors etc. They made their entrance by the cellar window & their exit by the front door. Emily Struth heard the latter but had no idea that the noise proceeded from strangers. They did not venture upstairs. The Constable, Lampard, appeared twice during the evening but brought no news of the plundered or their plunder.

November 2nd White, the constable from Lenham, called. Three men in haste, heavily laden had been seen the night in question returning through Bearsted 'Hollingbourne way'. Don the dog chained up in the house for the night.

5th We drank tea on The Hill, met Mr Wilder the clergyman of Thurnham & received the announcement of Mary Duppa's marriage with Captain Faunce.

6th Finished 'Oliver Twist', a book of terror. Continued my endless journal. *(This is the copy of the journal of the tour for Richard)*

9th Richard in Maidstone the whole day engaged in the cause of discovery.

10th Finished my journal! Mrs Disternell & I drove up The Hill & paid a congratulatory visit. Found them all in <u>the highest glee.</u> Captain Faunce & his youngest brother came in.

12th Drove to Maidstone & did shopping. Kent, Piety & Gibbons, the three receivers of stolen goods taken up & their houses searched, nothing of ours discovered.

13th Mr Thomas at Maidstone during the day, the culprits brought before the Mayor & after a little further evidence against them were remanded till Tuesday.

16th A day of preparation for little Richard's departure. Took leave of my husband's nephew this evening, the poor little boy in tears. *(He was actually 17)*

17th Little Richard departed for London & Mr Thomas to appear before the magistrates & then follow him. A lonely dreary day.

18th Another day of loneliness & dreariness of rain & wind.

19th Mr Thomas returned.

24th A letter from young Richard who is now in all the bustle of starting.*(He was setting off for the West Indies)* Mr Thomas out shooting. Myself with baby at Maidstone. The two thieves, Pearson & Bridger at last are taken. They were discovered by a tool left behind them in their fright at the return of a neighbour, while perpetuating a robbery at Sevenoaks.

December 24th St George and his troop made their appearance in the garden about 3 o'clock. There was the valorous champion himself in a cocked hat & paper trimmings & there was the king of Egypt in a nondescript costume, a soldier & a physician, old Father Christmas in a great coat, & another personage by name 'Open the door'.[37] The ringers of hand-bells came in the evening.

25th Richard went to morning church & I read my prayers at home over the fire, the cold intense. Drove up The Hill to dine with Mary Duppa, accompanied by Mrs Disternell. A family party consisting of all the Faunces besides The Hill folk. Roast beef, turkey, plum pudding & abundance of evergreens. The journey in spite of snow & ice performed in safety.

31st All the village in commotion on account of Mary Duppa's wedding. We started for the church at ¼ to 11, called for Mrs Disternell, all attired in lilac like an autumnal crocus. A little past 11 the bridal train appeared, the bride being led up to the altar by her old father. It was a most pleasing sight & she looked better than I have ever seen her. Favours were distributed immediately after the service & then Mr & Mrs Faunce departed immediately for London. I returned home to remain quiet till dinner while the rest of the party went to Hollingbourne House. Richard, Mrs Disternell & I went up The Hill at six, dined & danced in the New Year. Home by 2.

1841 January 9th Ice & snow everywhere. Our trial took place yesterday. Piety sentenced to seven years transportation & Pearson & Bridger to 14 years each. Gibbons I regret to say was acquitted. Nothing could exceed the recklessness of the two thieves who were quite young men not above two & twenty.[38]

12th *(To Brighton)* Snow during the night but a fine day ,& owing to Baby, impossible we found it to shut the carriage. The road slippery & in some parts very difficult to traverse. Took post horses to Tunbridge Wells & then on to Uckfield, where met our own & so reached Brighton about ½ past 5 having started from home about ¼ past 9. Richard retired early to bed & I sat talking with Mama.

17th Called with Baby on Lady Carhampton. Richard took his departure for London.

---

[37]   The 'Seven Champions' was the Kentish name for mummers plays, short, ritualistic & performed by men. Plays such as this were dying out in most parts of Kent. The last year Louisa mentions them is 1843.

[38]   Thomas Piety was a 60 year old fishmonger who had received the goods & sold them on. The two thieves Francis Bridger and Edward Pearson were just 19 and 21. Bridger and Pearson were responsible for a number of other robberies. Thomas Gibbons who was acquitted was a 38 year old porter.

19th Mulready called & offered to sketch Baby but I think she is all too young.

28th To the subscription ball which was pleasant, Sir Gardner Wilkinson, the Egyptian traveller, a short mustachiod man was there.[39]

February 1st Expected Richard who did not come.

2nd Richard appeared, he has seen Louis who is more tranquil & contented.

10th Went to the bazaar on the Grand Parade where Richard made me a birthday present of a rosewood tray for books. Emily Struth paid us a long morning visit.

11th Drove about the town. Milly gave me a little edition of Burn's poems & I treated myself to Blyth's edition of White's 'Selborne'.

14th To morning church to hear Mr Vaughan preach & called on Mrs Mostyn.

16th Adieu to dear Mama & Milly & on our road at ½ past 9, a fine day tho' the snow lay on the road in thick masses. We reached home at ½ past 6 having joined our own steeds at Tunbridge Wells.

19th Baby weaned, wrote to Mama & Milly. Mrs Disternell called.

23rd Mr John & Mr Julius Brenchley[40] breakfasted here & then went out shooting.

24th News of Mr Betts disappearance. Richard at Maidstone.

26th Mr Betts, the object of all the conjecture of all the village & neighbourhood returned home in the evening, half tipsy. Some thought he had hanged & some that he had drowned himself, which latter event I should have conceived very unlikely unless the Medway were flowing with brandy or porter. (*William Betts ran a small private boarding school close to the Thomas home. At this time he was in his thirties & it seems he managed to overcome his drinking problem for he continued to run the school into his old age.*)

27th Mrs Betts came in during the evening in great tribulation. She appears a very respectable nice sort of person. Richard at Maidstone.

---

[39]   Sir John Gardner Wilkinson is considered to be the founder of British Egyptology.

[40]   Julius Brenchley (1816-1873), traveller and author. Born into a wealthy family in Maidstone he had just been ordained. In later years he explored many countries & bequeathed his collections in ethnography & natural history to the town of Maidstone.

March 8th Planted ivy with Mr Thomas along the house & walls, continued my catalogue of the books. I have forgotten to say that last week Mr Thomas added to our library. Lodge's 'Portraits' in six volumes, Holbein's 'Court of Henry VIII', Crabbes 'Life & works' & Hasted's 'History of Kent'.

10th Passed two hours with Mrs Hassells in Sittingbourne & listened to her tale of woe.*(She was unhappily married)*

11th Walked with Mr Thomas as far as the Union.[41]

17th Ella's first birthday. Richard had an interview with Mr Betts. A letter introducing Major Burns, son of the poet, who is employed under government to enquire into the state of the children employed in the paper mills in the counties of Kent, Sussex, Surrey & Middlesex.

19th Major Burns here at intervals during the day between his visits to the paper mills. He is an intelligent Scotsman who has been the greater part of his life in India & seen much of the world.

25th Richard departed for London. Mrs Disternell drank tea here. I am more enraged against Charles Duppa than ever.*(He drank heavily & wasted money)*

27th Went to the school. I am glad to say that Mrs Ashdown has begun the singing as I wished, & that some of the girls can already sing the morning hymn.

April 9th Went to the school heard the children sing the evening hymn.

25th Mrs Disternell called thinking Richard had only transmitted to her £10 of her money instead of £15.

28th Mrs Hassells appeared at 11 & accompanied Duppas & myself to Maidstone.

May 6th The Duppas called. Dined at the Dollings where met Fanny & Harriet Duppa & Mrs Faunce. Much music.

June 24th Brewing at home so could not drive out, attended the school.

30th Mrs Hassells came & we all proceeded to the Flower Show at Maidstone.

July 5th Drove up The Hill. Harriet Duppa accompanied me to Maidstone where after shopping, Milly arrived & we brought her home.

6th Horses, servants & master decorated with orange & purple ribbons & at 11 started for Penenden Heath to see the

---

[41] The Hollingbourne Union workhouse was less than five minutes walk from the house.

nomination of Sir Edward Filmer & Lord Marsham. Much speaking but none that we could hear. Much people but all singularly quiet.[42]

31st Took luncheon at Mrs Hassells' where met the Duppas & Mr Grayling. A very agreeable intelligent person. *(Mr Grayling was a Sittingbourne doctor)*

August 2nd Mrs Hassells passing the day here & remained the night.

17th Took Mama & Milly to Maidstone saw them safely in the Brighton coach.

21st Began to sketch the ancient cottage on Eyhorne Green it is very rugged & picturesque. Ed Duppa called.

23th The new staircase appeared, a day of dust & turmoil.

24th At 5 o'clock the work of destruction began, & 9 saw the partition between the hall & dining room even with the ground, & the lower flight of the old staircase removed.

27th Drank tea at Duppa's & met Dollings & Dr Mantell the geologist. He talked of petrified teeth, crabs, dragon flies & was as eloquent as ever. It was a real pleasure to meet him again.

28th Luncheon on The Hill met the Faunces, & Dr Mantell.

September 3rd Dined at the Musgrave's just reached Borden in time to escape a violent storm. I like Mrs Musgrave extremely & their house is particularly comfortable. *(The Rev. George Musgrave and his wife had a large new vicarage)*

November 9th A letter from Milly containing the melancholy tidings of the deaths of Mrs Elliott & Mrs Alexander both of scarlet fever at Brighton a week after their confinements. It is supposed that Mr Taylor the medical man who attended them brought the infection from a patient at Worthing. Mr Alexander was so overcome with his affliction that he followed his wife to the grave almost immediately. They had scarcely been married more than a year.

11th Drove to the Duppa's paid a long visit, then went as far as Borden with Mrs H. Duppa.

December 6th Went to Brighton, passed a cold but pleasant five weeks. Went up to London by rail road. Spent a pleasant

---

[42]   The borough of Maidstone continued to be entitled to elect two Members of Parliament after the 1832 Reform Act. The votes were cast at this time in a small stone house on Penenden Heath.

fortnight with Uncle Albert.[43] Home again on 24th January 1842.

1842 February 22nd Chimney piece, hall chairs, carpets & curtains arrived.

March 6th Did little beside working & reading Crabbe's 'Life'. Richard dined at the Annual Hunt Meeting.

20th Went to church for the first time for months.

April 28th Watched the paper hanging & painting.

29th Drove to Sittingbourne to spend the day with Mrs Hassells & catch a glimpse of Uncle Albert, his wife & sister on their way to the Continent. It was a great pleasure to me to see them.

May 18th Called on Mrs Dolling her mother staying with her. Saw the 5th child. Richard at cricket at Penenden Heath.

24th Arranged the books in the new bookcase, no slight labour.

26th Began to arrange the new dining room & hall, worked very hard.

August 23rd To the Corn Exchange to hear a short & very agreeable concert all excepting the high backless bench on which I was perched.

27th Richard started at 5 in the morning to visit poor Louis & returned by ½ past 7 in the evening. He found him as usual in good health, but his mind the same. We called at The Hill & saw the whole party with the addition of their cousin.

October 19th All alone. Richard out shooting & I walked to the school.

20th Went to the school. Much time occupied, or rather idled away, with Ella.

22nd Mrs Hassells came here in her new little carriage Richard out shooting.

28th Went to the school to distribute a few little prizes for needlework. Fanny Duppa & Miss Savage called. Richard at Maidstone.

29th Mrs Hassells came to spend the day with me. We then called at the Duppa's.

1843 January 15th Yesterday quitted Brighton at nine after a stay of five weeks & reached this from rail road at ½ past one. Soon after our arrival snow & Charles Duppa appeared.

---

[43]   The London Brighton & South Coast Railway opened in 1841.

17th Settling accounts, Christmas bills etc. Called on Mrs Tennyson at Boxley, a lovely day but the poet *(Alfred)* himself not at home.[44]

February 28th In the afternoon went to the school & decided on those worthy of prizes.

April 5th Called at Boxley Hall saw the poet's mother, brother & brother-in law as well as himself. He looked ill, unkempt & unwashed. We then went to Maidstone.

10th Which was to have been the poet's day. We were disappointed & he did not come, only Mrs Hassells took luncheon here.

May 29th The day of the 21st anniversary of the Benefit Club, ten garlands there.[45] Those of Hollingbourne, Leeds & Harrietsham appeared here at 10 accompanied by the Hollingbourne Band. The rain poured, but by 12 o'clock they returned here from the church & serenaded us. It was a dreary ceremonial & the dinner in the dripping tent was the dreariest of all.

June 16th The first day of Hollingbourne Fair. Took little Ella there as a great treat who chose among all the treasures usually sold on such occasions, a box of ninepins. Much music & sound of revelry in the evening.

22nd Went to the school about the prizes. Mrs Hassells & Charles Duppa drank tea here & the H. Duppas called.

24th Tennyson & his mother & sister Mrs Jesse called. He was in great spirits & very odd. Then the Duppas came to tea & Charles Duppa afterwards.

29th Arrived Mrs Hassells for the flower show. Took luncheon at Mrs Tennyson's & Mrs Jesse & Miss Tennyson went with us to the show which was in a field near Rocky Hill. *(Maidstone)* The flowers were beautiful, particularly the fuchsias, geraniums & roses which were arranged in tents. Saw many whom I knew & was introduced to the Lushingtons. Julius Brenchley gave me a sonnet of Wordsworth & one by Hartley Coleridge in their own handwriting.

July 7th A visit to Mrs Tennyson & Mrs Lushington at Park House. *(Boxley)*

---

[44] The Tennyson family had moved to Boxley Hall in 1841.

[45] The Benefit Club was a funeral club. Payments were made weekly by the farm labourers to avoid the misery of a pauper's grave.

8th An evening visit to Mrs H. Duppa who accompanied us to Jennings where we found all the Savage party at home.[46]

10th Ella in so violent a passion was obliged to send her to bed.

12th Poor Mrs Hassells wrote to say that she is very ill.

15th Drove with Ella to Headcorn to fetch Mama & Milly.

18th To the Lushington's to a dejeuner & afterwards a dance in a tent.

24th Freddy Goulburn arrived from town.(son to the Chancellor of the Exchequer).[47]

25th We went to a most pleasant pic-nic *(sic)* at Aylesford Priory. Dined on the smooth green & afterwards danced in the dining room of the once monastery, now lodging house. The drawing room is richly panelled & decorated. The Medway winds sleepily close by the old walls. A party of 42, a military band, many officers.

28th A dinner party at home consisting of Miss Tennyson, Mr & Mrs Lushington, Charles & Ellen Duppa & more.

31st Took Freddy to Maidstone on his way home & on our road called on the Tennysons & took leave of Mrs Jesse. A cricket match in our field between the Upper & Lower village.

August 9th A pic-nic in Sharsted Wood, a very large & cheerful party. Dancing in the wood & in the evening in the Hall.

14th Pic-nic at Boxley consisting of Duppas, Faunces, Savages, & Lushingtons. After strolling everlastingly in the woods & dining in a most exalted & uncomfortable situation we quitted them about ½ past 8 & drank tea at Mrs Tennyson's. Decidedly the pleasantest part of the day. The poet was very dirty & agreeable & declared that a pic-nic was only another word for every inconvenience.

15th Drove to the cricket match at Leeds Park where the Gore Court club were conquering & Richard was the champion of the day. Mr Grayling & Mrs Hassells came & talked to us. Many to tea & then dancing to the village band.

17th Dined at the Tennyson's, sat between the barrister & the poet, a pleasant day.

---

[46]   Sarah, one of the Duppa siblings married John Savage a barrister.

[47]   Confusingly there are two young Freddy Goulburns in the family, one is Louisa's cousin & Edward's brother. The other is this one. Son of Henry Goulburn the Chancellor who was brother of Uncle Go.

30th Dinner party here. The party went off very well malgre the disappointment of not seeing the poet who was in town.

31st Julius Brenchley took luncheon here. Milly practising archery with the Duppas on the Hill.[48]

September 7th Dined at Boxley Hall, the poet in good spirits, sat at dinner between him & the Greek professor Lushington[49] who was there with his wife. Barrister Lushington & sister also there.

13th Richard to the flower show at Maidstone. In the evening to a musical party on The Hill where all the Duppas sang, a pleasant evening.

14th Mrs Dolling called, we drove to Boxley to visit the Tennysons.

22nd Mama & Milly departed & we are left all alone, retired early to bed not feeling well.

26th Drove to Boxley. Saw Mrs Tennyson & the young ladies & Ella had the long promised treat of seeing the monkey. Richard out shooting all day.

28th Horatio Tennyson here shooting with Richard. Poor horse died today.

October 2nd To Maidstone where called on Mrs Middleton but did not see her as we were told by Colonel M. that she is dangerously ill. Richard pheasant shooting. Dispatched a pheasant, a hare & a note to Brighton.

28th Richard at home all day. A circumstance so unusual as to be recorded.

November 6th Still more poorly, sent for Mr Day in the evening at 10, he came again & stayed till morning.

7th My second little daughter was born. She is blue eyed & fat with dark hair. A very strong, screaming baby.

26th Went downstairs for the first time since my imprisonment. Mrs Hassells has kindly lightened many heavy hours by staying here. Mrs Dis has called. Richard has been in town. Ann has departed & our new housemaid Sarah Tillman come.

December 2nd My second daughter was christened Louisa & Mr Hasted & Mrs Dis took luncheon here.

---

[48]   Archery was one of the few sporting activities considered proper for ladies at the time.

[49]   Edmund Lushington a great Greek scholar who had married one of the Tennyson girls.

6th Sent a brace of pheasants to Brighton. Mrs Dis called, drove to Harrietsham.

12th Finished Carlisle's 'Past & Present', work, painting & accounts.

13th Wrote to my Father. *(He has not been mentioned for years)*

21th The Seven Champions appeared early, also the Old Woman 'good-dencing' as they call it here.[50]

22nd Wrote tickets for a Christmas dinner for 35 poor families.

23rd A day of Christmas carols, hand-bells & music of all sorts.

24th To afternoon church. Mrs Dis was to have accompanied me but was suddenly ill & found by the maid on the floor. The Duppas accompanied me home from church & called on her, she was then better.

25th To morning church at which there were many present. Richard & I took the sacrament. The Duppa girls & Henry Duppa took luncheon here. Mrs Dis better.

26th A call before breakfast to say Mrs Dis was much worse. Sent for Mr Sankey instantly & went down to her, the poor old lady was in bed & much incapacitated. A visit from the H. Duppas. Went down to Mrs Dis again in the evening.

1844 January 3rd A most severe frost. Boys skidding about on the village pond when yesterday there was no ice.

5th Endeavoured to paint Ella's portrait, I fear an impossible undertaking.

9th Went to the ball. Saw many whom I knew. A Highlander & an Austrian both in uniform were the stars of the evening. Home by three.

15th Mrs Hassells came & accompanied me to Maidstone. Did much shopping & bought the prizes for the schoolchildren.

23rd Started for Brighton at 11 & by means of post horses, rail roads & flies reached our destination at ½ past 4. Dined at Silwood Place & returned to our own home, 24 Oriental Place.

24th Today introduced our new baby to her Grandmama.

25th Went to look at some pictures for sale on the Grand Parade, called on the Horace Smiths & Lady Carhampton.

26th To dine at Sir Gregory Way's. Afterwards to a ball at Colonel Blake's.

---

[50]   Goodening or Good dancing survived in this part of Kent. A tradition of widows begging on St Thomas" Day 21st December.

27th A walk down the town when met Julius Brenchley & the Blakes.

28th To Mr Vaughan's church where he preached an admirable sermon.

February 1st To dine at Lady Carhampton's where met Horace & Miss Smith.

3rd Milly & I had a long & agreeable potter on the cliff, Mrs Mostyn was our companion for some part of the way. Mama & Richard went to see & hear Love, the ventriloquist, & were disappointed.

6th A walk on the cliffs with Milly, much shopping & talking, visits to the Miss Halifaxes. A soiree at Mama's, very pleasant but not large.

8th Dined at Mrs Mostyn's. Afterwards we all went in procession to Lady *(Frances)* Hotham's brilliant house. Gold, mirrors, scrolls, crimson & paintings in profusion, the ceilings richly decorated. I should think that 200 people were present.

10th A present of two pairs of cuffs from Milly. Repaired to Mama's at 1. Afterwards called on Lady Strange & the Miss Friers who anciently kept a school at Kensington & whom I had not seen since I was 7 years old. No news of or from Richard.

11th A letter from Richard.

12th To Miss Bonar's ball at 10. No one had arrived but Lady Hotham & no fire in the drawing rooms. The doors too of course incessantly open & the thermometer at freezing point. A dull but pretty party, not too crowded. On my return home found a policeman in the house, who having found the doors open, had made his entrance, thinking that thieves might have preceded him. All was safe.

15th Purchased the works of Racine & Moliere. Richard arrived.

20th We at 9 departed for the rail road for home which we reached at 2. Charles Duppa soon appeared. The weather cold but everything wonderfully bright & clean when compared with Brighton.

24th News of Sir Gregory Way's sudden death from influenza, I can scarcely believe it having seen him so recently.

26th Captain Thorndyke & Charles Duppa at breakfast, the new horses tried by driving them up Hollingbourne Hill. Mrs Hassells came at one.

March 6th Mr Barling came to bring us a wonderful watch to see. Richard kindly ordered one for me just like it. The old clock too has gone to be set in order. Messrs Edward, Charles & Henry Duppa called. Richard gone to dine with Mr Fullock did not return till nearly 4. (*a.m!*)

14th Mr Day came & re-vaccinated the baby.

15th Mrs Hassells came & to Ella's great joy brought her the long-promised gold fish, also the Miss Duppas took luncheon here.

18th Mr Wilder breakfasted here & he & Richard rode to Sharsted, I drove accompanied by my two daughters to Maidstone to get the baby vaccinated from Mr Wilder's child but it was too late as the time for taking the lymph has passed.

20th Called on Mrs Middleton who is still always suffering dreadfully.

23rd Charles Duppa has hired Richard's house. (*Elnothington a three minute walk away on the Ashford-Maidstone road*)

Elnothington today

24th Ella's debut at church where she behaved very well. But the pouring rain coming on, we were compelled to take refuge at Mrs Roper's (*Hollingbourne Manor then inhabited by tenant farmers*) where we were regaled on home-made cake & with the sight of five children, till the carriage could be sent to fetch us.

27th Sent the baby to meet Mr Day & be vaccinated for the 4th time & this time actually from another child.

April 2nd Mr Whatman called to see baby's arm. Drove to Thurnham to see the Wilders. Found the whole family party at home. The new horse slightly lame, much examined by Mr Wilder.

5th Being Good Friday went to afternoon church. Of course Mr & Mrs Henry Duppa at dinner, Edward Duppa, full of agriculture as usual, came in to tea.

6th Mr Wilder brought me to read a pamphlet 'What is the church?' & 'Martin Chuzzlewit'. Took Mrs H. Duppa home to Boughton where we found her husband already arrived & much disconcerted by the recent loss of a favourite cow.

8th Milly arrived went to fetch her at Headcorn. *(railway station)*

9th Mr & Mrs Dolling called. Went to the Maidstone ball where danced with a young engineer officer, Mr Wilder & Mr Julius Brenchley, a pleasant evening. Ella poorly.

12th Started for rail-road for London with Milly. Found Uncle Albert & Caroline quite well & busy renovating their house.

16th Aunt Ella came for tea, we drove out together to the Soho Square Bazaar & called again on the Greatheds. I was truly glad to see them again. Aunt Ella & Mr Nat Goldsmid dined here & Richard appeared about 9. Much discussion of Popery & English history as relating to religion. Milly & Uncle Albert went to a ball.

18th Mr Nat Goldsmid at breakfast. The Miss Goldsmids called on me & we called on Aunt Ella. Started at 4 by rail road for Staplehurst. Reached our own home by 8, found the Kittens *(children)* tolerably well & everything as usual except that Mr & Mrs Charles Duppa are settled at Elnothington.

19th Walked up the Hill with Richard & visited *(old)* Mr Duppa whom I had not visited for nearly a year found him much changed for the worse.

23rd Paid my first visit to Mrs Charles Duppa at Elnothington.

29th Mrs E. Duppa accompanied me to Headcorn to fetch Mama.

May 1st The arrival of the garlands. Wild flowers particularly pretty.

2nd Mama & I drove to Maidstone & did some shopping. Called on Mrs Middleton who was wretchedly ill. Saw Henry Duppa in high spirits.

14th Last Saturday I have omitted to name that we went to Rochester, put up at the Crown Inn of Falstaffian fame, lionised the Castle & St Nicholas, a small & ancient church, & ended by hearing the cathedral service in that ancient edifice.[51]

20th Mrs Wilder & Mr Hill & Mr & Mrs Charles Duppa took luncheon here. Mr Hill gave an interesting account of Van Diemen's Land where he made his fortune, but he says that none are to be made there now without large capital. He has been twice round the world.

June 9th *(staying with Aunt Ella)* Went to Uncle Albert's where found Milly. Walked with the uncle to the Temple Church, a mass of decoration & very fine. The broken effigies of the Knights Templars recumbent on their grave-stones are very old & venerable. In the afternoon Caroline & Uncle Go called. Ella the little has been much admired. Drank tea at Uncle Albert's.

14th To the New Houses of Parliament which are splendid; Gothic & remarkably rich in decoration. Mr Trotter one of the Members for Surrey was our guide & in him Mama found a cousin.

15th Started with Uncle Albert & party for Chiswick; the gardens crowded, met manifold acquaintances unexpectedly. The Nawab of Arcot was splendid in shawls.

18th To the Botanic Gardens in the Regents Park with Mama where we sauntered about, sat beneath tents, heard the band, saw the model of the projected Winter Garden.

19th Again to dentist. Went to a soiree at Uncle Albert's. A blazing fire though the weather is so hot.

20th Freddy called. We started per rail road at ½ past 2 reaching home at ½ past 6 found Richard not a little glad to see us again.

23rd A letter from Dodo *(Palmer),* announcing her engagement to Mr Maunsell, a clergyman. But the marriage is not to take place until next year.

July 2nd Mr Grayling came early to fish; he & Richard caught seven brace of trout.

12th A pic-nic at Jennings with Duppas of Hollingbourne, Boughton & Elnothington, & Mr & Mrs Dolling. Mrs Whatman sang German airs beautifully. The military band was also in attendance & there was some dancing.

---

[51]   'Lionised' meant looked round as tourists.

13th The arrival in pouring rain of Uncle Albert & Caroline, both looking well.

16th Went to the school where Uncle Albert & Caroline gave trifling encouragement in the way of sixpences etc. Drove to Boughton & called on Mrs H. Duppa. Took a lovely shady walk with her towards Loose, gathered cherries & heard her sing.

18th Uncle Albert & I started for Sittingbourne, Caroline being disabled by her fall & Richard occupied with his hay, met there at Mrs Hassells & Mr Grayling.

August 16th Visits from Mrs & Miss Savage & Fanny Duppa who accompanied us to Malling Abbey, Mrs Losack's, where we saw the things for sale, much trash, but the Abbey is beautifully rugged & picturesque, the kitchen large & Gothic with vaulted roof. The staircase is of massive oak & the windows of painted glass.

19th To Maidstone early to fetch Freddy who arrived from Tunbridge Wells.

20th To the Duppa's musical party. A very pleasant evening, Duppas, Savages, Mrs Hilton, Dollings, Mrs Whatman, Sir John Tylden & the Musgraves formed the orchestra after which supper & then dancing.

22nd Domestic life after much dissipation.

28th To the Savage's archery meeting, very pleasant. Danced with Mr Dolling went to luncheon with Captain Faunce & supper with Mr Whatman of Vinters.[52]

September 2nd We went up in the evening to the Duppa's where the guests including Mr & Mrs Dolling were practising the Polka.

5th To the races at Chatham where were much people, much noise & much eating. The poor horse Rondo broke his leg & was obliged to be killed.

11th Freddy departed. To the Dolling's music party, very pleasant & well arranged.

20th To dine at Mr Lushington's, very pleasant. I sat between the squire and the Indian brother Mr Thomas Lushington. Alfred Tennyson was there combed & dressed like other people.

24th The opening of the rail road at Maidstone.[53]

---

[52]   This James Whatman was of the famous paper-making family of Turkey Mill, Maidstone & Vinters was his home.

[53]   This was the South Eastern line from Paddock Wood to Maidstone West.

25th Dined at Mr Pemberton-Leigh's, *(Torry Hill)* met there Mr & Mrs Gipps. The house is all gold & silk & luxury.[54]

30th Started at ¼ past 9 for Pluckley where met the rail road train & went on by that through a multiplicity of tunnels to Dover. As we approached the town the line of road ran along the shore & I never saw the sea look more bright & beautiful than when we emerged each time from the gloom of the subterranean way. It was covered too with vessels of all kinds, a great contrast to the extreme stillness of the sea at Brighton. We walked & sat on the pier & regaled ourselves at a pastry cooks. Richard & Milly ascended to the Castle & ancient remains, but having already seen them in days of yore, Mama & I preferred the less fatiguing & more populous paths of everyday life. When we reached Ashford found the Archbishop of Canterbury waiting at the station for the special train that was to convey him to Lambeth his visitations in these parts being ended. Saw our home this evening, lovely day.

October 1st Mr Wilder at breakfast preparatory to starting for Coxheath on a shooting excursion with Richard. Charles Duppa came in the evening, Edward Duppa's marriage to Miss Long in the paper.

4th Took Mrs Dis & Mama to luncheon with the Savages. Mary Faunce & her Belongings *(children)* there.

8th The day of our dinner party. Mrs Griffiths sang delightfully. Miss Savage & Mrs Dolling & her sister played & Mr F. Lushington also sang. Hassells slept here.

17th Richard at Coxheath & Maidstone. He brought home some of the new, but I should imagine almost useless coins, the half farthing. Frank Lushington called & talked of Miss Martineau who it seems instead of being confined to a sick room can now walk a mile by the aid of animal magnetism.

22nd Ella & I went to Maidstone where did much shopping & called on Mrs Middleton who lent me 'Life in a Sick Room'. Mrs Dis & her friend at tea & a short visit at same hour from the Hassells, a parting one, before his departure for Scotland.

28th A bright day, so started with Richard to call at Torry Hill, the view & the drive lovely but unfortunately Mr Pemberton Leigh not at home. On our way home called on Mrs E. Duppa & found the whole colony from all parts of the county

---

[54]   Mr Pemberton-Leigh was then the Chancellor of the Duchy of Cornwall, a middle aged bachelor with 11 live-in servants.

assembled. Mrs E. Duppa is very unassuming looking & her complexion singularly clear.

November 4th Called for Mrs Charles Duppa & took her to call on Mrs H. Duppa whom we found not looking well. Her husband has given up his farming.

7th The Kitten's first yearly birthday *(Louy)*, & the dear little thing is as fat & healthy as can be wished.

18th Drove up The Hill to call on Mary Faunce who had sent me the back of the chair she had worked for me. She had gone home, but saw Harriet & Ellen, & Mrs E. Duppa accompanied me to call on Mrs Dolling. I am <u>much</u> pleased with Mrs E. Duppa.

December 4th Ill in bed all day, a visit from Mr Whatman, a letter from Caroline.

8th Mrs Dis at tea. I felt very poorly & incapacitated & at ¼ past 3 on the morning of December 10th our third daughter was born, a slender little dark-eyed creature, as like Ella as possible. Milly's presence most cheering.

1845 January 14th A long void in my journal. The 3rd & last born has been made a Christian by the name of Bertha Jardine. Uncle Albert is godfather & Caroline & Mrs Hassells godmothers.

15th Drove Milly to Maidstone accompanied by Sarah *(Milly's maid),* & saw them both safe into the 'wood-built' Maidstone station.[55]

29th Called on Mrs C. Duppa, found her looking very handsome & her baby very flourishing.

31st Mr Wilder again here for six hours & talking as much as usual.

February 4th We went to Mrs Sibbbald's ball which I found very pleasant. Passed my evening with the Lushingtons, danced with the barrister & Frank, with Captain Gibson, & with Mr Julius Brenchley. Richard played whist. Home a little past 3.

22nd At 3 o'clock to Elnothington to assist at the Christening of Miss Edith Ellen *(Duppa)* which was performed by Mr Hasted; Richard being godfather.

25th Started from home at 10. Made a very prosperous journey to Reigate where we changed our vehicle & line & reached Brighton at 4.

---

[55] This was Maidstone West where trains ran to Paddock Wood eight times a day.

26th Settled ourselves a little in our apartment in Bedford Place. Walked down the town with Milly. Called on Mrs Mostyn, & Gertrude Halifax called.

March 2nd To Mr Vaughan's chapel where heard him preach an impressive sermon. Called on Lady Carhampton & saw her mosaic table formed of the various pieces of marble which her grandchildren had 'picked up' in Rome.

5th Dined at Mrs Mostyn's, we then proceeded to Mr Bowyer's ball which was very much crowded & pleasant, the supper admirably arranged.

25th Returned home to Hollingbourne. Richard went to see poor Louis.

29th The day of meeting of the Hollingbourne Leeds & Harrietsham Benefit Club & much rain, unfortunately for the assembled multitude. The garlands were almost entirely composed of field flowers on account of the severity of the season, there being but few garden blooms to be had.

A description of the event from the Maidstone Journal: 'At an early hour a merry peal from the church bells, firing of cannon & other demonstrations of joy, informed the inhabitants of its being the 29th of May and the anniversary of the Hollingbourne United Men of Kent Benefit society. The village presented an animated scene, the houses were decorated with oak boughs, & the Hollingbourne band soon made their appearance dressed in their uniform, playing in a party from Leeds. The members, nearly 200 in number, processed to the church, preceded by their band, the banners and three splendid garlands. Prayers were read by the Rev Edward Hasted. After divine service dinner was served in a commodious marquee near the Windmill Inn, & the members did justice to the good things provided. The chair was taken by R. Thomas esq, after the removal of the cloth the health of the Queen was drunk with enthusiasm. During the evening the company formed themselves into groups some were engaged in the old English games of kiss in the ring, cricket & quoits. The band played at intervals throughout the day.'

June 5th Called on Mrs Wilder en route to Maidstone. Maidstone so full of horned cattle the walking about anything but pleasant. Colonel Griffiths called. [56]

---

[56]   Colonel Frederick Griffiths then in his 40s, commandant of the Cavalry Depot in Maidstone. Lived in some style with his wife Lucy & eight live-in servants.

12th Richard at Penenden Heath in the cricket match against Tenterden.

13th Started early to join a pic-nic at Cobham. Richard & I were there long before the rest of the party appeared & enjoyed ourselves much in the stately rooms & amongst the pictures. The party at last arrived. Greatheds, Griffiths, Duppas, Savages. A most agreeable day & the weather hot & lovely.

26th To the flower show in the field by Rocky Hill at Maidstone, much people & many flowers. Talked to the Lushingtons, Savages, Duppas, Sir J. Tylden etc the fuchsias & roses lovely. Ella accompanied us.

July 10th Preparations for a dinner party. Milly arrived unexpectedly in the rain.

11th Colonel Griffiths took us to Cobham in his drag[57] drawn by four white horses. I went inside with Mrs Griffiths & Mrs Copland, Milly on the box with Colonel Griffiths. Saw the 'Old Hall' again. We dined under a shed & had a pleasant day. The party increased at Cobham by Mrs H. Duppa etc. Returned to the Griffiths where we drank tea & met the old Colonel Griffiths.

15th To Maidstone, called on the Griffiths & left them some strawberries & some roses for Mrs Middleton. Went to the Old College which has been repaired & rearranged by Lord Romney. The situation is lovely & the buildings ancient, ivied & very picturesque.

19th Mr Wilder met us at Bearsted & accompanied us to the launching of the 'Active' frigate at Chatham. Sat in Captain Shirreff's booth & afterwards went to luncheon at his house.

August 5th To Sittingbourne, on our way called at Mr Duppa's where saw himself, Harriet & Mr & Mrs E. Duppa, then on to Sittingbourne to pass the day with Mrs Hassells. Called on Dr & Mrs Vallance & Mr Grayling.

12th Dined at Colonel Griffiths. Went to the tea party at the Charity School where Ella distributed buns to the children.

15th Wrote to Jessy (*Goldsmid cousin*) to congratulate her on her approaching marriage. To see Mrs Dollng & her imitation of Brussells point lace, which was beautiful as she actually makes the flowers.

---

[57]   A private vehicle like a stage coach drawn by four horses with seats inside & on the top.

18th Milly started for London under the care of Mr Wilder. Hassells came at 12.

September 9th Mama & Milly's departure for Headcorn en route for Dover.

11th On our journey to Ashford with Louy at 6, then on to Dover where we were met by Mama & Milly thence to Walmer where paid a most agreeable visit with the Hulls & Aunt Ella. Took our leave, drank tea at Dover where bid adieu to Mama & Milly & dear little Louy *(Louy aged two is left to stay with Milly & Mama)* & had a most unexpected meeting with Edward at Ashford who had come to Kent to view the living of Elham.

13th Drove to Maidstone to fetch Caroline & Uncle Albert.

18th Uncle Albert & Richard went to see poor Louis; much the same.

19th Drove to see poor Hassells who is, & looks, very poorly.

October 1st To Maidstone, Mr C. Duppa accompanied us. Richard met us & we all went to see a collection of pictures for sale at The Star. A Gainsborough for which they asked £250, many copies & two little conversation pieces by Andrews which I should have much liked.

3rd Mrs Hassells passed the day & Mrs Dis drank tea. Richard attending a rail road meeting at Maidstone.

6th Richard in London on rail road matters.

8th Started at 8 for Dover, found the whole party quite well. Went to see the paintings of Waters, a Dover artist, on the whole much pleased with them. Shopping, walked on the esplanade at ½ past 6 left Dover with Louy.

12th Letter from Edward to announce that he had accepted the living of Elham & is most probably to be married next month.

14th Started early for Dover with dear little Ella. *(Ella's turn to stay with Milly & Mama)* Took her to the artist Mr Waters for her first sitting. Mr & Mrs Hull & Aunt Ella met us at dinner at Mama's. Sauntered on the esplanade.

27th Richard at Coxheath. Called on Mrs Middleton who lent me two novels.

31st Mr E. Duppa called. Mrs Hassells accompanied us to Maidstone & we went to see the models of the two atmospheric engines, Pilbrowe's & Samuel's, also a Mummy, a barometer, telegraph, pictures etc. Met Mrs H. Duppa & Captain Unett.

November 3ʳᵈ Mrs Hassells departed. Mr H. Duppa met with a serious accident out shooting, the ramrod of his gun passing quite through his hand.

12ᵗʰ At eight en route for the rail road. Left Maidstone at 9, our companions de voyage Colonel Griffiths & Captain Unett. Much discussion on the Polka, the elopement of Lady Adela Villiers & rail roads. Uncle Albert's carriage met us at the station & soon brought us to Park Crescent.

Park Crescent the best Nash terrace in London

The Uncle & Caroline remarkably well & Jessy full of purchases & preparations. *(Jessy was the daughter of Papa's brother Lionel Goldsmid & so Louisa's cousin. She married another related Goldsmid.)* A walk to many shops with them & a visit to Aunt Ella. Tea, dinner & whist ended the day.

13ᵗʰ Aunt Ella took a potter with Richard, Ella & myself. To Lewis & Allenby's *(department store)* where bought a gown, & to Madame Ryan's where decided on a bonnet. Drove out with Caroline, called on Kate, & the Struths, all away or out.

14ᵗʰ A drive with Aunt Ella to call on the Thomas Thomas's, left Ella there & drove to Lewis & Allenby's. A visit from Freddy who is looking strong, fat & well. A tea-dinner in Park Crescent & three rubbers. *(home ncxt day by train.)*

17th News brought in that Mrs Dis was very poorly, went to see her immediately & sent for Mr Sankey. She has also set herself on fire & is constantly falling.

19th Called on Mrs Dis & thought her very weak & indistinct. Rail-road people came in during the evening to make enquiries.

25th Started for London. At the Maidstone station met Mary Faunce who with Captain Faunce accompanied us to London. Milly met us at Tonbridge & on our arrival in town separated. She to stay with Uncle Albert & we with Aunt Ella.

26th Started early shopping & visiting, called early on the Miss Struths & on Kate found her in bed & Freddy not up. She looks ill & unhappy, dined at 3 called in Park Crescent, full of preparations.

27th At ½ past 10 met the wedding party at Uncle Albert's then to the church where Jessy married to Mr H. Edward Goldsmid. Returned to the breakfast, sat by Mr N. Goldsmid. Passed a quiet evening with Aunt Ella while Richard dined with Uncle Albert. *(Home on 29th)*

December 4th Drove early to Maidstone, Mr Wilder breakfasted here. Brought home Caroline to stay with us.*(Uncle Albert arrived next day)*

13th Yesterday a change of ministry announced, Lord John Russell is Premier. Today the arrival of Edward's wedding cake & cards.[58]

16th Started early for Dover with Ella. Went to Mr Waters where she sat for the last time for her portrait, passed the rest of the day at Mama's.

18th Took our leave of Dover at ¼ past 12. Dear little Ella thrown from the fly, took her into an hotel.[59] A medical man passing pronounced no bones broken so we pursued our journey, got home tolerably. Summoned Mr Sankey to examine her, put her to bed & from a fearful accident escaped most mercifully.

20th Called on Mrs H. Duppa, saw two portraits of her . The unfortunate Mr & Mrs C. Duppa came in & also Edward Duppa.

24th Mr & Mrs H. Duppa took luncheon here. Richard at Coxheath & returned laden with holly for the little girls'

---

[58] Cousin Edward Goulburn married Julia Cartwright of Aynho, Northamptonshire.

[59] A fly was a one-horse covered carriage let out on hire.

wreaths. In the evening we had the band, carols & hand-bells never ending.

1846 January 1st Dined at Mr Wilder's on a Norfolk turkey. Mr Wilder sang.

3rd Mr Rugg called to secure Richard's subscription to the school & left me 15/- for prizes for the children.

7th Preparations for Milly's dress as Queen Henrietta Maria for the Fancy Ball at Mrs Gifford's. At 7 set out for Borden, the children beautifully dressed, powdered heads & brocaded robes predominantly. Little Miss Dolling's dark eyes very brilliant with the aid of the powder. She wore an amber satin dress over an embroidered petticoat. The Miss Musgraves danced the minuet & gavotte twice over. After supper came a most noisy play acted by Mr Gifford, Mr Musgrave & Mr Gregg as an elderly French Countess. Then dancing again & a conjurer & then we departed, which no one was allowed to do till three o'clock. Danced with Mr Dolling, Mr J. Vallance, Mr G. Grayling & two Mr Prestons, one of whom personated an Albanian, the other Lord Rochester. Mrs Hassells looked much better & placidly happy.

16th A lovely spring-like day. Walked to Leeds to see the part of the old priory church that has been lately excavated, a few broken columns all that is visible.

18th Two rail road men called last night to obtain Richard's consent to the line in question, which he refused.

21st On Saturday a letter from young Richard announcing that he had purchased a farm near Brentford Canada West.

February 2nd Fetched Mama from Headcorn. *(railway station)*

3rd To Jullien's concert. Richardson played exquisitely & as to Jullien I enjoyed seeing him as much as hearing him. 800 people there.

9th Drove to Lenham to fetch Milly, the horses very restive & Hengist got over the traces & kicked very much. I was really frightened.

19th Called on Dis, went to the school. Wrote out the petition to Lord St Germans touching the post office. *(to establish one in the village)*

23rd The petition approved by Sir Edward Filmer, so sent it round the parish for signatures.

25th Dispatched letter & petition to Sir E. Filmer.

March 2nd Drove to Maidstone to fetch Dodo & her husband from the station, much pleased to see them. Mr Maunsell is very cheerful & agreeable.

3rd Drove to Thurnham found only Mrs Wilder & Miss Frances at home & lionised the church where is a remarkable window. Then to Maidstone to Mrs Griffiths where she took us to lionise the old church & very fine it is, but much ruined by pews & galleries.

4th Mr Maunsell went in the rain to the school & examined the children. We also walked to the church & Manor House & lionised all over them. Dinner party here. Mrs Duppa sang beautifully.

Hollingbourne Manor

5th Took our friends to the station at Maidstone, they gave us pressing invitations to their own home, Thorpe, But I fear that we shall never go that way. Began 'The Cricket on the Hearth'.

16th To Maidstone to fetch Miss Struth but first did much shopping. Saw Captain Unett again & took leave in good earnest as he was on his way to the station to depart immediately.

30th Dined at the Henry Duppa's. Harriet Duppa is to be married on Saturday.

31st Dined at Mr Cooke's where met Captain Douce. I went into dinner with Captain Douce who gave me a lock of the Duke of Wellington's hair – quite grey & very short.

April 1st To pass the day with Mrs Hassells at Sittingbourne, Mr Grayling there.

8th Ed Duppa called. Drove Miss Struth to Maidstone. Met Colonel Middleton who said that Mrs M was worse & in the most fearful pain.

13th To Pluckley to pass the day with Mrs & Miss Dering, a very agreeable one. There was much seeing & discussing relics, treasures, heraldry etc. A visit this morning from Edward Duppa who is on his way to Dover to paint Harriet's portrait before she goes.

16th Milly I regret to say departed, I took her down to the station & then called on Mrs Middleton & Mrs Whatman.

21th Started at 12 for Maidstone where met Captain Douce full of gossip as usual, reached Park Crescent *(London)* at 5. After refreshing ourselves Caroline & I walked to see Aunt Ella.

23rd Richard at Woolwich & Ella & I walked with Aunt Ella to the Pantheon where she was kind enough to order a dress & bonnet for the little thing. Drove out with Caroline & called on Kate, on Edward's wife & on the E. Goldsmids.

25th Richard who had returned last night came in & he & I went on a walk together & he gave me a beautiful dressing case & a tea chest. *(Richard then left for home)*

26th To St Johns Wood chapel to hear Edward preach which he did most beautifully, afterwards called on Kate. The Chancellor of the Exchequer *(Goulburn)* came in looking wretchedly – as thin & worn & grey as possible.

29th To the water colour exhibition where Caroline & I were charmed with some of the pictures 'Prayer' by Hunt was beautiful & also his 'Saturday' & 'Sunday' much admired. As we were coming out met Mr & Mrs H. Duppa. Dined at Aunt Ella's.

31st *(At home)* Mr Sankey called to say that Mrs Dis was very poorly having been suddenly seized in the night. Knight came, lent her £3 to advance her husband's business.

May 1st Little girls with wild flower garlands. Called on Dis who is better.

6th To Sharsted where saw the little new son, a most precocious & large child, long dark hair, in short clothes & without even a night cap & four teeth nearly through. Mary

(Faunce neé Duppa) looking very well. Ella had a most agreeable day.

25th The post office established & in operation. *(in Hollingbourne)* Mr & Mrs Bigge & Colonel Middleton at luncheon. Mr & Mrs E. Duppa called here.

27th To Sharsted found all its inhabitants well. Called in our way on old Mr Duppa who is very feeble & emaciated. Saw Fanny & Mrs E. Duppa.

June 16th Mrs Hassells came early. Went to the fair where we took Ella & Louy, weather sultry, at six the Wilders arrived to dine here.

17th The Wilders & I drove to Maidstone & did much in the shopping way. Mr & Mrs Duppa drank tea here. Much singing & dancing.

24th Brought home Eliza *(Horace)* Smith from the station. Colonel Middleton & the H. Duppas dined here & Eliza Smith sang beautifully.

30th To Sittingbourne to call on Mrs Hassells. On our way home met with a fearful accident which ended happily. The horses became frightened from the bits of one getting round the pole & dashed on, throwing Perfect *(footman)* down so that they really could not be held in. They were at last stopped by the ascent about two miles off & two men held them, but George *(coachman)* finding that they were very dull in arranging, dismounted from the box. The men let go & off they dashed again worse than ever. I thought that George would have been kicked to pieces but he held them in most manfully & at last succeeded in turning them into a hedge. Matters were then set right. Perfect came up much torn as to his clothing but unhurt & we reached our home most thankfully & most unexpectedly in safety.

July 4th To Maidstone to fetch Uncle Albert & Caroline.

28th This morning Uncle Go departed. Much has occurred since last writing my journal. The arrival of Mama & Milly from Oxford where they were much pleased with Edward & Julia. A pic-nic at Cobham to which we were conveyed by Colonel Griffiths & his drag a lovely hot day – archery, dining on the grass, & ending with dancing at Rochester. Started at 11 in morning from home & did not return till 1 a.m. the next morning. On 25th Uncle Go arrived, not in his highest spirits, but they improved by degrees. On Sunday he accompanied Milly to Leeds church in the morning & me to Hollingbourne church in the afternoon. On 27th walked to the farm with him

& drove him to Maidstone & Colonel & Mrs Griffiths dined here. All delighted with Uncle Go who made himself very agreeable & never ceased talking.

August 1st Taught Ella, finished my piece of worsted work.

7th Drove to Maidstone & called on Mrs Middleton, Ella & Louy accompanied me. Went to the school, called on Dis.

24th A walk to call on Mr Hasted & thank him for a second present of mulberries. The poor old man looked very ill.

25th Richard started early for Ticehurst. Mrs Hassells & Miss Grayling passed the day here & Mr & Mrs Gifford & Mrs Musgrave called. Took Milly to Boughton to stay with the H. Duppas.

28th Milly called with Mr & Mrs H. Duppa. Mama & I walked to the excavation of the old priory chapel at Leeds, a lovely evening.

September 1st Richard out shooting at 5 am. We drove to Wateringbury & took luncheon with the Bigges & did shopping in Maidstone, passing much time in Bunyard's nursery garden. Mr C. Duppa dined here after shooting.

14th In the evening Mr & Mrs H. Duppa & Captain Thorndyke called here, he to take leave on his way to Barbados for five years. Richard out shooting.

19th To the races at Sir Edward Filmer's, the races slow but the luncheon at the House *(East Sutton Place)* very pleasant.

October 6th Mama & Milly departed accompanied by Louy.

13th Drove to Sittingbourne to pass the day with Mrs Hassells. Mr Grayling called.

24th Dined at Mr Pemberton Leigh's to meet Uncle Go & Kate who had just arrived, of course a very sumptuous dinner, sumptuously served. Whist in the evening.

28th Uncle Go & Kate came to stay with us.

November 6th To the school to decide about the prizes. Drove to Maidstone to fetch Mr Thomas & Louy who arrived from Brighton much improved in looks.

9th To the school to give the prizes. Gave a dress to one Colegate & a pinafore to another & a dress to Bourne.

10th Began to teach Louy to read.*(She is three)*

11th Began a cushion for Mama in lambs wool & cross stitch.

15th I called on Mrs Dis who was as usual craving for more cash.

December 1st A letter from Milly & a present from Mama of £100. Forwarded a brace of pheasants to Brighton.

5th Fanny Duppa called & old Mr Duppa came to the door in his chair.

9th Too poorly to see any visitors. Richard returned in safety having had in going to town what might have proved a most sad accident but he managed to get out of the window of the rail-road carriage. Mrs Hassells departed.

23rd Milly arrived from Brighton.

26th Not feeling well, did not go down to dine. Sent for Mrs Kirby *(midwife who will stay six weeks)*, & at 6 in the morning of 27th the 8th anniversary of our wedding day, our 4th daughter was born, a small fat child.

1847 January 21st From that epoch till the present day most of my time has been passed in bed, but I am thankful to say that I am wonderfully & unusually well. Milly I regret to say departed today & Richard is still in town. Edward Duppa has just called. Snow fast falling. Richard returned this evening having seen Aunt Ella, Mama & Caroline & Uncle Albert.

23rd Mrs Kirby departed. Richard at Maidstone paying bills.

25th My first day for nearly two months of getting up at breakfast. Taught Ella & sent to Mr Rugg our yearly subscription to the school. Mr Whatman called.

26th Drove in the carriage with the three young ladies as far as Harrietsham.

February 2nd At 2 our little daughter was made a Christian by the name of Mary Julia Wilder, again a day of snow showers through which Mr Hasted came.

3rd Mr Wilder departed after luncheon.

5th Drove to Maidstone not feeling quite at ease about little Mary & consulted Mr Whatman. Ella & Louy accompanied me.

13th Wrote verses which I had not done for many a long day. *(This was the Floral Alphabet written for Mary – see below)*

19th Colonel Middleton, Miss Lushington & the two Miss Tennysons called. Little Mary much better. George, *(the coachman)*, shot in the orchard an uncommon bird which as far as I can tell by the aid of White's 'History of Selbourne' is the Hawfinch or Haw Crossbeak.

20th Henry Lushington is made Chief Secretary to Malta with £1500 a year. Purchased at Hall's the 'Illuminated Parables' cover in papier mache & exquisite imitation of wood carvings. Called on Dis after a three month cessation of visits, found her much the same.

26th A melancholy day for Mrs C. Duppa there being an execution at Chrismill. *(the bailiffs arrived with a warrant)*
27th The dismissal of the bailiffs by Edward Duppa. *(paid his brother's debts)*

WILD FLOWER ALPHABET.

TO MY LITTLE DAUGHTER MARY.

" Les prairies seront votre école, les fleurs vos Alphabets, et Flore votre Institutrice."

BERNARDIN DE ST. PIERRE.

A stands for Arum, with leaf broad and bright,
The crimson are lords, and the ladies are white.
But beware 'neath the hedge-row those berries so red,
For many have eaten and died it is said.

B stands for Buttercup, shining like gold,
Winter is gone, and the ice and the cold,
And the yellow blooms clothe all the field and the hill,
Mary may gather as long as she will.

C stands for Cowslip, the child of the spring,
When the trees are all budding, the merry birds sing,
Up, and to green lane and meadow away,
And twine you a garland to welcome May-day.

D stands for Daisy,—you need not go far
To seek and discover that white little star.
"And be sure you may know if the summer's come yet,
When your foot on nine daisies at once you can set."

E is the Eyebright that grows on the Down,
Where the earth is all white, and the grass is all brown,
Where we see not much else save the sea and the sky,
We greet thee, pale flower, with the dark purple eye.

N stands for Nightshade, of dreariest hue,
That deadly in name and in nature is too.
For like apple of Eden, its fruit hath beguiled,
Full oft to his death, the poor wandering child.

O is the Orchis,—just look in your walk,
For that strangest of plants which is found on the chalk,
Now a man, now a spider, a fly, or a bee,
All the forms that it takes, you will wonder to see.

P stands for Poppy, or else quite as well,
For that other bright blossom, the red Pimpernel.
Shepherd don thy thick cloak and thy cottage fast gain,
For it closes its petals to warn thee of rain.

Q stands for Quercus, the forest's great king,
The oak that from yon tiny acorn could spring.
Heart of oak are our ships that to nations afar,
Bear the riches of commerce, the thunders of war.

R stands for Rose, that is England's own flower,
The boast of the garden in summer's still hour.
Yet the white rose and red rose, as I understand,
Were once badges of discord in our sunny land.

The floral Alphabet

March 15th To Hollingbourne House for the meeting of the fox hounds. Took Mr & Mrs H. & Mrs C. Duppa up The Hill. Two foxes found & one passed quietly the drawing room windows, but none killed. Called on Mr Hasted.

20th Sudden summons to Mrs Dis who instead of one or two opium pills at a dose had taken eight. She was of course poorly & sleepy & Mrs Heady much frightened.

24th A general fast for the heavy affliction of famine & disease in the sister kingdoms of Ireland & Scotland. *(Irish potato famine)* Old Mr Duppa taken dangerously ill, reports of his death.

26th Mr & Mrs Bigge took luncheon here. Mr & Mrs Savage called. Little Mary so poorly that I called in Mr Sankey.

27th Little Mary still poorly but better. I drove with the two young ladies to call on Lady Filmer, found her & Sir Edward at home. Ella & Louy came in to play with their children.

April 5th Poor Mr Duppa died.[60]

6th To the Maidstone Ball in the evening where met Mr & Mrs Bigge & danced quadrilles & a polka & waltz with Colonel Griffiths with whom went to supper.

8th Visited Mr Hasted, he lent me a curious black letter book – Proctor's 'History of Wyatt's Rebellion' of which he said there were only five copies extant.

13th Ella, Louy & I started for Brighton. *(leaving baby Mary & little Bertha in care of nursemaids at home)* Drove to Tonbridge then got onto the train.

16th Made many visits but only found Lady Carhampton at home.

May 12th Took our departure from Brighton where we had driven & walked every day in spite of the dust & the bleak wind, after leaving the rail road at Tonbridge the country really looked lovely so green & blooming, found Richard & all our Belongings quite well except Bertha who had a little cold.

19th Richard at Coxheath & cricket at Penenden Heath. His new pointer, Doll, arrived from Mr Wilder. Called on Dis & sat with her in the garden.

25th Started for London to stay with Aunt Ella where remained exactly a week returning on 1st June. She was not very well, but as usual very kind. During our stay went to the Exhibition *(Royal Academy)* & also that of Water Colours. To the crowded bazaar at the barracks in the Regents Park for the Scotch & Irish where saw many of the belles of the day; Lady Clementine Villiers, Lady Aylesbury etc. To the House of Lords, a gorgeous mass of gilding, colour & decoration. To the Coliseum by night. The Panorama of London wonderful, the other parts of the collection a great melange of prettiness, ingenuity & trash. We visited Mr & Mrs Thomas Thomas *(Richard's brother)* at Kensington, & saw my old immense nurse Mrs Cooke. One day we dined at Uncle Albert's, another day we dined at Uncle Go's. Milly & Caroline called to say adieu, the heat intense.

June 12th *(At home)* To Sittingbourne with Ella & Louy to pass the day with Mrs Hassells, Mrs Musgrave rode up to the terrace there & talked.

---

[60]   When Baldwin Duppa died he left a complex will. Hollingbourne House & its lands were put into trusteeship, their use to be enjoyed by his successive principal heirs. The first of these was the eldest son of his own deceased eldest son. Young (Baldwin) Frank was 19 when he inherited.

24th Drove to Maidstone to the flower show. The show good, but not so many people as usual. Called on Mrs Middleton who was so very poorly.

30th To Canterbury with our guests where we were met by Mr Grayling & Mrs Hassells & saw the wonderful & beautiful cathedral, the college for missionaries anciently in the monastery of St Augustine & restored by Mr Hope, & the little simple church of St Martin, ivy grown with old stained windows. The stone coffin containing the dust of Bertha & the font of ancient date where her husband & consort Ethelbert was baptised by St Augustine. We turned from the wonders of past ages to those of a present one & returned to Ashford by train. Home at nine.

July 1st A dinner party at home consisting, besides our present guests, of Lushingtons, Duppas & Colonel Middleton.

4th To morning church where Louy went for the first time. Called on Mrs Dis.

5th Much rest & gardening. Drew our house from the field opposite. Fanny & Ellen Duppa at tea.

13th Mr Chetwynd dined here & afterwards accompanied us to a soiree dansante at Mrs Hassells', very well arranged. Danced & went to supper with Mr Gifford, home at 3, thoroughly tired.

15th Called on the Dollings who told us that the explosion of the gunpowder mills at Faversham which we heard yesterday was owing to carelessness & obstinacy in overheating the furnace & had been fatal to 18, 18 more being wounded.[61]

25th To afternoon church where Mr & Mrs Thomas Thomas & their little girl accompanied us, they arrived last Thursday.

31st Mr Griffiths called on the drag. Richard canvassing for Sir Edward Filmer.

August 3rd Donned purple & orange & with Louy & Ella went to the nomination, near enough to hear much but not to see. Sir Edward Filmer, Colonel Austen & Mr Hodges the three candidates. Mr Noel kindly gave the children cakes & currants. Charles Duppa looked more disreputable than ever, also saw his brothers.

6th Richard to Maidstone to vote for Sir Edward Filmer.

9th Drove with Milly through Maidstone where election & Freemason processions were going on.

---

[61]   Great explosion at Marsh Powder Works, 40 to 50 men killed.

23rd Called on Mr Hasted who was very poorly. He sent us in the evening another instalment of mulberries.

27th To Maidstone where did much shopping, saw Herbert Middleton who gave a better account of his father but a very sad one of his mother.

28th Mulberries from Mr Hasted, venison from Sir Edward Filmer.

September 2nd Colonel Griffiths, & Harry Duppa called on their way up The Hill to shoot. They dined here too with Mr & Mrs Dolling.

13th Drove to Maidstone to fetch Edward.

19th In the afternoon Edward preached on our changing our earthly body for a spiritual one, a very good & at times a very poetical sermon.

20th Edward & Julia departed, Milly taking them to the railroad station.

23rd Drove to Maidstone to fetch Frederic *(Goldsmid, Louisa's cousin & the brother of Jessy)* who took luncheon here & walked with us to Leeds Castle to lionise.

October 12th Accounts. Ella's lessons, arranging flowers, reading Howitt's 'Homes & Haunts of the British Poets'. Stringing beads & calling on Dis whom I found at dinner & the cat sharing it, filled up the day.

13th A mushroom walk & a more abundant harvest than usual. Called on the Dollings, took them pheasants & on Mr Hasted & left him one. On Saturday between 6 & 8 o'clock a.m. was the annular eclipse of the sun so long expected & talked of but which was not visible except in the darkness it occasioned, owing to the clouds & gloom of the morning.

20th Called on the Wilders whom I was much rejoiced to see again. He sent Richard half a dozen bottles of his Old Madeira & two old quaint stone monster's heads off his church. A very successful mushroom walk.

21st To the Assembly Rooms at Maidstone where Madame Dulcken & John Parry gave a 'Matinee Musicale.' Her playing very brilliant & with immense effect.

22nd Mr Wilder came to shoot with Richard. Dispatched pig & walnuts to Brighton.

25th Drove to Sittingbourne, called on Mrs Musgrave who was as usual sensible & agreeable, thence to take luncheon with Mrs Hassells. Mr Grayling came in, saw some specimens of minerals & one of stone from the Dropping Well at Knaresboro' in Yorkshire. All sorts of reports & realities, none of the most creditable description with regard to Mr C. Duppa.

30th Poor Dis had a slight paralytic stroke I went to see her. She was quite unintelligible & seemed not to understand what I said, sent for Mr Sankey.

November 2nd A steeple chase to which did not go as Richard said no ladies would be present, instead of which 'all the world & his wife were there'. *(A rare example of recording her annoyance)* Colonel Griffiths called with a large party on the drag.

7th Louy's fourth birthday. Ella & I drove to Thurnham to be present at the baptism of Mr Wilder's daughter who was Christened during the service. He preached a very good sermon.

22nd I went in the afternoon to meet Mr & Mrs Dolling at Mr Hasted's & lionised with them the church, the Manor House & the altar cloth worked by the Ladies Culpeper during the time of their father's exile with Charles II. Mrs Whatman sent Richard a very beautiful spaniel puppy, a retriever.

25th Richard at Maidstone at the sale of some meadows in Hollingbourne.

December 13th Mr & Mrs Wilder & Mr & Mrs E Duppa took an early dinner here. A bad report of Mrs Hassells.

14th To Sittingbourne, saw poor Mrs Hassells who was in bed & Mr Grayling who spoke very unfavourably of her case. She seemed quite aware of it but was not dispirited. Richard was at Maidstone where was the cattle show.

17th A note from Mr Grayling touching Mrs Hassells, saying that her case was a hopeless one but that he & Dr Locke had contrived to alleviate in some degree her suffering.

20th Mr Wilder at breakfast & he & Mr E. Duppa, Mr Wakefield son to Edward Gibbon Wakefield[62] at dinner. Mr Wakefield gave us a very interesting account of New Zealand.

27th Drove to Sittingbourne where found Mrs Hassells decidedly better but still in bed & her case still very uncertain. On my return home Henry Duppa was with Richard.

1848 January 7th A sad account of Mrs Hassells so went over to Sittingbourne, found her in a dreadful state. Her complaint

---

62   Edward Gibbon Wakefield, politician & driving force behind early colonisation of New Zealand.

cancer of the stomach which had been kept from her till then. Mr Wilder out shooting with Richard.

9th Mr Hasted too ill to have any service at all. Poor Mrs Hassells died at ½ past 4 this morning.

12th Mr Brenchley & his two brothers called for Richard to go out shooting.

13th Major Jardine wrote to say that poor Mrs Hassells would be buried either Saturday or Sunday.

15th A pouring day. Richard attended poor Mrs Hassells' funeral which was also attended by Mr Hassells.[63] Mr Walford *(vicar of Sittingbourne)* read the service. It was a most melancholy ceremony. She herself had written the inscription for the plate on the coffin omitting altogether the name Hassells. *(Helen Hassells died aged 42 estranged from her husband.)*

22nd Again much snow. The house is a complete hospital all the children being poorly & ill in bed except little Mary.

25th Up but very poorly. Sent to Sittingbourne for all poor Mrs Hassells' things which she had desired might be ours.

28th Richard at Sittingbourne, all our colds subsiding. A note from Mr Wilder announcing the dangerous illness of his little daughter. The account of her later in the day still much the same.

29th The 'Naturalists Library' came from Mrs Hassells' for little Bertha.

February 1st Called on the Wilders, saw Mrs Wilder & the poor little feeble & blind baby. She has water on the brain from her teeth. Mr Wilder returned with me.

5th Yesterday Mr Wilder's little baby died. Today Colonel Griffiths called for me unexpectedly in the drag & we went to see the stag turned off at Allington. It was so fat that it ran no better than a cow & was killed in about a ¼ of an hour. They all, ten in number came back to take luncheon here.

10th Drove to Thurnham to call on the Wilders, found her out of spirits & unwell.

11th A letter from Caroline giving such a very sad account of Uncle Albert who has been suffering from a severe attack of ague & fever & Dr Elliott in constant attendance. Sent Mrs C. Duppa some rabbits.

---

[63]   Ladies of Louisa's class did not attend funerals at this time. As Margaret Hale the heroine of Mrs Gaskell's 'North & South' said bitterly 'because they have no power over their emotions!' (1854).

26th News of a Revolution in Paris.

27th The abdication of Louis Philippe & the establishment of a republican government, much turmoil & some bloodshed.

29th Louis Philippe has escaped & it is not known what is become of him, some say he died at Haure in a fit. Duke de Nemoins in London, the Duchess not yet heard of. Mr Wilder was seated over the fire with Richard. Rain in torrents so he remained to drink tea.

March 2nd Yesterday Richard at the turnpike meeting at Lenham. Today I drove early with Ella & Louy into Maidstone where Mr Jones extracted for the former the two eye teeth. Louis Philippe & his Queen still unheard of.

5th Paris seems tranquil again. Louis Philippe & his Queen are in England, they landed at Newhaven.

15th Richard at the special jury (*the assizes)* & tomorrow is to be on another.

23rd Richard at the sale of books at the book club at Maidstone where he purchased several & also the book shelves. He dined at the Wilder's. Ella & Louy drank tea with me.

April 23rd On April 7th our little boy was born & now here I am on April 23rd.

May 2nd A letter from Mr & Mrs Hull kindly consenting to be sponsors to our little boy. Mama departed this morning after a stay of nearly 6 weeks.

3rd Taught all the lessons except music.

7th To church to offer my thanksgiving. Bertha's first appearance there.

9th Mr Hasted paid me a long visit & seemed wonderfully well.

10th To pass the day at the Dolling's, the three children quite worn out with pleasure.

21st To evening church, each day Edward Duppa has painted Louy.

22nd Today prepared for our dinner party. Host & hostess flattered themselves as usual that it went off very well.

29th The day of the Hollingbourne Benefit club and of music & garlands. Mr Wilder preached for it & with Mrs W & his little boy, Mr & Mrs Dolling & four of their children passed the day here.

31st Richard & I passed the day at Pluckley & went over Surrenden a most lovely place but not nearly finished. Many pictures & some very good.

June 5th Richard so poorly sent for Mr Joy who found him in bed suffering from a violent attack of influenza.

6th Richard not well enough to dine out so I dined at Thurnham alone, for all their great disappointment.

14th Passed the day in arranging the books, most fatiguing & dusty work.

20th Poor Mrs Middleton died last Saturday evening.

23rd Started for London with Ella & Louy, & found Aunt Ella quite well.

25th To Trinity church, Uncle Albert & Caroline & Miss Isabel Goldsmid called & I afterwards dined in Park Crescent where was Frederic. *(Goldsmid)*[64]

26th Frederic accompanied us in a morning walk, saw many dinner services but none to suit us. In the afternoon drove with Aunt Ella & saw some others which were more promising. Richard arrived.

27th Met Colonel Griffiths. Went to Madame Tussaud's where took the children.

29th Mr Wilder took luncheon at Aunt Ella's & we went to the exhibition afterwards *(Royal Academy)*. Some beautiful portraits. Dined at Uncle Go's, Kate ill in bed. To Almack's, Richard did not go having a bad headache.

30th To say goodbye to Uncle Albert & Caroline, met Mr Wilder on our way who accompanied us there. Then went to the Coliseum 'The Panorama of Paris' which was very true & made one quite melancholy in thinking of the horrors now being enacted there. Took luncheon at Aunt Ella's & afterwards started for home.

July 6th Drove to Maidstone & called on Mrs Griffiths & Mrs Lushington, brought Richard home with us from Maidstone.

7th Mr Wilder came in at luncheon. Richard very busy haymaking. Hollingbourne House *(home of the Duppas)* is let.

13th To Wateringbury where took luncheon with the Bigges. *(Orpins House)*

28th To Maidstone where the baby was vaccinated & Mama & I did much shopping.

---

[64]   Fellow of King's College London, orientalist and controller of Crown Lands in Egypt. When he was 21, in 1839, he had entered the East India Company's Madras Army and a year later served in China. He had a great flair for languages and over the next decade qualified as an interpreter of Hindustani, Persian and Arabic, also mastering several Indian vernaculars. When he was on active service in the Crimean War he also learnt Turkish.

August 3rd A visit from Aunt Ella who took luncheon with us & passed some hours here. She brought a frock for the boy & Mr & Mrs Hull sent him a silver cup.

11th To the grand 'Blow Up'.[65] Mr Wilder met us at Bearsted, & Mr & Mrs Bigge on the top of Blue Bell Hill. An immense concourse of people, much fire & smoke & noise. Saw many whom we knew.

15th News arrived of the approaching marriage of Emily Struth to Mr Harrison.

18th Started at ½ past 8 & drove to Ashford, from thence by the train to Ramsgate which reached at 12. Roamed about the town & pier with Aunt Ella & Mr & Mrs Hull. Dined with the former, a very pleasant day. Whenever we passed the potatoes in a very black & blighted state. *(Home the same day)*

September 7th To the theatre to see Charles Kean & Mrs Kean in 'The Wife's Secret' in which they acted beautifully, a very small theatre, the boxes being tolerably filled.

8th To Colonel Griffith's & proceeded in a large party to Chatham races. Sir Edward Filmer also took luncheon in the drag.

October 3rd To Wateringbury to call on Mrs Bigge whose son had just arrived from Australia after an absence of ten years.

5th To concert at Maidstone where we met the Bigges. The room crowded.

11th Charlotte departed after living here 14 years. *(housemaid)*

18th Mama so very ill that we sent for Mr Grayling who did not consider her dangerously so but promised to write to Mr Whatman about her.

19th Mr Whatman came & gave quinine & iron according to Mr Grayling's prescription.

November 2nd A walk in the road with Ella & Louy, Mama still better. Richard dined at the Wilder's.

4th Taught, walked with the children in the road & drove to fetch Milly.

15th To St Leonards *(West Malling)* to take luncheon with the Savages. St Leonards is a most comfortable & luxurious house.

17th A walk to call on Mr Hasted, his room & himself gloomy as usual.

---

[65]   This was the siege operations at Chatham. The local newspaper reported that thousands attended from all over Kent & London. The operation consisted of troops attacking and defending some trenches and lines.

December 19th To the County Ball. Many people & diamonds. Altogether the most brilliant assemblage that I have ever seen there. The Ladies Neville in pink & silver were the stars of the room.

1849 February 4th (*Next entry*) A long time has elapsed since I last wrote. Mama is rather better & is gone to reside at number 6 Bower Place, Maidstone.[66] Mr Branfill Harrison has the curacy of St Peters *(Maidstone),* & he & Mrs Harrison are now settled in Orchard Street. I have been in London with Richard for a week. We started on December 27th & stayed at Uncle Albert's. Frederic is married to Miss Mary Mackenzie Stuart & is to start soon for India. Began 'Sutram' in German & read a sermon of Edward's.

6th In the evening at 6 to a child's party at Mrs Dolling's where Ella & Louy behaved very well & wakefully. Dancing, singing & games whiled away the time. Supper at 10 when healths were drunk & songs sung. Danced with Mr Dolling.

8th Drove to Maidstone, Milly met us & Richard & Bertha accompanied us. Stayed some time at Bower Place.

12th Very bad report of Mama so started early for Maidstone. Found her up & rather better than I expected. Met Mr Whatman as I came away who says that all alarm is over for the present. Sent Mama some Jerusalem artichokes.

17th Drove to Maidstone to see Mama. Colonel Middleton walked with me to Bower Place, found Mama very tolerably well. Colonel Griffiths came in while I was there.

27th Drove to Maidstone in the afternoon found Aunt Ella in Bower Place.

March 6th George, after I had ordered the carriage & the horses were harnessed to it, went out into the field to shoot a rook, when the horses took fright & set off to Park Gate. Fortunately no accident happened as they cleared the corners wonderfully & they were brought home in safety.

12th A tarry-at-home day, George being employed brewing.

13th To Maidstone to take luncheon with Mrs Branfill Harrison & accompany them & their party to the Courts. Judge Parke on the bench & some very dull cases going on about rail road & houses etc. Very crowded & hot so we soon retired.

---

[66]   Bower Place, a row of large villas, was built during the 1830s off the Tonbridge Road.

16th Drove to Maidstone accompanied by the three young ladies & Miss Edmed to the Museum where Milly met us.[67] The birds appeared to me to be beautifully arranged & the room is a good one, but very cold with its pavement of tiles. Then went to Bower Place where found Mama better.

28th Mrs E. Duppa came & we drove to Sharsted together, found Mary & her children quite well.

30th Called on Mr Hasted who was feeble & much shrunk, & on the Dollings.

April 11th Uncle Albert & Caroline arrived to stay with us, she looking ill.

26th To Maidstone where with Mr & Miss Bigge & the Harrisons attended the band playing & military parade at the Depot, Colonel Middleton 'reviewing' the troops. *(He commanded the cavalry depot)*

May 2nd Mr Wilder sent us a turbot & came to take luncheon on it himself.

3rd Richard & I drove to Linton. We viewed the far-famed monuments in the church of Lady Cornwallis the 2nd & Lord Brome, they are both by Bailey. What struck us as pretty singular was an effigy in bas-relief of his Lordship himself in the attitude of resignation to his first & earliest loss. Richard went on to Coxheath.

4th A walk through the fields cowslip gathering with Miss Edmed & the children.

16th Visited Detling Hurdle Race, most agreeable day. Colonel Middleton took us to a tent where excellent luncheon was given by the stewards of the race & officers.[68]

19th To Maidstone where took Milly & Mr & Mrs Harrison to the Feu de Joie at the Depot on occasion of the Queens birthday, a very gay scene, about 60 or 70 sat down to luncheon afterwards.

24th Mama much better & in her <u>day</u> instead of her <u>nightcap</u>.

26th Miss Edmed went for a holiday so I had the charge of the young ladies.

28th To Maidstone where Milly & Miss Edmed met us to say goodbye & we started by the train for London where we arrived safely & Aunt Ella's carriage met us.

---

[67]   Miss Edmed is the governess.

[68]   The local paper listed the races which included the Garrison Stakes for all horses belonging to officers of the garrison.

30th Mr & Mrs Hull dined early in St Andrews Place & I took a morning walk with Richard. In the afternoon we went to the Exhibition & called on the Greatheds & Kate.

June 1st With Uncle Albert & Caroline to the Review of the Pensioners in Hyde Park. General Brotherton officiated & we had the satisfaction of seeing the Duke of Wellington who was present in plain clothes & gave the medals. Prince George of Cambridge & Lord Cardigan were also there.[69]

12th Today we went to the Botanic Gardens in the Regents Park accompanied by Mr & Mrs Hull & met by Mrs Mostyn. The gardens beautiful as well as the weather & the show of American plants unequalled, 6000 people visited them on that day including the Queen.

3rd To morning service at Trinity, dinner at Uncle Albert's to meet our own High Sheriff & his wife. They seemed pleasing, good-natured, people.

4th Some shopping, dined at Uncle Go's. Today uncle is much depressed & gouty.

5th Caroline & Mrs Hull came to say adieu, we started by rail-road to Maidstone. Aunt Ella most kindly gave me a colossal Dictionary, 'Clarissa Harlowe' & a very handsome pink flowerpot.

7th To Maidstone, drank tea at Bower Place. Mama much better.

13th Called on Mr & Mrs Dolling & on my way left Miss Edmed & the children on The Hill to find wild flowers. Mrs Dolling in much trouble on account of the sudden death of her mother from Bronchitis. Called on Mrs Dis.

14th A day at home correcting the printed copy of my Floral Alphabet.

16th Went to the fair at Hollingbourne. The children much pleased.

17th Wrote to Aunt Ella enclosing to her six copies of the Alphabet.

21st To the Maidstone Flower Show accompanied by Miss Edmed, Ella & Louy. Richard stayed at home haymaking, also took Milly.

July 21st Dined & passed the day with Mama while Milly went with the Bigges to the mock siege at Chatham.

---

[69]   The Times reported four battalions of veterans of the Peninsular campaign, numbering about 1,500 men paraded smartly & were awarded medals after which cheers were given for the Queen.

28th To Sittingbourne for a cricket, music & dancing party at the Walford's. The vicarage looked very pretty.

August 9th Miss Edmed summoned to Maidstone on account of her father's being suddenly attacked with cholera.[70]

10th Miss Edmed returned her father much better.

15th Sudden tidings arrived of the very sudden death of Miss Edmed's mother she was only taken ill last evening & died at 3 in the morning. Miss Edmed of course went to Maidstone. Colonel Griffiths called.

16th A hard day of teaching.

21st Richard employing everyone in his harvest so did not go out.

22nd To Maidstone, brought home Miss Edmed. Found Mama tolerable. Saw Waters, the artist, about Louy's portrait & did some little shopping.

September 6th To St Leonard's, took Milly up in my way. Luncheon with the Savages & an archery meeting afterwards.

7th Mr & Mrs Wilder & Mr & Mrs Grayling took luncheon here. The latter is a plain, dark-haired sensible person.

11th Mrs Disternell died.

17th Found Mama in her very pretty new house number 6, Bower Terrace.

19th Mrs Disternell was buried, Mr Ward, Richard & Mr Sankey attending the funeral. Mr Ward brought me Mrs Disternell's watch which had belonged to the Princess Elizabeth, sister to Louis XVI, & on which is a portrait of Marie Antoinette.

27th Mr Wilder at breakfast. He went out shooting with Richard who came home thoroughly tired, leaving me to the solitary enjoyment of Shakespeare's 'Julius Caesar'.

October 5th This being the day appointed by the Archbishop as the fast for the cholera, attended morning service. The commination, the collect, epistle & gospel for Ash Wednesday & the prayer against the cholera were all read. Mr Hasted also gave a sermon & the service was so long, (added to which he read the thanksgiving twice), that one can scarcely imagine how a man of 89 could get through so much unrelieved by singing & unassisted.

9th Drove to Maidstone to fetch Uncle Go, Edward & Julia who arrived by the train.

---

[70]   There were 26 fatal cases of cholera in Maidstone in 1849.

19th To Sharsted to take luncheon with Mary Faunce who was busy working & drawing as usual, Ella accompanied me & we on our way met the foxhounds & hunters, among the latter the round merry face of Mr Pemberton Leigh was conspicuous. Richard dined at Thurnham.

29th A present of some pinafores for Mary from Mr Wilder & also a barrel of oysters.

November 1st A sleepless night from ceaseless toothache, Richard at Leeds Castle about some fence or other.

21st A man calling himself a police officer, & perfectly tipsy, forced his way into the house & being turned out by Richard attempted to strike him when Mr Thomas shut the door against him & his stick was broken in the scuffle. On the appearance of Lampard with his baton of office he decamped, but we afterwards saw him still more intoxicated on the Road to Maidstone. We understood that he had been turned out of two other houses.

23rd Tidings that Mr Wilder is about to quit Thurnham for a living in Norfolk.

25th Poor Hobbs *(lady's maid)* lost her mother most suddenly she was taken ill at 7 & died at 12 last night.

28th A fifth daughter was born to us, as small a child as could well be.

December 20th *(Next entry)* Many events have taken place. Dr Thomson has paid Mama another visit & promises entire restoration feeling sure that her illness proceeds only from her liver. *(Cousin)* Edward has been appointed headmaster of Rugby though the youngest of all the candidates. Mr Wilder departs today.

21st A letter from Julia telling of Edward's election at Rugby & accompanied by his printed testimonial of the most flattering description.

23rd A bright frosty day Mr Hasted taken very ill in church & obliged to send for brandy, but managed to finish the service & also to have one in the afternoon besides. Wrote tickets for Christmas dinner.

27th Mr Hasted came to Christen the baby which he did by the name of Laura Charlotte after her two godmothers.

28th Mrs Kirby departed.

1850-1859: The social round

The 1850s began for Louisa with recovery from the birth of Laura her last child (always known in the family and journals as Lolotte), and ended with the approaching marriage of Ella the eldest.

Louisa's forties were a time of many pleasures. The regular enjoyable trips to London by train from Maidstone to stay with Uncle Go, Aunt Ella or Uncle Albert continued. Louisa was very fond of all three but she was particularly close to Aunt Ella with whom she had a deep temperamental sympathy.

From 1851 onwards there were occasional day trips to the capital. The arrival of reliable and rapid rail travel had made it possible for middle and upper class ladies from the Home Counties to spend a day shopping in the grand stores of London. Then there were the weeks at Brighton seeing Mama and Milly. Close to home Maidstone was losing some of its importance as a leading social centre for the county's gentry. The County Ball was kept up but London's importance for social events increased and it is interesting to see on just how many occasions Louisa encountered her Kentish friends when she was staying in London.

Richard and Louisa held regular dinner parties, rounded off with singing at the piano or games of whist. Richard's account books show that he kept a very plentiful stock of sherry, port, gin and wine in the house. He purchased 25 dozen (300) bottles of port and 10 dozen of sherry at a time. Louisa was in her element when entertaining for she delighted in lively conversation. New friends were made such as Henry and Mary Anne Gipps who became close when they rented the Duppa's home, Hollingbourne House. The children of the families played together and in later years Louy would marry one of the Gipps boys. The Duppa siblings were now scattered by marriage and fortune and were seen less by Louisa. When the Rev. Hasted at last died in his nineties the new vicar and his wife, the Carter Halls became friends.

Days when Louisa neither went out nor had callers were unusual. On such days she read novels, wrote letters, painted, played the piano and taught the children. On most Sundays she attended church. Occasionally at this period she would call at the school where she presented prizes. It was virtually unknown for her to call at the union workhouse which was very close by.

A craze for table turning swept England in 1853. It had arrived from America. Groups of friends would will a table to move by joining hands round the table in a seance. Louisa was briefly swept up in this which she termed 'magnetising a table'. She was confusing mesmerism and magnetism, for it was generally considered by those who investigated the phenomena that if the table moved it was due to some form of hypnotism or mesmerism.

Reading The Times ensured that Louisa was always well informed about national and international events. When the Crimean War broke out in 1853 it impinged on her life more than we might imagine because she knew the officers at the Maidstone cavalry barracks well.

The suddenness and frequency with which illness and death struck young and old alike amongst those Louisa knew is shocking to the reader, accustomed as we are to the relative security of modern medicine.

By now the fact that Richard was so much older than Louisa may have been making it hard for him to keep up with her busy social life. Family legend says that 'Louisa was his pride and joy, his torture and his torment.'[71] Quite frequently trips to London were made without him and were followed by his own trips to the capital. His financial affairs prospered and he continued to purchase local properties. One such was Godfrey House purchased in 1858. This handsome house had for many years been quite dilapidated, known as Rats Castle and occupied by farm labourers. Richard had it restored and then rented it out.[72] Louisa rarely mentions such business.

Richard was a respected, kindly neighbour and employer who was concerned for the welfare of those who worked for him. It was he who had instigated the Hollingbourne Benefit Club enabling the men to save for a decent funeral. As soon as he inherited Eyhorne House he had begun the custom of giving the ingredients of a good Christmas dinner to the families in the parish who could not afford one that year. Each family was given five pounds of beef, a pound of flour and a pound of

---

[71] 'Hollingbourne & the Thomas family.' B. Gipps, 1991.

[72] *Maidstone Journal* (20 Mar 1860)

raisins. Then there were the generous deliveries of winter coals to those in need. This generosity was doubtless prompted by his strong Christian faith. He gave freely of his time as a churchwarden over many years. So naturally his kindly generous character meant that he treated his family well too. He regularly sent money to young Richard in Canada.

Godfrey House Hollingbourne

Richard loaned money at interest to several people in the village as well as acting as treasurer for the village school.

Being a member of the turnpike trust and a magistrate made him a busy man, then there was the property to attend to, although this still left him with time to go to local cricket matches and shooting on Hollingbourne Hill with the cavalry officers. At harvest times Louisa wrote of how occupied he was and how he had taken on many extra hands.

The girls would not be debutantes as Louisa herself had been in Paris for they did not move in the highest circles. Most of the friends of the family were members of the upper middle classes, lawyers, vicars, army officers and it was amongst these that three of the girls found husbands.

Louisa's journal continued to be written daily with rare exceptions.

1850 January 5th Breakfasted downstairs for the first time for nearly six weeks. Drove as far as the Harrietsham turnpike, Mr Thomas up The Hill shooting.

7th Kept our Twelfth Day with the children & wrote characters for them.[73]

February 6th Started for London, Milly met us at the Maidstone station. On the London Bridge station Uncle Albert's carriage met us. Caroline retired early leaving Uncle Albert, Ella & myself together.

7th Called on Aunt Ella, drove out with Caroline, went also to Howell & James.

8th Took Ella to the dentist who extracted a tooth & in the afternoon she & I went with Aunt Ella to see the Panorama of the Nile with which delighted. It was like going to Egypt without the trouble of it. In the evening Caroline, Richard & I had a quiet rubber together.

21st *(At home)* Lent the lying in clothes to Mrs Fridd who bears a good character & is in great distress.(*Sarah Fridd's first baby was expected, her husband Robert was one of Richard's farm labourer's and they lived very close-by)*

March 5th A dinner party at home. After all the guests had departed, tidings were brought that Colonel Middleton's horses had run away & that the carriage was broken to pieces. It proved however to be Major Meyer's instead. The splinter bar was broken & one of the horses had made his way into Sir R. Martin's plantation. The vehicle was left there for the night & le petit Major, having borrowed Mr Thomas's saddle & bridal, rode home.

11th Drove up The Hill to call on the Dollings & found them in their church playing masses on the organ.

14th Got up with a bad cold, a drear cold day, snow on The Hill. News of the fearful explosion of powder mills at Hounslow on Monday which was heard by Mr Thomas & the children in the garden.[74]

April 2nd Went to the County Ball, a good but not a full one, danced with Lord George Beauclerck *(cavalry officer)* & talked & walked the remainder of the evening.

8th Drove to Maidstone to fetch Mr Wilder, a fruitless search. Came home. He arrived about 11pm whistling & shouting to let us know of his arrival.

12th Yesterday Mrs Tully departed having lived here 11½ years & our new cook Catherine Baker came.

---

[73]   Twelfth Night was traditionally a night for performing plays.

[74]   Eight people were killed in this powder mill explosion which was heard as far away as Brighton.

25th To Maidstone accompanied by the three children & Miss Edmed to meet Mrs Bigges & Mrs Murray *(Mrs Murray's husband was a cavalry captain)* & accompany them to hear the band.

30th To see the Branfill Harrisons & their 'new-born' who is a strong child. Brought home some of his christening cake for the young ladies.

May 10th Took our baby to be vaccinated from Mrs Harrison's boy. Went with Mrs Harrison to call on Mrs Whatman at Vinters.[75]

11th Mr & Mrs Whatman called on us. She is a pleasing, large, showy person beautifully dressed.

14th Started for London by the North Kent Line, driving to Rochester, which just reached in time for the train. To Seymour Street, Uncle Go rather gouty.

15th Walked with Hobbs to Uncle Albert's, found Caroline well & she & Uncle Albert preparing for a dinner party, visited Aunt Ella where Uncle Go met me.

16th Walked out shopping with Hobbs called on the Greatheds. After luncheon proceeded to Uncle Go's Court when he & I went to Covent Garden market & drove in Hyde Park together. A dinner party including Mr & Mrs Gosling of banking fame. *(Goslings were a City bank)*

17th Richard came to London today & we departed together for the North Kent Line.

21st Brewing, so a tarry at home day.

29th The day of the celebration of the Benefit Club much music with garlands.*(It was Richard who looked after the funds of the club, giving it to the stewards as requested.)*

June 5th To the Yeomanry Ball a most brilliant affair given by Lord Sydney & his officers.

13th *(In London staying with Aunt Ella)* Richard ill with lumbago, paid many visits.

15th Milly came up from Brighton to pass the day with us & we all went to the exhibition together & took her back to the station afterwards.[76]

18th To the Zoological Gardens early where saw the wonderful & hideous Hippopotamus with his Arab attendants. In the afternoon to Kensington to visit Mrs Thomas Thomas.

---

[75]   Vinters mansion lay in Boxley close to Maidstone. The house had been rebuilt in the 18th century & then just recently in 1849, greatly enlarged.

[76]   The Great Exhibition in Hyde Park.

19th To the dentist with Ella & then to call on Caroline. Left St Andrews Place loaded with presents from the dear aunt as well as kindness. All well at home.

26th Miss Bigge & her two brothers took luncheon here & we afterwards lionised the Manor House & the old church, Mr Hasted, & the altar cloth.

29th Wilkins came from Coxheath with the account of a wonderful storm that occurred last evening. A roaring in the air accompanied with intense cold & pieces of ice falling as large as fourpenny pieces & jagged at the edges. This was corroborated by others who intensified it. It was as it were the bursting of a waterspout over Maidstone, but no hail. At Bearsted there was the sound in the air for nearly ½ an hour & violent hail. Here we had scarcely more than a few drops of rain but the air was hot, dark & lowering.

July 2nd Mr Charles Duppa appeared at the door in the evening bleeding & drunk. He had been thrown from a cart on The Hill with two other men, Tom & Sam Sage. The former is severely hurt & is scarcely expected to live.

5th On Wednesday arrived the news of Sir Robert Peel's fall from his horse & death.

16th Went with the children & Miss Edmed to see Mrs Burkitt's collection of ferns of which plants she has the largest & smallest, & also visited their multitude of beehives of which they have all kinds.

21st To afternoon service at Wormshill. Mr Dolling has put up an organ in the church which Mrs D & the children play & which is admirably managed.

29th Went to Harrietsham to hear the Bishop of Toronto speak for the foundation of a new college there on religious principles. Mr Riddell *(rector of Harrietsham)* had decorated a barn for the occasion with evergreens flowers & banners & after the meeting we all returned to the vicarage to drink tea.

August 8th Went down to Brighton to see Mama, found her wonderfully well, riding daily & driving in flies. Saw many old friends & acquaintances. I had also the satisfaction of seeing Mary Duff, Lord Byron's earliest love, now Mrs Cockburn, a widow. Returned home last Tuesday & found all well.

21st A complete day of rain, but nevertheless went to the archery at Mereworth Castle & on my way halted at Mrs Bigge's. We dined in a very wet tent filled with people. After which we all proceeded to the Castle where, after three hours of sauntering & talking, the band arrived from London &

dancing began. A most agreeable evening & a magnificent room for dancing. Such a splendid Italian mansion that I had not half time to look at it.

23rd Dined at the Griffiths' where met Captain Steele, a man without a chin, whom I had seen before when visiting the hippopotamus & little thought that I should soon be seated next to him at dinner.

September 4th A dinner party on Sir Edward Filmer's haunch of venison.

17th A letter from young Richard announcing his marriage to a Miss Vaughan.

October 8th Yesterday Richard brought home a very young hare which Perfect is to bring up. *(It died within a couple of days)*

9th Dismissed Ellen Hayes who was so dirty that we could not keep her.

12th Wrote to young Richard & sent him £10 from Mama as a present. To Maidstone where met Colonel Middleton & brought home the Harrisons to pass the day with us. Miss Edmed went to pass a day or two at home.

14th To Sharsted with Ella, Louy & Bertha to pass Annie Faunce's birthday.

25th Walked with Miss Edmed & the young ladies as far as the Union.

November 6th Drove to Maidstone, Colonel Middleton in great spirits on account of the intended marriage of his son William to the daughter of Lady Julia Kavanagh with £30,000.

11th Started for Maidstone for London accompanied by Ella, Bertha & Hobbs. Met at the station Colonel Griffiths who went our journey with us & saw us into Aunt Ella's carriage.

13th Aunt Ella & I started for Brighton. Milly awaiting us, she was thin but Mama seems wonderfully well. Returned to London & found Richard at St Andrews Place.

14th To the dentist with Ella, he extracted two teeth. In the afternoon to call on Mrs Mostyn & to the Pantheon with the children. Dined at Uncle Go's.

15th To the British Museum where among the other wonders saw the new sculptures from Nimrod. In the afternoon called on the Greatheds.

29th *(At home)* Went to a very agreeable musical party at Mrs Murray's. Richard ill with lumbago & could not go.

December 1st To morning service. Mr Hasted was taken ill & fell down insensible at the bottom of the reading desk but soon recovered his senses & tried to go on but was unable.

20th To fireworks & dancing at the Gipps' accompanied by the three young ladies.

25th To morning service. Mr Hasted again taken ill when he reached the litany & the congregation compelled to return to their homes.

27th To the County Ball a very good one & very full, danced with Harry Bigge.

31st Mr Wilder sent us a Norfolk turkey weighing 18lbs.

1851 January 2nd To the Depot where Mrs Harrison & Mrs Bigge met us to hear the band.

9th The four elder Gipps children & their governess took luncheon here.

10th To a party at the Dolling's. Dancing & games. The three children went. Danced with Mr Walford. A most excellent supper at 11.

31st Drove to Maidstone. Went to the Bank for the first time in my life. Perfect gave warning.

February 26th Since writing my last journal we have been to visit Mama in Brighton & had the pleasure of finding her well. Went to a ball at the Pavilion, a dinner of 20 at Mrs Mostyn's & an evening party where met Harrison Ainsworth.[77]

26th Walked to Leeds with Miss Burkitt to see the altar cloth lately embroidered by her. The work beautifully done but the whole thing very tasteless.

27th To the Bachelors' Ball at Maidstone very agreeable & full. The supper most liberal, all the 300 guests could sit down at once. Danced.

March 3rd Looked over the plate with Perfect & Pearson the old & new servants.

13th Wrote to Mrs C. Duppa enclosing a £10 note as a present from Richard to his god-daughter Edith.

April 1st Out to see the foxhounds. Louy rode Gipsy the donkey for the first time. The foxes were seen & one killed. Dined at the Griffiths'. Major Unett has returned from India covered with laurels. He showed us some tricks after dinner.

2nd Walked up The Hill & called on Mrs Gipps accompanied by Miss Edmed, the children & donkey.

---

[77]   William Harrison Ainsworth was an extremely popular historical novelist, his books included 'Rookwood' & 'Crichton'.

22nd Mr Dolling's Oratorio. Gave our tickets away in the village & went to the Maidstone Ball. Danced with Colonel Griffiths & went to supper with Colonel Middleton.

23rd To take luncheon at St Leonards & then on with Mrs Savage to the meeting of the archery members at Malling. Obliged to come away early as I had to meet Mrs Greathed at the station at Maidstone where she & Minnie arrived at 4.

24th Took Mrs Greathed & Minnie a walk to see the church & the Manor House. Dinner party here. It was quite a day of misfortunes. First Mr Gipps' servant in coming down to borrow our harness threw down a valuable horse & broke its knees. Then one of Richard's cart horses fell & drove the shaft of the cart against Tassell & broke some of his ribs & his thigh, & lastly Mr Gipps' servant in turning broke the pole of the carriage & Mr Gipps was prevented from dining here.

May 1st The opening of the Crystal Palace. Otham church struck by lightning.

3rd Bertha had a sad fall from her donkey & came home with her face bruised all over & her nose so swollen that she was really not to be recognised. Sent her to bed & applied warm vinegar & water.

5th Richard returned in the evening having seen the Crystal Palace which he described as a large bazaar.

June 17th Have been to London & returned. Seen the Crystal Wonder twice. Went once to the opera to hear 'Fidelio', & also to Chiswick & saw the collection of orchids, & Mr Paxton exhibiting them to the Duke of Devonshire. Uncle Albert & Caroline so very kind. The dentist extracted two of Louy's teeth. On my return I found a new horse instead of Sir Edmund, & George the coachman with a broken finger. He had been kicked by Dinah & was quite useless so that my life has been a very stay-at-home one. Since then our maid-servant Jane Milner has been sent away for stealing, she having secreted my long lost black lace, Miss Edmed's sleeves & Hobbs' stockings. This morning Mary Ann Hooper came in her place. Yesterday went to the fair with the children.

27th Much teaching as Miss Edmed departed yesterday for her holiday.

August 3rd Mama & Milly have been & gone. Since their departure we have given a dinner party, & one luncheon, & we have dined at the Bigge's.

6th To London to see the dentist about Ella's teeth. Took luncheon at Uncle Albert's, found Caroline very anxious

113

about her mother who is ill. Mr & Mrs Burkitt were there.(*home same day*) Horse had met with another accident.

11th The little Gipps came to pass the day here & in the afternoon Mr & Mrs Betts of Preston Hall & rail-road fame called.[78]

12th Started early with Richard for Ticehurst, went over the establishment which is beautifully arranged. Saw poor Freddy. Richard thought Louis better. (*For reasons unknown this was Louisa's first visit to the asylum & she did not see Louis. Perhaps it was considered it would upset him too much. Cousin Freddy Goulburn who had been a Fellow of All Souls Oxford had also become mentally ill and become a patient at Ticehurst.*)

26th Drove to Maidstone. An accident occurred to the carriage, one of the horses having taken fright kicked over the traces, broke the pole strap & threw down a poor man of the name of Rolfe & broken his cart. Colonel Middleton kindly came to my assistance & did the needful. A dinner party at home.

30th A live turtle arrived from Domenica & is grazing in the orchard. The little Gipps walked down with us after church to see it.

September 1st Richard sent off the turtle to Sir Edward Filmer & went off shooting.

16th To Wateringbury where took luncheon with Mrs Bigge. Mr Wilder & Richard out shooting. Whist in the evening playing against Mr Wilder & Miss Edmed.

22nd My Swiss cousin De Bondely arrived & we had a dinner party.

23rd Took de Bondely to see the church & Manor House & also to call at the Filmer's. They were at home & we went over the house & grounds. The turtle is dead.

October 2nd Dined at Sir E. Filmer's. Went into dinner with him & I danced with Major Unett. The dining room promises to be beautiful.

7th A morning drive to Maidstone with Miss Edmed & my two young ladies to fit them out for the winter.

21st Meeting of the fox hounds at Hollingbourne House. Mr Stinsted thrown from his horse, the horse falling on him. He was found on one of the flinty hills at Hucking by Mr

---

[78]   Edward Betts was responsible for the construction of a number of railway lines in Britain & overseas. In 1848 he purchased Preston Hall & its estate at Aylesford. He demolished the old manor house & had the new mansion built.

114

Nicholson of Rochester & begged to be brought here where it was found by Mr Sedgwick that his collar bone was broken in two places. After it was set we sent him home in the carriage. We dined at the Gipps'.

24th Richard returned in the evening more light hearted than when he went away.

November 25th Took Richard to Maidstone on his way to London. Called on Mrs Griffiths & congratulated her on the Major's success. Major Unett took luncheon here, brought me some of his brother's sketches & played chess.

29th *(At Uncle Albert's)* Took Ella to the dentist, then went to get one of the fashionable Polka's, Aunt Ella having kindly said she would give me one.[79]

December 2nd Called to say goodbye to Aunt Ella. She gave me my grandfather de Visme's court suit of flowered velvet with the sword.

18th *(At home)* Mrs Whatman called. Last Thursday Hobb's foot was scalded by Jane upsetting over her the coffee pot of boiling coffee & she has been quite disabled ever since. Today Baker managed to drive a large splinter beneath her finger nail which was so closely wedged that it could not be removed without Mr Sedgwick's assistance & he had to cut through the nail to extract it. Mrs Tully is fortunately here to assist us.

24th To the Union to give a shilling from Mr Thomas to each of the eleven old paupers of Hollingbourne. *(first mention of setting foot in the Union workhouse)* Also to the school. Mrs Gipps called, drove with her to Maidstone.

29th To Mrs Gipps' with the three young ladies & Miss Edmed to pass the evening. The children enjoyed themselves much. Dancing to the village band.

1852 January 1st Heard them last night ringing the old year out & the new one in. Dined at Mr Pemberton Leigh's & met Uncle Go. A very agreeable party.

2nd To Maidstone, much shopping, met General Middleton. Wrote to thank Mr Wilder who had sent us a very nice cod fish & its accompaniments. Dined tete a tete with Mr & Mrs Gipps & played whist in the evening.

5th Preparations for a dinner party. Uncle Go arrived late, General Middleton came in late from Leeds Castle. *(This is the first time anyone mentioned as having been to call at Leeds*

---

[79]   A Polka was a tight fitting jacket for a lady.

Castle. The Wykeham-Martins at this period did not socialise with their near neighbours the Thomas family.)

6th Uncle Go & I went to call on the Filmers & saw all over the house. We went to the ball at 10 & had a very agreeable evening.

13th To the Stede Hill[80] juvenile party with Louy & Ella, beginning with dancing then supper & then the Christmas tree. I danced a country dance with Mr Baldwin after this in which old & young all joined. There was an Indian juggler.[81]

22nd Called on the Baldwins & Dollings, found Mrs D in bed with a little new red baby born yesterday.

29th *(At Aunt Ella's)* Edward took luncheon with us & accompanied us to the Zoological Gardens where we saw the young lioness Bertha, who is now allowed to run loose & also the new wingless bird from New Zealand. The orangutan too ill to see anyone. Today dined at Uncle Albert's.

February 1st To hear Edward preach at Park Street which he did beautifully.

2nd Went to the Soho Bazaar with the children & Aunt Ella, also in the morning to the dentist who extracted two long teeth for Louy. Dined at Uncle Go's & had the great pleasure of meeting Milly.

3rd Drove in the Park with Milly who passed the day in St Andrews Place, Edward bringing her.

12th *(At home)* Began to burn our Moderator lamp[82] which promises to be delightful.

March 18th Yesterday was Ella's 12th birthday, I began Italian with her.

20th To Maidstone, much carousing going on. Mr Whatman opposing Mr Dodd. *(election)* Richard accompanied me.

April 6th To Maidstone & then on to Aylesford to call on Mrs Betts. Preston Hall is magnificent.

7th Boy 4 years old.

10th The Gipps' boys passed the day here. Mr Gipps is about to stand for Canterbury.

11th Mr Gipps departed, the Gipps boys here again. We all went to morning service.

---

[80] The grand home of the Baldwin family in Harrietsham.

[81] The first mention of a Christmas tree in the diaries. Their use had become widespread in England during the 1840s.

[82] These were a new style of oil lamps advertised that year on sale in Maidstone as giving a light equal to eight candles.

12th Went to hear Fanny Kemble read 'The Merchant of Venice', a crowded room.

Preston Hall (Centre for Kentish Studies, Archive & Library History Service, Kent County Council)

14th To the ball which was not a very good one in point of numbers but very much so in point of company.
15th The young ladies & Miss Edmed drove with me to Maidstone. They walked home & after inviting Major Unett to dine here tomorrow I went on to take luncheon at the Savages & accompany them to the Archery Committee.
22nd To Maidstone where Miss Edmed, Louy & Gerard (*first mention of son by name*) accompanied me.
26th To Maidstone. On my return Miss Edmed had gone. Her father had dropped down dead in church yesterday & she had been summoned away.
27th Hard work teaching.
May 9th Went to afternoon service. The Boy at church for the first time.
19th The opening of the baths & washhouses in Maidstone of which we saw the processions with General Middleton. Shops shut & bands playing. Richard came home with us.[83]

---

[83]   *The Mayor and General Middleton presided over a meal for several hundred*

June 1st Dined at Barham Court, Uncle Go, Colonel Griffiths etc formed the party, everything most luxurious & the place beautiful.[84] Whist in the evening.

5th Drove to the North Kent railway station at Strood with Ella & Hobbs. We reached Aunt Ella's house in the afternoon. Ella had a tooth out. Called on Caroline, also to several shops in the vain search for a dress.

7th Went to the Royal Academy. There were some beautiful portraits & also some other remarkable pictures. One of the most so was the 'Drowning Ophelia' by Millais. In the evening we went for an hour to Uncle Go's.

12th *(At home)* Lady Frances Riddell called.*(She lived at the Bishop's Palace Maidstone)* Bunyard summarily dismissed.

22nd Horse suddenly taken ill so our drive to the Inspection delayed. Borrowed Mrs Burkitt's little conveyance & went with one horse. Took Miss Edmed for her holiday. Arrived so late at the Depot that the Duke of Cambridge was gone. A very recherché luncheon & a very agreeable day.

24th To the Flower Show accompanied by Mama, Milly, Richard, Louy, & Bertha. Enjoyed ourselves very much. Major Unett & the Bigges walked with us.

28th Went in the evening to hear Mr Ewart, Professor of Ventriloquism, perform at the National School room. A very small audience but his powers of voice extraordinary.

29th Major Unett at luncheon, he accompanied us to Mr Betts' house *(Preston Hall)* which I thought splendid, also saw the conservatories & gardens.

July 3rd Richard started early for Ticehurst with Uncle Go. On the whole a satisfactory visit.

14th *(At Brighton staying with Mama & Milly)* To Lewes to the Flower Show. Richard went to the Grand Agricultural meeting but we remained amongst the ruins of the old castle & the roses. A large party consisting of Mostyns, Scotts, & Harrison Ainsworth. The Comte de Cavour *(afterwards Italian minister)* introduced to me.

21st *(At home)* Dined at the Betts', a constellation of talent present. Among the numerous guests were Sir Edward Landseer. The house beautiful & everything princely.

---

people in the evening when a good deal of civic pride was expressed.

[84]   Barham Court had for centuries been a grand Kentish house, then owned by Lord & Lady Barham.

August 8th Bourne *(footman)* did not come home at prayers. Richard sat up for him & he appeared at 11, quite tipsy & with a dreadful black eye.

11th Rainy day but still we went to The Wilderness. *(near Sevenoaks)* A most agreeable day. Lord & Lady Camden received us in their tent where was no one but themselves & Dr Locock. Dinner in the beautiful library. Music afterwards, dancing in the evening & everything beautifully arranged.

17th Went to the school which has much improved under the administration of Orford & his wife.

18th Started at 2 for Canterbury which reached at 6. Mr Gipps met us at the Rose Hotel. He & Mrs Gipps & Mr Butler-Johnstone came to fetch us to the Ball, but Mr & Mrs Gipps were unfortunately called away by the death of a relation. Danced.

19th Mr Gipps came to see us early & brought us tickets for the theatre. At 2 went to the cricket match. A very gay scene & the cricket ground beautifully situated. In the evening to the theatre where were acted 'Simson & Co.' Mr Butler-Johnstone,[85] Mr Pemberton Leigh & his brother in the box with us.

30th Mr Austen, the architect from Canterbury, took luncheon here. He gave a most interesting account of the opening of the tombs of Queen Bertha & Henry IV both which he had seen. *(at Canterbury cathedral)* The body of the latter was as fresh as if just buried & his moustaches & tuft quite perfect. Of course it changed on exposure to the air. Queen Bertha was all dust. A very beautiful cross of straw however lay in the coffin but this also crumbled to dust on being touched.

September 11th Children delighted with new pony which Richard gave them.

18th The Duke of Wellington died on Tuesday.*(at Walmer Castle)*

24th Kate too ill to come but Uncle Go arrived at 5, dinner party here. Everything went well but that the mutton at dinner was <u>raw.</u>

November 15th Mrs Griffiths called, she is going to the United Services Club on the day of the Duke of Wellington's funeral where 500 ladies are to be entertained.

18th Day of the Duke of Wellington's funeral. Bells tolling, seven minute gun firing.

---

[85]   Henry Butler-Johnstone Conservative politician.

December 30th Uncle Go left us on Tuesday after spending the Christmas here. During his stay we had two dinner parties. On 21st to the Maidstone ball where I danced a quadrille.

1853 January 4th Dined at Mr Pemberton Leigh's where met Rt Hon. S.R. Lushington, & Uncle Go.

6th Made Twelfth Cake characters for the children.[86]

10th By the rail-road to London with Bertha & Hobbs. Reached Park Crescent in time for luncheon. Caroline & Uncle Albert quite well & also Aunt Ella.

11th Drove out with Aunt Ella who gave me a beautiful velvet cloak, ordered a pink bonnet.

15th A visit from Mrs H. Duppa looking very well & as nice as ever. Drove out with Aunt Ella. To the Haymarket Theatre with Richard & Caroline where saw a most interesting piece 'Masks & Faces' & 'Box & Cox Married' this last which was amusing enough depends entirely on the acting of *(John)* Buckstone & *(Mary Ann)* Keeley which is inimitable.

19th Bid adieu to London my kind friends & pleasures & reached home. All well.

February 6th To Leeds church where Mr Wilder accompanied us & assisted Mr Burkitt quite unexpectedly by preaching for him.

March 17th Major Unett took luncheon here as it was Ella's birthday. He & his dog very riotous.

7th Gerard five years old. He appeared at breakfast in a wreath of primroses.

26th To the Circus with all but Lolotte where General Middleton & Major Unett met us. Ourselves the only spectators. The dancing on the tightrope very good & very fearful & the performance quite long enough.

28th Took Mrs Murray to call at Preston Hall where we were fortunate enough to find Mrs Betts at home & see the two pictures which are now filling their respective compartments in the dining room.

May 13th To Sharsted accompanied by my four elder daughters to pass De Laune's birthday with him. The little people enjoyed themselves much.

---

[86]   Twelfth Night cake was a fruit cake enriched with brandy. In it were a dried pea & a bean. Whoever found these in their portions were crowned king & queen & little plays enacted.

15th Mr and Mrs Bigge have magnetised a table. They sat down as a joke and in about a minute it began to move slowly & in two minutes very rapidly.

16th On Saturday Mr Lee came in M.P. for Maidstone against Mr W. Martin, & today the town was crowded in consequence, blue flags flying in all directions & one heard everywhere nothing but 'Drink, drink, drink.'

Ightham Mote (Centre for Kentish Studies, Archive & Library History Service, Kent County Council)

18th To take luncheon at Mrs Bigge's where Mrs Murray accompanied us. Then Mr Murray, Major Unett & Mr Crawley met us. After luncheon we all went on to Ightham Moat. Major & Mrs Luard received us most kindly & showed us over the ancient mansion. We ascended the tower & saw innumerable & uninhabitable bedrooms. The hall & kitchen are very spacious & there is a window in the ceiling of the latter by which the mistress of the house may see all that passes among her servants.

We returned to tea at the Bigge's & there performed the wonderful & incomprehensible feat of magnetising the tables. The most wonderful part of this wonderful performance is that at the mere simple wish of the actors the turning tables change their course to right or left.

20th Saw the Duke of Cambridge inspect the troops at the Depot, all in grand costumes. Quite a gaudy day. Colonel Griffiths gave a luncheon. I went in with Major Unett accompanied by Gerard who ate what he called a 'glovers egg'.

22nd To afternoon service. Major Unett, Captain Nolan & Mr Crawley drank tea here, after which magnetised the tables. A lovely evening.

24th To the firing & parade for the Queen's birthday. Another gaudy day. Called on Mrs Murray & took Mrs Harrison to the Depot.

26th To London with Richard, Ella & Louy, found Aunt Ella quite well but poor Caroline in a most melancholy state. There had just been a consultation of physicians about her.

27th Poor Caroline much the same. A round of visits. To Mrs Gipps, at home & full of gaiety. To Kensington to call on the Thomas Thomas's. The daughter grown quite a young lady.

29th With Richard & the children to Westminster Abbey which is glorious. The music exquisite & Lord John Thynne's sermon on 'Be sure your sin will find you out' as good as possible. We walked home in the sun through the Park which was delightful after the chill of the abbey. Found Uncle Go in St Andrews Place. Caroline much the same. They have now two nurses for her. Went round with Yeats *(Goldsmid, Louisa's cousin)* to see Jessy in the afternoon. She & her children are very flourishing.

30th To Tottenham Court Road to make some purchases, then to the station at London Bridge to fetch Milly who gave a most flourishing account of Mama. Richard went to his brother's for the night & Milly slept with me. In the afternoon we went to the Water Colour Exhibition. Met Sir Lionel Darell, 'fat fair & forty', much changed since our early days.

31st Richard returned. The Wilders at luncheon. Mrs Wilder is looking thin. We magnetised the table after luncheon, as we have done two or three nights for Aunt Ella. Went to the Botanic Gardens which are lovely to see the Victoria Regia. The leaves are thin & very large. *(Huge water lily newly named after the queen)* The flowers not much exceeding the white water lily in size. Dined at Uncle Go's. Began to magnetise the table but people were afraid & impatient.

June 1st A morning walk with Richard. Yesterday we called on the Greatheds who seem most prosperous in their new house. To the National Gallery, Kate kindly called for me, where met Uncle Go. Left Milly & him at the exhibition & then went with the children to pay some visits.

2nd A little potter with Richard. Caroline still the same. They cannot decide about removing her into the country, the Doctors disagree. Milly at luncheon. Wished Aunt Ella goodbye. Reached our own door before 8, found all quite well and the country looking lovely & green.

11th Miss Edmed's room converted into a real schoolroom & Jane called upon to give up one of her nurseries. A day of arrangement.

21st An early drive to Maidstone. A visit to Mrs Murray in great spirits on his gaining his commission without purchase.

23rd To the Flower Show. Met there the General, Bigges, Savages, Mr Betts who is near starting for Canada, Captain Nolan & Major Unett. With Major Unett walked round the tents. Arranged a party to Rosherville on Saturday if fine.

July 1st Miss Edmed's sister at dinner. She, Miss Edmed, Jane & I turned the tables with great success. When we did not turn with it, it heaved backwards & forwards.

18th To the school with Mama to hear the children sing. Richard busy hay-making.

20th Major Unett called to bring us tickets to the launch of the 'Cressy' at Chatham tomorrow.

21st Richard. Milly & I started for Chatham at half past 9, the General & Major Unett met us at the Dock Yard & we sat in the superintendent's booth, saw the vessel named & all the ceremony besides, a magnificent sight. Then, joined by Mr Crawley, we availed ourselves of Richard's proposal & went on to Gravesend where we had a fish dinner & from thence to Rosherville Gardens, where Major Unett sat for his silhouette, where we lost Mr Crawley & Milly in the maze, where my fortune was told & we saw never ending sights. The dancing was in a room under the superintendence of Baron Nathan whose caricatures I have so often seen. On our return we reached Strood at 7 but we had not time to see half there was to be seen.

25th A fine day & bright promise for tomorrow's archery. Mr F Baldwin at tea. Most incredulous on the subject of table turning, he went away a little shaken from assisting in the operation.

28th Mama & Milly departed after a three week stay. I called on Mina Harrison to ask her about a house for Mama.

29th The archaeologists headed by Mr Ralph Bernal, late MP for Rochester, met at Hollingbourne church & went on to the Manor House. Mr Spurgin exhibited at the church a representation of the Holy Trinity on glass removed by Mr Hasted from one of the church windows, also the pedigree of the Culpepers in the handwriting of Hasted the Historian. They then went to dine at Leeds Castle where Mr William Martin entertained them. We drove on to the soiree at the assembly rooms where heard papers on the Earls of Kent, on architectural painting & on guilds & fraternities. There were two or more papers to be read but the hour was so late & so many of the party had to return to Rochester, that Mr Bernal who had been napping for some time, concluded the evening by thanking the Mayor, Mr Joy, for his kind reception & the Ladies for their attendance. Mr Joy then expressed the gratification it had afforded him, so ended the soiree. The room was well arranged & decorated with many antique & foreign specimens.

30th Drove to see Lady Strange who is staying at Ditton. She talks of illustrating my alphabet after the fashion of Henry VII's missal in the British Museum.

August 5th A letter from Milly to announce that Mama has taken the *(Bishop's)* Palace at Maidstone for three weeks from next Wednesday.

10th A letter from Aunt Ella to invite us to pass the day at Folkestone where she now is with the Hulls. Went to Ticehurst with Richard. Saw poor Freddy considerably worse than when I was last there, & Louis who was anxious to see me & whom I had not seen for 13 years. Met Mama & Milly at Tonbridge & got into the same carriage with them & saw them safe to their new domicile, the Palace in Maidstone.

18th To Folkestone, Richard, Ella, Louy & I started at ¼ past 8, reached our destination, (getting into the rail-road carriage at Headcorn), at ½ past 11. Found Aunt Ella & the Hulls quite well. Home after a delightful excursion at nine.

20th To the Palace to drink tea at Mama's where met Mrs Murray, Bigges, General Middleton, Major Meyer & Captain Nolan. A dinner party yesterday at the Brockman's. *(Rev. Brockman was vicar of Otham)*

22nd Aunt Ella, Mr & Mrs Hull, Mama & Milly passed the day here, a <u>great</u> pleasure to me.

23rd To Leeds Castle, the Bigges came to accompany us to the archery meeting held there. Mama remained at home. Mr

Crawley joined our party at dinner. I left at 7 & the rest went on to pass the evening at the Castle.

Maidstone Bishop's Palace today.

24th Major Meyer called & drove Mama home to her Palace accompanied by our two young ladies, drank tea with Mama.

27th To pass the day at Mrs Bigge's where took Mama & Milly & met General Middleton, Mrs Murray & Captain Nolan. As we drove home in the evening saw the Comet, Mr Crawley stopping the carriage to announce that it was visible. *(Mr Crawley is courting Milly)*

30th Mama, Milly, Miss Bigge & her cousin arrived, & as chaperone to the three last started with them for Surrenden where the archery meeting was held. A lovely day & a lovely place & people innumerable. Mr Darrell introduced me to a Swede, Captain of the king's bodyguard & there were other foreigners there besides. A most agreeable evening, home at ½ past 2.

September 7th The Flower Show where Mama & Milly met us. Flowers beautiful & latterly people abundant. Walked about shopping with Mama & Milly. Mr Crawley, passed ½ an hour at the Palace where Richard came.

16th Took Milly out shopping, saw the Duke of Cambridge at the Depot. Returned to the Palace & had some silks from Watts for inspection.

19th From the Palace accompanied Milly, Mr Crawley & Mr Leslie to Allington Castle. Much sauntering in the sunshine, reached the Palace again so tired out that I couldn't go with them to Mrs Griffiths to drink tea as I had hoped.

October 1st To a little & very pleasant party at the Palace consisting of Lady F Riddell, the Miss Riddells & General Middleton. Much talking, chess & whist.

3rd To the Palace to say goodbye. Found Mr Crawley there.

5th Dined at Mr Pemberton Leigh's. Uncle Go there. A most silent dinner.

9th To afternoon service where Mr Spurgin *(the curate)* preached an excellent farewell sermon & was much overcome.

11th Drank tea at Hollingbourne House with Mrs Faunce & Mrs E. Duppa accompanied by Ella, Louy & Bertha.

23rd To afternoon service where our new curate Mr Bowden officiated & preached a very good sermon.

24th Mr Crawley came to shoot rabbits with Mr Thomas. Mary taken very ill, screaming, struggling & insensible. Sent for Mr Sedgwick. Out. Mr Whatman fortunately at Mr R.W. Martin's. Put her in a warm bath & did the best we could. Colonel & Mrs Griffiths called. Mr Crawley at dinner. I like him much.

25th Mr Whatman found Mary better. We dined at the Riddell's, a pleasant day.

26th Mr Whatman did not think Mary better. Captain Nolan called & brought the children some sugarplums.

27th Mary better but the shivering fit comes on every day about 12. William Bunyard came to ask me to translate for him a French agreement as he is about to take a grocer's shop at Boulogne. He expressed himself very sorry for the way in which he had left us.

27th Mr Whatman finds Mary still improving & she is to begin quinine today.

November 2nd With Ella to pass the day at Mr Espinasse's *(Judge James Espinasse)* where we saw pictures, drawings, autographs, fossils etc.

7th The two little Miss Baldwins & their governess, Miss Burkitt, Captain Nolan, & Mr Crawley came to take luncheon here & pass Louy's birthday. All the children enjoyed themselves much & Louy had no end of presents.

9th Ella & I started for Brighton, met at the rail-road station Mr Crawley & Mr Murray. Found Mama & Milly quite well. Brighton looking very bright & full. Called on the Horace Smiths. Very glad to see Eliza Smith again.

10th Went out visiting with Mama. Called on Scotts who have taken a very pretty house in Brunswick Square. Called on Lady Carhampton who was painting away as busily as ever & projecting a series of little dinner parties. After dinner walked with Milly down the cliff, found Mr Crawley arrived on our return home.

12th Mama & I took a walk by the Western Road & home by the cliff. Mr Crawley after dinner escorted me home. Started from Brighton at 4.10 & reached Maidstone at 6.55, found all well & Mary looking better.

13th I miss little Ella much. She was in tears yesterday when we parted at the Maidstone station. *(She has remained in Brighton)*

22nd Poor Bertha thrown from Robin Hood & sadly cut in the face but not otherwise hurt. Sent for Mr Joy who strapped it up with adhesive plaster.

23rd Mr Joy called to see Bertha who is a melancholy looking little object. The poor little thing has borne her pain well.

28th Queen Mab's birthday, she is 4 years old today. (*Lolotte, the youngest*) She appeared in an ivy wreath & all the children drank tea with us. Mr Whatman found Bertha improving.

December 9th Another letter from Milly with a copy of one from a Mr Lansing, Watertown, Jefferson County, New York saying that my Father had had a fall from his carriage & had since been subject to fits & that his mind was much weakened in consequence.[87]

10th Started early with Louy, Bertha & Hobbs for town. I found Aunt Ella's carriage awaiting us & herself quite well. Drove after dinner to call on Uncle Albert.

16th To the British Museum with Hobbs & the children.

20th Sent the carriage for Milly who arrived not looking well. *(nothing has come of the courtship)*

21st *(At home)* Went to the County Ball with Milly saw many of my friends there & missed many, went in the Burkitts' char-a-banc.

24th Wrote last night the tickets for our Christmas dinner of which there are this year 40.

---

[87]   He had been director of the Watertown Bank

30th News of my Father's death at Watertown on the 1st of this month. Started with Hobbs in Mr Burkitt's char-a-banc to Maidstone to purchase mourning. Snow showers most violent. It is melancholy to reflect on anyone so gifted as my Father & all so completely thrown away.

31st Occupied all day as usual teaching, reading & working.

1854 January 1st Milly wrote to say that a notice of my Father has appeared in the Illustrated News among those of eminent persons lately deceased where he is said to be married in Watertown & has left a widow & two children!

8th Put on mourning.

28th Took Ella & Louy to Sharsted where we had a pleasant three hours, the children particularly as the Faunces had prepared a Christmas tree.

February 4th To London with Gerard & Lolotte. Heard that Mr Branfill Harrison has been presented with the living of Walmer, value £240. Aunt Ella's carriage met us at the station, found her quite well. Miss Isobel Goldsmid called & seemed to think that Mesmerism was having a beneficial effect on Caroline.[88]

9th Milly passed the day in St Andrews Place, I dined with Uncle Albert. Caroline mesmerised while I was there & in an excited state.

11th Dined at Uncle Go's & sat between the two Edward Goulburns.

13th Milly came up to St Andrews Place, then took leave of our dear aunt & returned home. Mr & Mrs Gipps travelled with us. All well at home.

14th A letter from General Middleton full of the war & other military matters.[89]

16th To Maidstone where found all my friends out. Even the barracks looked thoroughly deserted. Hard at work teaching in the morning as indeed I have my share of that every day.

19th A letter from Mama kindly offering to allow me £100 a year. Wrote to thank her. Did not go to church on account of the intense cold.

March 3rd Early to Ditton to see Lady Strange about her illustrations to my alphabet which are beautiful but the price of publishing (Cundell asks £700, the Ghent lithographer

---

[88]   A therapeutic system begun by Mesmer in the 18th century which he called 'animal magnetism'. From this developed modern clinical hypnotism.

[89]   The Crimean War had broken out three months previously.

£120 giving me 200 copies), is too great for me to undertake the speculation. Besides which to pay myself I could not ask for less than a pound a copy & that and the black letter printing would I think quite prevent it from being what it was intended to be; a child's book. Lady Strange's son was so ill that we had but a short time to stay there. Shopping in Maidstone.

13th Wrote to Lady Strange to give up the Alphabet.

16th To Maidstone where saw the entrée of the Judge. Also heard a man precipitated from the top of a van among a heap of crockery. The poor man was I fear hurt & was immediately taken to the Infirmary.

17th Ella's 14th birthday. Mrs Faunce & her children & Mlle Musard came to pass the day here.

April 1st Richard at Leeds to meet the other Commissioners for the building the vicarage there. Mr Wilder arrived last night, looking very well & bringing us a salmon, sugar plums, a scent packet for Miss Edmed & a puzzle for Mary. Today we had a dinner party to meet him; a most animated assemblage.

19th We went to the ball in the evening. A very good & full one. General Middleton introduced to me Sir Thomas Maryon Wilson & Mr Francis Bigge dined here.

23rd To afternoon service. Mr Bowden gave a very good sermon.

27th A letter from Milly telling of their safe arrival.(*in Brighton, she has taken Louy with her*) To Maidstone in the afternoon with Richard, called on Mrs Griffiths.

29th Mary struggling & shrieking. We sent off for Mr Joy. He considers her very poorly & says that she is a child requiring great care & rather keeping back than urging on in her acquirements. Wrote to Mama.

30th Poorly & anxious about Mary so did not go to church. Mr Joy came & found Mary a shade better.

May 1st Garlands innumerable. Richard off to London. Mr Joy found Mary better. On Saturday Richard dined at Mr Espinasse's & met Sir Thomas Maryon Wilson.[90]

2nd Mr Joy came & still found Mary improving.

4th Last evening called on the Burkitts about their char-a-banc which they are anxious to sell & today Mrs Burkitt called on us on the same subject.[91]

---

[90]   Sir Thomas Maryon Wilson was colonel of the West Kent Militia in the 1850s & a landowner.

5th Richard purchased the char-a-banc & it was brought home. Yesterday Mr Joy found Mary improving but in a delicate state. Richard dined with the Militia at The Star & invited Sir Maryon Wilson & three of his men to dine here on Tuesday.

12th Miss Edmed, Gerard, Ella & Bertha accompanied me to the Militia Inspection in the park at Vinters, a very gay & pretty sight. Richard dined with the militia at The Star to meet their inspecting officer.

15th To the Ball in the evening. Met Lord George Beauclerck there to our great surprise, fancied him safe in India. Many of the militia present.

16th To the Inspection by Sir Joseph Thackwell of the cavalry in the Barrack Yard. Arrived too soon for the performance & waited with Henry Gipps at General Middleton's when we went to the Depot & at 5 partook of a splendid collation.

21st Lolotte much better but towards evening again poorly, a letter from Mama who had most kindly offered to take Mary.

22nd Lolotte feverish & poorly so sent for Mr Joy. He finds her suffering from a sort of infantile fever much about just now. Packing up for Brighton tomorrow.

23rd I started for Brighton, Bertha & Mary going second class with Hobbs. Found Mama quite well & Milly too, & Louy much fatter & stronger, returned to Oriental Place at 9.

24th A good report of Lolotte from Miss Edmed. Walked with Mama. The children delighted with the novelty of everything. *(Louisa has rented rooms in Oriental Place, not staying with Mama)*

29th A much better report of Lolotte from home.

31st Eliza Smith sat with me. A letter from Ella to announce Richard's arrival today with Lolotte. They accordingly appeared at the rail road whither Louy, Bertha & I had walked to meet them. Took Lolotte to Silwood Place to see Mama & Milly.

June 1st Mary poorly & in bed. Called on Mrs Rooper, their house which formerly stood out of Brighton & in the country is now scarcely beyond the town. Sat with Mary while Hobbs & Bertha went to the concert at the Pavilion. A stroll along the cliff with Bertha in the evening.

3rd Left the children at the chain pier with Richard, & Milly & I went shopping. After dinner went to see the Talbot-type with

---

91   A waggon with long covered bench seats.

Richard, the likenesses are most perfect, & the execution very clever.[92]

4th To the old church which is beautifully restored & the memorial to the Duke of Wellington beautiful. In the afternoon called on Lady Abinger & Lady Carhampton.

6th A walk with Milly, dined with Mama, & at 3.30 started per rail road home which reached at 6.30. The children with us all well, & found all flourishing on return.

9th Book dusting assisted by Hobbs, Ella & Louy, thoroughly tired.

14th Drove to Maidstone met Colonel Griffiths who is to inspect the Yeomanry on Friday next in Lord Romney's park. (*Mote Park*)

16th Intended to go & see the yeomanry review but it rained, in the afternoon to the Fair, smaller than ever. Mary & Lolotte too poorly to go. Finished 'Cranford'.

19th Started early by Strood for London which reached at ½ past one. Drove out after dinner. Shopping & called at Uncle Albert's & Uncle Go's. No one at home. Captain & Mrs Hull called in St Andrews Place & took Louy & Bertha to see the animals fed at the Zoological Gardens.

20th To the dentist who took out four very large double teeth from Louy. I was almost afraid that she would faint but it all passed off & we went immediately afterwards to the German fair. In the afternoon Captain Hull accompanied me to the Royal Academy & the exhibition of the Old Masters.

20th To the Crystal Palace, a complete Fairyland with Aunt Ella & the Hulls. I never saw anything more beautiful. Dined at Uncle Go's only himself & Kate.

21st To Uncle Albert's where saw poor Caroline. Captain Hull took the children out walking with him & in the afternoon we all travelled home by Strood. Lolotte not well but the rest very flourishing.

July 20th Mama & Milly departed for Boulogne. During their stay we have had Mademoiselle Musard, Mary Faunce's governess here & Miss Edmed has gone for a holiday. We have also been to Ticehurst & seen poor Louis & Freddy. Another day we went to the archery accompanied by Francis Bigge.

---

[92]   Photographs named after William Henry Fox Talbot the photographic pioneer.

August 3rd On Friday news was brought of poor Cheesman's death at the Hospital in London & on Saturday Richard started for town.[93]

9th Mr Oliver's school treat to which our children went. Cheesman & old Tassell buried today.

12th Went on the char a banc to fetch Mama & Milly who were full of Boulogne.

14th This morning Mama & Milly departed. Poor Annie's brother died at one o'clock of cholera after a few hours illness. He had gone tolerably well to his work in the morning beyond Sittingbourne, was brought back home, & expired as he was being taken upstairs.

18th To Maidstone, called on Mrs Whatman, Mrs Griffiths & the Miss Betts. No one at home. Anne's mother taken ill with cholera today.

19th Mrs Hopper died last night.

20th To afternoon service. Mr Bowden preached well on the deaths of Mrs Hopper & her son who had both been to church last Sunday. She is to be buried today.

21st Mrs Burkitt called. Dined at Mr Taylor's. Susan Bunyard came in Jane Orford's place who has lived with us above nine years.

22nd To the Archery Meeting at Lord Romney's, took Miss Burkitt with me, a very large assemblage. Dined at the military table with Griffiths, Balders, Major Meyer.

30th To Maidstone where gave Colonel Griffiths Mr Thomas' invitation to shoot here on the 1st which he cannot accept being engaged with the Embarkation.

September 11th Mrs Savage called & Mr Frank Duppa came to stay with us.

12th Richard & *(young)* Frank Duppa up The Hill to look over his estate. Only Mary & Lolotte at home with me & we called on Mrs Burkitt.

16th Our new kitchen maid Mary Martin came. She is to be called Anne like her predecessor.

27th Dinner party here, it did very well. Yesterday Mrs Whatman called with two children and three nurses.

---

[93]   Richard noted the sad fate of Cheesman one of his workmen 'Cheesman left the infirmary at Maidstone and went to Kings College Hospital London, gave him a sovereign to pay his passage, underwent an operation and the poor fellow died in about a week after.'

October 7th Took Ella, Louy & Bertha yesterday for their first dancing lesson to Mr Philpott's Academy at The Star Hotel Maidstone.

13th Took the children again to Mr Philpott's Academy. The Baldwins came home & took luncheon here & passed the day. Dined at Vinters.

18th Mr F. Duppa departed & a London surveyor called. He had come down to look at Mr Duppa's estates.

21st Drove to Maidstone to fetch Richard. On my way called at Vinters on Mrs Whatman from thence to enquire after Lady Catherine Balders whose brother Captain Hare was killed at Alma & from thence to call on General Middleton with whom sat for some time.[94] He was feeble & complaining.

23rd Much shocked on receiving from Major Meyer a note to say that poor General Middleton had died on Sunday morning *(yesterday)* at 5. He had felt poorly & not gone to bed during the night. On attempting to lie down he died instantly. Only his servants were with him. Captain Middleton *(his son)* in Ireland & Mrs Bill *(his daughter)* in the Highlands of Scotland.

27th Took the children to the Assembly Rooms for their dancing lesson. Called on Mrs Griffiths & saw Major Meyer who had seen Captain Middleton & he wishes our carriage to attend his father's funeral.[95]

28th The carriage followed poor General Middleton to the grave. Miss Edmed & the children & Hobbs went to see the funeral which was very quiet.

November 1st A long visit from Uncle Go who came well & in good spirits & went away quite poorly.

3rd We dined at Mr Pemberton Leigh's where were Uncle Go & Mr & Mrs Faunce.

9th Mr Bowden called to consult Richard about the Patriotic Fund in the village.

12th Mr Bowden preached on the Patriotic Fund.

14th Poor Captain Nolan's name among those killed on the dreadful 25th.

15th Dined at Colonel Griffiths. Captain Nolan was the first killed in the fearful charge. *(The Charge of the Light Brigade)* Mrs Stacey said that he came to her in the beginning of the year & said that he had just been having his fortune told by

---

94   Captain Charles Hare died of wounds received at the battle of Alma.

95   It was the done thing for the upper classes to send their empty carriages to funerals to show their respect, whilst only those close to the deceased actually attended.

three gipsies who had each predicted that he would be killed in battle before the year was out.[96]

18th Richard at Chatham today & yesterday busy in assisting to collect for the Patriotic Fund.

27th Mr F. Wykeham Martin passed unhurt through the fire of Balaclava.

30th Met Mr Whatman who was full of sad deaths in the Crimea.

December 9th Our new kitchen maid Mary Martin came. She is to be called Anne like her predecessor.

13th With Ella & Bertha started for London by the South Eastern, found Aunt Ella's carriage awaiting & herself quite well.

17th To hear Edward preach at Park Street chapel which he did well, indeed I never heard a more striking sermon.

20th Edward at luncheon. Called on Mrs Mostyn. Edward sent me his book on the study of the Holy Scriptures & Aunt Ella gave Ella the best edition of Prescott's 'Works'; to Louy, Captain Marryat's 'Little Savage' & to Gerard 'Little Arthur's History of England'.

21st We drove down to the rail road & travelled home. Our compagnon de voyage an elderly man with moustaches who, instead of a hero bound to the Crimea, turned out to have been formerly a Commissioner of Bankrupts. Our new coachman David Roberts arrived.

23rd To Maidstone shopping. 40lbs of raisins for our village dinner.

25th To church with the children. In the evening assisted them in acting a charade.

29th To a meeting of ladies in the vicarage for the sending out necessaries in the way of clothing to the Crimea. Mr Stewart received subscriptions of money in the room. I gave £2.

31st Ella & Louy read with me in the evening 'Histories from the Old Testament in Latin' for the first time. A letter from Mr Wilder to announce that a turkey is on its way to us.

1855 January 3rd Drove with Uncle Go to Preston Hall. No one at home but we saw the drawing rooms, the new library & the beautiful statues in the garden.

---

[96]   Captain Lewis Nolan was intelligent, good-looking, an excellent horse-man. He was chosen by Lord Raglan to take the orders for the Light Brigade to charge to Lord Lucan. He may have misunderstood the order.

5th Uncle Go departed early & in the evening Ella, Louy, Bertha & myself at a Christmas party at Sharsted where were above 100 people.

9th Took Gerard, Ella, Louy & Bertha to a ball at the Baldwin's where was also a conjurer.

18th A letter from Henry Gipps from Boulogne announcing that Lord Hardinge has given him a commission. Took Ella, Louy & Bertha to a party at Mr Dollings.'

February 2nd Walked down beyond Elnothington, the road to Maidstone open but to Ashford quite blocked up.

9th Thanks to the snow plough managed to get to Maidstone for the dancing lesson. Yesterday Richard sent a cwt of coal to each of twenty one of the poorest families in the village. (*snow had started to fall on January 17th*)

18th Cold still most intense. The water in all the bedrooms frozen.

27th Drove into Maidstone to fetch Richard. Captain Crawley's wife is just 18.

March 16th Took the children to their dancing lesson. Met Captain & Mrs Cleve with whom I went to see Lord Cardigan inspect the troops going out to the Crimea. The men & horses of the 13th looked splendid & are to go out just as they stood, newly caparisoned for the occasion. The affair quite private, only one lady there besides ourselves.

25th Mr Bowden preached his farewell sermon as Mr Kirby *(new curate)* is to arrive tomorrow.

26th To Mrs Savage's & passed the day at St Leonards. Saw Miss Duppa's very clever paintings. Frank Duppa returned with me to Hollingbourne & gave me a very pretty little bronze lamp from Naples.[97]

April 8th Psalms sung for first time in church.

(On April 6th Louisa began to write the diary in French, no reason given, the whole of the rest of the volume is in French so this is a translation.)

21st Hobbs & I left for London. Found Kate at the station & at dinner Milly.

22nd Milly & I visited Caroline & Uncle Albert in Park Crescent & also saw Yeats there. Dined with Aunt Ella & found Mama in good health.

---

[97]   This Frank Duppa was the eldest son & heir of Frank Duppa the education reformer who died in 1840. He travelled for several years & was interested in geology and chemistry. He had a laboratory at Hollingbourne House.

23rd The Queen & Prince Albert were driving in Hyde Park.

24th With my uncle to the exhibition of amateur paintings for the Patriotic Fund.

25th Milly had luncheon here & we made visits together including Jessy, *(Goldsmid)* a widow now with five children, & went in Hyde Park.

May 10th *(At home)* Gave notice to Baker her temper is so violent that it is impossible to put up with any longer.

June 1st We left at last for Sydenham. When we arrived there were no rooms in the hotels or houses. At last we found three miserable little rooms where we are camped, & this done we went to the Crystal Palace where we met Mama & Milly.

7th *(At home)* Mr Kirby came about the organ, Richard gave him £15 & I £5. *(In old age she wrote that this organ replaces the various instruments which used to be played in the gallery of Hollingbourne church.)*

9th Baker has left after living here more than 5 years & Anne Bourne has come as cook in her place.

22nd Very sad news from the Crimea.

July 3rd Dinner party here. Lord Raglan has died of cholera.

August 6th Mama & Milly have left. Uncle Go also visited while they were here & we had a dinner party. Miss Edmed was absent 15 days for the marriage of her sister.

11th To Wateringbury to pass the day with the Bigges. Poor Fanny has a more delicate air. She gave me a bouquet of flowers made of feathers from Madeira.

14th We left for Folkestone, Richard, Ella, Gerard & I. There we met Captain Hull who accompanied us to see the horses of the Queen in the steam boat about to leave for France. Then to 13 Pleydell Gardens where my aunt is staying who was well in spite of the violent illness she has had. Then to Shorne Cliff to see the camp of the Foreign Legion mostly made up of Germans. We came back via Headcorn & Ulcombe & visited Mrs Ellis & Rosalind Smith.

September 4th Uncle Go & my sister arrived by rail road. Last week Mr F. & E. Duppa came to see us. I went to Maidstone with Mr Kirby to collect the Archbishop of Canterbury. Our Thomas a Becket is sweet & well mannered, Riddells, Espinasses, Kirbys, & Whatman dined here.

5th We went in the carriage to the church accompanied by the Archbishop who preached for the opening of the organ. It was a very good sermon, then he went to see Mr Hasted who is 95 & seems near death. From there he went to see the lovely ancient house where Mr Bachelor Roper lives. (*Hollingbourne Manor*) When we went back to the house we left again for the Kirbys' where they had put on a dinner with an infinite number of clergy & also lots of women. Then my uncle & sister left, I took the Archbishop back to Maidstone.

12th To the Flower Show at Maidstone, lots of people. On Saturday Lady F. Riddell & two children came & brought us the first news of the destruction of Sebastopol.

15th To Sharsted with Ella to take Mademoiselle Musard. Miss Edmed is returned from Hastings today. We asked after Mr Hasted who was very ill. Half an hour later came news of his death. *(he had been vicar of Hollingbourne for 65 years)*

October 25th Mr Thomas in Maidstone at the sale of some houses in the village.

November 22nd To Strood in char-a-banc & then by rail road to London, Louy Bertha, Hobbs & me to visit Aunt Ella. During our stay I dined at Uncle Go's & Uncle Albert's, to the Crystal Palace with Louy & Bertha, & also saw the Crimean photograph exhibition.

25th *(At home)* To church where Mr Carter Hall *(who is to be the new vicar)* took the office.

1856 January 6th To church where Mr Hall preached very well. Yesterday Mr Kirby came to tell us that the Archbishop has given him the parish of Appledore. They soon leave Elnothington.

February 18th To Brighton with Lolotte & Hobbs via Paddock Wood & Reigate.

20th Lady Abinger to see me. Captain Dennie was asleep on the canapé (*sofa*) having lost his feet in the Crimea.

21st Still looking for a boarding school *(for Ella)* but at last I decided on that of Miss Gilbertson in Brunswick Place. In evening dined with Mrs Mostyn.

25th A promenade with Milly, dinner with Mama, we left Brighton for home.

March 10th To Sharsted with Ella, Louy & Bertha, the old house has been much improved.

20th The induction of Mr Carter Hall as vicar of Hollingbourne by Mr Riddell. Mr Thomas was one of his witnesses.[98] The death of poor Fanny Bigge.

---

[98] The Rev. Carter Hall came full of good intentions for a parish which had been so long neglected. Unfortunately he quarrelled constantly with his parishioners.

24th We went to the Oratorio where there was an orchestra of 100 people.

31st To Brighton with Ella. We ate with Mama & then I took Ella to Miss Gilbertson's. *(school)* Poor little Ella was very sad. *(She is 16)*

April 1st I went with Mama to see Ella & then to some shops.

2nd Dined at Mrs Mostyn's where saw Miss Halifax & Colonel Yorke who was badly wounded at Balaklava & who cannot walk without crutches.

5th Said goodbye to Ella & travelled home.

May 4th It is the day fixed for giving thanks for peace.

6th Reading 'Little Dorrit' to Mr Thomas.

27th We left for Strood in the char-a-banc en route for London. Arrived at Aunt Ella's, went out in carriage. Everyone is occupied in preparations to celebrate peace.

29th All shops shut & everyone out looking for enjoyment. Mr & Mrs Carter Hall came, rode out in carriage. Richard & I went to see the illuminations in town & fireworks started at 9 which were superb like trees lit in flowers in all colours.

30th With Richard to the panorama of Siege of Sebastapol & then dinner at the Royal Academy; the paintings of the year 'Peace concluded' by Millais & 'The Scapegoat' by Hunt. I didn't like either of them. Uncle Go came in to see us.

31st Said goodbye to my dear aunt & en route for Strood with the Savages & home.

September 22nd *(She begins to write in English again)* Showery, but managed a walk in the road with Uncle Go. At 7 took Uncle to Mr Pemberton Leigh's & dined there. His house so changed again that I should scarcely know it. A spacious hall & a fine library with a gorgeous ceiling. Here too a large family party.

26th To Maidstone early accompanied by Louy, Bertha & Miss Edmed & ordered cloaks for the children & dresses at Paine & Evenden's.

29th Read for the 20th time at least 'The Clerkes Tale' in Chaucer.

October 1st Took Mrs Hall to see the Dollings, not at home, & on our return to see Hollingbourne House. Desolate & melancholy in the extreme. *(empty, the Duppas no longer living there)*

3rd Mr Kirby paid us an early & unexpected visit. He seems on the whole to like Appledore. Hobbs summoned away by her father's illness so our new maid little Anne Ambrose waited upon me on my return home.

7th Richard at Coxheath where he shot 3 pheasants. Mrs Cheesman *(widow of labourer)* has sadly fallen from her 'high estate' for tidings came that she had been confined in the night. The child arrived too soon & was dead. A dreadful vaut-nire *(scoundrel)* by name Whitehead the father of it.

12th To morning service which was read for the first time by the new curate Mr Bigsby, Mr Carter Hall preached. *(The Carter Halls were well able to afford a curate.)*

13th A beautiful eclipse of the moon which began about ½ past 9 & ending at ½ past 12. The children in a state of great excitement on the subject. Louy & Bertha sat up for the occasion. Mary & Gerard left their beds but poor little Lolotte, much as she wished for it, could not keep awake.

16th We dined at the Pepys', I went to dinner with the Crimean son of the family who had been through the Balaklava light cavalry charge. He has now left the army.

19th Mr Bigsby preached, I liked his sermon much, clear, earnest & simple.

21st Last week gave a flannel petticoat to Bourne's mother & today one each to Mrs Wisdom, Mrs Bottle & Mrs Peckham.

23rd Started for Brighton. Captain Hull & Milly met me at the station, the latter in her cavalier hat & feather. Found my mother looking poorly. Went out driving with Aunt Ella & called on Uncle Albert & Caroline, & Uncle Go & Kate, the former on his couch but he called in Silwood Place about ½ past 9. Little Ella too, who was looking very fat & well.

24th A walk with Milly to no end of shops, Mama & I drove out in Aunt Ella's carriage & drank tea at Aunt Ella's where met the Hulls.

25th Dear little Ella's confirmation at Hove church by Dr Gilbert Bishop of Chichester. The church crowded, nearly 300 children received the rite of confirmation. We brought Ella away with us in her white dress & veil & while we visited Aunt Ella she stopped to change & went with us to take luncheon at Silwood Place. Captain & Mrs Hull & Uncle Go & Kate called afterwards & Ella returned to Miss Gilbertson's. After dinner Uncle Go put a stop to all the music by saying it destroyed conversation.

26th To Christchurch where Mr Vaughan preached an excellent sermon. Called on Lady Carhampton almost in her dotage, telling the same thing four or five times over &

laughing at nothing. After luncheon Uncle Go, Uncle Albert & Caroline called. We dined at the Junction Hotel with Uncle Go & Kate.

27th To a literary soiree at the Pavilion, saw Aquariums, photographs, relics from the Crimea, medals, models of screw steamer, telegraph & other rail road inventions, the laughing gas, an amber cup dug up near Brunswick Square & supposed to be nearly 2000 years old. A very amusing evening.

28th Dined at Uncle Albert's, Caroline much the same. An Alma pudding at dinner.

30th Captain Hull called. Called on little Ella & Aunt Ella to say goodbye.

31st Captain Hull kindly saw me into the rail road. Waited at Reigate & Paddock Wood. The children all well. Richard to London.

November 2nd Forgot to say I called on Lady Abinger in Brighton in her very pretty house all summer & sunshine & Mrs Cockburn formerly Mary Duff the earliest love of Lord Byron & now a most agreeable old lady.

5th Richard so unwell that we sent for Mr Joy who prescribed leaches. Sat up till 2 o'clock applying them.

6th Richard better.

7th Dear Louy thirteen, took her & Lolotte to Maidstone to have their hair cut.

10th Drove to Harrietsham, found Mrs Riddell at home *(in the vicarage)* & the six 'young' children. The baby very nice & healthy looking.

11th Fanny Butler our little kitchen maid gave notice yesterday as she is going to be married.

15th Called on Mrs Hall, found Mr Hall restless as usual. Frank Duppa called.

18th Went to see old Mrs Butler who has been ill & took her some tea. Found her lying on her bed & very uncomfortable.

December 3rd Mr & Mrs Hall called. On Monday evening was the opening of the village reading room & library. *(the idea of Rev. Hall)*

9th To Maidstone accompanied by Richard, Louy, Gerard & Hobbs. The cattle show to which Richard & Gerard went & the town full of people.

10th Bertha 12 years old & the usual feast given with which all the birthdays are celebrated. In the evening went to the school where a meeting was held for the Conversion of the

Jews. Mr Hall opened the proceedings & then the curate of Egerton gave a long account of his missionary labours at Berlin. The room hot & crowded.

Louy at about this time painted by Louisa.

13th Gave a dancing lesson as usual on a rainy day.
16th Went to the school to see the meeting of the Clothing Club. 75 old women making their purchases from Hulburd & Oxley both of whom had brought their wares to the school room. Mr & Mrs Hall there. The latter came home with me & discussed the Jews. Fanny Duppa with her Swiss maid arrived about 4 & at 10 we started for the military ball. *(given by the officers of the Cavalry Depot)* Room full when we arrived. Stairs lined with soldiers, walls decorated with spears, swords & military trophies besides evergreens & flowers. Brilliantly lighted, dresses all new for the occasion, various uniforms, splendid diamonds, a most liberal supper, a boars head decked with banners & stuffed with truffles crowning the repast. In short nothing could be better arranged.

17th Walked with Fanny Duppa to the vicarage, & to see the other changes in the village. Called at the school on our way home & there met Mrs Hall. The reading room a failure as we anticipated. Frank Duppa came in for an hour & then Mrs Faunce took luncheon here. Fanny Duppa departed.

23rd Called on Mrs Hall found her making arrangements for their Christmas treat to the schoolchildren, 93 in number. Frank Duppa called. At 10 o'clock to the ball which was very well attended though of course not as brilliant as the military one.

24th Finished the tickets for our Christmas dinner, 39 recipients.

25th To morning service. Mr & Mrs Hall called to wish us a Merry Christmas. Our servants had a party in the evening consisting of Lowe & his wife, Mr & Mrs Lurcock, Jack Sage & his half, Ann Hooper, Charlotte Bourne & Robert's brother. Wrote to Mr Savage to get Mr Hall an order for the gaol to see the woman Wallace who murdered her child at Dover & who was formerly one of his congregation. Acted charades with the children.

26th Called on Mrs Hall to say that whooping cough at the school considered, I could not let the children attend the Treat to be given there by Mr Hall.

27th Snowy & slippery. Went to Malling to see Lady Strange & my Alphabet which she has illustrated. Her son Major Strange with her.

29th The Halls came to see my Alphabet which Lady Strange allowed me to bring home to show to Mr Thomas. They admired the illustrations so very much as indeed they are very beautiful, but they agreed with us in not liking the alterations that Lady Strange had made in the words & without naming it. So I wrote to her Ladyship on the subject.

30th Took the Halls to Maidstone to buy toys for their Christmas treat to the school children, they dined with us.

1857 January 4th To morning service. A poor man found dead by Jack Sage in Snarkhurst Wood. A complete skeleton & his clothing all decayed. He is supposed to be a half-witted man of the name of Carey who was missed from the Union about four months ago & later sought for in vain. A shell was brought, & in it he was taken to the Union.

5th Went in the evening to the school to see the tea party, the Christmas tree, the distribution of prizes by Mr & Mrs Hall &

the Magic Lantern. An evening of great enjoyment to the children.

6th At 5 the children went to the vicarage for tea & Magic Lantern & at 6 Uncle Go arrived. The children returned by ½ past 9 delighted with their evening.

7th Uncle Go, with Ella & Gerard walked into Maidstone & returned in a fly, the roads being so snowy that the omnibus did not run to Ashford. Mr Ellis came in the afternoon having walked over to say that the roads are so blocked up that he does not think it possible they can dine with us today. At 7 Mr Hall, Mr Bigsby & Mr Southwell appeared our other guests having all failed. Uncle Go never ceased talking the whole time.

8th Uncle Go went with us into Maidstone & departed on the train. Went to choose some books for the children which he had been kind enough to give them.

10th Drank tea at the vicarage to meet Mr S.C. Hall *(brother of vicar),* just arrived from London. Played two games at chess with him, he is very like our vicar but plump & sleek.[99]

12th Gerard, Mary, Lolotte & Louy poorly.

13th Intended to attend the County Ball but Richard so poorly that we stayed at home instead.

14th Today Ella, Ann Ambrose, Bourne & Bertha all invalided.

15th Hobbs & Sarah added to the sick list.

16th I was poorly & Richard went to dine at the Whatman's alone.

21st Mr Riddell called full of electioneering. Richard out with Mr Oliver canvassing.

22nd Mrs Hall took luncheon here & then we drove out to *(Detling)* to call on Mrs Cobb *(wife of the vicar)* whom we found dressed in a crimson brocade &, in her way, very smart.

23rd Richard out canvassing with Mr Riddell & Sir Brook Bridges.

26th Mademoislle & Ella went to see Mrs Hall who sent me a number of the Art Journal containing Mr & Mrs S. C. Hall's first paper of their forthcoming work on the Thames.

30th Richard & Ella started for Brighton by the 10.30 train.

February 1st Frank Duppa at luncheon. A friend of his, by name Perkins, has made a discovery of a very beautiful, durable lilac colour produced from coal tar.[100]

---

[99] Samuel Carter Hall was well known in literary circles & editor of 'The Art Journal'.

2nd Started for London by the North Kent. Uncle Go's carriage awaiting me at the London Bridge station. Fetched him from his court in Basinghall Street. Mary Chetwynd & Julia dined with us.

3rd Drove to see Aunt Ella who was very well. On my return to Seymour Street found Edward & he & Julia dined with us.

4th Went with Hobbs & had quite a morning of shopping. In the afternoon called on Uncle Albert & Aunt Ella where Edward met me. He & Julia again dined in Seymour Street.

5th Took luncheon with Aunt Ella & drove out afterwards. Called on Jessy & Dora & on Caroline whose maid is going to be very well married to a hatter in the City. Mary Chetwynd dined with us. Uncle Go in great spirits.

6th Uncle Go presented me with a photograph from his portrait by Richmond which some consider very like him. He says that it is like a pork butcher. Walked to Aunt Ella's & on our way we visited the German Fair. Took luncheon with her, the carriage came for me when I drove for Uncle Go in Basinghall Street. Edward, Julia & Mary Chetwynd dined with us. Discussed poetry; a very pleasant last evening.

7th I home on rail road, found everyone well except Miss Edmed who had a fainting fit last night.

9th Louy & I walked to call on Mrs Hall & in the afternoon Bertha went with me to Maidstone. Met everybody & brought home with us Mr Wilder who slept here.

16th To the nomination on Penenden Heath. Sir Walter Riddell made a good speech, straight forward & candid, which certainly could not be said of his opponent. Miss Savage joined us where Mr Savage took on for the first time his duties of High Sherriff. After the ceremony we went to Lady Frances Riddell's to take luncheon. Met there 50 or 60 of the Conservative party. A very pleasant day.

18th A portrait of himself arrived this morning from Edward. A wonderful likeness. It is an engraving from Pickersgill's portrait of him.[101]

19th Richard & Mr Hall to Maidstone to vote. Horses & servants with orange & purple ribbons, but alas Mr Martin

---

[100] Sir William Perkin discovered the first synthetic dye called mauveine or aniline purple. He patented his discovery which became a great success when the Queen wore a mauve dress to her daughter's wedding in 1858.

[101] Henry William Pickersgill was a successful London portrait painter.

returned by a majority of 440. *(The Martins of Leeds Castle were Liberals)*

20th Poor little Arthur Filmer has died at school quite suddenly. Lady Filmer was not in time to see him alive, but he left a message for her that he wished to be buried 'in his Papa's grave'. I took my children to the dancing school.

21st With Mademoiselle Musard, Mary & Lolotte to Sharsted where we took luncheon. Miss Duppa as usual busy painting in oils. The new library is very beautifully carved in oak panelling & opening into the conservatory.

March 4th Called on Mrs Hall. They have brought our children a Lotto game & Gerard a horn from London. Mrs Hall accompanied me to Maidstone & Boxley.

5th Mrs Hall & I walked by Primrose Lane. Richard at a Turnpike meeting.

6th Miss Edmed's brother is in the consumptive hospital & not expected to live. In the evening she announced to me that she wished to leave. She has been with us above eight years.

7th Walked with Richard to the vicarage where he had promised to give Mr Hall a lesson in pruning roses.

9th Miss Edmed received the news of her brother's death in London.

16th Went to Mrs Hall about the felt for the altar. She & Mr Hall came to the church with me & we made the needful arrangements. In Maidstone met Mr Duppa who showed us his newly invented lilac colour.

17th Dinner party here, Mrs Griffiths played, Mrs Ellis sang, & we flattered ourselves that our little festivity altogether did very well.

19th Drove Ann Ambrose to Harrietsham to recover a little after her illness.

20th Left Hobbs in Maidstone as her sister was ill. A fearful murder was committed there on Wednesday night. A lad of 18 by name Edwards had killed his own brother & was just taken.[102]

30th Started by train with Bertha, Mary & Hobbs for London, found Aunt Ella's carriage awaiting us. She had been very poorly.

---

[102]   Thomas Edwards aged 24 lived in Wheeler Street with his parents and brother. He was asleep when his brother George attacked him with an axe and killed him.

April 1st Went to the Zoological Gardens after dinner & saw the beautiful aquarium & all the wonder. It was feeding time & the noises, crunching & excitement quite wonderful.

2nd To Madame Tussaud's 'lifeless but lifelike & awful to sight' exhibition. Dined at Uncle Albert's with Yeats, his wife & her sister. Caroline in bed.

3rd Called on Mrs Thomas Thomas very ailing as usual. Dined in Seymour Street.

4th To a photographic artist in the New Road, Monsieur Louis, where Bertha & Mary were taken, not very successful however, but we are to go again. Did some shopping with Hobbs while Bertha & Mary went to the Coliseum with Miss Isobel Goldsmid with whom delighted.

6th Photographs successful this time, called on Uncle Albert & Caroline. Departed by North Kent line. Richard dined at The Star with Sir B. Bridges & other Conservatives to console themselves under their defeat as Mr W. Martin & Mr Whatman are returned for this division of Kent.

8th Mr & Mrs Hall went with me to Maidstone. Met Colonel Meyer coming to call. Visited Lady Riddell, the town in great tumult on account of the declaration.

10th A letter from Jessy who is to take Miss Edmed as her governess in June.

13th To the County Ball, about 170 people, a very good one. We were introduced to Lady Mildred Hope gorgeous in old point *(lace)* & diamonds. She is rather portly & very pleasing.[103]

16th To the Oratorio at the Corn Exchange. Mozart's 12th mass & the Messiah.

25th Letters from Mama & Milly about a German governess they think will do for us; Fraulein de Brocht, daughter of an artist at Wiesbaden.

May 1st Garland children. The wild flowers this year abundant in spite of the cold.

3rd A letter from Milly announcing that Mrs Mostyn had been taken ill in the rail road carriage on her way from Brighton to London & that on her arrival at the station Mr Mostyn, who met her there, had only just time to take her out of the train & lay her on cushions on the platform when she soon died. She had always wished for a sudden death. Mrs Daniel, her

---

[103]   Lady Mildred was a leading figure in London society, the wife of Sir Alexander Beresford Hope.

housekeeper, who had been with her ever since her marriage, was most fortunately in the carriage with her. She is to be buried in the family vault at Streatham.

4th Started early with Richard for Dover, house hunting. Found a house 18 Waterloo Crescent. Home again.

6th Drove to Leeds to say that the Burkitts might have the use of the carriage & horses during our absence. Mrs Ellis visited.

8th Took leave of Miss Edmed & started for Dover. A very comfortable habitation & the children delighted, the sea view lovely.[104]

22nd Our stay at Dover very prosperous. The weather fine. Saw several of my acquaintance. Two Scotch regiments quartered there, the 93rd & the 42nd which were quite an ornament to the town in their picturesque costume. Visited the castle, Shakespeare's Cliff, the Maison Dieu etc. Beachboro' is a beautiful & extensive place & the children & ourselves liked our day extremely. One night we went on the port & <u>saw</u> the salutes fired from the heights on account of the arrival of the Duke of Cambridge who rode out from Walmer to give the colours to the 93rd . The little Prince Alfred, just arrived from his foreign tour, went in the same train with ourselves & looked bewildered when our children surrounded him & fixed ten large eyes upon him all at once.

27th Miss Edmed passed the day here. I brought Fraulein de Brocht from Maidstone. She is a nice good-tempered looking person.

28th Superintended planting geraniums, sketched, Fraulein sang to us very nicely.

June 2nd Started with Richard for London to stay with Uncle Albert. Found him very well but Caroline in a sad state, more restless than ever. Yeats came round.

3rd To Aunt Ella, called on Mrs Hall at her sister in law's Mrs S.C. Hall. They inhabit a flat in Ashley Place Belgravia, 18 rooms beautifully & tastefully furnished. In the evening Isobel Goldsmid & I went to the Polytechnic & saw a diving bell, dissolving views etc. There was also a concert & a Ventriloquist. Richard came to us there.

6th Accompanied by Jessy we went to the Crystal Palace & heard the Cologne Choral Union who sang beautifully. Met Baldwins, also the S.C. Halls in the Ceramic Court who

---

[104]   Richard's notebook records that as well as five of the children they brought two servants with them.

introduced to us the Director. He went round with us & explained the treasures. Two plates were worth £600 each.

7th To Aunt Ella's pew at Trinity. Afterwards to call on her & Uncle Go. Edward has given up Rugby feeling that his health would stand it no longer. Jessy dined in Park Crescent & Yeats & his party came in the evening.

16th Hobbs is to go on account of her mother in law's approaching end, to take care of her father. A letter from Miss Edmed who is delighted with her new situation. I hope that Jessy will like her.

25th To the Flower Show at Lord Romney's accompanied by Ella, Louy, Bertha, Gerard & Fraulein. Richard came afterwards.

29th To Ticehurst. Louis worse than usual & Freddy no better. We had nearly three hours to wait at Tunbridge Wells on our return.

July 2nd Called on Mrs S. C. Hall. Ella went to Maidstone to fetch Mama & Milly.

8th Mama, Richard, Ella & I started for Charlton on rail road. Charlton is a lovely place & there was a most numerous assemblage to witness the variety of amusements there. The ascent of a balloon, ballet dancers from the opera, a dancing dog etc. The house not shown generally but Sir Thomas Wilson gave Richard a pass to admit him, so we went all through the beautiful rooms & only wished we had more time to see the pictures.[105] The collection of orchidaceous plants at the Flower Show wonderful. Home by 12 o'clock. Detained in Maidstone some time by the mob who had come together to welcome the news of the defeat of the election petition. Haranguing from the balconies going on at that late hour.

17th A dinner party here, Ella dined at table for the first time. Took leave of Hobbs with much grief as she starts early tomorrow for her own home.

18th My new maid called Philpott, but really Robert's sister, entered upon her duties.

27th Ella seized with chicken or glass pox, Mr Sedgwick saw her.

August 4th Drove in the evening with Mama to the archery meeting at Lord Romney's.

---

[105]   Sir Thomas Maryon Wilson had inherited the Charlton house from his father who had begun a private menagerie there.

8th Have lately read Trollope's 'Barchester Towers', which interested me much.

21st Drove to Maidstone with Uncle Go, Gerard & Mary. Uncle Go gave Ella a malachite bracelet & to the other children bows & arrows. Dinner party here.

22nd Uncle Go, Richard & I took luncheon at the Savages. A little archery afterwards. Mama & Milly are safely landed in Jersey. The second Miss Dolling is about to marry a Captain Walter Smith in the Indian army & go out to India. She is not 17.

27th To the archery at Lord Romney's where dined under the trees. In the evening Ella & I went to the ball at the assembly rooms which she enjoyed much & danced. *(Ella has now come out)*

September 3rd Roberts went for a holiday to recruit a little, he having been very poorly lately. Miss Edmed called.

4th Mr & Mrs Hall accompanied Ella & I to luncheon at the Savages. Mr Hall in a 'sea of troubles'.

15th Yesterday went through all the German lessons with the Fraulein.

17th Hobbs intends to set up a little shop in the village to take in dress making & millinery.

21st Called on Mrs Hall about Hobbs. Mrs Hall promises Hobbs a dress to make & that she will do all she can for her.

22nd To Mr Wright's *(vicar of Milstead)* flower show in the Milstead school. Quite a little rustic affair, but the schoolroom crowded & Mr *(Pemberton)* Leigh & the Lord Chancellor at the head of the elite there assembled. Kate appeared to my great surprise & more animated than usual, Uncle Go too poorly to come.

23rd Uncle Go & Kate at luncheon on their way to Tunbridge Wells.

24th Ella & I drove to Vinters where we took luncheon & then on to Boxley Abbey to call on Mr & Mrs Thomas Lushington. I like them both much. The door opened by a Hindoo who has been with Mr Lushington 18 years. Saw the nice old garden with its fountain & formal beds.

26th Colonel Griffiths is now a General.

October 4th To morning service. Mr Duppa took luncheon with us.

15th Dined at the Dollings & met all the family party, the bridegroom & bride. The former a grave, pale man, with a long nose. The latter rosy, cherry-like & chattering.

November 5th Guy Fawkes boys coming all day.

17th Hobbs opened her little village shop. Played chess with Mr Hall.

27th A dreary stay-at-home week. To the school with Ella where heard the new master teach very well.

December 5th To Harrietsham, left the children with Fraulein at Mr Riddell's for the dancing & went on to an out of the way farmhouse for the character of a servant. Not satisfactory.

11th Yesterday Bertha's birthday, she in bed from a cold. Bourne baked very good bread, but her last baking a miserable affair. Mr Bigsby has settled to leave Hollingbourne & has taken the curacy of Nonnington.

14th Called on Mrs Griffiths. Col. G so very ill nervously, that they have but little hope of him for a long time at least.

18th Went to the Union to see Mrs Tully who was in a long room with a range of many beds but very clean & well arranged & she has every comfort. She cannot however live many days. In the afternoon called on the Taylors at Boughton Place.

19th Walked with Richard to the Halls' about the Christmas charities. We were there for a very long time. Finn entered on her duties today as my maid.

21st To the County Ball, Ella enjoyed it much & danced all night.

25th Our Christmas dinner this year extended to 39. In the evening our servants had a little party.

26th Mrs Tully died last Monday morning.

30th Fraulein returned from Brighton bringing to Ella a fan & to Louy a Roman brooch from Milly. Both had belonged to Mrs Mostyn & will be valued by them.

31st Mr & Mrs Hall gave a dinner to 15 poor widows of Hollingbourne.

1858 January 4th In the evening to Mr Hall's school treat. Tea, Christmas tree, magic lantern & singing, a great many people present besides the children.

6th To Maidstone accompanied by Hobbs & Finn for shopping.

8th Richard dined at Mr Espinasse's one of his usual men parties.

9th To drink tea at the vicarage, magic lantern & elder wine, a pleasant evening.

12th To the County Ball where Ella danced the whole evening & enjoyed herself much.

18th Started for London accompanied by Ella & Finn. Reached St Andrews Place, found Aunt Ella tolerably well. Miss Edmed & Jessy's four boys called on us & Ella & I went & sat with Uncle Albert.

19th Called on Kate who is very poorly & has been confined to her room these three weeks. To the Greatheds, much rejoicing in Edward Greathed's success.[106]

21st Ella & Finn went to the Zoological Gardens & Uncle Go & Edward appeared at luncheon. Julia too came to pay us a visit. Ella & I dined at Uncle Albert's. The usual family party, Yeats & his wife & Esther Goldsmid.

23rd Edward & Julia came & we went to the Coliseum where saw the 'Earthquake of Lisbon'. Dined with Uncle Go. A very grand dinner, but Kate upstairs poorly.

24th To Quebec Chapel with Uncle Go where Edward preached beautifully.[107] Yeats & Dora *(his wife)* called on us, & afterwards Miss Edmed.

25th The marriage day of the Princess Royal. Ella went with Uncle Albert to the 'Great Globe'. Jessy called on me & afterwards Aunt Ella & I called on the Chetwynds with whom found Minnie Greathed, & then on to Julia at 21 Sussex Gardens where we were fortunate enough to see Prince & Princess Frederick of Prussia en route to the Paddington station. We dined at Uncle Go's.

26th Went to say goodbye to Uncle Albert & Caroline. Left St Andrews Place loaded with kindness from the dear Aunt. She had given Ella a ring, a watch, & a bracelet with my hair, besides many other smaller presents. Richard awaiting at Maidstone.

February 11th Yesterday heard from Mrs Hall. *(in London)* Mesmerism has hitherto had no effect on her. Mr Hall drank tea here & played chess.

18th All the children with Fraulein walked into Maidstone where I met them & we visited the museum in St Faith Street a beautiful old house. Many fossils, some pottery, a mummy & two or three pictures, also some corroded weapons.[108] Met Mr Riddell in Greens' shop ordering Edward's lectures.

---

[106]   Edward Greathed was serving in the army in India and had just been made a Colonel.

[107]   Edward became vicar of Quebec Chapel, Marylebone close to Seymour Street where his father lived. He & Julia lived at 21 Sussex Gardens Hyde Park.

[108]   Maidstone Council purchased Chillington Manor in 1857 & it was opened as a museum in 1858.

22nd To Maidstone with Richard & Ella, gave my weekly music lesson in the morning. Colonel Griffiths case is now quite hopeless.

26th Yesterday gave Ella her first lesson on the guitar.

March 1st Frank Duppa called. Richard sent for Mr Ball & gave him a month's notice to leave the school.

7th Mr Hall preached a very long sermon on Job.

8th Called on Mrs Hall who seems much better for mesmerism which Mr Hall now practises upon her. In the afternoon a snow storm but got to Maidstone in spite of the weather accompanied by Fraulein.

15th A nearly total eclipse of the sun, the air very dreary & chill but not so dark as we expected. We saw the approach beautifully, but the departure of the moon was not so visible.

16th Richard heard that Colonel Griffiths was dead.

22nd Drove to Sittingbourne, old familiar place, accompanied by Richard & Ella. Went to 'The Lawn' to see the pictures etc for sale. Two beautiful portraits by Sir Joshua Reynolds & Sir Thomas Lawrence. The former of Mrs Morgan the latter of Mrs Siddons. Mr Walford invited us to take luncheon, called on Dr & Mrs Grayling & saw their three children.

28th Richard has bought Yew Tree Farm on The Hill. Our horse Napoleon hung himself by his leg in the stable & on our return from church part of the stable was sawn down to free him which was then effected with some difficulty.

April 5th Mr Frederick Bigge arrived & we had a little dinner consisting of Riddells, Mr Hall, & Mr Blunt the new clergyman of Bicknor. A very eccentric person.

8th In the morning Gerard accompanied us to the vicarage to be examined in Latin by Mr Hall who most kindly offered it.

13th Drove early to Maidstone to take Richard on his way to London, then Mama Milly & I went to the museum. Found there Mr Bensted the geologist who went round with us & explained many of the fossils making us remark particularly a wonderful collection of stony seaweed which had taken him 15 years to make.

23rd A walk. Heard from Mr R. Martin that Mr Lushington at 83 has just married the maid of his first wife.

May 5th Took Ella, Louy, Bertha & Gerard to call on the Moores at Boughton Malherbe. Such a very pretty vicarage. (*Edward Moore was rector*) Also to see the old house where Queen Elizabeth visited Sir N. Wotton. The children brought away a piece of the yew planted by her.

7th Went to the school to see the new schoolmaster & mistress Mr & Mrs Hanlon.

8th To Maidstone, so many tipsy people about (*Saturday*) Mrs Faunce & Miss Duppa took luncheon here. The latter as lively as ever.

12th Started at 7 for London via Maidstone to visit the dentist in Stratford Place with Bertha, Mary, Gerard & Lolotte. Sat in his beautiful oaken room for some time. The children were examined, Bertha & Lolotte operated upon, & then we were conveyed in Aunt Ella's carriage to Uncle Albert's where saw him, Caroline, & Isobel. On to Aunt Ella's where met Captain & Mrs Hull. Edward came to see us & also Miss Edmed & the children. The dear aunt looking very well. En route again at 4.50 for the London Bridge station & reached home 8.30.

14th A photographer here who is occupying & amusing the whole house.

15th The final plan for our house arrived & trees are being cut down in preparation.

24th Called on Mrs Hall who was poorly & on Hobbs who was loaded with work.

June 7th Started with Ella by train for London, reached Aunt Ella's. Ella & I went to the Royal Academy, not a very good collection this year.

8th Captain & Mrs Hull & Fredrick Bigge at luncheon. The latter accompanied us to the French Exhibition. We then went to the museum at Kensington which contains a large collection of the curious & beautiful. Then called on Kate. Met in Seymour Street also Mary Chetwynd. Uncle Go better but poorly.

13th (*At home*) To church, Mr Bachelor Roper had tarred the grass of the church meadow to prevent people walking on it.

15th To a picnic given by Sir George & Lady Hampson in the ruins of Thurnham Castle, a very pleasant day. The military band was there & after dinner was coffee, lemonade, syllabub & dancing.

16th Drove up to Bicknor to see the little church. Mr Blunt (*the new curate*) met us there & showed us all its merits. It is early Norman & in a sadly dilapidated state.

20th To morning service. Mrs Hughes sitting down supported by her friends, on the pathway, having dropped down insensible on hearing a gun fire.

28th To Harrietsham to hear the bishop of Cape Town speak. Mr Riddell had fitted a barn up beautifully with flags &

153

evergreens. The bishop discoursed most simply & well. Sir E. Filmer returned thanks. We sauntered about the lawn before & afterwards. After tea I had the pleasure of a long talk with the bishop.

July 1st To Maidstone. Richard accompanied us & bought a few fields near our house & the first lime kiln going up The Hill.

6th Dined at Mr Brenchley's where met Colonel Meyer etc. Milgate beautifully furnished. Whist & dancing ended the evening.

Julius Brenchley (courtesy of Maidstone Museum)

19th The woman came to cut and fit the new carpet.

22nd The carpenter & bricklayer each took their departure so that our home seems now to be making a little progress.

23rd To the ball in the evening at The Star. Ella danced much.

August 1st Between that day & this Mama & Milly arrived, the former poorly. Richard, Ella, Milly & I went to the first Archaeological Meeting at Canterbury, started quite early from Maidstone with many other pilgrims. On our arrival at the ancient city, followed Mr Stanley through all his windings in & round the cathedral, treading principally in Becket's steps. Met there almost all our friends. After Mr Stanley had concluded his lecture he was our guide & together with him & Lord Stanhope the historian, we visited St Martin's church, the Dane John etc after which we dined with numberless others in St Georges Hall. Heard very good speeches from the Dean, Lord Stanhope, Sir Norton Knatchbull etc & returned home by railroad thoroughly tired.

September 20th Milly & Ella set out on a tour, beginning with Mrs Bigge at Neasdon where they spent a week, then for a fortnight to the Entwistles at Hinton-Admiral in Hants. From there to Mr Edward Trollope, Leasingham Lincolnshire & ending with the de Capel Brookes at Market Harborough, Leicestershire. Mama stayed with us during their five week absence & was better for the change. She & I went to the latter part of two archery meetings, we passed a day at the Savages, & took luncheon with the Gapes in their picturesque house. Another day we drove to the flower show at Frinsted which was very numerously attended. Lord Kingsdown more animated than usual. Mama & Milly departed about the beginning of September, since which we have given two dinner parties. Mrs Murray arrived to stay with us. One morning I took luncheon at Milgate & met Mr Julius Brenchley with a long beard & full of his wanderings. He exhibited to us a little specimen of aluminium.

27th Ella, Gerard & I went to the Swedish concert in the evening & heard the northern minstrels. We have gone each morning lately to sketch Godfrey House which Mr Thomas has purchased. Uncle Go has had a fall down some steps at Baden Baden & Edward was telegraphed for but he is not seriously hurt. Richard has bought a new carriage horse. He is called Comet after the magnificent one now visible.

October 6th Poor Mrs Hall so ill with the tic dolereux (*she often is)* that they could not dine here on Monday.

9th Started with Ella & Gerard for the Gate House *(at Mayfield)*. At Tunbridge Wells we got into a fly. The rooms beautiful, the drawing rooms gorgeously furnished & comfortably too, with books & gilded mirrors from Florence & treasures from Venice & carved oak. Mr Treherne very peculiar as usual. Dalrymple & his sister Florence very nice & Mrs Treherne so fat that I could scarcely recognise my former slim friend.[109]

11th Set off early for Brighton, entered the rail road at Lewes. Found Mama well, Milly very hoarse. At five went with Gerard to the College where left him with Mr & Mrs Newton who seem very nice people. The poor little boy, *(aged 10),* was very triste at parting. Aunt Ella came to see us.

13th Dined at Aunt Ella's to meet the Hulls, after dinner a drive in her carriage to see Gerard who appeared in good spirits. Uncle Go walked in last evening from Baden Baden. Thinner & dispirited from his fall but not otherwise ill.

15th To Mr Howell's the astronomer at Hove, to see the stars by daylight, but in vain as they were veiled in clouds. Went to his house & saw his wonderful stereoscope.

18th Ella & I started per rail road for home.

24th Very satisfactory letter from Gerard. He is living in a vortex of gaiety between Mama, the Halls, Aunt Ella & Uncle Go.

November 6th Edward had most kindly given Gerard a writing desk.

8th Heard that Mr Julius Brenchley is a Mormon & anxious to convert others.

17th Mr & Mrs Hall called, they are teaching at the school till the new master comes & Ella is to assist.

18th Uncle Albert has become General by the last Brevet.

December 10th Bertha 14. Brought Mr Wilder from the station today. He is very well, in good spirits & in expectation too of a ninth baby.

21st Ella & Gerard returned from Brighton. He is looking very well. At 9.30 Ella & I went to the ball where she danced all night.

23rd Finn went for a holiday. Wrote the tickets for our Christmas dinner.

---

[109]   Morgan Treherne was a magistrate & landowner. His son Morgan Dalyrymple Treherne was a   lieutenant in the West Kent milita. They had 10 live-in servants.

25th Mr & Mrs Hall dined & passed the day with us. The children presented me with a pretty little Lucifer Vase & Richard with a box of figs this morning. Gerard walking in his sleep in the night & coming <u>bang</u> against our door.

27th Today we have been married twenty years. We had a dinner party.

28th To the school to the distribution of clothing to the women of the Club.

29th Uncle Go arrived, very well, in very good spirits & laden with books for the children.

1859 January 3rd The new schoolmaster Mr Goldfinch has arrived. The church beautifully decorated with wreaths of evergreens.

6th Today to the ball at Sharsted. The fog on the hill so thick we could scarcely get on. A very gay ball & a very pleasant evening. Ella danced incessantly. Reached home at 5.15 on the morning.

7th Very tired & sleepy with last night's dissipation. Richard dined at Mr Espinasse's.

9th To morning & afternoon service. Disgraced myself at the last by snoring.

11th To a dance at the Dolling's accompanied by Ella, Louy, Bertha & Gerard who all danced much & were much amused.

12th The children much occupied with preparing for Mr & Mrs Hall's treat at the school. It commenced with tea & plum cake, next the Christmas tree & lastly fireworks in the schoolroom. The sparks, which seemed harmless, fell among the children some of whom were a little alarmed, when Dicky Miller three years old said 'You need not be afraid, it's only the stars from heaven coming down.'

14th Bertha very poorly with a violent sore throat, sent for Mr Charles Sedgwick.

16th To morning service. Richard gave away the money of the Norton charity.

17th To Sittingbourne with Richard & Ella where we took luncheon at the Walford's & met Mr & Mrs Grayling. Saw Miss Wickham & arranged to take her on trial as governess.

26th Called on Hobbs, found her looking quite well & happy & full of work.

29th Anne out for the day & did not get home for the night.

31st To London with Richard, Mary, Gerard & Lolotte. Started from home at half past eight & reached it at the same hour pm after having visited the dentist & witnessed the extraction of five teeth. Then to the Pantheon & Uncle Albert & to Aunt Ella with whom we took luncheon & where Edward, Miss Edmed & Uncle Albert & Caroline met us.

February 2nd Gerard departed for the College under the guardianship of Miss Simes. The poor little boy looked very pale & sorrowful.

4th Dined at the Gapes. Yesterday our new governess Miss Wickham came.

15th Ella & I started for London, found Aunt Ella quite well. Called on Uncle Albert.

20th Heard Edward preach beautifully at Quebec Chapel for the Cripples Institution. Uncle Go walked back with us & took luncheon. Yeats called.

22nd Took luncheon at Edward's. To the British Institution & saw some lovely pictures.

23rd Mr Attree came for us early & we walked to the British Museum for which he had obtained a private admission & saw the drawings of the old Italian Masters, Raphael, Titian etc, much interested. We also saw the new lion from Nineveh & the colossal horse from the tomb of Mausolas after which we called on Jessy. Dined at Uncle Albert's. Met Yeats & his wife, a pleasant party.

24th Caroline & Miss Edmed called. We bade adieu to the dear aunt who had loaded us with kindness & presents as usual during our stay. One day we went to see the luxurious Senior United Service Club with Uncle Albert.

March 4th *(At home)* Anne so poorly that I took her to her mother for a fortnight. Hired a girl by the name of Young to fill Anne's place for a fortnight.

14th Early to Maidstone to fetch Bertha. She is looking well & much stronger for her stay in Brighton. Mrs Hall is in Hastings.

23rd In the evening took Ella, Louy, Bertha & Mary to the Corn Exchange Maidstone where was first a little concert executed by four performers & the same four performers appeared in an operetta called 'Caught & Caged' very well got up, but the room was almost empty, a few officers & ourselves in the best seats.

25th Richard started early for London with Mr Beale to complete the purchase of Godfrey House. Called on Mrs Hall, very poorly.

29th Anne Ambrose came to see me. She was so very poorly that I was obliged to dismiss her. I fear hers is a hopeless case. Lolotte & I drove to Maidstone.

April 1st Ministers defeated on the Reform Bill.

19th A letter from Milly to say Gerard was still poorly & his coming uncertain. Mama too is rheumatic. A letter from Edward, his new appointment is St John's Church Paddington. The best piece of preferment but one in London.[110]

21st To Maidstone station to fetch Gerard, looking very poorly & with his nose so very sore. Richard went to the hop growers' meeting on Penenden Heath.

23rd Mr Walter the builder came in the afternoon when Richard & I walked with him to Godfrey House to look it over.

26th To the County Ball. Much people in the room on account of the approaching election. Lady North among the most conspicuous of the Dark Blues.

27th To take luncheon at the Espinasse's with Ella & Louy. Saw many of Mr Espinasse's treasures & drawings.

29th Went early to The Mitre to hear the speeches from the hustings. Mr Lee a wretched little specimen. Mr Wardlaw & Mr Vernon Harcourt very gentlemanly. Lady North in dark blue & gold.

May 1st The Liberals successful at Maidstone by 237 at Rochester by at least 100.

4th Started early for the launch of the 'Hood' at Chatham. Splendid. Mr Anderson & his sister met us there. Princess Bonita the Queen's African ward sat close to us. Luncheon at The Sun Inn. We then proceeded to Rochester Cathedral & heard afternoon service. From there to the inn to see the scene of Falstaff's revelries, but the room is in too ruinous a state to be safe. Returned to The Sun & visited Mr Espinasse in his room, full of the probable success of the election & in high spirits. On our way home the children visited Kits Coty House with Richard.

6th Took Louy & Gerard to the station on their way to Brighton. Ella & I went on to Malling to the Savages. That town as well as Maidstone brilliant with the election colours but especially purple & orange. On returning through Maidstone the Blues had nearly disappeared & Lord Holmesdale & Sir Edward Filmer were at the heart of the Poll.

---

[110]   This parish had some very wealthy parishioners and could afford three curates.

Took up Richard who had returned from his day's journey to London. Met the Brockmans, he looking very ill, had come from London to vote.

9th Horses & servants adorned with purple & orange & off to the declaration of the Poll. Got a very good place near the hustings, a splendid procession, such as Maidstone had never witnessed. A perfect grove of laurels, then banners of purple & gold, then the youthful MPs on horseback followed by a train of about 400 or 500 horsemen & these again followed by all the carriages of the neighbourhood. The Miss Maunsells in purple hats & orange feathers. Richard dined with the Conservatives afterwards.

14th To Maidstone, Mary & Lolotte went to purchase a cage for their dormouse.

22nd Started for Tunbridge Wells by train, got out at Paddock Wood & at Tunbridge, arrived at Gate House. *(the Treherne's)* Carts full of children with their mugs & bright with flags were travelling our road. The 50 foot high pyramidal pile for the bonfire was to be seen from every point. Ascended to the tents in a field opposite the house. Bands, banners, a baron of beef, bumpers of champagne, the beautiful & brilliant Miss Trehernes blended to do honour to the joint birthdays of Dalrymple *(he is 21)* & his sister. Lord Essex proposed his health on his coming of age, he returned thanks. In the course of the evening Lady Shelley, Milly, & Miss Dobson, made an unfortunate diversion by fainting. There were donkey races, punch, fireworks, & last & greatest, the enormous bonfire which lighted us home all the way to Tunbrdge Wells where we slept at the Kentish Hotel. Louy looked very well & happy with Milly.

25th Richard started early for Ticehurst & found Louis & Freddy just as usual. Ella, Bertha & I sauntered about The Pantiles & into the Tunbridge Wells shops & after dinner Ella & I went off on a long hot walk to see the Toad Rock & also the Loaf Rock & the Bleeding Rock. At 7 left the Wells & reached our own home.

June 8th A very poor report of Anne Ambrose.

10th Ella, Lolotte & I to the Yeomanry Review in Lord Romney's park. The ball in the evening was very pleasant. When we reached home at ½ past 3 the birds were singing & it was full daylight.

16th Finn gave me warning, I am sorry to say, as she is about to be married.

20th Uncle Albert, Caroline & Jessy arrived. They took luncheon here & then we went to see Elnothington & the Manor House. After tea they departed.

22nd To Maidstone & brought home Gerard from school looking very well.

August 21st A long interval during which much has happened in our little way. Mama has arrived & is still with us & much better for her stay. Milly & Ella have had pleasant visits at the Maunsell's & Sir William Brooke's & after returning here & partaking of the Filmer's brilliant archery meeting on the 10th August, departed again. Finn has left us & is become Mrs Randall & Wilson took her place. Sir Walter Riddell is married. Mlle Musard has been staying with us. We have also attended the first day of the Archaeological Meeting at Rochester. Received the first volume of the Transactions of the Society.

Sir Thomas Wilson & Dalrymple Treherne have dined with us & Jessy has stayed here a day or two. We have paid many visits, Gapes, Whatmans, Trehernes, Filmers, Hampsons etc. Gerard has donned a jacket instead of a blouse & has won a prize for French & returned to school after a week's holiday. Our well has now been deepening six weeks & has not yet come to a happy conclusion. The restoration of Godfrey House is begun. It promises to be very pretty. Aunt Ella is with the Hulls at Southborough near Tunbridge Wells.

September 2nd Mama departed early for Brighton & Ella came home.

17th Mr Wright & Uncle Go in the carriage with four greys, Mr Edward Pemberton driving & poor Major Dennie who had his feet frozen off in the trenches in the Crimea, called.

21st Uncle Go & Kate came in the afternoon & at dinner to meet them appeared Mr Espinasse, Mr Shaw & Major Dennie.

27th Dollings called. We dined at Mr Brenchley's, met there Julius the traveller, talked much to Julius of his travels.

October 13th Called on the Espinasses. Miss E. Espinasse is to be married to a physician, a Dr Barker of the 3rd Buffs. They have kindly asked us to the marriage.

19th Lent Mrs Miller a sovereign.

26th To London with Richard, Louy & Bertha. Passed the day with Aunt Ella & reached home again at ½ past 8. Edward came to see us.

November 3rd At ½ past 10 at Boxley for the Espinasse marriage. Everything very well arranged. At 2.30 after a sumptuous breakfast the bride & bridegroom Dr Francis Barker took their departure to cross to Dover tomorrow en route to Paris & Malta. Lowe so drunk that he could scarcely stand much less drive home.

5th Richard gave Lowe his dismissal.

22nd Comet fell on coming down Harrietsham Hill & cut his knees very much.

25th A letter from Mr Wilder enclosing autographs of Lord Brougham, Dickens & Layard. Richard shot & dined with Mr Brenchley.

26th Mr Shaw shot & dined here in the evening singing & playing chess.

29th To our great surprise an offer from Robert Shaw to Ella which she received very favourably.

December 1st Mr Shaw of Cuxton came over to see about matters, also his son.

3rd Mr Shaw of Cuxton here again to see Richard & the matter is now settled. Robert is in want of a curacy.

5th Robert Shaw slept here. Mr, Mrs & Miss Dolling dined with us & Colonel Meyer.

6th Much singing both days & all our guests sang.

8th Major Dennie dined here. Robert Shaw at tea, Mama has most liberally sent Ella a present of £500. *(Richard invested this for Ella)*

12th Ella & I started for Cuxton, Robert meeting us at Maidstone to be introduced to our new relations. Mr & Mrs Shaw received us most warmly, as well as their daughter Madge. The younger son Hugh, who is learning to be a banker, came in at dinner. Everything so very tidy & nice. The situation of the house beautiful but bleak.[111] One day to the cathedral service at Rochester, home on Saturday.

---

[111]   Mr Shaw was the rector of Cuxton in Kent.

1860-1869: Weddings and funerals

This decade when Louisa was in her fifties began with Ella's wedding and ended with the marriage of Lolotte. It was during these years that some of those dearest to Louisa; her dear Mama, Aunt Ella and Uncle Albert died.

As the girls become adults we begin to glimpse their characters. We know that all were, like their mother, well educated in literature, music, art and languages. They had been taught to dance well and never lacked admirers. They were attractive as their portraits show. Gerard being a boy required a different education. He was sent to Brighton College, in 1858, then in 1861, aged 13, he went to live with a private tutor, a clergyman, to be brought up to standard for Harrow. This succeeded and from Harrow he progressed, albeit with a struggle, to Oxford. Richard, surrounded by so many women in the house, must have been glad to have Gerard home in the holidays and to teach him how to shoot and improve his cricket.

Louisa and Richard were kind-hearted parents who did not stand in the way of Ella, Louy and Lolotte all marrying young for love. Neither Ella's husband Robert Shaw, nor Louy's husband Henry Gipps had money, and Richard and Louisa could have refused consent and asked them to wait for a wealthy husband. But in fact they set up annuities for the two girls and supported them in every possible way.

Robert Shaw, Ella's husband, was the son of the vicar of Cuxton in Kent. Robert was ordained himself and was rector of Danehill, a hamlet in East Sussex near Lewes. So Ella was often able to visit Hollingbourne and was also near to her Brighton relatives and friends.

It was with the marriage of Louy that the family became sharply aware of the demands of Empire. Louy was only 20 when she married her childhood friend Henry Gipps, a captain in the army. He was an eldest son but his father had many financial troubles and could not help him. Immediately after their marriage the young couple were posted far away to the Greek Islands where Henry's regiment was stationed. So Louisa missed Louy a good deal until the vicissitudes of military life meant that she and her baby came back to live in Hollingbourne whilst Henry was in China. It was always uncertain where Louy and Henry would be posted next.

Then in 1869, just before she was 20, Lolotte fell in love with and married Captain Harry Pierson of the Royal Engineers.[112] Harry was a very able man; he had been posted to India in 1860 and been noticed for his work on bridging rivers in Sikhim. In 1863 he was in Persia in charge of the laying of over 200 miles of telegraph. He and Lolotte had no need of financial support from Richard and Louisa although of course all the girls had a dowry. As soon as Lolotte was married she was to journey to Iran with Harry. It seems that Louisa worried more about her youngest child travelling the world than she had about Louy.

It is striking to see how close the six siblings were in adult life, constantly in touch by letter, frequently staying with one another and helping each other.

Louisa continued to paint and also wrote poems and had them privately printed. She and Richard were a hospitable pair holding many dinner parties and having numerous friends to stay, though hers was the driving social force.

Hollingbourne's vicar the Rev. Carter Hall and his wife left the parish in miserable circumstances in 1861. The problem was summed up by the Rev. Graeme Gibson who succeeded him: 'When at last the Rev. Hasted died, the Archbishop appointed one to take his place whom he believed to be a good man. But he was not wise and necessarily having a very difficult task to fulfil, failed utterly. He continually quarrelled with his parishioners until his effigy was burnt on the village green. When he left to reside for some four years on the continent, the church bells were rung.'[113] *(in celebration)*

As we have seen the ministry of Rev. Carter Hall started with every good intention. He tried to attract the neglected villagers to church, help the charity school, found a village library and a clothing club. Sadly in June 1860 when a depressed old villager hung himself Hall refused him Christian burial and this resulted in the 'rough music' on a night when the Thomas family were away. Hall and his wife saw his life-sized effigy burnt in front of the vicarage. Surprisingly they did not pack their bags and leave at this point when the relationship between minister and parishioners was broken but waited a few more months until a more minor dispute arose between

---

[112]   Harry was born William Henry Pierson in 1839, he was educated at Cheltenham College of which he became head boy.

[113]   Lambeth Palace Library VG / 33 / 5b

Hall and the postman over his allowing his children occasionally to deliver letters. It was then that the Halls departed. The parish was left in the care of a curate. Typically none of these details are recorded in Louisa's journal, only her sadness that her friend Mrs Hall was leaving.

1860 April 17th My dear & eldest child Ella was married to Robert Shaw.

September 17th *(Next entry)* Five months have now elapsed since that day & they are as happy as possible in their parsonage at Danehill which is lovely. Bertha is now staying with them.

October 13th Richard & Bertha arrived from Danehill. A good report of all there.

18th Mr Thomas dined with Mr Espinasse & met a large man party as usual.

25th An early drive to Maidstone, brought Miss Edmed back with us. Mrs Best called.[114] A dinner party *(here)*.

November 5th Boys of all kinds screaming & bawling all day & bonfires far into the night.

December 5th The annuity business settled. *(Ella is to have £100 a year from her parents as well as her dowry.)*

11th Pekin has surrendered & the allies are to winter there. The spoil in the Emperor's palace immense.[115]

13th Richard returned having slept at Uncle Albert's. Not a very favourable report of him & he must quit his house in February it being required for a railway station.[116]

1861 January 3rd In consequence of letters from Yeats & Caroline, Louy & I started early for London. Weather intensely cold. Found Uncle Albert almost worse than I had expected, a most melancholy house. He took the Holy Sacrament yesterday. Took luncheon with Aunt Ella.

8th *(At home)* Letters from Aunt Ella & Jessy telling of Uncle Albert's death. Such a sad loss he will be to every one about him.

---

114   Mawdistly Best of Park House, Boxley later became mayor of Maidstone and High Sheriff of Kent.

115   This was the conclusion of the second Opium War (1856-1860) between Britain & China.

116   Work on the Metropolitan Line began in February 1860 using the "cut-and-cover" method of construction. This caused massive traffic disruption in north London; some houses were demolished in the process, even the end of the beautiful curve of Nash's Park Crescent.

14th I went to Cuxton to see Mrs Shaw. Richard to London to attend Uncle Albert's funeral tomorrow. Returned with Robert who also came to Cuxton.

15th Richard returned from London but the funeral had not taken place as Caroline wished it delayed. He is to be buried on Friday.

19th Robert & Ella departed by train. I passed the day in bed & had on two mustard plasters.

25th Mr Thomas attended the meeting of the Infirmary Committee. Louy, Bertha, Gerard & I dined at the vicarage & ate wild goose spoiled by the port wine sauce.

27th Report says the bailiffs are in the Burkitt's house.

28th Louy & I started early for London. Found Aunt Ella's carriage awaiting us at the London Bridge station. She has been poorly & is weak. After dinner called on Caroline found her packing up & the house in a sad state of dirt & desolation.

29th To Lewis & Allenby *(department store)* for a cloak. Called on Kate & Julia & Dora. Aunt Ella afterwards drove with us to Lewis & Allenby's where she purchased a beautiful velvet circular cloak costing eleven guineas.

31st Mr Fred Bigge came to see us & we made an attempt to see Holman Hunt's picture of 'Our Saviour in the Temple' but it is not shown at present. On to the Burlington Arcade & then to a photographic exhibition where saw some beautiful portraits. Dined at Uncle Go's. *(Uncle Go was now in his seventies & he and Kate continued to live in style & sociability in Seymour Street looked after by nine servants.)*

February 1st A walk as usual down Oxford & Regent Streets. In the afternoon called on Mrs Murray. Aunt Ella kindly gave me a pretty black lace cloak.

2nd Called on the Greatheds, where found Colonel Greathed & saw the sword given by George III to the Emperor of China & brought by Wilberforce Greathed from thence. Took Mrs Hall to the German Fair where Louy walked with Mr Hall.

3rd To St John's Paddington where heard Edward's celebrated & beautiful sermon on the text 'Earthen pitchers & lamps within the pitchers.' Callers. Went to see Caroline who was much excited.

4th Aunt Ella presented Louy with a sovereign so we went to different bazaars in order to give her an opportunity of

166

selecting something but she could not decide on anything. Dined at Uncle Go's & met dear Edward.

6th *(At home)* Bourne gave me warning after living here nearly 6 years as she is going to be married.

Seymour Street today.

20th Mrs Burkitt called full of troubles. The bailiffs are in their house.

March 4th Mary & Lolotte started with Wilson in high glee for Danehill. She left them at the Reigate junction. Mr Frank Duppa called.

20th *(In London accompanied by Louy)* Edward has been taking Turkish baths lately & looks very well. Had luncheon with Aunt Ella who was rheumatic & weak. Drove out in her carriage to Howell & James where saw a magnificent Pietra Dura table value £400, the flowers & prints inlaid with precious stones. We then went to see Holman Hunt's famous picture. It is wonderfully painted.

22nd To call on Mrs Thomas Thomas, we returned home by the lane & Notting Hill House so that I saw all the haunts of my childhood, but much altered. After luncheon Edward & Julia called & Mrs Carter Hall. We all went to the Haymarket Theatre & saw 'A Duke in Difficulties', which was followed by a pantomime.

23rd Louy & I took luncheon with Julia & Edward, drove back with Julia & saw the new omnibuses on the tram roads from the Marble Arch to Notting Hill. Much crowd & commotion. After going to some book shops Julia set us down at the top of Portland Place & we made our way to Aunt Ella who is better today.

April 2nd *(At home)* Caroline is off to Australia with her nephew, Miss Jekyll & the butler.

3rd Teaching, drawing & gardening before dinner & afterwards a drive to take Mrs Hall to have her dresses tried on. Uncle Go called in our absence. The children walked up The Hill with him.

5th Richard took luncheon at Lord Kingsdown's to see Uncle Go. Louy, Bertha, Mary & I went to the Oratorio in the evening. It was 'St John' composed by a Maidstone organist Mr Gilbert. About a hundred performed & assisted. Well attended & for the benefit of the Infirmary.

11th Caroline has given up her voyage to Australia & is now at Brighton again.

18th Mrs Hall, Richard, Robert, Ella & I started early to take luncheon at Sharsted.

20th Our children departed for Danehill laden with plants. Lolotte & I accompanied them to Maidstone & did some shopping.

29th To call on Mr & Mrs Hall, I grieve deeply to say to take leave. Even Mr Hall does not talk of returning. It made me quite sad to see the house all in confusion & wretchedness & all so sudden too. In the afternoon the bells were rung.

May 1st To dine at the Ellis's, Louy accompanied me as Richard had toothache.

13th To London with Richard & Lolotte. Met Gerard at London Bridge looking well & strong. At *(dentist)* Lolotte underwent severe discipline & nearly fainted twice. Then on to Aunt Ella who is well but weak. Edward called on me but I had gone out to the Pantheon & Alexandra bazaars with the children. Left London at 7.15.

17th Brewing, & Benfield managed to upset nearly all the beer.

23rd Went to the Depot with Louy & Bertha to see a ride & take luncheon. A very pleasant day.

30th *(At Danehill)* Mr Jones called early *(Dr)* & thought Ella not safe a minute. She was out watering her flowers at ½ past 9 & at 10 retired to bed, well but we had only been there about 5 minutes when we were called up again. Mr Jones was summoned & at 5 minutes past 4 on the beautiful morning of May 31st our *(first)* grandchild was born. A very small, thin, very red boy but apparently very strong & healthy. After seeing Ella alright, Mr Jones, Robert & I perambulated the lawn at 6 in the morning & I then retired to bed until 10 o'clock. Ella doing very well. I wrote many letters. Went to bed early thoroughly tired.

June 1st Mr Jones called & found Ella doing well & the 'little minnow' too as Mrs Coleman the nurse calls him.

3rd Robert & I started early for Brighton where found Mr & Mrs Hall sitting in Silwood Place, Mama I grieve to say poorly. Milly & Gerard very well, reached Danehill about 8.

8th Left Ella well & flourishing & at Haywards Heath met Milly who travelled with me as far as Reigate. Louy & Bertha met me at the station. At home found a large parcel awaiting me from Jeffs the foreign bookseller in the Burlington Arcade. It contained 'The History of the Mormons' etc by Jules Remy & Julius Brenchley.

9th In the afternoon to church where Mr Watts did the duty. Very common, both reading & preaching.

10th Called on our new clergyman *(curate)* Mr & Mrs Watts. A a very quiet man.

11th A letter from Robert. The boy's name is to be Robert Reginald Monson (S*haw)*. Took Louy, Bertha, Mary & Lolotte to Yeomanry Review at the Mote, altogether a very pretty sight. Mrs Riddell came into our carriage.

21st Gerard returned from college looking strong & well.

28th Started at 8.45 for Staplehurst with Richard, Gerard & Louy & Bertha. There got into a fly & went on to Ticehurst. Louis as usual. Freddy I thought much emaciated.

July 3rd Major Dennie called. *(Major Dennie then in his 30s was barrack master at Maidstone)* Taught Gerard. Latin very bad.

August 18th Recommenced my journal finding it indispensable as an aid to memory. Dearest Mama with us & very well though weak at times. My foot still feeble from the inflammation of the cartilage which came on more than a month ago, so did not go to church. Milly at Homburg as well as Uncle Go & Kate.

21st To the archery meeting at Hadlow. One of our horses fell at Mereworth, (for we had taken a fly from Maidstone), & dragged down the other. We were obliged however to go on with him. Dined with the two Miss Riddells. A fine ball after the archery & supper too. Ballroom eighty feet long. Hadlow *(Castle)* is a modern castellated mansion with a lofty tower. Home rather before 4.

23rd Richard, Louy, Bertha & I went in the evening to hear the Christie Minstrels. Their faces all blackened & a charming performance it was. Ballads sung beautifully besides much comic uproar.

September 5th Milly walked in this evening the fiancée of Baron von Gremp. She was tired but in good spirits.*(Milly was now 47 years old and must have long been resigned to dying an old maid)*

9th Dined at Lord Kingsdown's & played two rubbers, he being my partner. A tarte & venison feast. This morning Ella, Robert & the baby came. Uncle Go & Kate took luncheon here.

11th The Volunteer Ball in the evening. Ella too poorly to go. A very bright meeting. The room well lighted & decorated & the variety of uniforms made it very brilliant. Louy danced all the evening. A great mixture of people.

12th To the Volunteers Review at the Mote Park. A beautiful sight the number of volunteers 2800 & that of the people present said to be 15000.

13th Ella & Bertha in bed poorly but Richard, Robert, Louy & I passed the day at Cuxton. They presented Ella with almost all the short clothes for her baby beautifully made by themselves which we brought home for her.

14th Robert & Ella departed today, Lolotte with them, so we are now reduced to a very small party.

28th Fetched Lolotte from the station which was swarming with hop pickers. The noise, confusion & drunkenness dreadful.

October 3rd To Maidstone shopping & also to see Holman Hunt's picture 'The Light of the World'. A wonderful work, both in expression & colouring.[117] Mr Watts called about a school meeting & a school clothing club. A dinner party here.

---

[117]   Hunt's painting of Jesus was so popular that it went on tour. It is now in Keble College Oxford.

26th To Brighton, the four girls & myself, accompanied by Anne & Wilson, found Uncle Go there & made the acquaintance of my future brother in law Baron von Gremp. Milly had taken for us a very comfortable lodging in Bedford Place, number 8, kept by Mrs Mostyn's late butler (<u>French</u>.)

29th Milly became the Baroness Gremp de Frendenstein. Edward married them. Richard gave her away, Louy & Bertha were her bridesmaids. The ceremony took place at 8.30 & by 11.30 they were en route to Hollingbourne we having lent them our house. The breakfast took place at 8 Silwood Place, & at 3 the children & ourselves dined with Mama. We remained on at Brighton five weeks & after a fortnight Milly & Leopold returned & we took the house together. His little German boy Ernst & his nurse were also there. I had the pleasure of seeing many of my old friends. Saw Kean & Mrs Kean in 'Hamlet'. At the end of the five weeks Gerard caught the scarletina, so sending the rest home I remained a few days with Mama, till he was through the worst of it. I returned home on December 4th.

7th Jessy & little Caroline *(her daughter)* arrived to stay with us.

14th The sad & unexpected death of Prince Albert of gastric flu.

16th To Maidstone. Shops & people as black as possible & everyone buying mourning.

19th Gerard arrived from Brighton at Elnothington where he is to live with Mr Betts for the present, as it is not considered safe to have him home.

26th Walked in the road with Gerard as usual.

1862 January 1st To call on Mrs Riddell found her surrounded by her children & in the midst of New Year's gifts.

6th Bertha & I drove to Maidstone & did some shopping.

8th Robert, Ella & the baby arrived from Cuxton. Richard dined at Sir George Hampson's, a whist party.

17th I took Bertha, Mary & Lolotte to a juvenile party at Vinters. First tea, then Magic Lantern, then dancing. All 'went merry as a marriage bell' till Johnny Riddell & his cousin Mary, being pressed upon by the throng, managed to waltz against a magnificent vase to throw it down & break it in 1000 pieces.

18th Robert & Ella departed & Gerard emerged from quarantine & returned home.

21st A sudden thaw set in while we were at the Maidstone ball. A very gloomy one on account of the mourning. The red uniforms the only relief from the universal black & white.

February 2nd A letter from Aunt Ella telling of the death of Captain Hull. *(her brother-in-law)*

15th Wrote to Mr Howlett enclosing him the first quarter's pay for Gerard. *(Gerard is boarding with the Rev. Fred Howlett, private tutor)*

22nd Walked as far as the Union. We dined at the Gape's. Miss Gape's 'future' sang comic songs, many & well, 'Nancy in the Strand' etc.

March 12th To Maidstone, much shopping. Yesterday Wilson gave notice.

20th Bertha & I started for Brighton, left Louy en route at Danehill & reached Silwood Place in time for luncheon. Mama looking very poorly. Caroline called.

21st In the evening accompanied Milly to the rail road & saw her off to Newhaven.

22nd A lovely day for her to cross. I hope that all will go well.

25th Dr Pickford came to see Mama. He does not, I grieve to say, think very favourably of her. Yesterday wrote to Milly who has arrived safely in Paris & found Baron de Gremp.

April 3rd We returned home leaving my mother decidedly better.

10th Bertha & I passed the day with Aunt Ella, found Aunt & Mrs Hull pretty well. Edward very well. Home by 10 o'clock.

20th Letters from Uncle Go with his photo, like him in his gloomiest mood. *(she is often now sent photographs of friends & relatives)* To morning service.

21st To Maidstone, brought Louy home, saw Robert, Ella & the baby for a moment.

23rd To Maidstone to fetch Ella & Robert etc. Yesterday my new maid Hinde came.

1863 May *(A gap of over a year in the journal, this is the next entry)* On the 4th of November 1862 at eight in the evening died my dearest mother after a lingering illness fortunately without much suffering. She lies in Preston churchyard. Edward read the funeral service.[118] On the 29th April 1863 our dear child Louy was married to Captain Henry Gipps of the

---

[118]   Mama left £7000 equally between Louisa & Milly, knowing they would pay for Louis' care.

172

9th Regiment now stationed in the Ionian Islands. They left for Zante.[119]

July 31st (*Next entry*) In the morning began a sketch of the miller's house & pond.

August 4th Bertha & I went to the archery meeting at Vinters. A cricket club projected amongst the boys of the neighbourhood to be called 'The Kentish Stars'. To the ball in the evening. Bertha danced incessantly.

6th Mr Thomas went to London & found his brother better. Gerard to the first meeting of the 'Kentish Stars' at Malling. Miss Edmed passed the day here.

13th Gerard played among the 'Kentish Stars' against Maidstone Grammar School.

17th To Maidstone to fetch Lolotte whom Robert & Ella brought from Danehill en route for Cuxton.

September 2nd To Maidstone shopping accompanied by Ella & Bertha, en route home to see the 'Kentish Stars' play cricket at the Mote.

7th Wrote to Anne *(Woollett, Mama's old maid)* & sent her a post office order for £1. Robert & Ella returned.

16th Gerard left for Harrow. *(Richard's account book notes that he was accompanied as far as London by Mr Riddell and Edward.)*

18th Drove to the Maidstone races on Detling Hill, altogether very amusing.

October 21st Miss Gape *(of East Sutton)* came to accompany us to the Sittingbourne Ball. The ball a very good one. Bertha & Miss Gape danced all night. Home at ½ past 4.

November 6th Richard, Bertha & I started early for London. Aunt Ella's carriage met us at the station. Did some shopping at Howell & James & Lewis & Allenby. Found Aunt Ella very poorly & on the sofa in her dressing room. Mrs Hull there. Home by 10 o'clock.

7th Louy's birthday. A letter from her. The Ionian Islands getting very much disturbed since the cession to Greece.

9th A letter from Mr Wilder with autographs of the Duke of Marlborough & Lord Brougham.

18th Passed the day at Maidstone. A service in the old church to hear the Archbishop preach for the National Society. To take luncheon at the Palace where were the Primate & most of

---

[119]   The Ionian Islands were then under British rule though soon to be ceded to Greece. The island of Zakynthos was then known as Zante.

the neighbourhood. After luncheon we all went to the Town Hall where the archbishop was in the chair & others spoke.

20th Jessy arrived with little Caroline. A dinner *(party)*.

December 9th Started early for London. Richard went to the cattle show. Mary, Lolotte & I to dentist. Aunt Ella with whom had luncheon was <u>much better.</u>

15th Bertha & I to the County Ball. Bertha danced incessantly.

18th Gerard made his debut in shooting.

25th Bertha presented me with a very pretty pair of slippers worked by herself. Mary & Lolotte gave the same to Mr Thomas.*(Richard noted that he gave ten shillings to each servant who had been with the family for more than a year, and five shillings to the rest.)*

28th Richard, Gerard, Bertha & Mary went early to Maidstone to greet the arrivals from Cuxton. Bunyard went for a holiday for two days. A ball at the Baldwin's about 80 people. Music & lighting very defective.

29th Gerard rode up to Torry Hill & Uncle Go came to see us in the afternoon.

30th Bertha went to Leeds to learn of Mrs Burkitt how to play the organ.

1864 January 1st Went to the school treat. Tea & cake to begin, then Christmas tree & prizes. Snap dragon *(a game)*, singing the national anthem & a wind up of bread & cheese.

6th Richard attended a rail road meeting. Robert, Ella & Bobbie arrived.

8th To the church to hear Ella & Bertha practice the organ with the school children. Gave coals to twenty poor old people.

10th To morning service. Ella & Bertha took the organ playing & acquitted themselves well.

12th Richard was in London for the day. (*He only ever goes for the day now*)

13th A letter from Louy. The two battalions of the 9th to be quartered shortly at Gibraltar. Henry still trying for India.

25th Mrs Rodney *(the new tenant of Godfrey House)* & I walked to call on the Burkitts & then went to Elnothington.

27th Mr Gale the rail road enquirer took luncheon with us & discussed the various points with Richard.

28th A letter from Frank Duppa begging us to let him know when we go to London as he will then procure us tickets to hear the principal scientific men of the day lecture.

February 2ⁿᵈ War has broken out between Denmark, Austria & Prussia.

10ᵗʰ Intense cold. The Thermometer in our room one degree above freezing point.

18ᵗʰ A large box of things arrived from Zante. Reptiles, shells, skins, drawings etc. Much interest & pleasure in unpacking.

26ᵗʰ Sent off some more things, soap etc to Zante.

27ᵗʰ I saw Mr Fowler in Maidstone yesterday & gave him Mr Thomas's message that he will belong to the new County Cricket Club. Wilson departed.

March 3ʳᵈ The new piano arrived, it is by Kirkman & a great beauty. Price £42, nearly as good as new having only been used three months.

11ᵗʰ Richard, Bertha & I to London. First went to the Bank, & then to Aunt Ella; found her I grieve to say looking very ill. Richard seized with violent lumbago.

13ᵗʰ *(At home)* Did not go to church as Richard too poorly to get up the whole day.

14ᵗʰ Richard rather better & up tho' he could scarcely crawl.

April 1ˢᵗ To the County Ball in the evening. Bertha abounded with partners.

2ⁿᵈ Robert, Ella & Bobbie departed for Danehill. Lolotte, Gerard & I went to the museum to see Thomas's Statue of Godiva.[120]

7ᵗʰ Lurcock gave warning after living here nine years. Dined at the Riddell's, Mr Thomas, Bertha & I.

11ᵗʰ Richard went up to London about the rail road committee to the House of Commons & saw General Garibaldi. Well. Mary & I did some shopping in Maidstone & went to see Thomas's Statue of Godiva at the museum.

14ᵗʰ To Sharsted to meet Mr George Duppa, Mr Frank Duppa also there. Mr G. Duppa has just returned from New Zealand with a fortune of £100,000.[121] Bunyard & Gibbons departed & Wilson & Frances Gibbons came.

19ᵗʰ Letter from Gerard to announce his removal into the 5ᵗʰ & his promotion to tails.[122] Major Cubitt called. Mary & Lolotte at croquet at the Blunt's.

---

[120]   A popular statue by John Thomas.

[121]   This is equivalent to over four million pounds today. George had spent 24 years in New Zealand. See my 'Farewell to Kent' for an account of his life there.

[122]   At Harrow, having worn a short jacket, he was now allowed to wear a tail coat.

21st Bertha & I drank tea at the Rodney's & saw Mrs Rodney make an omelette.

George Duppa (courtesy Margaret Parsons)

26th Richard & I went to Ticehurst & saw Louis & Freddy, found the latter certainly better. A new physician is added to the establishment. Our new maid Anne Brisley has arrived & the old & much valued Anne gone.

May 7th Bertha & I off to London, took luncheon in Seymour Street. Called on dear Aunt Ella & found her very poorly. Uncle Go very glad to see us.

8th To church at St John's where Edward preached beautifully, then went to Jessy & saw her father very ill. His state hopeless. Then on to Aunt Ella who was better.

10th To the exhibition at the Royal Academy. Millais' 'Second Sermon' & 'Charley is my darling' are beautiful. Uncle Go met us & we came away thoroughly tired.

11th Left Seymour Street for St Andrews Place. Dined with Edward & Julia. Edward read to us some poetry.

13th Dined at Caroline's, a superb entertainment. Caroline very gay & looking very well & fat.

14th To see Herbert's 'Cartoon of Moses' at the House of Lords, a most striking picture. Dined at Yeats & met there Jessy.

16th Mrs Hull in St Andrews Place. Aunt Ella still very poorly & Mr Newton in daily attendance. Left for home, Miss Edmed & Mary at the station.

June 6th Mrs Burkitt at luncheon, she drove with us afterwards to make calls.

7th Drove for the first time in our new carriage. It is very comfortable.

16th Mary & I to London to the Royal Academy, then to call on Kate who was looking very well, then to dear Aunt Ella suffering sadly & much wasted. Caroline called & Edward came & prayed by our dearest aunt. Home by ten.

30th Bertha, Mary & I en route to London where Aunt Ella's carriage met us at the Charing Cross station & took us to Harrow. Everyone on the road standing out to catch a glimpse of the Prince & Princess of Wales. Bertha taken in by Mr Vaughan to the Speech Room, saw Lord Palmerston arrive. I thought him very infirm. No end of celebrities were assembled besides. Lord Brougham, Archbishops of Canterbury & York, Bishops of London, Oxford & Ripon, Lord Cardigan & last of all appeared the Royal Pair. She very pretty & interesting. Then followed recitations by the boys in Greek, Latin, French, German & English Then the prizes were given & afterwards we retired to Mr Vaughan's for luncheon. A better report of Aunt Ella.

July 2nd The long looked for letter from Corfu arrived & Louy has a son born on the 18th June.

4th To the regatta at Wateringbury. The regatta itself a very dull affair, but the company pleasant. Herbert Gipps there with the Chatham officers.

31st Since writing the above entry, Milly has paid an unexpected visit from Homburg & remained above a fortnight. Caroline has run down here for a day. Robert & Ella have passed a few days here with Bobbie. I must not forget that Uncle Go has been here too from Saturday till Monday.

Dearest Aunt Ella is becoming gradually weaker & suffering fearfully. Henry & Louy are at Gibraltar & their child is soon to be christened. Mr Watts is to leave before long. We have been to a beautiful ball at the Depot, to several croquet parties, to a picnic arranged by the Moores, in a dirty out of the way field, & an archery meeting.

August 17th A picnic with the Baldwins at Stede Hill, about forty people. Dinner under the larches, tea in the shady walk near the grotto & dancing on the lawn by moonlight.

21st A letter from Mrs Hull telling of the death of our dearest Aunt Ella, calmly & peacefully after her great sufferings.

23rd A letter from Mrs Hull saying that dear Aunt Ella's funeral was fixed for Saturday & begging Richard to attend.

27th Richard started early for dear Aunt Ella's last journey on earth & returned home by 6. She was buried in Kensal Green cemetery. Edward read the service.

September 1st Richard & Robert out shooting & Bertha & I to London to see Mrs Hull. How dreary the house I cannot describe! Mrs Hull most kindly gave me an original sketch by Reubens & a magnificent blue vase. Mary, Lolotte & Ella at tea at the Rodney's.[123]

3rd Took luncheon at the Moore's at Boughton Malherbe. Tried to make a sketch of the house which is very picturesque. Yesterday dined at Lord Kingsdown's.

4th Mr Thorpe *(new curate)* preached his first sermon here.

20th Mrs Thorpe accompanied us to Maidstone where we called on the Espinasses & Mary had her ears pierced.

22nd A letter from Gibraltar proposing that Henry & Louy should go out to New Zealand which after having seen the Rodneys & George Duppa we positively refused. *(Henry & Louy needed to ask permission because they could only afford the fare with the help of Richard & Louisa.)*

October 2nd An unexpected visit from Canada. *(Young Richard)*

5th 'Canada' left.

6th A letter from Henry saying that he had exchanged to the 2nd Battalion to go to China & Louy is coming to us with her boy.

---

[123]   Aunt Ella had no children & left her estate of over £35,000 equally divided between Louisa, Milly, & their cousins Edward & Freddy Goulburn. Her sister Jane (Mrs Hull) was left all her clothes, paintings and jewellery.

17th Early to Maidstone with Mr & Mrs Thorpe. Richard got out at London Bridge, I at Charing Cross. To Mr Kensitt's to look over the plate *(Aunt Ella's).* Here Edward & Julia met me. Then to Edward's to luncheon & on to St Andrews Place where we were met by Mr Thomas. The dear old house looked very desolate. Great bills on the columns of the entrance & people going in & out. A dinner party at Edward's.
20th To Cuxton to be present at the celebration of the restoring of Mr Shaw's church. Luncheon in the schoolroom. Sat by the Bishop of Rochester who preached a very dull sermon. The church very well restored.
28th At the ball last night Mary came out & enjoyed herself much. Fred & Herbert Gipps *(Henry's brothers)* accompanied us.
November 4th Louy came in the evening about tea time with her boy & his Maltese nurse. She is looking ill & worn.
1865 January 1st Since writing my journal last time we have passed above a fortnight at Dover & met there Milly, the Baron & little Ernst. We have also been to Walmer & seen my old & dear friend Mrs Branfill Harrison. Since our return Milly, the Baron & Ernst have passed Christmas with us. They left on the 28th taking Mary to Homburg with them. We dined at the Riddell's, went to luncheon at the Gape's, dined at Lord Kingsdown's & met Uncle Go. Whist, billiards & punch.
2nd To Maidstone to fetch Louy from Danehill. She is looking much better.
6th Went to a very fine Twelfth Night Party at Preston Hall. Games, a conjurer, a splendid Christmas tree, a ball & supper. About 120 present. Louy, Bertha, Gerard & Lolotte accompanied me.
18th Gerard left for Harrow in very low spirits.
30th A letter from Ella telling of the alarming illness of Mr Shaw. Robert telegraphed for to go to Cuxton. A telegram from Robert to beg us to send for Ella.
31st Richard up the Hill shooting. Another telegram from Robert. His father is attacked with smallpox.
February 3rd The Christmas tree at the school beautifully decorated.[124] Tea & cake & Mr Thorpe read poems & told a

[124] It is interesting to note how much later than the 25th December Christmas trees were up & being enjoyed.

short ghost story. I fetched Ella & Bobbie from the station, both well & happy. Mr Sedgwick called & vaccinated Ella.

11th Took Ella & Bobbie to meet the train & Robert who had just left Cuxton & his father very weak but as well as could be expected. Shopping in the midst of snow.

18th To Maidstone, purchased a silver cup for my god-daughter Patricia Goldsmid. *(Frederic's daughter)* Took Louy & Jessy to see 'Lady Godiva' at the museum. Mr Thorpe took tea here & sang 'The Araby Maid'.

22nd Called on a few old village women. In the afternoon drove to Maidstone & called on Espinasses, Claytons etc. The present Military depart & the Artillery enter Maidstone on Ash Wednesday. Mr Rodney & Mr Hamilton in the evening.

27th Walked to the Kings Head to take Mrs Sellen some sal volatile. In the evening we went to the Engineers' Ball at Chatham, a very good room, music & supper, a blaze of scarlet. Bertha danced all night. A throne (which had been taken from the Emperor of China) of rich carved work under a canopy at the end of the room. Did not reach home till past five.

28th Breakfast at nine as usual.

March 2nd Finished a little portrait of Willie which was dispatched to Shanghai to Henry.

7th Began a portrait of Bertha in her grey coat & hat with yellow feathers. Drove to Maidstone, took my Wild Flower Alphabet to be reprinted. Mr Rodney came to smoke with Mr Thomas.

11th The proof copy of my Alphabet sent from Grundy. Not quite correct.

12th Mr Thorpe preached almost a funeral sermon on Mrs Lampard, young Hadlow who died last night 12 years old, & Taylor who has also just died suddenly leaving a widow & child. Mrs Rodney called on me & gave Louy a letter of introduction for Fred Gipps *(Louy's brother-in-law is emigrating)* to her brother in New Zealand who is comptroller of the Customs.

13th Louy, Bertha & I attended Mrs Galton's concert, a good one. The two last pieces from Beethoven, beautiful. Took Miss Espinasse, much mismanagement & confusion with regard to the seats. An audience almost composed of ladies except the Artillary officers lately arrived at the Depot.

17th A letter from Constantinople from my cousin Frederic *(Goldsmid)* containing a photo of himself & some of the new

Turkish stamps for Bertha. Little Hadlow is to be buried tomorrow. Mr Thorpe was at luncheon, he asked Bertha to make a snowdrop wreath for the bier. Drove to Harrietsham to call on the Riddells.

22nd Miss Edmed arrived. A most romantic missive from Albert Goldsmid which we of course 'blighted in the bud'. *(Richard & Louisa were not in favour of Bertha marrying a second cousin)*

27th Went to see Mrs Sage in her new cottage & also Mr & Mrs Sears. *(village poor)*

April 7th News of poor Kate's *(Uncle Go's wife)* sudden death from bronchitis. Wrote to Uncle Go. Went to Maidstone for mourning.

17th Robert & Ella have been married five years. Went to Maidstone as large party & met them there with Bobbie. Passed the afternoon with the Claytons at croquet.

20th A letter from Edward with a very poor report of Uncle Go. His depression is so great. Went to the ball, Bertha, Gerard, & I. Bertha danced all night.

28th Mr Thorpe called & told us Mr Hall had obtained another year's leave.

29th Richard & I went to Ticehurst & saw Louis & Freddy both well in health of body & Freddy very rational. He & Dr Newington walked back with us as far as the village of Ticehurst. Home to tea.

May 3rd Gerard left for Harrow. Yesterday Richard & Mr Rodney out canvassing.

13th Took Mrs Branfill Harrison to the station *(she has been staying)*, called on the Espinasses. Collected Richard & Mary looking very well & fat.

30th To London early with Mr Thomas, Louy, Bertha & Mary. Business at the Bank. Luncheon at Caroline's. Miss Edmed there. To the exhibition where we were met by Mrs Hall & Uncle Go & Miss Chetwynd. Very ill on our return home.

June 2nd The Shingles which had been making me so poorly developed itself thoroughly & kept me in bed.

18th Frederic is made director of the Anglo Indian telegraph.

21st Bertha & I, with Wilson, started for London. Edward's carriage met us at Charing Cross station, but missed it. A warm welcome in Sussex Gardens *(cousin Edward's home)* Uncle Go at dinner.

22nd Drove out in the afternoon with Julia. Called on Jessy & Mrs F. Goldsmid. They were just starting for Paris. Dinner in

Sussex Gardens after which went to hear Edward give a most charming lecture on Confirmation.

Sussex Gardens today

26th Shopping with Wilson. Dined at Mr Gibb's in Hyde Park Gardens a party of 22 & a magnificent reception.

29th Went on with Edward & Julia to the Paddington Station where met all the Gibb's party, Mr G having hired the Saloon Carriage to convey us to Windsor. On our way rain began so instead of the pic-nic to Virginia Water we walked up to the Castle. Edward called on the Dean, Dr Wellesley, & he showed us no end of wonders. The Wolsey Chapel in progress of restoration with its gold mosaics like St Marks at Venice. Two Italian workmen were busy on them. St George's chapel, the Queens private chapel, the golden beard of Edward 4th in a locket & the still more golden hair of Elizabeth Woodville his queen. The water colour drawing of the coffins of Henry 8th, Jane Seymour & Charles I. The portrait of Charles I's head when it was taken out of the coffin in modern times, all in perfect preservation but the nose. The window overlooking the cloisters where Henry VIII first saw Ann Boleyn & where they afterwards used to sit. Edward then wrote to Sir Thomas

Biddulph in order that we might have a private view of Windsor Castle. So taking our leave of the courteous Dean & his delightful home we proceeded to the Palace of our kings & wandered the gorgeous & spacious rooms. After which returned to the rail road carriage where ate the liberal luncheon supplied by Mr Gibbs. On our return to Nottingham Place rested till the evening when we went with Jessy to a party at Lady Whitehead's.

30th Gerard arrived & accompanied Bertha to the Crystal Palace to the Handel festival 'The Israel in Egypt'. We dined at Yeats, & Jessy & Bertha went to the Italian opera at Covent Garden.

July 5th *(At home)* Richard, Bertha & I went to the Yeomanry Review then to Maidstone to fetch Louy, then back to the cricket match.

10th Richard started for London. (*his brother Thomas Thomas has had another paralytic stroke*) Walked to Leeds for a nurse for Ella.

12th The day of election for Maidstone, we drove to call on Mrs Ellis. Lady Holmesdale called. The dining room carpet laid down, it is green with gold stars.

17th Went to the Nominations, bright with purple & orange. Drove, & Richard rode in the procession. Did not hear much beyond the usual election noises but Lord Holmesdale & Mr Dyke were said to speak well.[125]

18th Breakfasted early & Richard started for Faversham to vote for Sir Norton Knatchbull & Sir B. Bridges.

20th When Ella's nurse disappointed me I wrote to Mrs Kitchen who called today & settled with her to go to Danehill on the 5th August. Mr Thomas at Maidstone for the polling. All sorts of rumours but it ended successfully for the Conservatives & Mr Dyke & Lord Holmesdale became our M.P.s.

22nd Fortunately the afternoon proved fine as we had a croquet party consisting of Riddells, Claytons, Baldwins, Dennie & Captain Tatham now in command of the 'Bellerophon' at Chatham.[126] He slept here.

25th Richard on the Grand Jury & stayed to dine with the judges.

---

[125]   The local paper reported that the High Street was filled end to end with carriages, the procession then set off for Penenden Heath

[126]   The Bellerophon was a new iron clad ship built at Chatham in 1865.

27th To the archery meeting with Louy, Bertha & Mary. The ball in the evening.

31st To see General Tom Thumb, his wife, her sister Minnie Warren & Commodore Nutt, the dwarfs. They are to exhibit two days at Maidstone. Mrs Tom Thumb is really rather pretty, was beautifully dressed & sang & acted. So did her sister & the Commodore. Tom Thumb, whose voice is very unpleasant, merely acted. Among other things he personated Napoleon the great. It was a most curious sight. The room very full.[127]

August 2nd Richard & I dined at Lord Homesdale's. Everything lovely.

10th To Danehill to receive a third grandchild who was longer in appearing than was expected & did not arrive till August 26th. A very fine strong boy & Ella doing well. On 28th Richard came to fetch me. We went round by Brighton, saw the house, number 8 Silwood Place looking desolate, empty & dreary, & dearest Mama's grave so still & peaceful in the quiet church yard of Preston. Left Brighton by a late train & having missed the S.E. one were obliged to take up our quarters in Reigate, a very small but clean room. The trains snorting & screaming all night quite close to us. Wandered out into the very pretty garden of the hotel. Home, Louy & Mary awaiting us.

September 1st Gerard's first day of partridge shooting. Mr Thomas & Mr Rodney also went out. We went to Maidstone.

8th A croquet party here, Riddells, Moores & Dollings.

18th In the evening we went to the Amateur Theatricals at the Corn Exchange by the Artillery Officers now in Maidstone. There were two good actresses from London.

23rd Ella, & her babies & nurse arrived from Cuxton.

October 4th Robert out shooting with Mr George Duppa. A telegram arrived to him during the day of the death of *(his brother)* Mr Edward Duppa.

14th Mr George Duppa called, also went to the church to see the decorations for the harvest home, our children had made wreaths of autumn leaves.

15th Mr Edward Duppa who was reported dead is still living.

16th Richard well enough to go to Maidstone, so we drove there with Mrs Rodney. Mary, Lolotte & me & went to see Holman Hunt's picture of 'Our Saviour in the Temple'. The

---

[127] The show was advertised in the local paper as 'the same as given by command of her Most Gracious Majesty the Queen, by the four smallest beings in the world.'

composition I now think much too crowded. Many there to see it.

19th The death of Lord Palmerston yesterday at 11 a.m.

24th To the Sittingbourne Ball, Louy, Bertha, Mary & I. Met all or nearly all of our Hill acquaintances. Bertha & Mary danced all night. *(The local paper reported that the ball was held in the Corn Exchange & attended by about 150 people including the Leigh Pembertons. Music for dancing was provided by Mount's Quadrille band from Canterbury & dancing was kept up with spirit until about four in the morning.)*

25th Last night started for Sittingbourne at 9 & reached home at nearly five this morning. Going & returning met but <u>one</u> man.

November17th House filled with Chinese treasures sent by Henry.

18th Rifleman, the horse, taken ill so obliged to send for a fly to convey us to Lord Kingsdown's where Richard, Louy, Bertha & I dined to meet Uncle Go.

29th Bertha, Mary & Lolotte went to the Penny Reading.[128]

30th Began my sketch for 'Solitude' a subject given by the Claytons.

December 1st Continued my <u>nun</u>, Lolotte rode to call on the Riddells.

2nd Went to the Clayton's to give in the drawings. Many & various were the ideas of solitude. The collection of drawings was won by Lolotte. Richard up The Hill with some of his tenants shooting.

8th To Aylesford, Louy, Bertha, Mary & I to be present at the opening of the New Organ in the church when the bishop preached, took coffee at Archdeacon Grant's.

12th Gerard arrived. To the ball, very agreeable, music, supper all good. Home at 5.

13th Mr Thorpe called & begged me to read at the Penny Reading tonight which I did. Bertha sang. She & Louy played a duet. Mrs Thorpe read. *(they then became regular during the winter)*

14th A Ball at Linton. Lady Holmesdale looked very pretty in grey & silver. Lady Filmer beautiful in black & silver. Diamonds glittered on all sides.[129]

---

128   Penny Readings began in the 1850s. Working class people paid a penny & were entertained by being read to by those higher up the social scale. Dickens himself gave Penny Readings from 1853.

21st To the County Ball the room newly decorated & very brilliant with the white & gold walls & rose coloured curtains.

23rd Called on the Thorpes to congratulate them as the Archbishop has just given him the living of Herne Hill. Yesterday wrote tickets for 30 poor families.

27th Uncle Go arrived to a late dinner. In great spirits & looking very well.

1866 January 1st Gerard shooting on The Hill. Farkins did not return from Maidstone where he had asked leave to pass the afternoon.

4th All our olive branches but Lolotte went to a party at the Betts at Preston Hall. Dancing & conjurer. Bourne appeared with her baby.

11th The first snow of the year & very deep. Nephews of Mr Thorpe drank tea here & amused us much with their singing of comic songs.

22nd Bertha, Wilson & I started for Brighton to stay with Mrs Hull. Went to the large Fancy Ball at the Pavilion. Bertha wreathed in hops & cherries as the 'Fair Maid of Kent'. Saw many of my old friends. Visited my dearest Mother's grave & went to look at the Old House in Silwood Place which is now a Foreign Governesses Instruction. *(stayed a week)*

February 1st Louy received a telegram from Henry in Bank Street to say that he had just landed & about 10.15 pm he arrived looking brown but not well.

5th Took Wilson to Maidstone to select the poor people's testimonial *(a leaving gift to which they had all contributed)* for Mr Thorpe. She chose a lamp.

6th Mrs Thorpe called early to ask if Mr Thomas could give a Christmas tree for this evening at the school which he did. Our party went to assist.

17th To Maidstone to fetch Lolotte, looking very well. Henry up The Hill shooting.

27th Over The Hill & far away in the brake with Mary through mud & mire & flints till we came to Hucking Hill the residence of Mrs Edward Duppa where found her in a very inaccessible house. Edith Duppa was with her.

March 5th To Maidstone met Mr Moore who said Richard was a most valuable man & that he had just recommended him for a magistrate.

---

[129]   Lord & Lady Holmesdale lived in their splendid mansion, Linton Park, looked after by 18 servants.

11th A very long sermon on the eternity of punishment.

13th Captain Hunt gave his lecture on Japan in the schoolroom in Chinese costume. A full audience. He & the Dollings drank tea with us before & after with the addition of Mr & Mrs Thorpe who came in for wine & cake.

16th Richard off to London. He gave but a poor account of his brother.

April 1st Easter Sunday, took the sacrament with Louy, Bertha, Mary, Gerard & Lolotte. 98 communicants, so large a number can never have been in Hollingbourne church.

5th Richard sworn in a magistrate. To the County Ball, much dancing & the room very brilliant.

8th Mr Thorpe's farewell sermon. He wept aloud & some of his congregation too.

11th Lionised Mr & Mrs Bigge through our parish, church, old houses & all.

14th Mr Hall arrived to dine & sleep. Bertha, Mary Gerard & I to the Engineers' Ball at Chatham to which we had been invited by Major Harrison. Home at 5.30 am Broad daylight & morning lovely. Mr Hall left.

20th Gerard departed for Harrow. Two rail road officials came to see Mr Thomas.

May 4th Miss Burkitt took luncheon here & examined the state of the Culpeper's altar cloth & the repair that is required.

7th Richard attended the magistrates' monthly meeting. Mrs Duppa & Edith at tea.

9th Richard went to London to attend the railway meeting. Mr Hall at breakfast. He & Henry went fishing, Mrs Hall passed the day here.

16th Started early for Staplehurst, Richard, Bertha, Mary & I, the fly awaiting us there which carried us on to Dr Newington's. Found Freddy better & fatter. Louis the same, voluble & excitable as ever.

17th Uncle Go at luncheon, well, but I thought more infirm & easily tired. He took me, on his way back to Torry Hill, to call on Mrs Hall & I then went to Mrs Rodney.

18th Yesterday Richard purchased a new horse to be called 'the Serjeant' as Uncle Go was here at the time.[130] Mrs Hall here at tea.

---

[130]   Uncle Go was a serjeant at law.

23rd Brewing. Mrs Hall & I walked to call on the Burkitts & she took luncheon here, Mr Hall called in the evening on his way from London & brought us a turbot.

June 19th Since writing my journal last we have been in London with Jessy. A matinee musicale at her house. To the Crystal Palace accompanied by Gerard. Also went to the Botanic Fete at the Regents Park. A dinner party, one evening to see Kean & Mrs Kean, another day to take luncheon with Edward, & to the Royal Academy.

26th Mr Hall & Henry out fishing in Leeds Moat. A hand cart was necessary to bring home the fishing spoil.

July 1st Wrote to Milly in Homburg I fear that she is in the midst of the war.[131]

3rd Drank tea at the Hall's to meet our new vicar & his wife, Mr & Mrs Gibson.

13th Lolotte & I did much shopping. Henry all day up The Hill shooting.

14th Richard returned having been to the Harrow & Eton cricket match & seen Gerard. He also took his brother to the Bank & settled his affairs for him.

16th Went to the Pusey's *(The Rev. William Pusey was rector of Langley near Maidstone)* to meet Queen Emma of Hawaii. Everyone was in turn presented to her & I had the additional honour of sitting by her. She is most gentle & pleasing. Rather dark but not altogether so foreign as I had expected. A most agreeable morning. Tea & refreshments in the garden.[132]

25th Saw much of the Halls. On Tuesday took Mrs Hall to Maidstone to see 'Lady Godiva' by Thomas & on Wednesday Mr & Mrs Hall drank tea here.

27th Richard on the Grand Jury yesterday, & we today at the Speech Day at Sutton Valance at the Grammar School. Prizes given. Pieces of poetry badly recited. Many of the neighbourhood present, a luncheon for at least 60 guests. Mr Kingdom supported on the right by the Master of the Clothworkers & on the left by Sir Edward Filmer who took me in. Healths drunk, speeches made, a walk in the garden & then home. So ended an agreeable but 'curious' day.[133]

---

[131]   The Austro-Prussian War.

[132]   Queen Consort Emma (1836-1885) was a widow by this time & had visited Queen Victoria.

[133]   Sutton Valance school was founded in the 16th century by the Clothworkers Company & remained under their control until 1910.

28th The Atlantic Telegraph laid & a message of congratulation already received from India & Egypt.

30th To Maidstone, very much shopping for The Cottage.[134]

August 1st Yesterday Mr Gibson arrived at the Vicarage.

2nd Mr Gibson called. Message by the Atlantic Telegraph from New York from the President to the Queen in one hour & nine minutes.

11th Ella & her two bairns arrived from Cuxton to stay with us. A letter from Mrs Hall, she finds the Vicarage House an Agean Stable to clean.

19th A very good sermon from Mr Gibson.

22nd At work at The Cottage all day. Henry, Louy & Emma (*Henry's sister)* arrived, much pleased with their new home.

'The Cottage' Eyhorne Cottage today

September 2nd Jessy arrived with Caroline. 'The Cottagers' at dinner & tea.

7th Jessy & the Blunts departed & our house is now vacant & en repos.

---

[134] The Cottage was Eyhorne Cottage, far from a cottage this is a large house a couple of minutes walk from Eyhorne House. Purchased by Richard it was to be for a time the home of Louy and Henry.

9th Henry, Louy & Emma at dinner. Farkins out & came home after prayers drunk.

25th Called on Mrs Ellis who is out of spirits & no marvel as her eye is beginning quite to fail her, called also on the Gapes & ate some wedding cake.

October 7th A great commotion in our house at 4 o'clock this morning. I was summoned from bed & Attwood brought a son into the world without pain or struggle & before Mr Sedgwick could arrive. (*Sarah Attwood had become the cook a year earlier. In August her pregnancy being apparent she was given a month's notice but in September she had married her sweetheart by special licence, although still called Attwood at work and allowed to remain a little longer.*)

15th Our new cook Susan Barton arrived & Henry's orders to leave.

16th To Maidstone early to take Henry to the station en route to London where he went to transact business. Called on the Claytons who kept Bertha to stay with them. Called on Mrs Rodney.

17th Henry received a telegram from Pembroke to summon him there at once.

18th Henry left. Such a sad parting! Mary at The Cottage. (*Richard noted in his account book that Henry left to take charge of a detachment of his regiment in Japan.*)

24th To the Ball at Sittingbourne. Bertha & Mary danced <u>all night</u>.

November 1st We were to have gone to the Engineers' Ball at Chatham but Chapman was suddenly taken <u>very</u> ill & we passed our evening at home instead. Wilson returned. (*she has been away looking after her sick mother*)

3rd Mrs Hull has been most dangerously ill. Henry has command of the 9th Depot during his stay.

6th Henry leaves Pembroke for Portsmouth on 9th. Edward is the new Dean of Norwich & Frederic Goldsmid is made a C.B.

13th To Brighton, Richard, Bertha, Mary, Lolotte, Louy, Willie, Wilson & Anne for a fortnight. Our lodging is 17 Montpelier Road & very clean & comfortable, but for the fact of sending our maid out to sleep & she not being able to procure more spacious accommodation. Horace Smith just opposite. Called on Mrs Hull the first night. The new pier an immense attraction & crowded every morning. Went to the theatre to see 'The School for Scandal,' went to an afternoon tea at the Horace Smith's. Robert & Ella came over for a day & Richard went over to Portsmouth & brought back Henry with him, but he was forced to return the next day. He is now really gone to Japan by the 'Golden Fleece'. One day drove to Preston to see dearest Mama's grave. Left the gaiety of Brighton for the comfort of home.

30th Mr Allwork called to see Louy, & fixes <u>the</u> event about Christmas.

December 7th To Maidstone early trying on dresses for Bertha & Mary.

Just what the girls were wearing

11th To the County Ball, chaperoned the Miss Timmins. Lady Holmesdale gorgeously attired in amber crape spangled with silver, wreathed with grapes & vine leaves. Wilson very poorly.

12th Gerard returned home from Harrow with a knee much injured by football.

13th Richard, Bertha, Mary & I went to Lady Holmesdale's Ball, a most brilliant affair, home at 4 o'clock.

17th Took Gerard to see Mr Joy who said his knee will be a very tedious affair.

18th To the Amateur Theatricals at the Corn Exchange. The performance lasted from 8 till past one. Far too long.

22nd Martha Waghorn came on trial as my maid. Bertha, Mary & Lolotte busy over evergreen decorations for the church. Mary quite ill with them.

24th To the church to assist in erecting the cross made by our daughters. Went to see Mr Hoare with Gerard. He says his leg will require great care. 33 had our Christmas dinner this year.

26th To Maidstone with Bertha & Gerard. Mr Hoare & Mr Joy both saw his leg & bound it up tightly.

28th Mr Allwork was sent for & at 11.45 a very large boy was born to Louy. I returned home at 1.30 through the still orchard which was very damp & dark though the sky shone bright with stars. Wilson carried a lantern.

1867 January 1st Mr Crawford came to read with Gerard & took luncheon here. *(private tutor who is giving regular help)*

8th Gerard tried his crutches which he hired yesterday & made his first expedition to The Cottage & saw his Godchild. Went to the County Ball in the evening, a very pleasant gathering. Home at three.

12th Too cold & snowy to go to church, thermometer in our room two degrees below freezing point.

February 6th Gerard left for Oxford where we hope for his success. Mrs Burkitt called. Did some shopping in Maidstone.

9th Gerard returned, I grieve to say unsuccessful.

12th Richard at Turnpike meeting at Lenham. Mr Crawford came to Gerard. Called on the Gapes, Mrs Gape goes up to London on Saturday for a dreadful operation.

17th Gerard walked to church for the first time since his accident.

24th To afternoon service where Louy's baby was christened by the name of Frederick George de Visme Gipps. The noise he made was quite dreadful.

March 4th To Malling & took luncheon at the Savage's. Went on to Dr Lowry's & saw his establishment of which we heard a most favourable report. *(A private asylum, Malling Place, St*

Leonards Street West Malling, to which Louis was then moved from Ticehurst so that he was closer for visiting. However his cousin Freddy Goulburn, remained for the rest of his life at Ticehurst Asylum visited regularly by his brother Edward.)

18th Ella & her babies arrived from Cuxton.

25th Gerard left for Oxford. *(this time he passed the exams)*

April 3rd Richard & I went to West Malling Place & saw poor Louis who really seemed as happy & comfortable as his state can allow.

5th Gerard left for Harrow. Met Mr Shaw in Maidstone & heard of the awfully sudden death of Captain Cheeve. He had just got out of his carriage yesterday in Week Street nearly opposite the Club, when he staggered, dropped to the ground & never spoke again.

15th Richard to London. Took Mrs Burkitt to Maidstone & went to the museum & saw Mr Lightfoot the curator who exhibited to us some curious manuscripts. Another brother of Captain Cheeve is just dead. This made the third in about three weeks.

20th A long letter from Frederic from Tehran. During the last four years he has traversed 40,000 miles, 3,500 on horse & camel back.

28th I waited in Maidstone to see Dr Lowry *(of Louis' asylum)* & during that time we went to the museum where Mr Lightfoot showed us much in the way of coins, rings & drawings.

30th To the concert at the town hall for the organ of Trinity Church, very well attended. Gerard much pleased with Oxford.

June 2nd Took Bertha to London & saw her safe on board the steamer. *(She is going, chaperoned, to Homburg to stay with Milly.)* Took luncheon with Uncle Go & there met Lord, Lady & Miss Chetwynd. Then to call on Jessy.

8th *(At home)* Mr Rodney escorted us to Preston Hall which is really beautiful though much of the furniture & many of the pictures are removed.

15th (In London with Mary, staying at Jessy's) To call on Caroline, ill & in bed & on Mrs Treherne. To the Haymarket Theatre after dinner to see Southern in 'A Wild Goose'. He acted so charmingly that it was not acting.

16th Called on Uncle Go, then to Kensington to see the Thomas Thomas's by the underground railway. *(the first time she has used it)*

July 2nd To Maidstone accompanied by the Rodneys. Left our carriage to be renovated & came home in a clumsy old machine. Mr Rodney at dinner.

4th Yesterday the laying down gas pipes in the road opposite our house was begun.

10th To West Malling, Richard, Jessy & I. Found Louis as well as we can expect him to be but as usual very wild & incoherent.

12th Richard & Gerard to London. In the afternoon we went to Mr Gibson's school treat which was a great success. Almost all the inhabitants of Hollingbourne there. After the children had been regaled we had our tea at various tables on the lawn, flags innumerable, also singing.

14th Jessy departed leaving little Caroline here. Mr Gibson at luncheon.

23rd The archery meeting at Vinters; the wind so high that the arrows were blown about everywhere except in the targets. Louy went with us. In the evening Lolotte made her debut at the ball & danced much.

25th To the speeches & dejeuner at the Sutton Valance Grammar school. The patrons, the Clothmakers, gathered in great force. Then there were present Sir E. Filmer, Mr Wykeham Martin, the High Sherriff etc. Mr Kingdom received much approbation for the success of his school & many good wishes on his approaching marriage. The boys' recitations were rather doleful.

27th Took little Caroline to Maidstone where her maid met her to see her safely home. Mary, Gerard, Louy & Willie at croquet & tea at the vicarage.

31st Began a sketch of the house for Gerard. Mr Baldwin, Mr & Mrs Gibson & Colonel Meyer at croquet. Brewing.

August 2nd A cricket match in Leeds Park between Leeds & Yalding. Gerard played for Leeds which was victorious.

13th The second archery meeting of the season. We dined with the Timmins *(the vicar of West Malling & his wife whose vicarage was just doors away from Louis' asylum)* & Robert & Ella met us there. A dull ball in the evening.

14th Mrs Barton *(the cook)* gave me warning on account of my administering to her a lecture on Truth.

22nd To the 3rd & last archery meeting with Louy, Gerard & Mary. Gerard won a prize for the highest score at 30 yards. The prize given in the evening at the Ball proved to be an inkstand though of larger size than the former one.

24th Called on Lady F. Riddell who has become <u>very old</u> & infirm. The Palace now all thrown into one instead of being divided as formerly.

31st Ella, her maid & bairns arrived.

September 2nd Still poorly & in the evening so ill obliged to have Mr Sedgwick. Louy & Mary sat up with me. Fainted away.

13th To Sittingbourne to take tea with Dr Grayling, Gerard, Mary, Lolotte & I. A very agreeable party, Mr Anderson, Mr & Mrs Walford & Mr Robertson the curate of Elmley. Croquet & music.

27th Mr Anderson came to stay, Captain Hunt called & played croquet, also Blanche Rodney. Mr Anderson sang & acted the 'Dwarf'.

October 2nd Kate Gibson & Mr John & Mr Julius Brenchley dined here. The latter gave us some account of his travels. He is an immense man.[135]

11th Mrs & Edith Duppa came & stayed the night. Whist & music in the evening.

21st Richard, Louy & I drove to Headcorn & then entered the train on our way to Dover. Established ourselves in very spacious lodgings, 21 Waterloo Crescent.

22nd To the Admiralty Pier to meet Bertha who arrived from Calais full of Homburg stories & songs. Much improved in her singing.

24th The inspector of the Custom House came to say that the luggage had arrived in the night. Bertha off to Headcorn to meet Mary, & Lolotte came to Dover in her place. Much strolling about on the esplanade & in Snargate Street & on the pier.

28th Left Dover returning by the London, Chatham & Dover line in order to see Canterbury. The cathedral seems more beautiful each time I see it. Went all over the cathedral & down into the crypt, walked to St Augustines, then took luncheon at a pastry cook's. Purchased photographs. Then to the rail-road station, got into the train for Sittingbourne where the carriage met us.

November 7th Louy 24 today. Richard sent her a dozen of port wine.

---

[135]   It was this year that Julius Brenchley gave his collection to Maidstone & £400 for an extension to be built to the museum.

8th Richard went up to the sale of carriages, horses & dogs at Torry Hill. (*Lord Kingsdown has died*)

12th Walked to Leeds Castle with Agnes Gibson, Lolotte & Mary to look at a sketch of 'the Maiden's tower' made by the former, very incorrectly.

13th Wilson came to work here. (*she comes to stay to do needlework jobs*) Sat up till two & Mary & Lolotte till 5 to see the meteor shower but only four or five made their bright appearance.

16th Louy heard from Henry. For a wonder we did not see her the whole day.

18th Mrs Ellis's face is drawn by the paralysis & it is feared that it may reach the brain. Louy, Bertha, Mary & Lolotte drove to Linton to see Lady Holmesdale's poultry. They say that some of their own are as fine. Wilson finished her work.

29th Bertha & I dined at the Palace at Lady F. Riddell's. Farkins quite tipsy.

30th Farkins 'took the pledge' before Mr Gibson.

December 12th Took my verses on Hollingbourne to Grundy to have them printed.

Louisa's poem 'Hollingbourne' was written in 1851 for her children. A verse will give a flavour of it:

> *You see our village Hollingbourne,*
> *That high bleak hill below*
> *They say the name meant 'running brook'*
> *In long, long years ago.*
> *Green pleasant fields, and orchards rich,*
> *And clustering hops are there;*
> *And the clear stream that gave it name*
> *Reflects its pastures fair.*

14th Today's paper brought the dreadful news of the blowing up of the prison wall & houses at Clerkenwell (4 people killed & 60 wounded) by Fenians to attempt the release of Burke & Casey who are imprisoned there.

15th Gerard arrive most unexpectedly, smallpox having broken out at Magdalen College.

17th To the County Ball, Lolotte's first. They danced very much.

20th Walked to see the steam plough but it was under repair.

28th Richard put two half sovereigns in the servants' cake last night which caused much laughing. They were won by Crayford & Anne.

29th A letter from Ella that she is likely to require Mrs Kitchin (*midwife)* at the beginning of March to my great surprise. The explosion (*that we heard)* was at Mr Hale's powder mill at Faversham. 10 or 12 men have been reported killed.

30th Eleven men blown quite to atoms & their remains undiscoverable. Drove to Malling, Richard & I & saw Louis much as usual. Took luncheon with Mr & Mrs Savage.

1868 January 1st Heard the Bells last night. Indeed it seemed as if all the frosty air were full of bells for the night was so still that both those of Hollingbourne & Leeds appeared quite near together. Walked in the road while the small hard snow was falling.

8th Richard gave away a ton of coals to the oldest & poorest villagers.

18th With Crayford to London. Found my Uncle I grieve to say very much altered but better than he had been. A dinner party.

19th To St John's Paddington with my Uncle, quite missed Edward. Called on Jessy.

23rd Milly appeared at breakfast looking very well. She & I walked to see Gustave Dore's three wonderful pictures & to Christie & Manson's auction rooms. Then left Seymour Street, & met Richard at the Charing Cross station.[136] Instead of coming home to a pleasant quiet evening, found Captain Hunt & Mr Baker who had come over unexpectedly to shoot & Gerard had invited them to stay & dine.

31st Started for Brighton, Louy & Willie with us, passed a most agreeable time, had lodgings next door to Milly & Leopold, saw all our old friends, went to balls, to a soiree, to a luncheon at Caroline's & returned home on St Valentine's Day.

February 18th Arrived Milly, Leopold & Ernst. Gerard came the same day to meet them here. Ella brought into the world another son.

March 9th Richard at the Grand Jury. We went into the Criminal Court where Mr Justice Byles was sitting. Three poachers condemned to imprisonment with hard labour.

11th The three Miss Gibsons at tea, *(daughters of the vicar)* who with their Mother, Bertha & Lolotte went to a dull but

---

[136] Gustave Dore (1832-1883) a French illustrator. His work was very popular in Britain & he was a regular contributor to the Illustrated London News.

crowded concert at the Union. Today I went up to Godfrey House & looked over it, Jane being there to clean the grates.

21st A day without a letter coming to the house!!! Lolotte passing the day at the vicarage as it is Ellen Gibson's birthday.

24th Called at the Palace, it is not expected Lady Riddell will leave her bed again. Gerard arrived. Met Mr Shaw of Cuxton in <u>immense</u> spirits.

April 2nd To Maidstone in a fly the horse being still invalided. Brought back with us Gerard's Magdalen friend Mr Paulson. Dinner party here with much singing.

3rd Gerard to Leeds Park for first cricket practice of year. Others to the vicarage for croquet.

10th Frank Duppa is engaged to Miss Dart whom we met at the Sittingbourne Ball she is an only child. Mrs Coveney's hand better.

14th All our olive branches drank tea at the vicarage so we had a very still evening.

16th Mr Gibson at luncheon, Kate *(Gibson)* in the afternoon making up wreaths of pyrus japonica for our three daughters at the ball. A very good one.

30th Robert & Ella came with their three boys.

May 1st Great excitement with garlands. Bobbie & Willie up at ½ past 6 collecting flowers.

15th A very sad account of Uncle Go who has some interior complaint. Captain & Mrs Moore came to see Godfrey House again. *(from East Grinstead)*

16th Robert left for Danehill & Lolotte & I for London. Reached Leinster Gardens about one. *(home of Yeats & Dora Goldsmid)* Took luncheon with Dora walked across Kensington Gardens to the Loan Portrait Gallery. Such wonderful treasures are there brought together! I wish that I could see them again. Met there Mr & Mrs Hall. Yeats at dinner.

17th To the church at Lancaster Gate. After luncheon went to see Uncle Go. He revived on our going up to see him & told me that 'the oftener I came the better'. He is feeble & much wasted. Afterwards we went to see Mrs Bigge, she looks very well & is now 82. Lolotte went with Dora to see Westminster Abbey.

19th Again called in Seymour Street but Uncle Go too sleepy to see us & they did not like to disturb him. Saw Mary Chetwynd & Julia. Then on to take luncheon at Jessy's where Dora met us. Went to the Prince of Wales Theatre.

20th Called on Mrs Hull who took us in the afternoon to call on Mr & Mrs S. Carter Hall *(brother of vicar)*, then to Kensington. Mr Thomas Thomas much the same. Today Edward called on us looking well but very lame.

21st Early to the Royal Academy which is not considered a good one, but some of the pictures are lovely. Bought a fan each for Bertha & Mary in Regent Street. A large dinner party. The dinner was most recherché & magnificently served.

29th *(At home)* The day of the Club garlands & bands made our village very gay.

30th In the afternoon to the cricket match at Mote Park between the club there & the Aborigines. Some of 'the darkies' played very well. The numbers of people were large. After the cricket, boomerangs were thrown & darts & a man displayed wonderful agility in warding off cricket balls which were thrown at him from all sides.

June 11th To Oxford, Richard, Bertha, Mary, Lolotte & I. Reached the ancient learned city in time for tea. Gerard met us at the station. As we drove up the High Street thoughts & memories of bygone days made me quite sad. *(memories of brother Louis)* Went to Magdalen College & to Gerard's pretty little comfortable rooms looking into the lovely park. One day took luncheon with him & met many of his friends. Another day breakfasted with him when we met John Riddell. On Saturday to the concert at Queens. Claret cup & ices most liberally supplied. Sprained my knee in a walk to the Church Meadows to see a Boat Race & became almost disabled by rheumatism succeeding the wrench for the rest of the day. On Monday evening drank tea with Cecil Maunsell & went to the St Johns Theatricals where was acted 'She Stoops to Conquor'. Claret & Champagne Cup in abundance.

16th To the Harrow & Eton Ball. A very good one. In the morning we breakfasted with Mr Grant at Balliol. On Wednesday was the theatre, dinner in the Hall at Magdalen to which we went & met Cyrus Field of telegraphic fame & the Freemasons' Fete in the garden of Worcester College, a concert at Magdalen & the University Ball to which Mr Robinson chaperoned our daughters.[137]

18th Bertha & I took luncheon at Dr Bailey's the President of Magadalen, after which all our children joined a large picnic.

---

[137]   Cyrus West Field, American entrepreneur who helped to create the Atlantic Telegraph.

19th Concluded my sketch of the opposite side of the street. Went to Guggenheim the photographer & purchased some views, after which we met, by Gerard's arrangements, a musical party at Magdalen & passed a most agreeable evening.

24th *(At home)* The Flower Show at Lord Romney's. Roses lively & abundant, company scarce. Yesterday Mr John & Mr Julius Brenchley called. The latter brought me some beautiful egg-shell china & for Lolotte stamps.

July 4th Mary left with Gerard to embark for Homburg tomorrow & to sleep at Jessy's.

18th A letter from Mrs *(Edward)* Duppa announcing her intended marriage with Mr Green.

22nd Letters from Mary & Milly announcing themselves in the Bavarian Tyrol & telling of their most charming tour. Louy also heard of Henry's arrival in Ireland. Richard on the grand jury. Judge & barristers without wigs from the heat.

23rd To meet the Clothworkers at Mr Kingdom's luncheon & see the giving of the prizes. A carpenter's son, was the most distinguished boy at the school & took a scholarship. They acted a scene from the 'Bourgois Gentilhomme' (such French!).

25th To archery practice at the Timmin's. I went on to Dr Lowry's & saw Louis in the distance.[138]

28th Archery meeting. Louy went as chaperone in the morning & I in the evening to the ball. Gerard won first prize at 60 yards, a pair of candlesticks.

29th Mr Gibson's school treat which was a great success. Tables on the lawn for the tea-drinking of the guests, after the children had finished theirs. Mr Thomas instituted races amongst the boys & girls which were most popular.

August 9th Henry, Louy, Emma & Willie at dinner. After tea Dora & Yeats left us.

16th Too rainy for morning service so went in the afternoon, when I grieve to say, we all slept. Much music in the evening.

25th A letter from Edward this morning to say that Dear Uncle Go passed away at 1.30. yesterday, very quietly & surrounded by all he most loved. To Maidstone to arrange mourning.

29th Gerard at Uncle Go's funeral. He returned in the evening. My Uncle was buried at Kensal Green.

---

[138]   Seven staff attended to the 20 patients under the supervision of Dr Thomas Lowry and the matron.

31st Robert & Ella & their three boys arrived looking very well. Henry, Louy & Willie at tea in addition.

September 2nd Took luncheon with Mrs Faunce at Sharsted. A French artist there painting portraits of herself & her children.

3rd To London to see Edward who was much harassed. Julia in good spirits. Saw all the old servants who were very sad. Henry left for Ireland.

28th Packing case arrived *(items from Uncle Go)* containing Spanish books, portraits of myself & Milly as children by my Aunt Jane de Visme. Engravings, & a little sketch of my mother.

29th A letter from Cecil Maunsell telling of the death of his poor mother. (*Dodo.*)

October 2nd Henry arrived from Ireland. Monsieur Rougeron came & began a sketch of Louy.

4th To morning service to which Mr Rougeron accompanied me though he did not understand a word.

15th Mr Rougeron continuing his portraits as usual. Lolotte's most successful.

16th Craddock recovering, so we went to Maidstone accompanied by Henry & Louy. In the evening arrived Robert quite unexpectedly to announce he had been presented with the living of Madehurst. It seems to be a charming little affair & the country very beautiful.[139]

21st Bertha, Lolotte & Kate Gibson walked up The Hill to see Mrs Duppa's trousseau.

23rd Henry, Louy & Willie at luncheon, the latter with short hair & in knicker bockers. Mr Rougeron very successful with Lolotte & improving Bertha.

24th Mr Thomas' portrait begun & Lolotte's concluded.

28th Henry & Louy started for the Isle of Man.[140] Kate Gibson, Mrs & Miss Burkittt came to see the portraits.

31st Mr Thomas went early to London for his brother's funeral. He was interred in the same grave with his daughter in the Brompton Cemetery. Many of the shops were closed & much respect shown to his memory. Monsieur Rougeron departed having been here a month. He returned to Sharsted on his way to Paris & Madrid. We brought back Mr Gibson

---

139   Madehurst is a village in West Sussex close to Arundel.

140   Henry was appointed adjutant to the Isle of Man Volunteers.

from Maidstone who had solemnised Mrs Duppa's marriage this morning.

November 5th Called on the Burkitts, saw Miss Burkitt's altar cloth she is embroidering for Ripon Cathedral from the design of Mr Scott. Gorgeous.

6th A walk through the village. Called on Mrs Craddock *(wife of their coachman)* Mrs Sellen *(wife of the landlord of the Kings Head)*, Mrs Roper of the Manor House whose son is delirious & dying, and Mrs Gibson. *(wife of their gardener)*

10th A letter from the Isle of Man telling Henry he can if he likes take the adjutancy.

20th Warning from Mrs Coveney who certainly did not distinguish herself in the dinner yesterday.

21st To Maidstone with Lolotte. Richard & Gerard accompanied us to vote. The town all purple & orange, scarcely any blue to be seen, bands playing & colours flying. Went to see Mr Lightfoot about Henry's Japanese treasures. Mr L is to come over. Conservatives successful.

29th A letter from Mrs Green from Florence, signed 'Mrs E. Duppa'! Louy chaperoned Bertha, Mary & Lolotte to the Engineers' 'Ethiopian serenades' & Mr Thomas & Henry dined at the barracks, so I passed my evening in silent solitude.

December 10th Bertha is 24. Went to the ball, Henry, Louy, Herbert, Gerard, Bertha, Mary & Lolotte. Returned at 2.30.

11th To Maidstone, Gerard to choose a <u>breech loader</u> promised him by his father in acknowledgement of his success at Oxford. We went to the first exhibition of the school of art, at the College, <u>very poor</u>.

14th Dined with Bertha, Mary & Gerard at the Balston's.[141]

16th Craddock threw down Prince Alfred on his way to fetch coals from Maidstone & brought him home with his knee severely cut.

21st Our new cook Mrs Chambers came. Henry, Louy & Gerard off to London. They returned thoroughly tired but successful in purchasing a breech loader for Gerard.

23rd Wrote tickets for our Christmas dinner. Called on Mrs Moore at Godfrey House. The horse's knee still in a bad state.

24th Louy very poorly, Henry thinks it may be scarletina.

25th Church <u>beautifully</u> & fully decorated. Mr Sedgwick sent

---

[141]   The Balston family owned Springfield paper mill which employed hundreds. They were staunch Anglican Tories and amongst the richest families of Maidstone. They lived in Springfield House.

for, Henry is right.

26th Louy rather better.

30th Yesterday sent off Mrs Chambers in haste, & much rejoiced to be free from her. Gerard & his three sisters to Amateur Theatricals at Maidstone.

31st A very grand Ball at Torry Hill which we all much enjoyed & where we met numerous friends. The house was so much changed that we scarcely knew it. Magnificent chandeliers glittering all around etc, the conservatory beautiful.

1869 January 1st To Maidstone. Turnpikes at an end. Brought home Louy's coat with the Japanese buttons. Left at Tapley's her Bird of Paradise plumes.

9th To Maidstone to have a tooth stopped, dreaded it as if I were going to be beheaded, but I suffered no pain.

11th A nosegay in my room of yellow jasmine, coltsfoot, snowdrops, stock, polyanthus, anemones, violets & the yellow aconite!

22nd To Malling with Richard, saw poor Louis. My visit to him was more satisfactory than any I have ever yet paid. He seemed less excitable.

25th Bertha & I started for London, did some shopping, took luncheon at Very's & then on to Mrs Bigge who gave us warm welcome. *(they stayed with her)*

28th Took luncheon at Caroline's, her little house in Brook Street 'a perfect bijou.' The drawing room carpet pale blue sprinkled with pale pink roses. To the wonderful pantomime, the scenes of enchantment astonishingly beautiful. 'Puss in Boots' was the story, & on this was built a superstructure such as our ancestors never could have dreamed.

29th I called on Jessy, & took luncheon with Miss Chetwynd. She spoke much of the pleasant life & social society she had enjoyed at Uncle Go's & also at Edward's which had all ceased.

30th Returned home after a most delightful stay. Mrs Bigge is now 82 & a most charming old lady. I can only say if I live as long may I be like her.

February 2nd Called on the Moores *(who are renting Godfrey House),* with Richard.

11th Confirmation of the sad report of Mrs Hall's death. My best & most valued friends are daily diminishing.

March 1st Richard to the Sitting & Mary & Lolotte on their way to Madehurst.

7th The Cottagers & Herbert Gipps at dinner. Reports that a man was found dead on the road near Maidstone. A tailor by name Finn & that he had been shot.

8th The report too true. The poor young man was shot dead by the wall of Vinters & just opposite the Turkey Mills at little after midnight. Gerard returned.

12th No further tidings of the murderer of Finn.[142]

16th Henry & Herbert at Chatham for the Medical Board.

17th Henry & Gerard went up to London. Gerard for the Oxford & Cambridge Boat Race, Henry returned in the evening. Gerard stayed at Yeats.

19th Breakfasted at 7.30, & at 8, accompanied by Louy & her two dear little boys & Bertha, drove to Maidstone, saw them all safe into the train. The former en route to Liverpool *(for the ferry to the Isle of Man)* & Bertha to London. Gerard met them at Charing Cross & saw them safe to Euston Station & off. Henry & Herbert met them. Gerard & Bertha called on Mrs Gape, took luncheon with Caroline, visited Madame Tussauds & home by 7.30. All so still today at home.

23rd Louy & Henry reached the Isle of Man safely & are busy house hunting.

April 1st To the County Ball accompanied by Gerard, Bertha, Mary & Lolotte, a very good one. Lolotte considered the belle of the room.

7th Gerard 21 today. Fred Goldsmid, (Jessy's little boy), came to stay here. He has been trying hard at the Exam for the Indian Civil Service but will not know his fate for six weeks.

8th To Maidstone. Tapley's shop crowded for the purchase of the new bonnets from Paris. Took one for Bertha & intend Vidian to copy it for Mary & Lolotte.

10th Gerard left for Oxford. Brunette *(new horse)* went very quietly & well. She is as thin as possible, not much more than a 'frame' as Benfield would say.

19th Mr Thomas, Mary, Bartle *(Goldsmid)* & I started early for London. Shopping & took luncheon with Mrs Treherne in Stratford Place. *(back same day)*

May 1st Garland children as usual. Kate Gibson here, we read 'The Iliad' in Italian.

8th To London with Lolotte. At Leinster Gardens Dora received us most warmly.

---

[142]   John Finn was a respectable young man on his way home to Boxley from Maidstone with no known enemies.

9th Called on Mrs Bigge & Jessy. Passed 37, Dorset Square where much of my childhood was spent.

10th To the Charing Cross station where Mary met us. Then to the Royal Academy in its new home.[143] The pictures seen to much more advantage than formerly. Richard met us in the refreshment room & took Mary home.

12th Made up my mind yesterday to return home on business. A great disappointment to me. Bertha came in my place.

19th (At home) A visit from our old well-remembered friend Colonel Crawley. Looking well & stouter but grey headed. It was a great pleasure to see him. How much sorrow & trial he has gone through public & private since we met. His wife has died which I was not aware of.

June 3rd Bertha left for Homburg forgetting her through ticket to Cologne. But Gerard arriving later in the day informed us that all had gone well & that he had seen her safe under Mr Aylward's care.

5th Went to the consecration of an addition to the church at Harrietsham the service for which the bishop read most distinctly. After this we all proceeded to a garden tea at the vicarage. Mrs Riddell had assembled all the neighbourhood.

8th Started early with Mr Thomas for Madehurst. Reached Arundel about 2.30 where Robert & Ella awaited us. He took Mr Thomas in his little carriage & Ella & I proceeded in a fly to their charming vicarage. Everything as nice as possible & the country lovely tho' not quite as picturesque as Danehill. The church is very near & reached by their own garden. School covered with China roses & pyracantha.

9th Walked up through extensive & beautiful woods to Dale Park, & on our way called on Mrs Brenchley our former coachman's wife. In the afternoon made a little watercolour sketch of the vicarage.

10th Sat in the churchyard with the two boys who are much grown & sketched the church which is beautifully restored by Gilbert Scott.

11th Set out on our homeward journey, again drove through the lovely scenery of Arundel Park & saw the magnificent castle overlooking the town of Arundel.

15th To London early Lolotte, Vidian & I. Went at once to the National Gallery. The Turners there are exquisite. Some are

---

143   Burlington House, Piccadilly from 1868.

hung side by side with Claude Lorraine & I thought them superior. Then took a cab to Nottingham Place & found Jessy.

16th To a most crowded fete supposed to be given by Prince Teck in the Botanic gardens, about 12,000 people present. Followed 'Dizzy' & Lady Beaconsfield.[144] He is very peculiar looking in his long drab coat & black ringlets.

18th Lolotte accompanied Jessy to a first rate concert. I went to take luncheon with Mrs Bigge & met there Mr & Mrs Frederick *(Bigge)*. Jessy's dinner party was very agreeable. Yeats & Dora, Frederic, & Captain Pierson R.E.

19th Walked with Frederic to the House of Peers went over & saw again Herbert's grand fresco in the Robing room. Also saw the models for Woolner's Statue of Lord Palmerston now standing on the Abbey Green. It appeared to me very good. The likeness perfect & the attitude very easy & natural. Dined at Yeats, a large party.

21st Jessy's immense party. Such a lot of people! Stairs as well as rooms quite crowded. The Persian Ambassador there among the number & he is so plump that he occupies a considerable space. In the evening Frederic gave us a box at the Prince of Wales's for Robertson's piece 'School'. –very cleverly written & beautifully acted. Captain Pierson there.

22nd To the Promenade at the Horticultural Gardens. Went by the Underground Railway to which I am now becoming quite accustomed. A ball in the evening at Lady Clifford's to which Jessy kindly took Lolotte, accompanied by Bartle & Captain Pierson. An event there occurred which may greatly affect Lolotte's future life.

27th *(At home)* Yesterday a letter from Frederic giving Captain Pierson a very high character. Chivalrous, well principled etc. Mrs Green & her two little girls at luncheon.

28th The anniversary of the Queen's Coronation & much firing in consequence.

30th Drove into Maidstone & brought out with us Captain Pierson, who left us again in the evening.

July 2nd Took Mary to Maidstone on her way to the Isle of Man & brought Captain Pierson out. Mr & Mrs Gibson at tea.

5th Captain Pierson left early. Richard at the sitting of magistrates.

8th Captain Pierson here for the day.

10th Captain Harry Pierson came by his usual train.

---

[144]   Benjamin Disraeli, Lord Beaconsfield

15th Harry & Mr Pierson *(his father)* arrived & passed the day here.

19th Drove to Maidstone to fetch Frederic & Lisa & Major Champain who passed the day here leaving with Harry. Major C. corroborated all we had heard in Harry's favour.

20th Went to Maidstone & began purchasing for trousseau.

23rd Lolotte & I in London at Madame Elise's etc. Met Jessy & Caroline in Oxford Street. A letter from Edward who cannot perform the ceremony as he will be absent. Arranged the wedding dress.

27th Harry came. Attended sports of Artillery in Mr Whatman's party. Tea & ices in a tent. Everyone there & universal congratulations on Lolotte's approaching marriage. Harry departed.

28th Cricket match in the front meadow between 'married & single'.

August 3rd Went to very pleasant ball where Harry & his brother Jack met us.

4th Richard & I went to the Gibson's school treat. Tea, singing, games & a balloon.

5th The archaeological meeting at Malling to which Lolotte, Gerard & I went. First visited the Abbey then the church, then St Leonard's Tower after which I went to see poor Louis & Mrs Savage.

8th Harry left this evening in order to fetch Bertha early tomorrow. Wilson came.

11th The shooting for the archery prizes at Vinters. Last Sunday Harry & Lolotte's banns published for the first time. Edith Harrison to be our 6th bridesmaid. Magnificent presents arriving on all sides for Lolotte.

16th Letters from Man announcing the birth of a daughter to Henry & Louy. All going well.

17th Gerard had what might have been a most fearful accident & was a most merciful preservation. The new horse just as he was starting on a ride reared & fell upon him. Mr Thomas was fortunately there & says that he can scarcely tell how he escaped with so little injury. He was however quite stunned & could not at all remember anything. His elbow & hip are bruised, the former too is deeply cut. He was immediately put in bed & had a warm bath which relieved him.

18th Mary arrived under the escort of Harry. Gerard better. To the archery meeting.

22nd Lolotte's banns published for the last time. How near is the event!

23rd On Saturday Robert, Ella & Bobbie passed the day here & brought Lolotte a ring. Today we went early to Maidstone for signing the deeds at Mr Beale's & to the station to fetch the grapes & peaches sent by Robert. Brought home Edith Harrison. People coming all day to see the presents. In the evening arrived Mr Pierson & his two sons & in the afternoon Mr Cuyler Anderson. Mr Gibson joined us at dinner. Kate Gibson here all day arranging flowers. Mr Pierson brought Lolotte a beautiful bracelet & earrings set with pearls & from Granny a brooch of gold & carbuncles. None can tell our deep anxiety for the event of tomorrow.

Hollingbourne church today

24th The day dawned in mist & the broke into glorious sunshine. All the village was on holiday. The house constantly filled with people. Lolotte looking lovely in her bridal attire & tearless but she had promised Harry that none should be shed. The bridesmaids bright as roses in their pink & white dresses. The guests began to arrive about 10.45, Baldwins, Riddells, Moores, the envoy to Persia etc. Robert & Mr Gibson performed the ceremony. The church & churchyard were decorated with flowers & when the bride entered the church led by Mr Thomas & followed by her six bridesmaids the quire burst forth in the wedding hymn. After the service the wedding march was played by Kate Gibson, the bells rang merrily. The band met the procession on their return & everyone was in Commotion. Then came the breakfast, the speeches, the healths, the departure of the bride & bridegroom for Dover, the throwing the slipper, a bridesmaids' & groomsmens' quadrille on the lawn & the parting & dispersion of all. The Persian envoy brought a beautiful casket of Dresden china & the Persian servants of himself & Harry with their swarthy foreign faces looked very strange among our villagers.

25th Edith Harrison departed. I ought to have said that Harry gave gold locket sets with turquoise & pearls to all the bridesmaids. Such a day of arrangements & heat.

26th Wrote to Mrs Hull & to Milly. (How we miss our little child!) & to Louy.

27th Today they leave the Grosvenor Hotel for Scotland.

28th Sent wedding cake to many of the villagers.

31st Called on the Gibsons. The church alteration begun. Robert & Ella arrived.

September 5th Mrs Hull sent Lolotte another bracelet. To Leeds church with Ella, Gerard & Bobbie, ours being closed for repairs.

9th Ella, Bertha, Mary & Gerard all went to fetch Harry & Lolotte who arrive to a tea dinner & looking very well & in great spirits.

11th Harry left to pass the day in town & Robert & Ella for their Madehurst home.

13th The departure of our bride & groom delayed till next Tuesday I rejoice to say.

15th Mr Thomas very poorly during the night. In the morning of 16th I was obliged to send for Mr Sedgwick.

21st Lolotte & Harry left for Tehran. They sleep tonight at the Cannon Street Hotel & he takes out government dispatches.

27th A letter from Harry & Lolotte in Homburg. They had had a rough passage but she & Jenner *(her maid)* had borne it well.

28th I forgot to say that Frederic had seen them off from London & had presented Lolotte with a beautiful seal-skin muff & bag combined & Harry with a cigar case. Letter from Dr Lowry saying that poor Louis's want of sight is increasing. Letter from Man. *(where Gerard is staying with Louy)* In driving home Henry's horse, Gerard was run against by a grocer's cart (the latter was driving the wrong side of the road) & nearly killed.

October 2nd Gerard is detained in Man to appear as witness in the affair of the accident to Henry's horse.

5th Letter from Frederic with the dates of postage for letters to Tehran. Hired a little maid yesterday by name Isobel Tomline to take Jane's place.

7th Gerard arrived from Man giving a good account of the inhabitants of Greeba *(Louy & Henry's house)* & looking better himself for the change.

17th A letter from Dr Lowry saying that Louis had gone well through the operation of removing the cataract from one eye. It was done under the influence of chloroform.

22nd Called on Mrs Pusey, found her & Miss Pusey in great afflction on account of the great uncertainty with regard to the fate of the ship 'Metola' by which the eldest son was to arrive from New Zealand about the 4th August & which had not been heard of yet.

28th The 'Metola' the vessel in which young Pusey was to return is considered 'hopeless' at Lloyds.

30th To Maidstone with Mr Thomas to see Bertha into the train en route to Madehurst. Took Mary who is not well to see Mr Joy.

November 10th Richard at the last Turnpike meeting at the Dog & Bear Lenham.

12th Called on old Mrs Sellen & on Mrs Williams to take them each a flannel petticoat. Robert again out shooting.

14th To morning service. The pew-less chancel a great improvement.

19th Bertha & I drove to West Malling & took luncheon with the Savages where met Mrs Faunce & called on the Timmins. I went to see my brother but Dr Lowry would not allow me to have an interview with him for fear of excitement so he walked in the garden & came quite near without his seeing me, I saw him well. He does not look out of health but walks much bent.

20th Walked to the church with Mary. Mr George Duppa paid us a long visit.

23rd A letter from Mr Pierson saying that yesterday the long looked for telegram arrived & that on the 21st Harry & Lolotte had reached Tehran safely.

27th Gerard has passed <u>well</u> through the divinity school. Farkins went wrong last night.

28th Dear Lolotte 20 today we drank her health. Read some of Edward's 'Pursuit of Holiness'.

December 9th Since writing my journal we have given a dinner party, I have written to Anne Woollett & sent her £2, one from Milly & one from myself. We dined at the Best's. Many beautiful things about the house. Two magnificent Dresden china vases on brackets in the drawing room, brought from thence by Major Best etc.

10th I dreamt of dear little Lolotte & that I heard her speak as plainly as possible & the morning post brought a letter from her. She is delighted with her white Arab steed Jupiter, & gives a very interesting account of her travels. Bertha, Mary & I took luncheon at Milgate with Mr Brenchley & his brother Julius who showed us his museum of countless treasures. Seals of rock crystal from Russia, emus' eggs set in silver, Chinese carvings of the finest description, vases, china, costumes of the various nations etc. He is sending much to the British as well as the Maidstone museum.

13th Mr Thomas & Gerard out beagling.

16th Went to the ball at Linton with Bertha, Mary & Gerard, a very small party. The house looked lovely & so brilliant in lighting & decoration. The Prussian minister there & the Duchess of Cleveland gorgeous in green satin & diamonds. Lady Holmesdale looked very ill & much wasted.

21st Drove to Maidstone which was loaded with the wealth & abundance of Christmas. Met Captain Maunsell. A dinner party & a very successful one.

28th Expected Frederic & Lisa but they did not appear. We went to the Ball given by the R.H.A. beautifully decorated with banners & other such war-like implements, the stairs & passages lined with soldiers & evergreens & the evening very bright. Warm & cheerful within, but out of doors bitterly cold.

1870-1879: Keeping in touch

Although Louisa's daughters were now scattered, the efficient postal service meant that letters could be promptly and frequently exchanged even with Lolotte when she was in Persia or India and this greatly eased the anxiety and loss of parting. Not a day passed without letters being written and received from family and friends. All are noted in the journals. In 1870 Bertha and Mary still lived at home whilst Gerard was setting out on his legal career in London. By the end of the 1870s only Mary lived with her parents although Gerard was about to return to Hollingbourne with his bride to live in The Cottage.

When Bertha eventually married at the age of 29 in 1873 Louisa missed her more than she had Ella, Louy or Lolotte, for after each of their weddings the younger girls had remained to accompany her to dinners, balls, luncheons and archery meetings. Of all the girls Bertha was the most like her mother in her vivacity and love of social life. In some families a mother getting on in years would have been glad to relinquish attending such events but nothing was sweeter to Louisa than to be at a large social gathering. Of course Mary was still there most of the time. She was spared to stay with her sisters when they were having a baby. She also departed on purely pleasurable visits to see Aunt Milly in Germany or cousin Edward in Norwich. When at home however Mary preferred spending time on her chickens and on church matters. She did take after Louisa in that she kept a diary and these volumes remain in the possession of the family. Of all her siblings she was the most involved in local good works such as helping with the Sunday school, running the soup kitchen and visiting the sick. The regular winter making of soup for the village poor was instigated by Mary at this time and faithfully kept up. Of course she did not make the soup herself, that was a job for a servant, but she oversaw its making and distribution. The money for the ingredients was contributed not just by the Thomas family but also by others in the village. The poor paid a penny each for their helping.

Richard was an old man of 78 in 1870. He no longer attended balls and had ceased to dance many years earlier. This decade saw a dramatic decline in his health. Louisa continued to go to London as often as possible, the railways making it straightforward to take day-trips to shop and see friends and relatives. When Louisa met her old friend Colonel Horace Rochfort an M.P. for Ireland, in London in 1876 they had not seen each other for 40 years and it is clear how stimulating she found his company. Colonel Rochfort was the same age as Louisa, owned a large estate, Clogrenane House in Ireland, and was long married.

Louisa always enjoyed having many people in the house and we hear her lament how still and quiet the house is when the visit of one of the girls and her children comes to an end. As the girls each set up home Louisa often organised the appointment of servants for them. She got on well with her sons in law, Harry Pierson being a particular favourite. Harry is one of the few characters that we truly catch something of in the journals. We see his sense of fun, his artistic abilities, and athleticism. Back in England in 1874 he worked for a while at the regimental headquarters at Chatham as an instructor in field works. That same year he returned to India as secretary to the defence committee. Louy's less successful husband Henry Gipps often wrote to Louisa for advice on job applications.

When grandchildren became of an age to converse, Louisa enjoyed their company and all of them called her Nonna.[145] She faithfully kept up regular visits to her brother in his private asylum where he was well cared for and able to wander in its pleasant gardens.

Hollingbourne's vicar, the Rev. Gibson and his daughters were close friends of the family, Kate Gibson in particular became almost another daughter to Louisa.

1870 January 1st Heard the bells ring most cheerfully last night.

2nd The church temporarily heated with gas.

6th Bertha, Gerard & Mary dined & danced at the Moore's of Boughton Malherbe.

7th A visit from Mr Gibson about a subscription towards warming the church with gas. Bertha, Gerard & I dined at the Maunsell's, singing, dancing & Vingt-un.*(pontoon)*

13th A letter from Captain Pusey. They go to the south of France on Saturday for Miss Pusey's health. No tidings of the missing ship.

---

145   Italian for Grandma.

19th To the Sittingbourne Ball, not nearly light enough & a great mixture of people.

22nd Departed for Brighton & comfortable lodgings, 15 Oriental Place. Called on Mrs Hull & the Horace Smiths.

23rd To morning service at the parish church where Mr Wagner preached as usual. Five curates were in attendance. Called on Miss Moore & Mrs Hull.

28th Drove out in the afternoon Mrs Hull having lent us her carriage. On our return found an invitation for the ball at the Pavilion this evening. Gerard & Mary too ill to go but Bertha & I went. Such a lovely ball, warm & bright. Abundance of uniforms naval & military. A supper with every luxury, returned home at past 4.

29th Gerard left early, he was very poorly & seemed unfit for the journey. Called at the Halifax's, Gertrude 94, & very well but her mind fails much.

February 2nd The Fancy Ball at the Pavilion very amusing but hot & crowded. Bertha & Mary looked very well in their pink & silver wreaths. There were two Frosts, one Christmas, two or three Knights, one Bo-peep, one Red Riding Hood, and one Charles II.

4th Anne Woollett came again to see us. She looks very well & has an increase of £4 a year from the Percy Alms House fund. Saw a maid likely to suit me as Vidian is contemplating marriage. Bertha went to a ball.

5th Called on the Horace Smiths & bade farewell to them & Brighton. Delightful letter from Lolotte. Tehran seems the gayest place possible. Races, dances, cricket matches, dinners etc.

12th Dr Lowry enclosed the oculist's bill - £52-10 for nothing. Poor Louis is as blind as ever. Water in several of our rooms frozen.

March 2nd A great gulf in my journal, the greatest event has been the birth of Ella's first daughter on the 18th February. Both most flourishing.

3rd Richard went to the Quarter Sessions. We drove to call on Mr Leigh at Barham Court. Received dear little Lolotte's parcel from Tehran containing two Astrakhan lamb skins for Bertha & Mary & embroidered slippers for Richard, Gerard & myself.

23rd Richard & I drove to Malling. Saw poor dear Louis & took luncheon with the Savages. Bertha & Mary drank tea at the vicarage.

April 1st Took Gerard on his way to Madehurst. Such a still house.

3rd Richard & I went to morning service, Mr Gibson still preaching on Abraham.

15th Gerard, Bertha & I dined at the Maunsell's & met Mr Waller who is going to enter Gerard at the Middle Temple & give him all possible advice in the matter. He is to go to him to dine & sleep on Friday in Chester Square.

27th To London with Bertha, much shopping. Luncheon at Jessy's home.

May 4th Mr *(John)* Brenchley has left over £10,000 to the Maidstone Infirmary, the same to the Bishop of London's fund, £500 each to seven schools in Maidstone, £1000 to his clerk, £500 to his lawyer & £70,000 to his brother & sister.

7th Gerard is to be entered at the Inner Temple today, Frederic & Mr Waller being his sureties. Mr Minter attempted to drown himself at Sutton but was taken out just alive.

9th A letter from Mrs Minter begging me to fetch her poor husband out of jail.

10th Called on Mrs Bachelor Roper about Mrs Minter.

15th Gerard is admitted a student of the Middle Temple & has eaten his three dinners.

16th Mrs Valance, late Bourne, called. Then came the Dollings. Then came Vidian with some flowers she had learned to make in wool. Then we went to call on the Blunts & to the Dolling's for croquet.

23rd It is to be arranged that Mr Minter should emigrate as soon as he is released from gaol.

25th To the Yeomanry Review at Lord Romney's Park, to the ball in the evening.

26th Mary taken very ill after tea. Had to send for Dr Sedgwick. Richard in bed.

July 18th Such a void in my journal ! Bertha & I have stayed with Yeats & Dora in London. Mary has been very poorly, unfit for anything but to stay at home & today Dr Grayling has seen her & pronounces her better. And he has undertaken to be displayed at the Sittingbourne Archaeological meeting four coins found hereabouts & the old key from Godfrey House. There is a village cricket match between 'Married' & 'Single' in the front meadow in which Gerard is playing & the band is very gay under the trees.

The staircase in Louisa's home (courtesy Bryan Gipps)

19th Richard to London. Heat intense. Vidian wrote to announce her marriage to Mr Chittenden in London today.

20th Miss Edmed called to see us looking very well. Mr & Mrs Cobb halted at our gate in their drive & said that Bertha was called 'the Flower of Kent.'

21st Wrote to Milly to beg her to come here & leave the horrid war-ravaged land.

23rd Letters from Lolotte from Tehran. Jenner *(Lolotte's maid)* likely to come home as she still continues poorly. They are at their country house. Kate Gibson, Mary & I walked to the Union & saw the Matron about the boy Hudson.

August 2nd A letter from Edward who is gone to South Wales for a holiday. He has lost £2000 by Sir R. Hervey's bank, £1000 of which, a legacy, he desired to restore one of the chapels in Norwich cathedral.[146]

3rd To Sittingbourne to the Kent Archaeological meeting. A very grand luncheon at Dr Grayling's. First went to the church where Mr Scott Robertson lectured very well & where

---

[146]   During the years that Edward Goulburn was Dean of Norwich it is calculated he spent about £10,000 of his own money restoring the cathedral, largely from earnings from publishing his books.

he was met by Lord Amhurst, Lord Fitzwalter, Sir Walter Stirling, etc. Then the carriages appeared to convey the pilgrims to survey the Castles of Tong, Bayford, Murston etc. I stayed in Sittingbourne & called on the Walfords. Home about 7. Mary & Bertha made the grand tour with Mrs Riddell.

6th Mr Waller (*Master of the union workhouse*) came about Robert Hudson the boy for Henry. Wrote accordingly to the Isle of Man. *(He is to be sent to be a servant for Henry)*

8th A fearful battle. The French defeated.4000 prisoners taken & Paris declared in a state of siege. *(The Franco-Prussian War)*

11th Called on the Brasseys *(Preston Hall)* & Savages.[147] Gerard & I saw Louis.

13th Jessy came to stay & young Caroline. *(her daughter)*

16th Walked to the Union. Saw Robert Hudson in his new clothes. He came to see me again about 2 o'clock before starting for Man.

19th Milly seems to be in the midst of the wounded at Homburg & the Baron unceasing in his attentions at the hospital. Jessy & Caroline departed.

20th Henry & Louy highly approve Robert Hudson.

29th To the Russell's for luncheon & croquet, a very pleasant party. Robert & Ella arrived in the evening. The new baby very fine & fat & nice.

September 6th We went to Mary Dolling's *(daughter of vicar of Wormshill)* marriage to Mr Robertson. A pouring day unfortunately. The bridal party passed beneath the canopy of hops erected by the villagers & Mr Dolling ended the service. Then came the breakfast in a tent. Such a downpour the whole time & the poor bride quite overcome. Mr Dolling spoke well. Choir, farmers, schoolchildren & all were most liberally entertained, but the weather spoilt all.

9th At 8pm arrived Henry, Louy & their suite, such a houseful. Never had it contained so many souls before. We had much difficulty in finding a resting place for all, but we managed at last & in the midst of all our exertions we were without a cook for Hopper left yesterday & Anne Woollard did not arrive till this morning.

---

[147]   Henry Brassey M.P. (1840-1891) replaced Preston Hall, the old manor house of Aylesford,with the large new Gothic mansion. He was a great benefactor to Aylesford. The Brassey fortune had been made in railway building.

19th The Gipps children are lovely, especially Freddie. Mona, a very fine large-eyed child that can neither walk nor talk. Willie tall & fair & delicate looking.

23rd An early breakfast & Henry, Louy & their Belongings accompanied by Bertha left for their island home. Such a still house.

October 3rd Richard at the Sitting & Gerard & Mary off to Sheerness to meet Captain & Mrs Maunsell & see the 'Great Eastern'.

30th Mrs Green & Edith Duppa at luncheon. Craddock brought the tidings of Mr Wykeham Martin's death. *(of Leeds Castle)* The church bell of Leeds tolling.

November 2nd Richard out with the beagles. Killed 38 rabbits & two hares.

5th Letter from Bertha announcing that Louy's second daughter was born on 3rd & that the mother is going on most satisfactorily. Drove to Maidstone, shopping.

8th The bell at Leeds tolling very slowly for Mr Wykeham Martin's funeral. A letter from Mr Joyce who writes to say that he has forwarded a bottle of insects from Lolotte from Persia. Mary at luncheon at the Moore's at Boughton Malherbe.

9th Mr & Mrs Gibson at luncheon. Mr Wykeham Martin buried at Broomfield yesterday. Today the meeting at the school to decide whether it should be a rate school according to the government plan or not. The decision was to retain it as it is at present, adding 15 feet to each schoolroom. £30 subscribed in the room.

15th Letter from Lolotte, poor Jenner died at Shiraz while on her way home with Mr & Mrs Walton. She sank at last from sheer weakness without pain or suffering. Sent the news of it to her Father who came up in the evening to see us. A letter from Frederic who cannot say enough in praise of our dearest child in Tehran. Sent his letter to Mr Pierson. *(Harry's father)*.

21st Robert & Bobbie arrived, Bobbie very small & thin.

December 12th *(To London)* I reached Jessy's, found her quite well, dined at Yeat's.

19th *(At home)* We went to Mr Henneker's morning concert. Miss Sherrington literally <u>screamed</u> her songs though she has some good notes in her voice.

20th Bertha & I called on Mrs Walford whom we found sitting in her drawing room at Detling covered with rose coloured ribbons. The room much improved & enlarged. *(The Rev.*

Humphrey Walford had now left Sittingbourne & become vicar of Detling)

22nd Saw Mrs Andrews & hired her. (*for Louy as a nurse*)

27th Mary's birthday & today we have been married 32 years. The first thing that greeted us on our going down to breakfast this morning was a lovely table decoration. A vase of frosted glass with three shells at the base. The gift of our three dear children, Bertha, Mary & Gerard. Saw Mrs Andrews & arranged for her to go to Liverpool tomorrow en route for Man.

29th Sent off Mrs Andrews. Dora kindly promises that she shall be met in London.

30th The first distribution of soup to about 60 of the most needy of the parish.

1871 January 6th Bertha & Mary's third distribution of soup to the poor. 70 quarts given away.

9th Mr Wright the engineer of the projected railway & Mr Hughes the solicitor took luncheon here. Things still seem very uncertain. Bertha, Mary & Gerard dined at Captain Maunsell's, so Richard & I had an evening alone. I read to him.

12th Walked to Leeds Park to see the very few skaters, Gerard among the number. Mr John Roper *(Hollingbourne farmer)* buried today & his unjust will much talked over. His eldest son, quite without cause, not even mentioned in it.

13th Went to Lord Romney's park to see the skaters. Mr Gibson at luncheon full of Mr Roper & his horrid deception. Gerard skating at Leeds Castle by torch light.

24th Miss Edmed came to stay & Gerard departed. To a dance in the evening at the barracks, very pleasant, & though there were but few men Bertha & Mary had much dancing. The room was bright with light & scarlet coats.

24th Richard to London. Bertha & I to Malling to pass the day with the Savages. I also saw my brother, he looks healthy in body but rambling in his talk as usual.

27th Soup distribution of 88 quarts today at which Mary presided.

February 2nd To Maidstone with Bertha & Mary to the meeting at the Town Hall on the vagrancy question. Lord Sydney in the chair, magistrates innumerable.

17th Richard better & very rebellious as to medicine.

March 8th Richard more suffering but still refusing to see anyone. Mrs Wykeham Martin called.

18th Visited the Burkitts found Miss B busy with some very ugly ecclesiastical work designed by Gilbert Scott the younger.

Richard (painted by Louisa)

23rd To church, brilliant with gas & the congregation numerous.

24th Gerard & I walked to the Castle (*Leeds*) & went all over it with Mrs Wykeham Martin & her friend. Too large to live in, & the papers of the rooms frightful, but very warm & comfortable being heated with hot air. *(they had never been inside before)*

April 3rd The census taken last night. *(A night when Richard, Louisa, Bertha, Mary, Gerard & five servants were in the house. Craddock the coachman & his family were next door in their cottage which adjoined that of Gibson the gardener and his family.)*

15th Took Gerard to Maidstone on his way to Oxford & brought home Bobbie who had been left at the station en route from Cuxton.

19th To the ball given by the 7th Dragoon Guards. Poor Mary not well enough to go.

29th Bobbie has been here a fortnight. Crowhurst returned on Thursday after a week's absence. Mary is regaining her health & losing her rheumatism daily. The country is brilliantly green with almost constant rain. Wrote a week ago to Mr Walton about Jenner's box but have not received an answer.

May 7th A visit from Jenner (*deceased maid's father*) as stubborn & thankless as usual.

9th To the conversazione at the museum. Dr Monkton, Mr Brett the astronomer, Mr Wood the naturalist. The old building was quite lighted & illuminated for the occasion & there were numbers of the learned & the learning, male & female pacing the old halls, listening or contributing to the discussions & looking over the scientific machines & treasures of art & nature. We left at 10.30 in the midst of a lecture on Singing Flames, Sirens etc but which we were too far away to hear distinctly.

18th To the luncheon & inspection of the Militia, tea in the mess room of the barracks after the inspection. A very pleasant day.

30th Early to Maidstone to fetch Robert who has come in quest of Bobbie. Andrews has given notice.

June 3rd Jenner's box arrived by Honey the carrier.

5th Mr Gibson came to assist at the opening of Jenner's box. Little packets for all of us including Miss Edmed. Mine a beautiful silver saucer. Poor Jenner's sister. I quite pitied her in having to open her sister's box & look over all the little remembrances of her. We went to cricket & afternoon tea at Chilston.

7th The head of the telegraph works here came about the posts up this lane which seem to be satisfactorily arranged.

12th Left early for London, met Gerard at the Charing Cross station. Called on Mrs Treherne & then went on to Jessy. Then house hunting with Gerard. Such wandering up & down. At last fixed on one in Devonshire Street well situated & apparently well furnished. Home by the train reaching Maidstone at 11.15.

13th The bells ringing for the arrival of Mrs George Duppa.[148] Telegraph posts lying in front of our house.

---

[148] George Duppa married the beautiful Alice Miles who was 33 years younger than he. George had come to an arrangement with his nephew Frank whereby George took on Hollingbourne House & the estate.

16th To London, 56 Devonshire Street our lodgings, & very comfortable they were. We hoped to enjoy ourselves much & so we did.

24th Went to the opening of the new Conservatory in the Botanic Gardens. Such pouring rain that we delayed our going & missed the Royal Party. Richard started earlier & saw them all.

25th I took Crowhurst while the rest went to St Paul's, & attended service at the little old church in High Street Marylebone where my grandmother had a pew when we were children. After luncheon Yeats & Dora came to see us. Called on Mrs Bigge who was too ill to receive us. Colonel & Mrs Crawley called.

27th We went to The Row & saw all the gay people. Dined quietly with Yeats & Dora.

July 31st *(At home)* Mr Gibson's school treat, Mrs Gibson too poorly to appear. Visited her in her room. A very full party, 160 children besides the guests. Mrs Duppa, Mrs Green & her children were there.

August 2nd Joined the archaeological excursion to Knole. Most interesting, the old house so very beautiful & the relics it contains in the way of pictures, furniture etc innumerable. A Mr Calthorpe whose picture of 'The School for Scandal' is in the Exhibition of the Academy this year was our conductor. About 600 present & 300 at the dinner where Lord Stanhope presided.

27th Robert & Ella have been staying with us a few days & departed with Jack & Eleanor. There has been another archery meeting & Gerard has won the prize for the centre gold. The Miss Roopers from Ouseley Lodge *(Windsor)* have been staying here & accompanied us. We have also had two dinner parties at home. There has been a large meeting & dejeuner given by the military, a croquet party at the Dolling's & the invitations have been countless. Today, Sunday, I did not go to church till evening when Mr Edwards preached, a worn elderly man but his sermon on Christian love very good. It is said that he really practises what he preaches & that he will dine on dry bread to give his dinner to a poor man. He is curate at Maidstone.

27th The Flower Show but did not go, sent our four maids instead. To the archery ball in the evening a full & bright one. The 7th Dragoon Guards leave today.

31st I went into Maidstone & brought out Ella & her baby & nurse. The rest came in a fly.

September 4th Richard at the sitting, Gerard & Robert up The Hill. Ella, Bertha the two boys & I shopping preparatory to Bertha's departure for Scotland.

18th Started for Malling with Gerard & Mary. Left Mary at the Savages & G & I to Dr Lowry's. Louis better in heath, in very good spirits but full of the Queen & soon dismissing us. Went all over the grounds & gardens of St Leonards. Saw them filling the hop sacks by machinery. Left cards at Preston Hall.

22nd Went to the Mote Park cricket match. The Gibsons *(the vicar's daughters)* in their scarlet & blue shawls gave quite a mass of colour to the picture.

October 5th Crowhurst & I started early for London. Much shopping for Lolotte.

20th Frederic cannot come tomorrow but Gerard's appointment decided.[149] Telegraphed to him.

21st Gerard arrived from Oxford.

23rd Gerard departed early for London. I visited Mrs Sage, Mrs Warman, & Mrs Seers. *(poor old village women)*

24th Mr Rigden thrown from his horse yesterday while out hunting & killed on the spot. Gerard arrived.

25th Immense shopping in Maidstone for Gerard who has much to prepare.

27th Frederic wrote to say that Gerard will leave with him in a few days & Gerard started early for London. His boxes arrived from Oxford yesterday. Such a scene of ruin when the porcelain was unpacked.

November 1st Gerard off to London. About 4 o'clock like a shell burst among us a telegram from Gerard announcing his arrival tonight & that his things must all be ready for packing to depart early tomorrow. He arrived about 10 & half the night was spent in packing & arranging.

2nd Gerard departed at 8 to breakfast with the Persian Ambassador.

3rd Went to see Mrs Sellen, Mrs Chapman & also visited Mrs Gibson. Gerard returned at 10 o'clock having eaten his

---

[149]   Gerard was appointed Frederic's private secretary. Sir Frederic had become a commissioner for the delineation of the boundary between Persia and Baluchistan. In India he had been on the staff of the Chief Commissioner. He then became involved in the vast scheme to connect Europe and India by overland telegraph. He had negotiated the Anglo-Persian Telegraph treaty in 1865, and in 1866 had superintended the construction of the telegraph line across the whole of Persia.

Persian breakfast yesterday & been very busy all day in London & at Harrow.

Louisa's drawing room (courtesy Bryan Gipps)

5th Frederic a 'Knight Commander of 'the Star of India'.

7th Sir Frederic came down to meet me at Maidstone by the 12 train & was off again at 12.35. "Bright tho' brief", for he is so very happy in his new appointment & honour.

9th Gerard left on his long tour. A lovely still night. He will have a fine passage from Dover to Ostend.

11th Sent Ella a bonnet by Crowhurst who is gone to see her relations for a week. Kate Gibson called.

12th Heard Harry is appointed director of the Persian telegraph.

19th At church saw Mr George Duppa who seems to have had no end of anxiety about Mrs Duppa. Kate Gibson at luncheon. Mary still very poorly.

22nd Mrs Green & Edith Duppa at luncheon, Dr Prothero Smith had £150 for coming from London to attend Mrs Duppa. *(at her confinement)*

24th Yesterday a letter from Mr Pierson to say that Captain F. Pierson *(Harry's brother)* had just sent home a tiger skin shot by himself for Lolotte & that he had had it made into a rug which he wished us to keep for her.

25th A letter from Bertha telling that another son was born to Henry & Louy on the 22nd A very large child & Louy is going on well. An immense tiger skin arrived.

26th Heard from Gerard from Alexandria. He is as well & happy as can be & much enjoying his 'roving'. Mary rather better.

December 11th Today the papers announce that all hope is over for the Prince of Wales but he still lingers. Busy all morning repairing broken china with Coagaline.

14th Australian Beef for dinner very good.

15th Heard from Lady Goldsmid that she had received a telegram of the arrival of Gerard & the rest of the party at Karachi. All well.

21st To the Poultry Show early. Met the Maunsells there. A most wonderful gathering of chickens. In the evening went to the Linton Ball which was a most pleasant one. The Duchess of St Albans, the Duke & Duchess of Montrose, & Lady D. Beauclerk making herself very conspicuous, small as she is. Made a promenade to supper with Captain Roberts. Stayed till the last & reached home at 4.

22nd Walked up The Hill to call on Mrs Duppa. Saw her looking just like 'wax-work' & the Baby magnificently attired in embroidery & lace.

23rd To Maidstone early for Mary & Willie's teeth. Poor Willie *(Bertha has brought back Louy's son Willie with her)* had to return as he went & he is very poorly. The town in great confusion & dirt but full of Christmas crowds & preparation.

26th We gave 6lbs Australian meat yesterday to the poor instead of our usual gift of 5lbs English beef. Mary Riddell at luncheon & Kate Gibson in the afternoon.

28th A magnificent ball at the Henry Brassey's Preston Hall. The house gorgeous. All gold & light. Music & supper perfect & our daughters much enjoyed themselves. Home at 4.30.[150]

29th Letter from Lolotte. Harry is acting director of the Persian Telegraph at a salary of £1600 per annum & horse allowance.

30th A letter from Gerard from Bombay. All well. But no gun boat ready for them at Aden a great disappointment.

---

[150]   It is no wonder that everything was magnificent for the Brasseys had 27 servants living in the house & 12 living in the stable block caring for the horses.

1872 January 2nd A loving telegram from Lolotte wishing their relations a Happy New Year. The message travelled 6000 miles in 4 hours. [151]

8th Called on the Burkitts. Miss Burkitt hard at work as usual. She is now embroidering an altar cloth for India.

20th Gerard is at Muscat *(now the capital of Oman)* on the point of being presented to the Sultan.

23rd To the Sittingbourne ball, rather empty & rather mixed. Mrs Duppa looked very beautiful in her new diamonds.

February 3rd Mr & Mrs Duppa sent £3 for the soup club & Mr J. Roper *(farmer)* a sack of potatoes.

4th Between 6 & 7 a wonderful Aurora Borealis lasting till 12. The stars brilliantly white through the red vapour.

6th Willie & I walked to Leeds to see Miss Burkitt's work, white silk with roses, fleurs de lis, wheat ears & grapes embroidered on it. The upper part crimson velvet set with passion flowers.

10th A memorable day to me. God grant that I may amend! *(She must have said some terrible things)*

11th The worst headache I ever had.

12th Sent Valentines to Ernst, to Madehurst & to Man. Bertha, Mary & I dined at Captain Maunsell's. A very agreeable dinner.

18th A letter from Lolotte at Isfahan she is very well & <u>very</u> happy. They rode for Tehran by journeys of about 20 miles a day & did much to relieve the starving population on their way.[152]

27th The thanksgiving day for the recovery of the Prince of Wales. London in such a commotion & we are so still!!

March 18th A confirmation here by the Bishop of Dover of over 100 from the surrounding parishes. Luncheon at the vicarage afterwards, Riddells, Duppas, etc.

19th Mary & I, with Crowhurst, left early for Brighton where we saw many of our old friends – Horace Smiths, Guinesses, Lady Abinger, Miss Halifax. Mrs Hull was better than I expected & kindly lent us her carriage to go to Preston to see my dearest mother's grave. Anne Woollett drank tea with us one evening. We were located at 25 Oriental Place, the first house we ever inhabited in Brighton. We heard Mr Vaughan

---

[151]   The first telegram sent within Britain was in 1845 & by 1850 they were known as telegrams.

[152]   There was famine in Persia in 1871. Harry gave all his energy to helping the starving population.

preach a very good sermon. We went to Madehurst & saw Robert & dearest Ella & their blooming children. Bobbie much grown. March 26th found ourselves again at Hollingbourne.

April 4th To the Military hurdle race on Detling Hill. Weather gloomy & cold but Bertha enjoyed it much & was in the officers' waggonette from whence she could see all well. The luncheon in a tent. Everything beautifully arranged but the clay soil was very damp & the chairs sank deep into it. Everyone there but Mr Thomas & Mary who remained at home.

6th A stag turned out in a field called 'Bricketts'. Carriages, people on foot in numbers & about 300 horsemen. The stag went up the hill by Harrietsham & Lenham to Torry Hill & then came back & was taken in the Moat at Leeds Castle.

7th Gerard 24 today. Where he is we know not but we fancy that he is near Tehran & Lolotte. Drank his health.

10th Mary rode to Boughton Malherbe to arrange about travelling to Germany with Mary Moore.

16th Ella's little daughter born on the 13th. Bertha & I dined at Major Bertie Robert's.

29th To London early with Richard & Bertha. Shopping first then a visit to Mr Reginald Palgrave, Speakers Court, Palace of Westminster. Thought him & his wife very agreeable. Richard met us at the Charing Cross station.[153]

May 14th Train for London, Bertha, Crowhurst & I. Found our way to the St Pancras station & left for Norwich. Such a flat country! Passed the distant spires of Cambridge & the nearer & most beautiful Ely cathedral, otherwise all was flat & marshy in the extreme, pollards, poplars & rushes abounding. At Norwich Edward's carriage & two plump grey horses awaiting to take us to the Deanery. Such a a delightful old house! Full of ancient remains. Julia & he all kindness. In the evening he & Gussy sang comic songs. Prayers in the library.

15th With Edward & Julia to Eaton a neighbouring village where the Mayor, Mr Chamberlain was to lay the first stone of a new church. Edward preached beautifully on the occasion at the old parish church, much painted & decorated & then walked in procession from the house of Mr Bolingbroke, the ex-mayor, to the scene of the ceremony where hymns &

---

[153] Sir Reginald Palgrave (1829-1904), Clerk to the House of Commons lived in an official residence within the Palace of Westminster.

227

prayers were sung & said. A silver trowel was given to the mayor, the coins placed beneath in a cavity & the stone descended on them. We repaired to a sumptuous dejeuner at Mr Bolingbroke's house. A dinner party at the Deanery. The Master of St Katherine's College Cambridge, Dr Robinson & his wife there, a very pleasant evening. Mrs Robinson & Bertha sang & Edward made himself very agreeable.

Edward Goulburn Dean of Norwich
(with thanks to the Dean & Chapter of Norwich cathedral &
Ben Smith Photography)

17th Today was another dinner. In the afternoon Julia & I called on Mrs Canon Heaviside. Such a charming view of the

Cathedral from her garden, & then we walked round the old town & saw the Castle & Market Place. Bought some point lace patterns & some photos. Yesterday I went all over the fine cathedral with Edward & saw his restorations.*(Edward was a very sociable man, immensely hard-working and scholarly. He had considerable private means inherited from his father in particular. In 1877 on the death of his brother Freddy he inherited more. He had a special affinity with the sick, the dying & the bereaved.)*

18th Mr & Mr Wilder came in during the afternoon.

19th Took the sacrament in the grand cathedral at 8 o'clock. Attended morning service at 11 when Edward preached, & afternoon service with only the litany & anthem.

20th A thanksgiving for the Prince's recovery & also the celebration of the Queen's birthday by a review, athletic sports, the mayor's great dejeuner of 550 in St Andrew's Hall to which we went with Edward & Julia & fireworks. Edward spoke very well.

22nd (At home) Preparations for Mary's departure tomorrow.*(to stay with Milly in Homburg)*

29th The village all alive with the club & bands & garlands. The sunshine very bright. Willie delighted.

June 6th To Maidstone accompanied by Willie, & Anne Woollett. *(who is staying)*

7th Gerard & Lolotte met at Tehran yesterday. What a happiness for both.

29th A letter from Mr Frank Bigge telling of the death of his dear old mother.

July 3rd Richard, Bertha & I dined at the Douglas's, dancing in the evening.

8th News that Miss Pooley had been killed at Sutton Valance by the sail of Mr Robinson's windmill which proved to be only too true.[154]

12th Little Miss Pooley buried. Bertha set a wreath of white roses & lilies for the coffin, Agnes Gibson a larger wreath, & Mrs Laurence a cross of hot-house flowers. The poor little woman was at church & well last Sunday & next Sunday we shall pass her grave.

---

[154]   The local paper reported that Louisa Pooley, daughter of the plumber, was universally beloved for her constant kindness to those in need of help. The children of the Sunday school were in the funeral procession and every house in the village had the curtains closed as a mark of respect.

14th Mr Gibson alluded in his sermon to Miss Pooley's death. Her grave as we passed it near the church meadow gate was covered with flowers. She bore the highest character possible for active goodness. *(Louisa Pooley was 37)*

16th To a ball at Linton to meet H.R.H. Prince Arthur. Lady Holmesdale so ill that she was lying on the sofa the greatest part of the evening & retired early to bed. Prince Arthur looked very nice, like most of the Royal Family.

18th The first archery meeting, held at Mr Brassey's Preston Hall. Such a lovely ground! And a very pleasant day.

19th Richard & I to London, went to the Royal Academy where passed the most agreeable morning by myself. Met Louy & her child Mona at the Charing Cross station. *(coming to stay)*

23rd A letter from Mr Carter Hall to announce his approaching marriage with Mrs Starbuck.

29th The first flower show of Hollingbourne held in Mr Lawrence's field. Very successful. Mrs Duppa called & asked us to chaperone Maud to it.

August 3rd Letters from Gerard & Lolotte in Tehran, so very happy. Called on the Maunsells & took them a couple of chickens of Mary's breed in return for their mixed Dorkings.

10th Lady Goldsmid, Lisa & Patricia passed the day here from Folkestone.

12th Louy & her bairns left us for London en route to Liverpool, Willie looking very poorly & pale. He has been here now nearly 8 months. Richard accompanied us to Maidstone.

15th To the school treat which went off very well, tea on the lawn. Some mountebanks & acrobats but they did not stay long.

22nd Took Bertha to Headcorn. She is gone to stay at Folkestone with Lady Goldsmid.

23rd Walked up the village with Richard to see the repairs & renewal of the Kings Head & the Malt House. The timber of the latter not dark enough.

26th Robert & Ella & the three younger children arrived & Bertha an hour later, so the house is now full again.

27th Robert went to Cuxton early, & Bertha & I attended the last archery meeting.

28th To a cricket meeting at Major Bertie Robert's. Tea made & served in a tent & the kettle boiled, gipsy-like on the ground.

September 2nd We went to a croquet party at the Russell's. I heard from Mary that Gerard was very ill in Berlin & the Baron, all kindness, went to fetch him.

9th In the evening while we were at tea, quite unexpectedly, appeared Mary & Gerard. The former in robust health, the latter pulled & thin, but not much tired with his journey. How much we shall have to talk of!

The dining room in Louisa's house
(courtesy Bryan Gipps)

20th Gerard out shooting & so poorly & chilled on his return that he retired to bed.

28th Sent for Mr Sedgwick as Gerard was still so ill & still keeps his bed. The chills & heats he suffers from are extreme.

26th Gerard still so far from well that we telegraphed for Dr Grayling who pronounced his fever 'an exotic' arising from paludial *(malarial)* poison. Changed the medicine & put him on a new system. To the archery ball in the evening.

27th Drove to Maidstone with Bobbie, Lewis *(Bobbie's brother)* & Crowhurst & called on the Maunsells. Gerard better but still weak & poorly.

30th To Maidstone with Bertha, Bobbie & Lewis. To the museum new rooms & gardens which Mr Julius Brenchley is to give to the town. A most munificent present & they will be very fine.

October 3rd Letter from Lolotte who has had her first attack of Persian fever but now seems quite well again. Brewing. Mr Gibson at luncheon.

7th Out sketching with Mary. Prepared a parcel for Lolotte. Called on the Duppas & saw the baby, also on the Dollings just departing for 6 months.

10th To Maidstone to fetch Frederic who passed a few hours with us, & then carried away Bertha to Harrow. He looks very well.[155]

21st Gerard not feeling well. Sent for Mr Sedgwick.

November 1st A telegram for Gerard from Frederic asking him to dine today to meet Sir Bartle Frere.[156] Mary & I took him to Maidstone.

5th The village carnival & all the little boys in masks & a horrible noise all day long.

6th Gerard arrived last night quite well. 250 present at Sir Bartle Frere's dinner & the ladies, among whom was Bertha, came in the evening to hear the speeches.

December 6th To Malling, found Louis much as usual & not nearly so excitable as formerly. He walked about the grounds with us & tho' quite blind poor fellow, is not depressed. He seemed delighted to see Richard.

12th Went to the passage of arms at the Depot. We also saw boxing, fencing, single stick, broad sword, quarter staff etc. The leaping, swinging etc was <u>only not</u> flying but came very near it. Richard & Kate Gibson accompanied us.

24th Richard, Gerard & I to Maidstone to fetch Mary. Carols & hand-bells in the evening.

25th Just as I was ready for church Gerard taken ill so I remained at home with him.

27th To Maidstone with Mary, no end of shopping to be done preparing her for Man & Ireland.

1873 January 3rd Started early, Richard, Gerard, Crowhurst & I. Drove to Headcorn where got into the train & about 12 found ourselves at Dover. Took a fly & went to each house with tickets in the window & at last decided on 20 Waterloo Crescent. Very clean & nice. Many acquaintances. Saw Prince

---

[155]   In 1870 Frederic resigned the directorship of the Indo-European Telegraph. Later he was asked to investigate the claims of Persia and Afghanistan to the province of Seistan and it was his impartial conclusion which kept the peace. He wrote about this in the two volume 'Eastern Persia'. He retired from the army in 1875 with the rank of major-general.

[156]   Sir Bartle Frere (1815-1884) was an acclaimed British colonial administrator.

Arthur who embarked for Calais during our stay which was also rendered memorable by the death of the French Emperor. Went one day to the pier to see the arrival of all the French who came to be present at his funeral.[157] Richard departed on 14th & we followed on the 17th having been at Dover a fortnight & inhaled all the sea air we could. Gerard seems much better for the change. Bertha has had the chicken pox but is well again & Mary is gone to the Isle of Man. Mr Frederick Bigge & his brothers have kindly sent me a turquoise ring as a remembrance of their dear old mother.

23rd News of another Gipps grandson. We went all over Leeds Castle with Mrs Martin who was a capital guide, but it is an immense undertaking & I was quite worn out though I did sit down by the clock instead of mounting the tower.

24th Bertha full of preparation for Jessy's ball. Poor Mary has the chicken pox at Greeba. *(Louy's house)* Henry's new appointment to the South Lancashire Volunteers is at Bury. They say it is all smoke & blackness & manufactures.

27th Bertha & Gerard departed to be at the meeting of the Geographical Society.

28th Gerard returned home having been too ill to be present at the meeting.

31st Heard from Bertha, Jessy's first ball a delightful one. Gerard left for Oxford.

February 18th Charlotte Summers who once lived here as housemaid came to see me. We had not met her for 24 years. She has been 11 years in service in Berlin.

25th Bertha began her first distribution of soup to the poor.

28th Bertha's second distribution of soup. Mr Gibson at luncheon. He told us that Mr Brenchley is to have a public funeral at Maidstone.

March 3rd Mr Brenchley buried at All Saints today. A letter from Gerard who had been to the House & heard Gladstone, Cardwell & Goschen.

14th Went to see the soup distribution, Mrs Hilton & Kate Gibson assisting Bertha.

22nd On arriving at Sir William Mahon's, Craddock drove too near the gate, it is a very bad entrance, took the wheel off the carriage, gave us a tremendous shake, & for some time we were unable to get a wheel. However this was accomplished

---

[157]   The French Emperor Napoleon III died at Chislehurst on 9th January.

after some difficulty & we took luncheon with our friends. The carriage being bound up with ropes, conveyed us home.

April 1st To London with Bertha, much shopping & took luncheon with Jessy. She very gorgeous in mauve satin & black velvet.

7th In the afternoon Crowhurst & I left for Ostend, Bertha accompanying us as far as Headcorn. Reached Dover that night & slept at 20, Waterloo Crescent.

8th Boat to Ostend, wretched weather & a very rough passage. Towards the end became very sick. The Baron & Milly awaiting us. Went to the Hotel de Prusse. Milly & the Baron looking much as usual. Ernst poorly with a cough. Dinner at 6 in the public room. Everything very nice.

9th Breakfast in the same room with the same companions as last night. Sauntered about Ostend, into the fine old church, old curiosity shops etc.

10th At 12 left for Bruges, hired a laquais de place & saw all the churches & pictures that were to be seen. The cathedral & its treasures, Notre Dame & its wonderful monuments of Charles of Burgundy & his daughter. The hospital of St John, the chapel of the Holy Blood. A delightful but tiring day.

12th To Bruges as before, Milly, Crowhurst & I. A very fine day, saw no end of old lace & china hoards, bought some beautiful lappets & hundreds, I might almost say thousands, of Delft plates.

14th Bade farewell to my dearest Siss & to the Baron & Ernst. Embarked on board the steamer. Such a lovely day & passage. Carriage awaiting us at Headcorn.

16th To the Military ball. Very brilliant. Went to supper with George Duppa.

28th A concert in the evening at the Manor House, kindly lent by Mr & Mrs Roper. The performance in the hall. Mrs Kingdom, Bertha, Kate Gibson, Emmy Gibson, the performers. Among the audience, for the hall was crowded, were Balstons, Riddells, W. Martins, Miss Burkitt. The Gas was brilliant. The platform decorated with flowers, the stone floor carpeted, in fact all was as well arranged as possible.

29th A walk with Henry to Leeds to call on Mrs Burkitt. Bertha & I dined with Major & Mrs Bertie Roberts. A first rate dinner, a table overspread with flowers.

May 2nd Henry left for London. Went to the museum. The Brenchley collection wonderful, stuffed birds, shells, china etc. A telegram from Henry to tell that Renfrew was all but certain.

5th Letter telling of poor dear Anne Woollett's death.

16th Drove to Sittingbourne & left by train for Canterbury where Mr Petley (*of the East Kent Militia who had invited them to the ball & trooping of the colours*), met us & we took up our quarters at The Rose a nice clean hotel & very full. To the Militia Ball in the evening, a very good one.

17th To the colour trooping. Walked with Mr Petley to the Faussett's House in the precincts. After the ceremony called on the Graylings at 'The Priory' & saw Mrs G, a very pretty & placid old lady aged 86. Mr Petley came to The Rose to fetch us to a very grand militia luncheon, about 80 people. No dinner party at the Duppa's, Mrs Savage *(neé Duppa)* being scarcely expected to live from hour to hour. A letter from Henry. They leave for Glasgow on Monday.

19th Carrie Goldsmid arrived at 12 & Ella & her three younger children at 4.

21st Ella beginning to look better than at first. She is still however very thin & worn. The baby, her namesake is a lovely little child.

25th Jack *(Ella's son)* went to church for the first time, under Mary's care & behaved very well.

June 7th Orders arrived from Robert for Ella to return home on Monday.

9th Ella I grieve to say departed. We went to an archery meeting.

17th Drove to Maidstone to fetch Mary. A letter from George Duppa to ask us to see the Shah *(of Persia)* land.

18th Started early with Mary for Dover. Took luncheon with Mr & Mrs G. Duppa at Number One, Esplanade. Such a glorious day! Such a sight! The sea deep blue & alive with shipping. The yachts lovely, & when the mighty Ironclads appeared round the South Foreland the sight was beyond words. Then all the guns sounded when the Shah came in sight & when his foot first touched English ground they positively boomed from all points of the compass. Mrs Duppa looked beautiful. Dover quite en fete & swarming with people. Our return home tedious.

21st A letter from Louy, Henry much likes his corps, officers & men.[158] A telegram from Gerard who has passed most successfully.

23rd Ellen Woollett came to see me in sad trouble from the loss of her sister.

25th A letter from Bertha who had seen the Shah pass down the Floral Hall to the opera, all gems & splendour. Gerard arrived.

July 7th A letter from Gerard who is now M.A., he returns today.

14th To London early with Richard. Met Gerard & Bertha at Waterloo House. Then on with them to the Royal Academy where we were joined by Mr Morgan whom I liked much. Luncheon at Frederic's & home. Bertha's answer to be given tomorrow. *(Bertha being older has not asked permission to marry)*

16th A letter from Bertha to say that Mr Morgan is to be our future son in law & will be down today. So we fetched him from the station & conveyed him to the archery meeting where Mary won a prize for best gold.

17th The conversation with Mr Thomas took place & went off very well & Mr Morgan left us after luncheon.

August 6th Bertha has been engaged for some weeks to Delmar Morgan & now all things are progressing.[159] Yesterday was the 2nd archery meeting, held at Leybourne Grange. Today I have heard from Mrs Balston that Mr Surtees says 'Bertha will be a crown of glory to her husband'. To the school treat at Mr Gibson's.

12th To a croquet & archery party at Barham Court, very pleasant. The table spread with fruit & cakes & about 60 people present. Mrs Morgan arrived.

15th To Maidstone with Mrs Morgan. She gave Bertha a magnificent brooch of aquamarines & diamonds which had been given to her by the Emperor of Russia.

16th Mrs Morgan & Delmar departed. She also gave Bertha a gold chain. The wedding dress arrived from Elise, & Bertha sent Delmar's wedding present; an inkstand & some candlesticks.

---

[158]   Henry has become adjutant of the Renfrewshire Rifles. They have moved to Paisley.

[159]   Edward Delmar-Morgan was then 33 & wealthy. After leaving Eton he had lived for some years with his parents in St Petersburg. He was a linguist & traveller.

18th Delmar appeared most unexpectedly & took Bertha back with him to Herne Bay. (S*he stayed so his mother must have been there)*

23rd Frederic & Katie arrived from London & Bertha & I went to fetch them. Frederic very poorly. Delmar came yesterday bringing Bertha home.

25th A walk to Leeds Castle with Sir Fred, took him to Maidstone & saw him off.

26th To the archery meeting at Mr Brassey's, very full. On our return in the evening found Delmar bringing gifts from Mr Morgan *(his father)*. A belt of gold & silver thread studded with silver, a dress of Persian silk, malachite candlesticks, an amber necklace & gorgeous diamond earrings.

28th To a garden party at Mr Douglas's, all the neighbourhood there. The delightful band of the marines played beautifully. In the evening the archery ball.

September 3rd Mrs Balston came to afternoon tea & brought Bertha a lovely present for having tea in the bedroom, combining both cup & plate.

9th Delmar arrived bringing a beautiful bracelet of stones from the Helmund for Bertha from Frederic. A letter from Lolotte who expects to be on the 'Lord Warden' in Dover October 14th.

24th A dinner party to which came Edward, Frederic & his daughter Lisa, Delmar & his cousin Mr H. Morgan rector of St Johns Newbury. Bertha Clayton, staying here, Henry & Louy also staying here, Mr Gibson & Captain Wright of the 9th.

25th The sun dawned on a bright day when, attended by six bridesmaids, Richard gave his third daughter in marriage to Delmar Morgan. Jessy, Carrie & Bartle Goldsmid, Ella & Mr Egerton Hubbard arrived at cock-crow for the early breakfast. & later appeared Mrs Morgan & many more. Edward read the service beautifully, assisted by Mr Gibson & Mr H. Morgan & then arrived bell ringers, band playing, flowers etc. After a sumptuous breakfast the newly married, accompanied by Wilson, left for the Italian Lakes & Venice. The bridesmaids were Mary, Kate Gibson, Lisa Goldsmid, Bertha Clayton, Cordy Hamilton & Flora Lancaster Lucas. The best man Egerton Hubbard, the other grooms-men Gerard, Captain Bingham Wright, Jack Hamilton, Mr Akers, & Bartle Goldsmid.

Since this day all sorts of events have occurred. Milly arrived unexpectedly from Germany & stayed over a fortnight. Louy remained a month. Robert Shaw came one week. Gerard has taken up his abode in London, & last but not least Harry & Lolotte have arrived from Tehran & accompanied by Milly we went to Charing Cross to meet them. Poor dear Lolotte had fallen out of a window, one very dark & stormy night on to a pile of bricks. One can scarcely imagine how she escaped, but God in his mercy preserved her to us. She & Harry have been staying here with their friend Mr E. Ellis (Lord Howard de Walden's son) & she seems already better for the change. Last Thursday they departed for London.

November 9th Received a present from Edward of his new work 'the Gospel of the Childhood'. Mr Ellis gave me one of the ancient beads or cylinders from Babylon at least 2000 years old.

13th Started early with Richard for London, he left us at Canon Street & I went on to Charing Cross where Gerard met me. Then to Gerard's rooms at 8 Jermyn Street. Next went to Gustave Dore's wonderful pictures. It is impossible to describe the light & shadows, the countless figures, the depth & grandeur of almost all his productions. From thence we returned to Gerard's to luncheon where we were met by Lolotte & Harry who had just taken the rooms beneath him, & by Delmer & Bertha in great spirits.

18th Mr & Mrs Frederick Bigge came to stay. Dinner party went off <u>very</u> well.

19th Poor Mary still with her face swollen. Gerard out shooting all day & left in the evening. We took luncheon at the Duppa's accompanied by Mr & Mrs Bigge.

24th Larkin's men packing all day for Bertha & Delmar who departed by train.

25th The house seems now quite empty, both of the animate & inanimate. So much has disappeared with Bertha.

27th Shopping with Mary & Mr Thomas, called on Miss Edmed taking with us Bertha's present, a mosaic brooch, with which she was much pleased.

28th Gerard is to be made a Fellow of the Royal Geographical Society & has also been admitted a member of the Universities' Club.

29th To Maidstone to fetch Harry & Lolotte, she is not looking well.

December 1st Harry & Lolotte packing & departing.

3rd Mary being better today we drove to the poultry show, the birds wonderful in size, condition & noise. Mr Ellis arrived with Gerard, dogs, photographic equipment etc.

4th A very dull misty day but still did not prevent our photographer from attempting the house from the lawn meadow & in this he was very successful. He brought me some blue Egyptian beads from a tomb, the view of the house from the window of which Lolotte fell, & some bricks from Babylon with the name Nebuchadnezzar inscribed on one.

6th Mr Ellis, Mary & Gerard left for Jermyn Street, our house is now very still & empty. Richard & I had our quiet tea together & heard no voices but our own.

10th Bertha 29 today. Called on old Mrs Bolton & took her a pair of knee caps. Mr Gibson at luncheon & Mrs G, Kate & Agnes called afterwards.

13th Mrs Balston came & we started in her little carriage for Leeds Castle where many met on horse & foot & after seeing the Meet we drove towards Greenway Court over ruts & clods & clay & saw the stag followed after a while by the dogs. Lost sight of both. Kate Gibson called on me & we had a long talk on heraldry.

22nd Started for London, at Charing Cross was met by Bertha & Delmar who kindly carried me off to see Holman Hunt's picture 'The Shadow of the Cross'. Then we went to take luncheon at Mrs Morgan's, 19 Queens Gardens, where soon appeared Harry, Lolotte, Mary & Lisa. My day was only too short, & a great happiness it was to see Bertha so thoroughly appreciated.

24th Mr Ellis sent Gerard some mummied heads & embalmed bits from Egypt.

25th The church very nicely decorated. A most unhappy Christmas to me. (without Bertha)

29th Drove to Maidstone with Mr Thomas & Gerard, purchased a clock as a present to Frederic & Lady Goldsmid on their silver wedding. It is I think very beautiful, porcelain & old. Barling is to forward it in perfect order.

30th Took the little Craddocks some presents. A tea party at the Wesleyan chapel for the children, also at the vicarage for the church children & a Penny Reading.

1874 January 1st Gerard took the mummies to the museum at Maidstone.

2nd Continued my portrait of Gerard, he & I dined with Mr & Mrs Hilton.

3rd Delmar & Bertha arrived to tea, but no Mary, She had remained in London for the Pantomime.

6th Delmar & Bertha left. They start for St Petersburg on Thursday. Gerard, Mary & I went to a Christmas tree at Captain Maunsell's. It was a pleasant evening with games, dancing & supper & the tree was very brilliant.

9th Robert came early & took luncheon. He does not look well & seems quite upset. Besides the death of his father he has much to try him.

10th Gerard departed for London. Crayford the gardener is to leave on Monday but before going has made an immense commotion in the house, bringing accusations against Mary, but especially against Craddock.

12th Crayford departed after having given utterance to a string of falsehoods & blackened the name of everyone within his reach. Harris arrived. A letter from Mrs Dolling announcing that the Dean of Waterford has taken the living of Wormshill for the winter.

27th Mrs Duppa came & in about half an hour after she had left, she returned with her nurse & two babies having been thrown out of the pony carriage. The pony kicked, but how otherwise the accident happened no one can tell. The carriage is entirely destroyed, children bruised & bleeding. Mr Sedgwick was sent for, but tho' everyone was much alarmed, no bones were broken.

28th Drove up The Hill called on the Dean of Waterford (Hoare) & his wife, & afterwards to see Mrs Duppa whom we found quite well only a little stiff. Mr Duppa was lying on the sofa in a dressing gown still very poorly. Miss Edmed left this morning.

29th A letter from Bertha describing the Russian marriage at which she was present & close to the altar. Anything so gorgeous it will never be her fate to see again. Also another letter from Lolotte who is very gay at Cheltenham. To Maidstone, banners flying & the town full of people in consequence of the approaching election.

31st Drove with Mary to Maidstone the town all in an uproar & blue & purple on account of the election which ended in the triumph of the Liberals, Sir John Lubbock & Sir Sidney Waterlow.

February 5th Gerard arrived to give his vote to the Conservatives tomorrow.

6th The thermometer two degrees below freezing point in my dressing room this morning. At 12.30 went to the polling place, the school room Harrietsham (the carriage & horses very gay with purple & orange ribbons), where Mr Thomas & Gerard having voted, we drove to Maidstone. Sir David Saloman the Liberal candidate driving his landau up & down all about the town which was full of Conservative colours.[160]

7th Sir D. Saloman was the rejected one. Captain & Mrs Maunsell called & I lost my half crown bet with him on the subject.

12th Took Mary to Maidstone to embark for Scotland *(to stay with Louy)* ultimately, for London today. Crowhurst went to see Dr Monkton.

14th A letter from Gerard telling of his ball at Mr & Mrs Davidson's, Queens Gardens, where on taking his partner to the ice room, he beheld the waiters & tables sinking, & very soon realised that the flooring had given way & they were all precipitated into the kitchen beneath. No serious injury to any one but many bruises & cuts, Gerard's knee rather the worse & his dress suit completely ruined.

17th Mr Gibson here about the board school which is now shortly to come to pass.

23rd A letter from Mary announcing the birth of a 5th son & 7th child to Louy. Called on Mrs Craddock & took a prayer book to Polly Craddock.

26th Left Maidstone for Brighton by the 9.50 train, drove to our lodgings 29 Oriental Place. Called on the Horace Smiths.

27th Called on Mrs Hull & saw her looking very ill & in bed.

28th A walk in the morning with Richard to the Aquarium, very wonderful to be introduced to & become intimate with so many fishes in their life, not as they are generally know to us, in their death. The sea anemones are really like flowers of every different colour, some in full bloom some only budding. The pike looked as savage as possible but not condescending to notice the fishes in his tank, & the octopuses beyond description ugly save when they are swimming.[161] After luncheon Miss Edith Duppa having lent me her carriage Tizey *(Elizu)* Smith & I went off on a round of visits. Called on Mrs Hull, dined at Mrs Green's.

March 3rd Went to meet Ella who with Bobbie & Lewis arrived by train. Took them to the Aquarium where Richard met us.

---

[160]   Sir David Goldsmid-Stern-Salomons (1851-1925) High Sheriff of Kent. He inherited Broomhill near Tunbridge Wells in 1873, now a museum. He was a motoring pioneer.

[161]   The aquarium opened in 1872.

Then home to luncheon. Then to the skating rink & then to call on Mrs Hull after which & a little tea dinner they all departed much pleased with their day.

8th A letter from Miss Edmed announcing her marriage. Took tea at the Horace Smith's. Mr Thomas amused himself with following d'Israeli *(sic)* on the Cliff.

11th Called yesterday & today on Mrs Hull, she seemed better & less wandering. Wound up my visits with Lady Abinger, she was 72 today, her house full of people.

20th *(At home)* A Mrs G. Thomas, the widow of an artist, will take Godfrey House.

28th Mrs G. Thomas appeared with her son-in-law of the great firm of Lucas Builders.[162] She chose papers for Godfrey House & signed the agreement. Kate Gibson came for her drawing lesson.

30th Mrs Balston called with some frightful needlework in worsted but which she much prizes.

April 9th Gerard & I went to the Maidstone Ball, very full & very pleasant. Diamonds & magnificent lace in abundance. How I missed my children!

15th Harry & Lolotte arrived, she not looking well & living on iron, cod liver oil, porter, wine etc.

17th To the Ball at the Assembly Rooms given by the 7th Hussars. Beautifully decorated with banners, weapons & trophies. A block of ice in one of the open windows over which passed the gelid gales wafting in the fragrance of the flowers around. A pyramid of ice on the supper table also surrounded by flowers & flanked by cups of gold won at various races in various countries. The Ball was very animated & the dresses new & bright. Lolotte one of the dancers in yellow.

19th Walked to church with Mrs G. Thomas & party. The restoration of the church begun & the gallery removed which I think a great improvement.

20th Richard to London & Harry to Chatham. Lolotte & I amused ourselves with a little shopping.

22nd Richard went off canvassing for Henry. *(a vacancy had arisen for governor of Maidstone prison)*

23rd To Maidstone early to fetch Datie Clayton. Wrote no end of letters for Henry.

---

[162]   Messrs Lucas Brothers were important London building contractors throughout the period.

26th To Leeds church accompanied by Harry & Datie, Lolotte too poorly to go.

30th Last night we went to the Volunteers Concert at Leeds Castle & heard some very good glee singing, the band <u>fearfully</u> loud & near. The room full of everyone in the immediate neighbourhood.

May 1st A letter from Lord Holmesdale, also yesterday one from Lord Fitzwalter, very encouraging for Henry. The children with garlands, not so many as usual.

2nd Lolotte went to Maidstone to fetch Harry & his brother Fred & also Datie Clayton. Crowhurst departed. Poor thing! I really pitied her but she has made her own fate. *(almost certainly she is pregnant but not to be married)*

7th Craddock went for coals in the morning & in the evening distinguished himself by drinking too much & thrashing his wife. Her screams alarmed the neighbours & they called in Mr Thomas.

10th Gerard & I went to church & after dinner he came up to my room & unfolded what gave me great pain. Told Richard Gerard's communication which annoys him much. *(he is in love with an 'unsuitable' woman)* Harry left for Chatham.

18th Shopping with Ella *(who is visiting)* took Jackson *(new maid)* to give her a little insight into matters of fashion.

22nd Militaire inspection at which Prince Arthur was present.[163] Luncheon at The Star given by the Militia officers to their friends. Ella & Lisa accompanied me. Gerard dined with them & in the evening I took Lisa to the very pleasant Ball. Rooms beautifully decorated with flowers, wreaths of ivy & muslin festoons. Supper very good. Prince Arthur again there.

23rd Luncheon at Mr Duppa's, Mr & Mrs Duppa both very agreeable.

June 14th Last Tuesday returned from London after a very agreeable stay with Yeats & Dora. Bertha's home quite close. Gerard too there & a great delight it was to have them both. A large family dinner at Yeat's consisting of Jessy, Carrie, Bartle, his fiancée, Sir Fred, Lady Goldsmid, Lisa, Gerard, Delmar & Bertha. The latter looked <u>very</u> well. Another day to the South Kensington Horticultural Gardens, another to the Royal Academy. Today Lolotte is in London with Bertha. A

---

163   Prince Arthur, born 1850 was an army officer.

letter from Henry who is in camp & rejoicing that he was not appointed to the gaol.

17th A croquet party at Mrs Douglas's. Gerard is much pleased with his lodgings.

23rd To Malling with Mary. Poor Louis much as usual but I thought more incoherent & hurried. Took up Harry at Maidstone on our way home.

27th Delmar & Bertha arrived & a great pleasure it was to see them.

30th We went in the evening to Godfrey House when Mrs G. Thomas showed us some drawings by her late husband.

July 6th Bertha & Delmar departed I grieve to say, leaving behind them most pleasant memories & a model of a Russian house.

16th The first archery meeting of the season, very scantily attended as many of the members have not returned from town. We dined with the Timmins.

24th To a garden party at the Douglas's where the band of the Engineers played & we wandered about in the garden & ate ices & grapes & met numerous friends. In the evening we went to a ball at the Brassey's, a very gay one.

28th Harry & Gerard departed. The latter is not well but he would go.

August 1st Harry arrived just as we were going to dine having narrowly escaped a severe accident by the train running over a herd of oxen.

3rd Sketching Lolotte in her fancy dress on the stairs. Harry busy on the same subject.

6th Anne Cooper having been our cook about 10 months & Mary Tomline our housemaid the same time, left our services. They were so careless & discontented that I was forced to dismiss them.

8th To St Leonards Malling, to pass the day with the Miss Savages. Missed poor Charlotte extremely. Went to see poor Louis who is much as usual, his hair longer & whiter than ever.

15th Yesterday Hopper came to be our cook. Lolotte brought Gerard back & Jack *(Pierson, Harry's brother)*.

16th Gerard, Jack, Freddie *(Gipps grandson aged 8 has been staying for some weeks)* & I went to morning service.

20th Yesterday a Miss Pittman called with a male friend & took The Cottage as a school for a year.

24th On Saturday our old servants Charles Goodwin & Anne came back to see us. They have a lodging house at Tunbridge Wells & are very prosperous.

31st To Maidstone with Gerard. Robert & Bobbie arrived, the latter much grown & a very nice boy.

September 5th Robert & Bobbie left. Harry & Gerard up The Hill shooting.

17th Walked with Lolotte & Freddie to call on the Burkitts. Miss Pittman our new tenant in The Cottage & her friend Mr Henry took luncheon here.

27th Gerard, Freddie & I to morning service. The church beautifully decorated for Harvest Home. The pulpit festooned with flowers, grapes, apples & tomatoes.

October 8th Maidstone was quite full of beau monde & gayer & brighter than I remember it for ages. We drove to Detling to call on the Dowager Lady Hampson.

10th Farkins went early to Brighton for the christening of his child tomorrow. Dr Grayling took luncheon here & found Lolotte much better.

15th Young Gilbert Scott here to see the church.

21st Went to the school to see the village show which was most rich in gourds.

27th Much packing in the house on account of Harry & Lolotte's flitting tomorrow. Called on Mrs Sellen & the Gibsons. Mrs Sellen too ill to get up.

November 4th Richard & I started early for London. He left me at Canon Street & I proceeded to Charing Cross where found Harry, Lolotte, Delmar & Bertha awaiting me. Shopping with Bertha & purchased a cloak. Sir Fred came to see me. A very pleasant day.

6th To Maidstone early with Mary, purchased a bonnet. Kate Gibson in the afternoon. In the evening arrived Delmar, Bertha & Gerard.

18th Kate Gibson & I started early by the Sevenoaks line for Victoria where we were met by Bertha who took us immediately house hunting. Went to two in Roland Gardens, & one in Southwell Gardens, preferred one of the first which was most convenient. Took luncheon with Frederic & Mary & all their party. Bertha very well. Gerard saw us off at Victoria to which we went underground from Gloucester Road.

December 24th Harry & Lolotte arrived. Harry building a snowman for Freddie. *(first mention of sending Christmas cards)*

26th Skating on the moat at Leeds Castle. Harry, Mary, Lolotte & Freddie all there twice during the day.

27th Mary's birthday & we have been married today for 36 years! Colds all through the house & the fields white with snow. Two partridges pecking under the cedar on the lawn. The only clear spot they could find.

31st A most triste letter from Henry. Louy's emerald & diamond ring that belonged to my mother has been stolen.

1875 January 1st Gerard appeared last night, his moustaches white with frost. Water frozen in my dressing room.

8th Second soup day, went to taste it. Read sermons to Mr Thomas on 'What shall I do to be saved?'

14th Farkins went early to Brighton.

16th Farkins did not return. Mary & I went to a singing matinee at the Riddell's.

18th To London, met Bertha at Waterloo House. Much shopping with her & luncheon, called upon Yeats & Dora. Farkins returned.

30th Drove to pass the day at Sharsted. De Laune as usual removing large trees. His sketches in Egypt, Madeira etc very clever. The little de Launes nice, bright, brown-eyed children.

February 13th Richard met the school inspector at the school. Sent no end of Valentines to the grandchildren. (*Just as in Edward Goulburn's home Valentines seem to have been exchanged in as great a number as Christmas cards & were sent to all loved ones.*) Heard Freddie's lessons.

March 3rd A letter from Bertha. They are to have the house, 15 Roland Gardens (*South Kensington*) this week. Two men called about the S.E. Line

9th Richard to the Grand Jury. Jackson nearly out of her mind with toothache.

13th Freddie & I walked to call on the Gibsons. Saw Kate who has had 20 teeth extracted & suffered much.

15th Poor Miss Burkitt caught the scarlet fever from the children of a parishioner which flew to her brain, over-anxiety too, they say, hastened her end. (*Elizabeth Burkitt, the talented embroideress was 42*)

16th A letter from Robert telling of the sudden death of his mother from bronchitis. She died before he could reach her. I went to the re-opening of the church at Sutton Valance after its restoration. A very good sermon, an excellent luncheon & amusing speeches afterwards. Tea at the Kingdom's.

20th To London to buy furniture with Bertha. Went through avenues of bedsteads & carpets at Heals & Shoolbreds. Bertha very well. Her house very nice & Wilson presiding there. Afterwards took luncheon at Mrs Morgan's. Delmar saw me to the station & Gerard met me there. On my arrival at home found Robert sealed with Mr Thomas.

30th Gerard & I dined at Hollingbourne House. (*Mary is staying with Edward & Julia in Norwich*)

April 16th Bertha gave us our 13th grandchild. I was present at his arrival which occurred at 3.45 pm & Mr Thomas was also in the house, having come up to London for the day. Mr Harpur was her medico & Mrs Epps her nurse, an old Kentish woman celebrated in that line. During my stay in London I took luncheon twice with Caroline, & dined once with Sir Fred & once with Yeats whom I thought looking ill & feeble. I also saw the Scotts.

June 14th Bertha, Mary, baby & nurse arrived. All in good health & the baby much improved. Farkins left about three weeks ago having lived as our footman 9 ½ years & we now have Frank McNalty who formerly lived with Colonel Griffiths.

16th The evil reports of our cottage tenant seem confirmed by a letter from her to Mr Thomas this morning.

25th To take luncheon at Mr Hollingworth's (*Turkey Court*) such lovely roses, a collection just being sent off to the Crystal Palace Show. Walked with them all round their plantation & ponds which are very beautiful.

26th Mowing machine at work in the hay field.

30th Lolotte arrived yesterday looking thin but calling herself well. Jackson & I went up to London & after some shopping reached the Scott's, 16 Montagu Square, a most delightful house. A dinner party & Gerard there who was quite astounded to see me. A very pleasant evening & a meeting with many old friends.

July 2nd Gerard at luncheon & afterwards went to the Royal Academy.

3rd To Marshall & Snelgrove with Jackson, met there Jessy & Caroline full of purchases. In the afternoon drove out with Ellen Scott, called on Sir Fred & Lady Goldsmid. Last evening Sir Sibbald Scott & Mary Struth dined here. The latter wonderfully unchanged. It is a great pleasure to see all my old friends.

4th To the old Marylebone church with Ellen Scott. Very interesting to me from the recollections of early days. Sir

Sibbald Scott paid me a long visit & I called on Mrs Treherne who was alternating as usual between smiles & tears.

8th *(At home)* Mary & I went to see Mrs Featherstone & her rheumatic legs.

13th Went with Bertha & her Belongings to the Week Street station & saw them off.

20th To Maidstone shopping in loneliness, Mary being too ill to go.

23rd Gerard at the Assizes. The furniture all carried off from The Cottage & the high & loaded vans tottering down the road. Dined at the Balston's.

27th Mary & I went to Leeds, she remained sketching while I walked to call on the poor Burkitts. Mrs Burkitt had her sister with her but she is sadly changed & broken since her daughter's death.

August 2nd Ella & her two daughters arrived, Florence shrieking with shyness.

8th A cricket match at Barham Court. 33 gardeners work to keep it in order.

12th A cricket match in Leeds Park between the boys of Hollingbourne & Harrietsham, Gerard one of the umpires. Lolotte is delighted with Exmouth.

20th Ella & I left for London, Bertha met us at Charing Cross, drove about the town, did some shopping, tried to see the National Gallery which was closed, took luncheon at Roland Gardens & saw Bertha's charming & large baby. The house gaining in furniture & comfort. On our return Craddock told us that one of his children had the scarlet fever so Ella made up her mind to depart tomorrow.

30th The new horse taken out to try, but as the brake came out of the gate at Godfrey House he rushed off down the village & ended by running into a van. Both horses fell & Craddock was thrown upon them. Cincinnatus fearfully cut & Craddock much strained & bruised. The cause of all the mischief alone uninjured. Robert arrived laden with grapes & peaches.

September 2nd Craddock's child still very ill.

3rd Craddock's little girl Tita, died. *(Harriet Craddock was three years old)*

5th To morning service, Mary & I remained for the Holy Communion. Met Craddock in the church meadows following his little girl's white coffin carried by two men.

6th Mrs Craddock very poorly with sore throat, much fear of her having the fever.

10th Robert left. Mary & I called on Mrs Burkitt. Craddock's wife very poorly.

11th A telegram just arrived to tell of the death of Mr Dolling. He has held the living of Wormshill 40 years & will be much missed as a good man, & a very clever & <u>universal</u> one.[164]

12th Lolotte, with Harry, has returned to Cheltenham. Mr Gibson preached a good sermon & referred to poor Tolhurst's suicide which took place during the week. Met his funeral as we returned from church. Mrs Craddock is much better.

14th A letter from Jessy who finds London very dull after Homburg dissipation.

21st To Leeds early where made a miserable sketch of the dwindling yew.

25th Agnes Gibson came to see me in her nurse's attire & looking very nice.

October 7th Gerard, Mary & I went to Malling & took luncheon with the Miss Savages & went to see poor Louis. He appeared to me more tranquil & less unreasonable than I had ever seen him, but he looked rather thinner.

19th Answered Lolotte's letter, Poor child! She is still suffering much from boils on her face. Painted all the morning.

27th Richard & I started for London to stay with Bertha but he feeling gouty returned home the next day & I remained till November 6th. Found the inhabitants of Roland Gardens quite well & flourishing. The baby very fat. Dined with Caroline a gorgeous repast at Claridge's Hotel, Brook Street. Dined with Yeats, the guests Bertha & Delmar, Gerard, Frederic & Lisa. Dined with Frederic. Passed a day at Whipps Cross near Epping with the David Morgans. Delmar's father is very nice & gentlemanly & the house most luxurious.

November 7th To morning service, sat in the chancel with Mrs Gibson as our own seats are not ready. Read a lecture to Mr Thomas on the Parable of the Talents & wrote to Gerard that his father does not approve of his going to Rome at present.

8th To the church to see about the cushions for our new seats. I was mistaken yesterday, the change is certainly not favourable to us, & ought not to have been made as Richard

---

[164]   Rev. Robert Dolling's obituary in the local paper recorded that his parishioners 'always found in him a sympathising and charitable friend.' He was 67.

is turned out of the place he had occupied for 80 years & his uncle before him.

13th Having finished 'Our Mutual Friend' began to read aloud 'The Tale of Two Cities'.

15th Drove to call on Mrs Dolling, poor thing, she looked much worn & broken, they leave about Christmas. Mary left to stay with Bertha en route for Norwich.

December 1st Went to see Mrs Sage who is still poorly. Harry & Lolotte arrived.

3rd Snow very deep. Gerard & Harry built a gigantic snowman in front of the house. Harry painting Lolotte in a yellow dress. Old Bodiam died.

7th Harry began to make a snow elephant in the front meadow.

8th In spite of the snow went out walking. The elephant a wonderful performance & attracts immense attention. Mrs Duppa, Gibsons, all there to view it.

13th Delmar & Bertha came just as we had finished dinner.

16th The Hunt Ball to which we all went, a very pleasant & amusing mixture of all castes & classes. Mrs Duppa looking beautiful. The High Sherriff *(George Duppa)* only in pink. He took me to supper. A very full room & the people enjoying themselves immensely.

18th Harry composing a Christmas card, a holly spray borne by Cherubs.

23rd Richard early in Maidstone for magisterial business. Gerard & Harry up The Hill shooting. Wrote tickets for Christmas dinner.

24th To Maidstone to fetch Mary who arrived looking very blooming & well. Kate Gibson came in the evening with her quire & they sang carols in the Hall. Band, hand-bells etc all in due course as usual.

25th Edward has sent me a most magnificent prayer book. He & Julia have also written to me most delightful letters on the subject of Mary whom they thoroughly appreciate.

30th Harry hard at work illustrating Mary's poem 'William of Dawdleland'.

31st Gerard, Mary, Lolotte & I drove to take luncheon with the Moores at Boughton Malherbe.

1876 January 6th Took Harry & Lolotte to Maidstone on their way to London for the Pantomime.

12th To Leeds Park where Harry & Lolotte skated.

13th Brewing. The school treat in the lower village. Mary & Harry there. The latter conjuring for the amusement of the children.

18th Gerard wrote to say that his L.*(Love)* affair was quite at an end.

25th Mr & Mrs Duppa came to see Harry's drawings.

27th Much domestic disturbance & Craddock & Tom in utter disgrace. *(drunk)*

28th Harry, Lolotte & I started early for London, Bertha & Delmar met us at Charing Cross station which we reached through a dense fog & fog signals resounding all around us. We literally could scarcely see our way but we managed to reach Waterloo House & from thence Howell & James's where Lolotte made some very grand purchases in the way of dresses. Had a very good luncheon & then left again for the Charing Cross station where Gerard met us.

February 2nd Hunting Breakfast at Hollingbourne House for the Meet of the stag-hounds. A very large gathering, Lord & Lady Harris, De Launes etc.

4th Harry, Lolotte & I went to Sharsted to take luncheon & meet Mrs Faunce. De Laune busy removing a large yew tree about 200 years old. He manages these matters very successfully & many an ancient tree has under his auspices changed its 'local habitation'.

7th Mary & I went to Maidstone & got through an immensity of business. Franks left on Saturday. It is quite a relief to be without his 'drinking, dawdling & dirt.'

18th Letters from Ella & Louy, the former very happy the latter in troubles again. When will they end? Harry returned from London.

25th Heard that poor old Mrs Sage was very uncomfortable in her new house at Broad Street. *(a hamlet in the parish)* She has lived with us 25 years & at her age the change is hard.

March 3rd Kate Gibson & Mrs Kingdom took luncheon here & Gerard & the engineer came down from London about the new Railway. Should it take place he promises that the station shall be in a more convenient position.[165]

April 4th Since writing the above, Harry, Lolotte & I have been in Brighton & I have seen Mrs Hull, not much changed, & my

---

[165]   In 1875 a railway was planned to run from Sittingbourne to Maidstone. Hollingbourne would have been one of the stops. A tunnel was to be cut through the North Downs. The line was never built.

dear old friends the Horace Smiths, & Lady Abinger, & Cecil Maunsell. Brighton immensely grown. Ellen Woollett came to see me & I went to my dearest mother's grave. About a fortnight ago, Louy with her two children Mona & Richard came to see us & to meet Harry & Lolotte, Louy not having seen her sister for seven years. Yesterday I grieve to say Harry & Lolotte departed after a stay with us of over four months. We shall not I fear see much more of them before they leave for India.

8th Early to London with Louy, she leaving to go to Bertha, & Mona remaining behind with us. Bertha met us at the station. After our shopping was over Bertha & I went to her house to luncheon where we were met by Lolotte, Louy, Delmar & Harry, the former seeing me to the station. Mary & Mona met us.

26th Lisa arrived from London. Sir Fred too busy to accompany her.

27th Mary better so we all went to the Bachelors' Ball. Gerard wore his little white rosette & did his part as one of the stewards thoroughly. The band of the Royal Marines & flowers to decorate sent in profusion by Mrs Brassey.

May 5th Afternoon tea with Mrs Balston. Craddock's child (*Charley*) died this morning, about a year old.

17th Gerard & I en route to the ball, driven by a drunken fly man, were dashed into a traction engine coming towards us. The fly shattered. Harwood & the driver hurled from the box. My head most fearfully bruised & battered, & after the horrid accident were obliged to walk home. Such a scene of fright & confusion on our arrival!

18th Gerard departed, my face a fright to look upon.

20th Jackson & I left. Delmar & Bertha awaiting me at the station & quite shocked at my appearance. Found all well & Edward *(Bertha's son)* immensely grown.

21st To take luncheon with the Miss Scotts, then Mr Rochfort came whom I have not met for 40 years!!!

24th Took afternoon tea at the Palace of Westminster with Mr & Mrs Palgrave, then to call on Miss Greathed & Miss Chetwynd.

25th A walk in the zoo with Mr Rochfort. There were the tigers Moody & Sanky, but the prettiest things were the little cows.[166] Dined yesterday with Yeats & today with the Miss Scotts. Sir Sibbald Scott very agreeable.

26th Went to hear Sir Fred lecture at the United Service Institution Whitehall on the powers & education of military men which he considers fit them for any post. Sir Bartle Frere in the chair. A very interesting lecture. Afterwards went over the institution with Colonel Vaughan & saw numerous models, & the skeleton of the horse which Napoleon rode at Marengo & Waterloo.

27th Sir Sibbald Scott having procured us tickets, Gerard & I accompanied him & his son to the Trooping the Colours at the Horse Guards. We saw the Princess of Wales & her children, the Prince Imperial, Prince Teck, the Duke of Cambridge etc after which Gerard & I went to the Royal Academy.

26th Went with Gerard & Mr Rochfort to the Aquarium & then afternoon tea with Mrs Acton Tindal the authoress, agreeable & eccentric.[167]

29th To Whiteley's with Bertha.[168] In the afternoon to walk with Mr Rochfort in Kensington Gardens & the Row. Saw the golden statue of Prince Albert glistening in the sun.[169]

30th A letter from Mary saying that Mr Thomas was getting very impatient so made up my mind to return home tomorrow. Called on the Scotts & put off my visit to them. Went to dress Gerard for the Lady Mayoress's fancy ball. He went as a courtier of the olden time in blue satin & silver waistcoat & altogether looked just like the bridegroom in Hogarth's Marriage a la Mode. His tie was white lace & his shoes had cerise rosettes & silver buckles. Mr Tindall was Charles I. I rushed back from thence with Delmar to dinner at which Sir Fred present.

31st Mr Rochfort came to say Goodbye & at five I left the charms of London for the dullness of the country. Mary met me.

June 1st Passed the morning with Gibson & the geraniums.

10th Fetched Gerard who is anxious to go to St Petersburg with Delmar, I think Richard will consent.

---

166   Moody & Sanky were American Evangelical hymn writers.

167   Mrs Henrietta Tindal, minor poet.

168   Whiteley's department store was created by William Whiteley in Queensway, Bayswater. By 1867 it had 17 departments & by 1890 employed 6,000 staff.

169   Opened in 1872 by the Queen, architect Sir George Gilbert Scott.

14th Gerard & I went after dinner to Malling by train. Walked from the station to Dr Lowry's & saw poor Louis, scarcely a gleam of reason & I thought him thinner but he talked the whole time & was very cheerful.

29th Gerard departed early. He leaves London tomorrow for Hull & in the night embarks for Sweden. *(A great number of letters have been exchanged with Mr Rochfort & this continues for a few weeks.)*

July 4th Took luncheon with the Miss Hollingworths, Richard, Mary & I. Saw their beautiful roses & also went over the paper mills & saw the whole process of making from the commencement of the dirty rags to the transformation to the lovely white smooth substance destined to receive so many & so various traces of so many minds & hands.

6th To Maidstone early to meet Bertha & her Belongings. *(baby and maid)*

12th Old Sam Sage thrown from the hay wagon at Lampard's & killed on the spot.

14th Charlotte Eade *(maid)* discovered stealing.

15th To a cricket match on Bearsted Green where Miss Mayne gave us tea in a tent. Sent off Charlotte Eade & our new maid Annie Matthews came.

27th Went to the celebration of the Tercentenary of the Sutton Valance Grammar School at which about 180 were present. The Clothworkers came down by special train from London. Mr Wykeham returned thanks for the House of Commons & spoke very well, but Sir E. Filmer blundered as usual especially when he came to the word 'centenary'.

August 1st To the archery meeting at Barham Court. Gustave Dore was at our table with his party. Went up to the house & looked at the chimney piece in the dining room sculptured by Lady Barham which is very beautiful. They say that it is not finished & that her ghost is heard endeavouring to come in every night at the window to complete it.

2nd Took Mary & Mona to Maidstone on their way to Scotland.

9th To the archery meeting at Vinters for the after dinner shooting Bertha & I. I thought it very inferior to what it used to be when green jackets & hats & silver badges used to be worn.

11th A letter from Mary to announce the birth last Tuesday of a 6th boy to Louy.

14th To a lawn-tennis party at the Riddell's, about 80 people present. Weather intensely hot, sat & drank tea under the shade of the trees & found it very pleasant.[170]

23rd To Mr Leigh's Harvest Home & Flower Show at Barham Court accompanied by Kate & Ellen Gibson. A lovely day & everything bright. The church with flowers, the grounds with gay people & the tent with fruit. Admiral Englefield the discoverer of Smith's Sound & who has been three times to the Arctic regions was much with us & was very agreeable. Everyone there.

27th Harwood was taken ill with congestion of the lungs & is in bed.

31st Gerard arrived *(from Homburg)* & Bertha departed. Kate Gibson accompanied her. A letter from Robert telling of the birth of a son to Ella yesterday her 6th child. Gerard left Milly very well but triste & dreading the winter. The Duke of Cambridge had sent for him to hear about Russia.

September 6th Mrs Gibson *(wife of the vicar)* has had another heart attack.

9th Robert left. To Maidstone to see about a cook, who took the place & afterwards wrote to say that she declined as we live in the country. In the evening arrived Harry & Lolotte both looking very well.

11th Harry began a painting of the book room, Gerard shooting. Lolotte trying on & Anne making no end of dresses for her. Mushroom walks every day & returning home laden with them.

12th Lolotte & I to call on Mrs Gibson who was too ill to see us.

15th Lolotte & I to Maidstone when she did much &, I grieve to think, final, shopping.

17th We all, except Mr Thomas, who is too deaf & too rheumatic, went to morning service.

18th Harwood returned yesterday escorted by his uncle. He is decidedly better but looking feeble. An afternoon tea consisting of Riddells & more, a great success.

---

170   Lawn tennis was only a few years old. It was taken up with great enthusiasm by the middle & upper classes who had space & money to lay out private courts. It rapidly overtook the less energetic & more decorous game of croquet as a game which young men & women could play together.

21st A sad day, tho' very bright externally, as it was that of dearest Lolotte's departure. She, Harry & Gerard left & I accompanied them to Maidstone.

24th Very rainy so could not go to church. Read one of Edward's lectures to Richard but my powers of reading above my voice & his of hearing do not last long.

October 3rd Called on Mrs Sage with Kate Gibson & went to see Colonel Lester's drawings which are very clever. Yesterday drove with Mrs Duppa in the pony carriage to Maidstone where she did no end of shopping. *(The Lesters have moved into Hollingbourne Manor & the old house began to go back up in the world)*

4th Old Mrs Sage in the village again, Mrs Sam Sage having fetched her from Broad Street. Gerard arrived, he had taken luncheon with Harry & Lolotte & seen them off to Southampton.

5th In the morning called on Mrs Sage who tho' she has trouble walking is better than I expected.

6th A last farewell letter from the 'Mongolia' from Lolotte & a photo of the ship.

12th The new cook Anne Stitchman came today. Drove to luncheon with the Miss Savages. Went to see poor Louis who was more excited & more insane than usual.

16th A telegram arrived to say Bertha's confinement was over & to beg me to come up to town as soon as possible which I did accompanied by Jackson. Found Bertha very weak & with a little daughter but going on well.

17th A great improvement in Bertha. Took luncheon in Southwell Gardens *(Jessy's home)*. Delmar arrived unexpectedly about 7 from Russia.

21st Delmar, Lisa & I went to the United Service Institution to see the Naval Testimonial, a Chronometer watch given to Commander Cameron the African traveller. Sir G. Sartorius, Admiral of the Fleet, in the chair who had this day 71 years been at the Battle of Trafalgar with Nelson. He is a very venerable old man with a long white beard. Admiral Ommanney chief speaker & very dull. We went to the Aquarium to hear the music & read the paper, principally the article in the Athenaeum on Southern Persia the book lately edited by Frederic.

23rd Bertha & baby going on well but she is not to get up till next Monday.

24th In the evening we dined, Delmar & I with Yeats & Dora. Frederic, Carrie, Lisa & Jessy all there.

27th Took luncheon at Southwell Gardens. Sent a sewing machine as a present to Lisa & Carrie. *(two of Sir Frederic's daughters)*

30th *(At home)* Gerard shooting. Colonel Lester called to say adieu as he leaves for India tomorrow.

November 5th A scrap from Mr Wilder to tell of the death of his 3rd son George, rector of South Ealing, Herts from the typhus fever. Poor Man! What a sad blow for him.

9th To Mrs Best's ball, Gerard, Mary & I. House lovely, so entirely changed & the ball a charming one in every respect. Went to supper with Mr Duppa. Met there a Captain Collins editor of the 'Engineers Journal' who perfectly raved of Harry.

11th Kate Gibson at luncheon, she, Mary & I drove to say farewell to the Riddells who leave for San Remo this next week.

15th Wrote to Gerard who had written to us that from having been Mr Browne's pupil he has become his 'devil', & that in consequence he is the envy of all his young legal friends. Called on Mrs Warman & Mrs Bodkin. *(poor village women)*

December 2nd Harwood so ill sent for his uncle, the poor young man looks quite death-like. Gerard arrived.

4th Took Gerard to the station. Saw the new servant Russell who is to be Harwood's locum tenens for the present. The latter poor man is to leave tomorrow hoping to return. He came in to say good night, pale & feeble but thinking that he will recover.

5th Harwood left with his uncle & aunt. Dellelston *(the uncle)* came in during the evening to say his nephew has seen the physician at St Thomas Hospital who hopes to do him good.

24th Yesterday sent piles of Christmas cards to Ella & Louy. Today dispatched more to Bertha, Mr Rochfort, & the children of Gibson & Craddock.

1877 January 5th Drove to Maidstone with Mr Thomas paid bills & brought home Gerard from one station & Bobbie from another. A very nice boy.

13th Arranging my museum with Bobbie, placing the specimens in the hall.

16th Mary's second soup day & all the village children on the alert with Cans.

18th To Harrietsham to call on Bishop & Mrs Tuffnall *(he is acting as curate for Rev. Riddell)* thought her very agreeable, we had many friends & subjects in common.

19th Richard & I left for London, he disembarked at Canon Street & I at Charing Cross. Met Bertha at Waterloo House did some shopping & then went on to Howell & James to see the Lambeth Pottery. Made Bertha a present of a specimen, took luncheon with her, saw her charming children.

23rd A walk in the village & went over Taylor's premises & saw him take about 150 loaves out of his oven, & then visited Jemmy Taylor's stuffed birds etc.

24th To Maidstone & brought home Edith & Ida Branfill Harrison. Gerard & his friend Mr Broadmead arrived, & Mr & Kate Gibson, Bishop Tufnell, & Mr & Mrs Balston to dine. The party a great success.

February 10th Mary is in Norwich staying with Edward & Julia. Russell left having given satisfaction & Harwood returned looking well.

15th Canadian Richard wrote that his wife is dying. Richard sent him a £50 note. Kate tells me that her sister Emmy has been appointed matron of the Wisbech hospital.

March 1st Mrs Rule neé Edmed came to luncheon, very pleasant to see her again.

13th Russell went to Roland Gardens. *(the temporary footman is now to work for Bertha)*

29th Richard, with Gerard, went to Maidstone about a sale of cottages in the village when he purchased the row by the Green.

14th To dentist who cleaned my teeth by machinery, an American patent, & a most curious operation.

17th Started early with Richard for London. Bertha met me at Waterloo House. Took luncheon in Roland Gardens where Gerard met us & Mr Thomas had already arrived. Everyone well & the children charming.

18th A great & disagreeable discovery of misconduct in our house. Craddock & Stitchman dismissed. *(Stitchman the cook & Craddock the coachman were having an affair)*

27th A letter from Julia to say that to my sorrow Brighton is given up. So there is another disappointment, Milly's not coming to England being the first. Mr & Mrs Duppa called. Saw a coachman, C. Fuller from Bexley Heath whom we decided to take if his character suits. *(it did)*

June 13th *(At Bertha's)* To the Royal Academy which much enjoyed all to myself. Tuffnells & Riddells called, also Sir Fred.

14th Sir Fred came again. He leaves on the 25th for the Island of Reunion. Bertha & I drove out & went to Howell & James, called on Minnie Greathed.

15th A morning at Whiteley's no end of commissions for Lolotte, saw the dressmaker yesterday about her Coat-Dress.

20th To a garden party at Sir Joseph Hooker's at Kew where were assembled all the savants of the realm to meet the Emperor of Brazil.[171] A very fine-looking man who made himself universally agreeable. Sir William Guise introduced to us. Professor Huxley was there, Sir John Hawkshaw[172] etc.

21st To the Grosvenor Gallery with which much disappointed. *(home next day)*

27th Kate Gibson at luncheon, she accompanied me to a show of lovely roses at The Star & afterwards to a lawn tennis party at the Mayne's. *(the vicarage Bearsted)*

July 24th Brilliant fireworks at the Hollingbourne Flower show given by Mr Lawrence. Mr Thomas & I alone in the house having given the servants leave to go to the fete & Gerard & Mary being there too.

August 6th Ella arrived, Gerard playing cricket with the Hollingbourne Eleven against Mr Lawrence's Eleven. Dellelston came to see me, arranged that Harwood should leave on Wednesday. The poor man is becoming very ill.

7th To Maidstone with Ella to fetch Bertha & her children home with us, sent them on to Godfrey House. *(Bertha & family are staying at Godfrey House)*

8th Harwood left accompanied by his uncle & much grieved we are to part with him & for his sad state.

30th A very agreeable archery ball to which Delmar & Bertha & Gerard & I went. Poor Mary as usual had a headache & was obliged to remain at home. Ella departed with her bairns.

September 10th Mr & Mrs Gibson in a frightful accident in Mrs Lester's waggonette which was crushed by two runaway driver-less horses in a travelling carriage. They escaped with most severe injuries but wonderful to say with their life.

---

171   Sir Joseph Hooker, botanist, was Director of Kew Gardens.

172   Sir John Hawkshaw was a railway engineer.

15th Kate went to stay in Scotland with Louy & Henry. Held a tea party. No end of cook disappointments. Called on old villagers Mrs Sage & Mrs Bolton.

29th Left for Brighton with Jackson & after much effort found very nice clean lodgings, 36 Lansdowne Place. Dined with Edward & Julia on roast goose & very delightful it was to be with them after so many long years. Called on the Scotts.

30th With Edward & Julia to hear him preach at St Peters. Called on the Horace Smiths, also on Mrs Hull who is old & shrunken. One day I went with Edward to Rottingdean to the vicarage & here Edward & I renewed all our old recollections of Dr Hooker's school & Mrs Hooker's parrot.[173] Another day went over to my dearest mothers grave at Preston. The stone too thickly overgrown with ivy & too many evergreens round. Saw Ellen Woollett & charged her to plant there some China roses. Another day Edward & I went to Chichester, took luncheon at the Deanery after which the Dean & his sister lionised us over Chichester cathedral.

October 8th We made a pilgrimage to some of the Brighton churches. Every day I have dined & lived with Edward barring breakfast. Gerard too ran down to see me for two days. In fact my stay at Brighton has been too pleasant & I only grieve too much to leave it. Returned home on 9th & found Gerard & Mary awaiting me at Maidstone. Bertha's two children & two nurses here while her house is in disorder from workmen.

16th Bertha's babies & their suite departed. They are charming little children & good as gold. (*Mary is staying with Ella at Madehurst*)

20th Willie arrived unexpectedly with Kate Gibson from Scotland. Mary returned.

25th To a very gay Fancy Dress ball at Major & Mrs Best's. The costumes brilliant & the whole affair a great success. Gerard looking very well in his blue & silver as Charles Surface.[174] Mary as Queen Anne in pale yellow & black velvet & pearls with a pearl coronet & the blue ribbon of the garter, myself in pale bluish silk over a white muslin fully trimmed skirt a white muslin kerchief with Mechlin lace, ditto ruffles & a light lace cap with lappets fastened under the chin with a

---

[173]   Louisa & Edward were pupils at Dr Thomas Hooker's school. He was vicar of Rottingdean & the school was in his house. Cardinal Manning & Lord Lytton were his most famous pupils.

[174]   A character in Sheridan's 'The School for Scandal'.

diamond. Kerchief & cap both with a pale pink bow, & calling myself by the name of my thrice great grandmother Marquise de la Mijonelle. Dalrymple Treherne as Henry VIII was perfect, & Mrs F. Balston very well got up as Katherine Parr in a family dress of the time. Major Ross as his ancestor Sir Thomas Cornwallis.

30th To the Barracks to see the ceremony of Lady Sydney presenting the colours to the 2nd Battalion of the Militia. A carpet was laid in the middle of the barrack yard & on this, in chairs, were ranged most of the ladies. A hymn was sung, prayers were read, Lady Sydney made a speech & then Colonel Larkin made one in return, then to luncheon.

November 10th Called on the Bests & old Mrs Sage. Willie is being tutored by Mr Morris at Leeds. *(the vicar)*

15th News that Gerard has the appointment of private secretary to Frederic & that he leaves for Paris in a few days.

December 13th Took Willie to Sutton Valance & left him there to try for the scholarship.

15th Robert left, Mary fetched Willie, his case seems to be hopeless as one of his rivals was so clever & so fast. (*Willie did not get the scholarship*)

30th Willie's illness has developed itself into measles. Sent for Mr Sedgwick.

1878 January 6th A letter from Milly who is at Sorrento, oranges lying under the trees like apples, and having read this sunny description I quite waded to church thro' a slough of mud & mire below, & above, an atmosphere of dense white fog.

7th Drove up The Hill to see Mrs Duppa's painting on china. She has improved immensely. In the evening went with Kate Gibson to see Charles Matthews in 'My Awful Dad', a piece he has written for himself. His acting was simply perfect.

18th Discovered that our new housemaid can scarcely see so that we must part with her.

21st Richard & I started early for London, *(for day)* he on business, I on shopping & pleasure bent. Bertha met me at Charing Cross & then she & I went to Waterloo House & Howell & James. Roland Gardens wonderfully changed for the better & much enlarged. I thought Harwood, who is there, looking very poorly.

24th To the noisy poultry show with Willie & Mary having promised to meet Lady Howard there, after which Mary departed for London on her way to Norwich.

March 26th Left home for Roland Gardens. On 7th April I was present at the birth of a 2nd son to Bertha & Delmar & on 13th I took my departure leaving mother & child most flourishing under the care of Mr Harpur & Mrs Epps. During my stay I called on the Alexanders (Aubrey House), Miss Chetwynd, Mr & Mrs S.C. Hall, Jessy, Yeats, Frederic, Mrs Morgan, Lady Scott etc. Went to the Aquarium with Gerard & saw a man swallow eight swords. His name is Bernadetti. Also Zarzel take her famous leap & fired from a canon & walk on a wire at the top of the building.

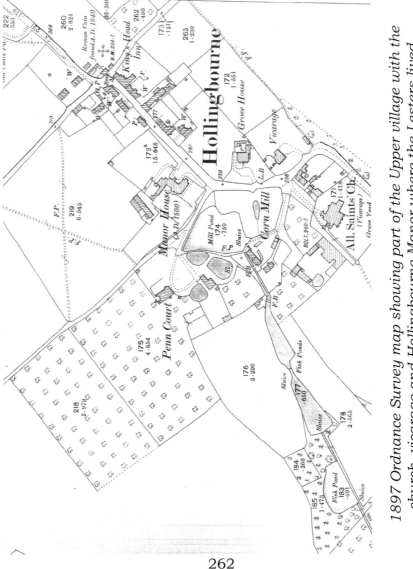

1897 Ordnance Survey map showing part of the Upper village with the church, vicarage and Hollingbourne Manor where the Lesters lived.

April 22nd Went to see Mrs Lester & then to view the decorations of the church. Mary was the sole artiste for the font which she arranged beautifully, a cross above of sloe blossom & a cross of white hyacinths floating on the water.

May 14th A fortnight ago this morning at 2.30 a.m. I had a fearful fall down the backstairs from our bedroom onto the front landing. Our night light had gone out & hearing Mr Thomas trying in vain to find some, I rushed into my dressing room for the purpose. The night was pitch dark, not a ray of light, & on my way back with the matches, I had the accident. Jackson, followed by Mary, fortunately heard my call for a light. I made my way upstairs streaming with blood & much battered & all over bruises. My head soon began to ache violently after I returned to my bed & to shiver. However I managed to find a little brandy in my dressing case & with that I slept an hour or so. The next day I passed on the sofa & in bed. My finger too was so much strained that for the last fortnight I have been almost incapable, besides my eyes & my forehead being so black that I have almost been ashamed to appear.

21st The annual cleansing of the dining room & the early stir in the house produced by chimney sweepers.

31st Mr Wykeham Martin *(of Leeds Castle)* died most suddenly at the Houses of Parliament in the library there while writing a letter. *(M.P. For Rochester)* He will be much missed for his kindness to everyone without exception.

June 1st The bell of Leeds church tolling for the arrival of Mr Wykeham Martin's body at the Castle. In the village old Mrs Wisdom & old blind Mrs Jenner died.

8th To London to stay with Bertha. Whilst there went to service in the Brompton Oratory, called on the Horace Smiths. One day walked in the Row with Mr Rochfort, one to the Royal Academy, another the Botanic Gardens. My last evening in London Captain Rochfort & I went to see 'Olivia' at the Court Theatre. Visited poor Yeats, looking worse, played backgammon with him. Luncheon with Ellen Scott, passed a morning with Jessy.

19th Returned home & Mr Rochfort came to wish me Goodbye.

July 9th Mary, Willie, Freddie & Ann left for London & the house seems empty.

11th Mrs Balston & Miss Long called & afterwards Gerard & I went to the vicarage. *(for the school treat)* The bride elect *(marrying the vicar's son young Gibson)* Miss Dyke, nice looking & like a gentlewoman. Mrs Marjoribanks there with Mrs Duppa, flags, cakes, children & old women in profusion. Old Mrs Tolhurst broke a blood vessel & died suddenly in the Church Meadows.

14th Gerard walked to Hollingbourne House in the afternoon & found Mrs Duppa sitting on the haystack which she had mounted by a ladder.

21st Attacked with violent pain in my hip & back & in fact one half of me. The agony continued so much that in the evening sent for Mr Sedgwick.

August 23rd *(Next entry)* Left with Jackson for Margate after a long & weakening illness. Sir Fred met me at the station & Bertha was at 42 Athelstan Rd when I arrived so that she & I were lodged in the same house, she having the larger share. Frederic opposite to us. My time was passed chiefly on a quiet esplanade exposed to all the delightful sea air which is the charm of the place but I also went on the jetty & saw the regatta, the fireworks & the Grotto which last I certainly did not appreciate. And on the extensive sands which I most truly enjoyed with the white cliffs & the rocks covered with brown & green seaweed. I returned home on Tuesday September 10th accompanied by Mr Thomas who had been in Margate a week but whom I do not think very well. Bertha left before I did.

September 21st Fainted away twice in the night & could not get up today. Yesterday called on Mrs Kingdom, Miss Pusey, Mrs Strong & Mrs Balston.

24th Mary & I went to Maidstone which was full of hoppers, noise & tumult.

28th Robert departed early. The death of Mrs Hull, the last of my old ties.

30th To a concert at the Riddell's school for their schoolroom furniture, went afterwards to drink tea at the rectory.

October 2nd Mary attended the Girls Friendly Society meeting in Maidstone.[175]

12th Walked with Gerard to the church to see the decorations, en route home Mr Snell showed us over the new Board school.

---

[175]   The Girls Friendly Society was founded in 1875 'to bind together ladies and working girls for mutual help sympathy & prayer.'

18th Richard & Gerard to town early. To meet Richard in Maidstone & there I saw an enormous elephant perambulating the town followed by four smaller ones.

21st Took Mary to Maidstone, she & Gerard leave for Paris tomorrow.

22nd Walked with Kate Gibson to Leeds Castle found Mrs Martin at home & deploring the dullness of their immense home.

December 11th The County Ball very cold & dull & empty, no fires in the ballroom.

1879 January 2nd To Maidstone with Mary & brought Blanche Rodney back. An evening treat at the board school for which General Lester had a Magic Lantern.

6th Mary & Blanche to a little dance at Captain Maunsell's. Gerard remained at home, Mr Thomas not having been well during the day. He was attacked with partial blindness.

12th Richard is better but his sight scarcely improves.

February 3rd Visited Bertha for a week with Jackson. Shopping. Dora Goldsmid & her sisters have taken a house in Lexham Gardens not far from Bertha. Called on Ellen Scott & Jessy. Had luncheon at Mrs Morgan's whose house is gorgeous – crimson & gold chairs etc. Also to a brilliant party there where a Mrs Clay walked about with a real living golden beetle on her sleeve imprisoned in a rosette of tulle & wearing golden feathers. Frederic dined & escorted us to the Court Theatre.

12th Mary went to stay at Norwich. The man who clothes himself in sheepskins & fancies himself the prophet Elijah is now at Deal.

18th Kate G & Edith Lester came to read French.

March 1st General Lester came in the afternoon & played chess & backgammon.

2nd Harry is with Lolotte again at Simla after an absence of two months during which time he has travelled 7500 miles.

6th A bad report of Louy from herself & from Henry.

7th Henry wrote a most desponding letter so I wrote to him & also to Mary to go to Scotland.

8th Sent our carriage to follow Mr Riddell's funeral, about 30 or 35 clergymen present. The service done by Bishop Tuffnell.

11th Bertha arrived with Edward & his nurse. Mary wrote that a miserable little girl was born which only lived twenty minutes. Louy going on well.

12th Bertha & I drove to call at Chilston. Mrs Douglas out. On our return found Richard very poorly & Gerard most anxious. It seemed to be a kind of bilious attack as he was able soon to walk upstairs.

16th My face very much inflamed & I did not feel well so Gerard sent for Dr Monkton. He recommended the constant use of cold water applied by wet linen & the application of the new remedy 'Vaseline' at night.

17th Took Anne to Maidstone en route to Bertha from whom I had a letter giving a poor account of herself. *(Maid Anne is sent on loan to help Bertha)*

21st Called on Mrs Duppa whom I found as usual painting china. Kate Gibson came to stay with me.

April 12th To luncheon with the Miss Savages with Gerard & visited poor Louis.

May 2nd Dr Monkton called again & thinks we must have a nurse for Mr Thomas.

3rd Nurse came, Adelaide Anstee by name, tall & nice looking. Mr Thomas likes her much. Bertha & Delmar arrived.

7th Louy & Mary arrived accompanied by two charming little boys with wonderful heads of hair, Leo & Louis. Richard better & in my dressing room.

16th Richard came down into the dining room for about an hour and a half. Louy & I to Maidstone shopping.

26th Mr Thomas being better I left for London & reached Roland Gardens in time for luncheon. Shopping with Bertha at Waterloo House & dispatching our acquisitions to Lolotte at Simla.

27th Mr Rochfort came to see me in the morning & in the afternoon Bertha & I went to a musical party at Jessy's.

28th Met Mr Rochfort at the Royal Academy who escorted me to see the pictures & afterwards in a walk in the Park & Kensington Gardens.

29th Sir Fred, Lady Goldsmid & Mr Rochfort came. In the afternoon I went with Bertha to see Velasquez pictures, very wonderful.

June 20th *(At home)* Went with Gerard to tennis at the Mayne's. Agnes Gibson elected Matron of the Sussex County hospital at Brighton one of 64 candidates!! She called a few days later.

July 2nd Louy, her boys & Mary departed early. Mr Thomas much depressed.

14th An early drive to Maidstone to hunt out a cook & housemaid & to fetch Gerard.

15th Kate, Edith Lester & Violet & Daisy Waddington came to read Moliere with me.

19th Went yesterday to the G.F.S.(*Girls Friendly Society*) meeting accompanied by Mary & Kate. Archdeacon in the chair. Mr Nepean & Mr Collis each read papers written by ladies.

August 10th With Gerard to luncheon with Mr Surtees at Boxley Abbey. A charming old monkish place with smooth lawns, rugged stones & sheltered arches. A long, dark, rat-infested refectory remaining entire.

12th With Mary to the school treat at the vicarage, numerously attended by high & low, rich & poor, flags flying, children screaming & rushing.

14th To Bertha's & stayed to 28th being present at birth of a second daughter. London as to people was a desert but green & bright with trees & flower beds. Drove to the People's Park at Battersea & by the wonderful Thames Embankment to Cleopatra's needle.[176] With Delmar to see some art students at the Kensington museum. Saw Frederic, Jessy & Carrie.

29th *(At home)* To a tennis party at the Best's with Mary. Walked with Gerard to the new paper mill & found there Mr Wilson the engineer & Mr Colley.

September 8th Ella & her youngest born arrived.

9th A young woman by name Annie Fagge came for the lady's maid place. She is tall & respectable looking. Too young but time will mend that defect.

11th Henry has become a Major. To a tennis party at Best's.

24th Ella & her boy left early, in the afternoon came Kate, Edith Lester & Daisy & Violet Waddington to read Moliere.

October 7th Fagge is hopeless, took another maid, by name Frances Pyman.

8th General Lester called for a lesson in perspective.

10th Jackson married Farmer but continues in service for a few days.

14th To Dover & found Delmar & Bertha in their lodgings at 1 Marine Parade, took lodgings at number 19. Dover looks as charming & picturesque as ever. While there had luncheon with Mrs Branfill Harrison at Great Mongeham.

---

[176]   Sir Joseph Bazelgette's great engineering work, The Embankment was designed in 1862, & then recently opened.

23rd *(At home)* New lady's maid Pyman arrived.

25th Pyman very stupid. Found another a pretty little maid Lizzie Short. Told Pyman I could not keep her & sent her back to her own home. Her dullness increases each day. Mary to London for a few days

29th Mary brought back Gussie Cartwright.[177] The archery club to be wound up. After 30 years Bockingfold archery club ends for ever.

31st Jackson left to my sorrow after living here 5 ½ years.

November 9th A great event occurred in the evening in Gerard's life as well as our own. (*He proposed to & was accepted by Gussie Cartwright the adopted daughter of Louisa's cousin Edward.*)

10th Gerard & Gussie departed. Richard had a very bad attack.

20th I left for town, Bertha & Delmar quite well also the bairns. Dined with Edward & Julia at the Grosvenor Hotel, Park Street & talked over matters.

30th Have written to many friends touching Gerard's marriage. Mr Thomas was last night seized with violent bleeding at the nose & we had to send for Mr Sedgwick in the middle of the night, but today he seems no worse. Mrs Sage is now here for night work.

December 2nd Richard very poorly. Sent for Mr Sedgwick but there is nothing to be done. In the afternoon Kate Gibson, Daisy Waddington, Edith Lester & Miss Scott finished reading with me 'L'avare' by Moliere. Thick snow.

5th Gerard shooting at The Mote. I went round to see The Cottage. *(where Gerard & Gussie are to live)*

10th Yesterday Miss Jarrett the nurse for Mr Thomas came. Gerard left early for Norwich.

12th Richard's first distribution of coals under the management of Mary & Kate Gibson who took luncheon here.

16th To Maidstone early with Mary. Began to buy linen for Gerard's ménage.

18th Richard had a bad attack & was only up about two hours.

23rd Edward arrived looking very well & wandered over to The Cottage of which he had heard a bad reputation, & seemed

---

[177]   Edward and Julia had no children of their own & adopted Gussie in 1862 when she was orphaned aged nine. She was related to Julia.

quite satisfied. A very busy day writing Christmas dinner tickets etc.

24th Band, carols all the day & in the evening arrived Kate & Grace & all their singers looking very nice in their red hoods, Kate travelling with her harmonium in Potter's vehicle & the rest on foot bearing lanterns.

26th Cold extreme. The school treat to take place at the paper mill in the large room which in the future is to be devoted to rags.

27th Mr Knatchbull Hugessen came here disguised in the evening as a countryman with his carol singers. We had them in the Hall & very well they sang.

31st Kate Gibson came to announce the engagement of Agnes to a Rev. Stafford. Emmy Gibson brought her betrothed Mr Burnett *(also a clergman)* to introduce him to us, Mr Thomas saw them & was also well enough to see Kate tho' at times very wretched.

1880-1889: The lively widow

This decade of Louisa's seventies began with the happy occasion of Gerard's marriage. The young couple set up house almost next door to Eyhorne House in Eyhorne Cottage. The Cottage as we have seen was not a cottage at all and had space for five or six live-in servants and half a dozen children. It was Gerard and Gussie's marriage which led to more contact between cousin Edward and Louisa than they had enjoyed since childhood.

By the start of 1880 Richard was requiring nursing day and night as he declined into confusion and in 1881 he died, as did Louisa's sister Milly. Saddest of all, at the same time, was the death of Lolotte's husband Harry.

Once Louisa had become accustomed to it, she enjoyed her widowhood. There was no diminution in her status. She had more freedom to come and go, could spend money on the house as she wished, and was the matriarch of a large and affectionate family. Loneliness did not feature in her new life. When they were at home Gerard or Gussie saw her daily as did Kate Gibson. Louisa visited her beloved Paris once more in 1882. Her day trips and stays in London became more frequent. Bertha's home was always buzzing with activity and her sociable vivacious nature made staying with her a particular treat. Louisa had always taken an interest in politics and now Mr Rochfort, being an M.P., kept her even better informed. Ever sociable and with many friends, Louisa also kept in close contact with most of her lady's maids when they left to be married and some she helped with small amounts of money when they were in need.

As the decade progressed Gerard's health became once again a cause for serious concern and resulted in long spells of time when he was confined to his room at home or convalescing in Margate.

Louisa maintained her life-long habit of writing her journal daily as well as weekly letters to those of her children not with her at the time. Some friends such as Mrs Treherne, Mrs Branfill Harrison and Mr Rochfort were constant correspondents. Over the years her grown-up grandsons Lewis, Bobbie & Willie had also become regular correspondents.

1880 January 1st Mr Gibson called & kindly brought Mr Thomas a little box of cigarettes but he has not smoked now for some time.

2nd Richard today very poorly & much excited.

3rd Richard only up about two hours & full of dark forebodings.

5th Rose by candlelight & at 8.20 with Short started for London. Met Bertha at the Charing Cross station & proceeded to Waterloo House & then to Howell & James where purchased a dark green velvet dress for Gerard's wedding. After much shopping again embarked on the train. Found Gerard at Maidstone station.

7th Early to Maidstone with Gerard about a nurse & to meet Julia & Gussie. They passed the day here & saw The Cottage etc. Mrs Duppa called. Gerard left with Julia & Gussie for town. Mr Thomas much better & walked as far as the upper landing.

9th Early to Maidstone nurse hunting & brought Kate & Gerard home.

10th At The Cottage in the morning taking dimensions.

18th During the last week I have called on Lady H. de Walden. Mrs Hurd has come & gone & is to return to nurse Richard. Gerard has received many presents.

19th Kate Gibson called & Bobbie, who has been here a week, left.

28th Left early, met Gerard & Mr Tindall at Paddington station & travelled with them to Mr Fredrick Cartwright's where stayed at the rectory Aynho. A dinner party consisting of ourselves, Edward, Julia & Gussie.

29th Dearest Gerard was married to Gussie in the little parish church. No end of Cartwrights present & Bertha, Delmar & Sir Fred who stayed with Major Fairfax Cartwright for the occasion. Laying aside all maternal feelings I must say that no one at all was to be named with Gerard & Bertha for personal appearance. Our host was most kind & Edward made a very good speech at the breakfast. Oh but I felt in another world! The bride and bridegroom having departed, we left about 3. Bertha, Delmar, Sir Fred & I, in intense cold, stopped at black, dark fireless stations & reached London in such an impenetrable fog about 6 that we only found our way to Roland Gardens in about two hours by the aid of torches.

30th Saw dear Gerard & Gussie for a moment in Lower Belgrave Street where I went to take his great coat which had been left behind. At 4 left for home where found Mr Thomas not well & Bobbie gone. Since then we have heard from Ella that he has an appointment in the City Bank, £40 a year to begin with.

February 5th Gerard & Gussie at home again. They had a most brilliant reception, a triumphal arch of evergreens nearly opposite our house, illuminated with gas & the motto 'Welcome to the bride,' crowds of people & the band going down to the corner to welcome them & the horses taken out of the carriage, which was drawn by the villagers in triumph to the door. Poor Richard even came down stairs to witness the grand doings.

13th Mr & Mrs Gibson called. A whole cargo of Gussie's puss-cats arrived.

17th Mary went to Maidstone to attend her G.F.S. meeting & Gerard went to see about no end of things from Norwich. Gussie & I walked in the road.[178]

23rd Arranged the dining room for the display of wedding presents.

24th Such a concourse of high & low to see 'The Gifts' filled the dining room all day that it is impossible to numerate them. We were all quite worn out.

26th Mary departed for Bertha's, Gussie & I remained to shop in Maidstone.

27th Gerard's furniture arrived from Whiteley's. Delmar is on his journey to Tashkent.

March 3rd Drove early to Maidstone with Gussie. Much shopping & called on Jackson & Anne in their damp homes in Grecian Street.

6th To Maidstone on my way to Malling where took luncheon with the Miss Savages & met Mrs Henry Duppa, also saw Louis whom I thought looking decidedly better & far less excitable. Richard was not well on my return.

8th Arranged carpets at The Cottage, Gerard & his wife in Maidstone.

11th Gerard at an election meeting at The Star. Bertha & her boy arrived.

12th Walked with Bertha & Ed to the vicarage. Gerard out canvassing.

---

[178]   To celebrate his marriage Gerard gave a dinner for all his father's tenants, who numbered over 40, at the Sugar Loaves pub in the village and the wives of the tenants were given a week's rent.

13th Walked with Bertha to Elnothington. A magnificent silver belt, necklace & bracelet came from Harry & Lolotte for Gussie.

18th With Gerard to see the paper mills. One giant boiler has arrived & two more are to come. They cost about £650 each. Gerard attended the election committee in the afternoon.

19th All the morning at The Cottage arranging furniture.

20th Gerard to London. Richard much disturbed in the night, pacing the room & stirring the fire.

21st Gerard & Gussie returned last night. A long political letter from Mr Rochfort.

22nd The third & last colossal boiler passed the house to the paper mill.

29th A stag hunt meeting at Penn Court, Bartle & Amy, Mrs Lester & Mr Cecil Lester, & Colonel & Mrs Waddington & Kate Gibson took luncheon here.

April 2nd Mary came to me at 7 to say that her father had a fall during the night. It seems he overbalanced himself in rising from his chair. Gerard's glass arrived from Homburg & he & Gussie moved from our house to The Cottage.

6th Sir W. H. Dyke & Sir E. Filmer elected for Maidstone. Gerard went early to Harrietsham to vote followed by all the Conservative voters in the parish. Edward & Julia arrived to stay, Edward looked round the paper mill. An afternoon tea including Mrs Whatman & Mrs Balston.

17th Anne Rodwell's baby arrived early, she is very ill. Mary went to ask after her. Ella & Henry *(her son)* arrived.

21st With Short to stay with Bertha, Sir Fred & Lisa came to dine. Home on 24th. Mr Thomas a little better.

25th Called on Anne Rodwell in Maidstone found her improved. With Gerard & Gussie to subscription concert in Maidstone.

26th Mary to the village concert & I passed three hours in Richard's room. He was very uncomfortable & feeble.

May 1st At least seven garlands & all so brilliant with wild flowers.

8th To Maidstone early with Gerard horse hunting, for Cincinnatus seems quite broken down. I went to Gerard & Gussie's tea party.

13th Gerard & Gussie left for Norwich. Mr Thomas wonderfully well.

17th Harwood came to see me. He is superintendent in an insurance office with a salary of £120 a year.

20th To a very beautiful ball at Linton. Scarlet geraniums strewn over the supper table & every lamp & candle on it had a rose coloured shade.

23rd *(With Short to London on 22nd)* A visit from Mr Rochfort & a walk with him in the park.

24th With Bertha choosing carpets. Also purchased a bed-rest for Mr Thomas. Frederic came to see me in the afternoon & we settled to go to the Lyceum on Wednesday to see Irving & Terry in 'The Merchant of Venice.'

25th To the Royal Academy with Mr Rochfort & a walk & sit with him in the park.

28th A farewell visit from Mr Rochfort. An afternoon garden party with Savants at Sir Joseph Hooker's at Kew. *(home on 29th)*

June 5th The girls came to read French. Mr Thomas wretched & excitable.

6th Edward & Julia to stay.

July 1st It is more than three weeks since I have written my journal & yet the days have been a shade more unpleasantly eventful than usual. Fuller *(coachman)* being angry at being dismissed, accused Gibson *(gardener)* of dishonesty & Sanderson *(footman)* became fierce on the subject & then apologised to Gerard. In fact the whole house seemed in flame. Last Monday we hired a temporary coachman by name Hollands who is like a cabman.

4th Gerard & Gussie as usual at dinner.

8th To London & found Bertha awaiting me at Charing Cross, much shopping.

10th Mr Sedgwick, Kate Gibson & Mr Wilder called in the morning. Gerard sat up with Mr Thomas & we sent Mrs Hurd to bed.

15th Mary & Gussie went to a large party. Gerard was haymaking, Mrs Hurd in bed & I sat during the hot afternoon with Mr Thomas.

16th My pupils came over to read French & I think that they improve.

20th Mary gave a pic-nic tea to her schoolgirls in the orchard. She & Gussie presiding & Kate Gibson & Edith Lester assisting.

28th Much has occurred since I last wrote. A Malling nurse by name Couch came to Mr Thomas last Friday. She is to take the night work & Mrs Hurd the day. On Saturday Mary dined at Godfrey House & Sanderson went for her in the evening so intoxicated that he could not ring the front door bell. He rolled over the fuchsias & begonias breaking them down in his fall. Mary & I went to Agnes Gibson's *(one of the vicar's daughters)* wedding today. Agnes looking very nice in her dove-coloured silk with ecru lace, & Gloire de Dijon roses. There were no bridesmaids. A tent was pitched in the garden for the breakfast.

31st Heard from Lolotte Harry is made a First Grade Executive which gives them great satisfaction & the new Viceroy Lord Ripon is making himself popular & giving dinners & dances wholesale.

August 2nd Jackson (now Farmer) called. Old Sellen died. Alice Wood, Gerard's cook seized with scarlet fever so she was conveyed home in Bath chair & Gerard & Gussie off to Folkestone. Holland the coachman's child seized with the fever.

6th Louy arrived looking very thin. Mary has scarlet fever & Gerard unwell in Folkestone.

10th Louy helped to look after Mary & Mr Thomas. Gerard returned while Gussie goes to Norwich.

26th Mary & Louy left for Hythe to stay in lodgings. Mr Thomas better but sad & discursive in his talk. Visited Jackson & her child. Alice Cooper *(housemaid)* gave notice, she is about to emigrate to Canada with her family.

September 2nd Kate & I went to Barham Court, a very large lawn tennis party & very hot. The tables beautifully decorated & the peaches & grapes in golden vases.

3rd Kate breakfasted here & left early for Headcorn to meet Louy & take her place with Mary at Hythe, & Louy reappeared here looking much better.

10th Mary & Kate returned from Hythe. Mary looking much better but still weak.

13th Louy left for Scotland. She looks much better for her stay here but is still thin.

15th Left for Brighton, found lodgings at 5 Oriental Place, wandered by the sea, Short & I, to inhale all the salt we could.

20th Ellen Woollett came to see me & I went to see dearest mother's grave at Preston & settled with Ellen that the yews should come down.

23rd Took a last walk on the esplanade & left Brighton. Found Richard wonderfully well on my return, far more tranquil than when I left him, & Robert staying in the house & delighted to be here again.

25th Took Robert to Maidstone on his homeward journey. Gerard on the Ophthalmic *(Hospital)* Board & appointed one of the visitors for next month.

28th A letter from Lisa *(Goldsmid)* telling of the death of Caroline at Brighton & how Sir Fred had been telegraphed for to Paris. A telegram from Gerard to say that Delmar was coming with him today. Delmar very well but darkened by travel.

October 1st Mr Thomas depressed. Gerard went to Caroline's funeral, a melancholy one at which only himself, Sir Fred, Major Albert Goldsmid, Delmar, the lawyer & Caroline's maid present at Isleworth. New cook, Collins, arrived.

6th To London shopping with Bertha for a dress for Lolotte, brown, embroidered with gold, & brought home grand-daughter little Ella Gipps. All Bertha's children have chicken pox. Bertha is immense.

10th Kate Gibson & the Lester girls came for Italian lessons. Mrs Green to tea.

11th Gerard & Gussie to Sunday dinner as usual. A daughter born to Bertha.

12th Gerard & Gussie left for Norwich. Called on Mrs Kingdom & Mrs Balston.

19th Went with Mary to see Bertha & baby for day, a very nice little brown child.

November 1st Mary departed for Brighton. Gerard returned.

4th A telegram to summon Gerard to Norwich as Gussie not well. Another one hour after to say that she had a daughter.

5th Walked to the church meadows to see where the new rail road is to pass. Met no end of Waddington children making their parting gifts to the villagers preparatory to their leaving tomorrow. Mr Thomas very excitable.

11th Harry is on the Viceroy's staff & Lolotte is going with him to Lahore. Gerard arrived from Norwich.

19th Mary, Gerard & little Ella at the chrysanthemum show in Maidstone. Mrs Lester, then Kate then Mr Gibson called. Mr Thomas's bed moved, by his own especial wish, from the bedroom he has so long inhabited overlooking the stables to the one opposite overlooking the garden.

26th Made another change in the house by removing the nurses to the workroom. No nurse available at the Malling institution so Couch must remain for the present.

28th Couch called me up in the morning about five as Mr Thomas was in a most painful state of excitement, stayed with him till 7.30 when he became calmer.

30th Ella & her good-looking boy Lewis came quite early & left again in the afternoon. Mary & little Ella at a birthday party at the Lester's.

December 1st I write to Gerard every day with a report of his father. Girls came to read French & Italian.

3rd A fearful accident occurred in Maidstone. The explosion of a steam engine. One man blown up a tree & killed instantly. Two windows in the old parish church destroyed & some tombstones forced from their places.[179] Two of the men died later in hospital. With Kate visited Mrs Balston, Mrs Mayne, & Mrs Cave Browne. Mr Betts came to see Mr Thomas, a mutual pleasure.

10th Gerard returned looking very ill.

11th A telegram on to say Gerard's baby very ill, then that she improves.

12th Heard an explosion which proved to be the Faversham powder mills, no lives lost. Gerard's baby very ill.

13th Baby died in Norwich. Gerard set off tho' ill.

20th A glowing account from Lolotte of the Viceroy's gorgeous progress, his receptions, his silver ladder, his elephants & his golden throne. Little Ella still here. Nurse Wallace arrived, Couch left.

22nd Gussie & Gerard returned. Wrote tickets for 40 Christmas dinners. Richard very still & torpid.

24th Our carol singers in their red hoods came & sang very well.

27th We have been married 42 years, Mary dined at The Cottage, I remained at home & thought over old times. The hand-bells came playing the same primitive airs they did when we were first married. This was to me a very sad day.

1881 January 1st The first day of the New Year. It has not dawned brightly for us & yet we have much to be thankful for.

2nd To morning service, made good resolutions & took the Holy Sacrament. Richard had a disturbed day. Gerard & Gussie at dinner.

---

[179]   A traction engine exploded as it passed All Saints church. The engine was not old and was pulling two trucks laden with manure up from the wharf by the river. Three men accompanied the engine and 19 year old Frank Underwood was killed instantly.

6th To my deep sorrow Emily Harrison cannot come to visit. Mary's first soup day.

7th General Lester at luncheon & we played backgammon afterwards.

13th Went to the old school to see the second soup distribution. Austen & his wife stirring, Mary directing, Ella receiving the pence & an Austen girl filling the cans.

17th A clerk called to ask what we felt on the subject of the S.E. Railway line through our land, to which of course we are strongly opposed.

21st Mr Thomas's first gift of coals to the poor. The thermometer in my bedroom stands at 27. The ice on the widows remained un-melted during the whole day.

25th Drove through banks of snow & deep drifts to Maidstone in the afternoon.

February 2nd A week in London with Short, shopping & staying with Bertha & family. Called on Jessy & Carrie & Ellen Scott. To the Old Masters exhibition with Bertha & Delmar. Called on Dora in her new house in Lexham Gardens. To Marshall & Snelgrove with Bertha. Called on Lady Goldsmid in Observatory Avenue. Home on 9th after a pleasant stay.

15th Tried to improve my old verses on Hollingbourne. Mr Gibson & Kate called.

March 4th Fanny Bolton was sent home at once, (*seems to have stolen Gerard's boots*) her mother came twice, poor woman, to see Mary & me.

9th Mary left for Norwich accompanied by Harriet. (*Edward noted in his diaries how she helped him by writing letters he dictated, a job which Gussie did before her marriage. Edward had a fond nickname for Mary which was Pom.*)

14th The horrid news of the Czar's assassination.

22nd Gussie & I went to the consecration of the bells at Boughton Monchelsea by Bishop Tuffnell. I was very glad to see the Bishop again.

25th Mrs Faunce (*neé Duppa*) was buried on Wednesday, another of my old friends gone! It makes me very sad to think of the rapid diminution of their number.

27th Gerard very poorly so did not go to church. Sent for Dr Monkton who considers that he ought to be <u>very</u> careful & that he requires universal strengthening. Jackson brought her very strong baby to see me. I did not see much of her however on account of Dr Monkton's visit.

April 2nd Gerard better. Kate Gibson has been very poorly. Holllands dismissed. 10th Mary returned after nearly five weeks. Girls came for their Italian. Concluded revising my little Hollingbourne ballad which wrote in 1851 & to which Gerard has added some interesting notes.

May 6th A telegram from Leopold telling of dearest Milly's death last night at 12. Oh that I could have seen her again! She is to be buried on Monday. Delmar will attend the funeral as Gerard is too unwell to go & so is Mary. Nurse Carnell left today I am glad to write, & we have Law, on trial. *(Cousin Edward underlined in his diary 'the sad tidings of Melia's death' & wrote immediately to Louisa)*

8th Milly is to be buried tomorrow.

9th To London accompanied by Gerard & Short. To the bank & Mr Hills the broker, both useless. Bertha met me & I took luncheon with her charming children.

10th Letter from poor Ernst who is quite overcome by the suddenness of Milly's death. He writes that a more dear & good & noble mother no son ever had.

17th To London early with Short. First to Lewis & Allenby to buy Mary a dress & then on to Roland Gardens to receive poor Milly's things & read her letter containing her last directions. It was more sad to me than I can express. Met Gerard there. *(on his way to stay with Edward & Julia in Norwich)* Saw again things that had belonged to my Mother & Grandmother that I had not seen for years & that I had known from my childhood. During my absence Law departed & I brought home Jones. She is a most precise elderly maiden & will I trust suit Mr Thomas.

19th All over Maidstone nurse hunting as Jones declares that she has broken her back. Much division & arrangement of Milly's things.

27th My dear husband was better in the morning but just as he was dining was seized with strong convulsions ending in epilepsy. Heavy sleep followed & on Monday at 10.15 he breathed his last so peacefully that we scarcely knew he had gone & as I held his hand I felt his pulse beat some little time after his breath seemed to have ceased. He was sensible at times & knew me in the morning & spoke to me very faintly. Henry Gipps had come during the day, this sad day when the spirit that had lived so long within these walls passed from earth.

31st I cannot realise that my dear husband is gone & the stillness of everything is quite wonderful & all is so sad. I went to see him as he lay in his bed.

June 1st A hot brilliant day but the stillness and gloom of the house dreadful. Henry went off yesterday to fetch Louy who came this night.

2nd Saw my dear husband in his coffin many times, so placid & peaceful & his face smooth & unfurrowed after all the wear & excitement & turmoil of the last two years. A wreath of hawthorn that he had bushed lay upon his breast, & some kind hand had placed there too a bunch of lilies of the valley. Saw him for the last time on earth about 3 o'clock after which the lid was closed.

3rd The funeral. Robert & Bobbie came & Delmar & Bertha accompanied by Willie. And at 11.30 covered with a purple pall, my dearest husband left the house he had inhabited for at least 84 years. Bertha sat with me & when the luncheon was over Louy came to my room & asked me if I could bear any more & then told me that dear Harry had been taken. Mr Gibson kindly came to say a prayer by my side & all who had followed the bier (which was covered with flowers), departed including Mr Sedgwick. *(Edward noted in his diary 'Wrote to dear Lou about her three-fold bereavement.)*

9th Left early for Headcorn, Mary & I on our way to Deal & Walmer. A most delightful clean lodging found. A telegram from Gerard saying that Mr Pierson was expected at Simla on Sunday. Mrs Branfill Harrison came to see me. Such a pleasure to see her.

10th Mrs Branfill Harrison & Ianthe *(her daughter)* at luncheon, much talk of old times.

11th Mary & I spent the morning on the beach poring over the pebbles & scarce shells. Mrs Harrison in the afternoon.

13th To Sandwich where Mrs Harrison & Ianthe met us & where we at once proceeded to view the very curious old church of St Bartholomew connected with a brother & sisterhood for the decayed trades-people of the place. The church is wonderfully old & picturesque. One of the brothers was very communicative, we next went to St Clements. The churchyard was full of flowers. All the windmills quite reminded me of Holland. Much firing at Deal today & seven ironclads in the Downs for the Duke of Edinburgh arrived in his yacht 'Lively' & took luncheon at the barracks.

14th The railway to Dover is to be opened today. A telegram from Colonel Chapman that Lolotte is to remain at Simla a month or two.

15th An early walk with Short down the quaint old narrow-streeted town of Deal. A hamper with butter, flowers & vegetables from home. A visit from Mrs Branfill Harrison.

16th To Dover with Mary & Short by the new railway through many tunnels which was only opened on Tuesday.

17th Letters from Lolotte. Poor child! They were just when she was receiving telegrams that Harry was ill & overworked & were dated May 21 & 22nd .

20th Drove over with Mary to take a quiet luncheon with Mr & Mrs Harrison, the vicarage at Great Mongeham is very nice.

21st Mrs Harrison came to fetch us for a drive to Ringwould to see the old place where I had often been in childhood. (*Home next day*)

30th Saw Mr Edmed about renovating the drawing room.

July 5th All seemed so sad.

6th A letter from dearest Lolotte & from the Viceroy's Military Secretary. She had travelled from Simla to Bunnoo a journey of five days & nights without rest in the dreadful heat & arrived just in time to be with him two days & one night before his end. He burst into tears when he saw her & said that 'now he did not mind dying in that lonely place.' He & his poor father-in-law were buried the same day in their far off graves.[180]

8th To London with Gerard. We parted at the station at Canon St & then Short & I went to Waterloo House & reached Roland Gardens for luncheon. Frederic came to see me looking very well, but uncertain of his plans.

13th Drove out with Bertha & saw a landau which pleased me, black & yellow.

15th (*At home*) Much painting going on in the house.

19th Gerard in town looking at carriages for me, he purchased one I had seen.

20th Lolotte is staying, poor child, with a Major & Mrs Sergeant & talks of returning home on the 16th. Mr Pierson sent a letter from Colonel Close telling of poor dear Harry's

---

[180] Harry had been appointed commanding Royal Engineer of the field force proceeding against the Mahsud Wazirs. Throughout the expedition the Royal Engineers were exposed to great heat whilst road-making and mining. On his return to Bannu, Harry had succumbed to dysentry.

last days & how weak he was & how he suffered from the want of proper food.

23rd The coach arrived. Hanging pictures in the drawing room. Gerard in town for the day about probate duty.

26th Letters from Lolotte who is to leave Bombay on the 16th of August. The Viceroy has placed his country house at her disposal. Poor child! She is bringing home carefully every smallest remembrance of her husband, & she has left her home which he & she had made so pretty.

27th Today is the Village Flower Show & the Leeds bells are ringing merrily.

30th Arranging my own room as I have now returned to it. It seems far more natural to me than being in front of the house.

August 2nd Leopold & Ernst arrived to stay, & talked much of my dearest sister.

5th Went to London with Leopold & Ernst & saw Bertha. Ernst stayed with Bertha.

8th Gerard & Gussie left for a holiday to Brussels for his health. To see the paper mill with Mary & Leopold, Mr Wilson took us all over & explained everything & very interesting it all was.

September 6th Bertha & her children departed taking Kate with them.

18th Sent £500 to Richard.[181]

22nd Our dear little daughter returned to us & I fetched her from Maidstone. She looks very sad. *(An obituary for Harry appeared in The Times on June 11th enumerating his many talents: 'an ardent soldier, an accomplished engineer, a first-rate linguist, a beautiful musician, a distinguished painter and architect.')*

26th Fetched Edward & Julia who arrived in high spirits & health. Took them to The Cottage where left them. *(Edward in his diary wrote that 'Gerard is looking much better & our darling also looks well, Pom came across to dinner')*

27th Edward & Julia here all morning. I dined at The Cottage. Edward & Julia left.

---

[181]   This is Richard's illegitimate son in Canada to whom he had left £500 in his will. Louisa was left everything for her life or until she remarry and then the house would go to Gerard. On her death her dowry of £10,000 would be converted into money and divided equally between their six children. Richard's estate was valued at £63,179 which had the same spending value as £3,052,000 today.

30th Took Lolotte & Gerard to Maidstone en route to London on her business.

Lolotte (painted by Louisa)

October 18th To London with Mary & Lolotte. We parted company at Charing Cross where Bertha met us & I passed my day with her. She, Delmar & the children most flourishing. Much shopping at Waterloo House.

20th The tea party for 'the Mothers Meeting' given by Gussie & Mary.

24th In the evening came Louy & two children, Richard & Bryan. Bryan is an odd little light-haired child of five years old.

25th Gerard & I went to Malling, took luncheon with the Miss Savages & saw poor Louis who was less wandering in mind. Robert & Lewis arrived at the cottage.

November 2nd Emmy Gibson (now Burnett) died in Bath, her body returned to Hollingbourne for burial. Ella arrived to stay & all my children are round me except Bertha.

23rd To London with Gerard & Gussie, shops with Bertha & spent time with Mrs Treherne who is overwhelmed with sorrows. All my friends will soon have passed away. Mrs Gibson very seriously ill. Harriet Sellen came as cook.

30th Lolotte left to stay with Bertha & then on to Cheltenham.

December 5th Dined with Gerard & Gussie, a very pleasant party & much singing.

11th Did not go to church. A letter from Canada which answered. It was certainly not a pleasant one. Walked to the vicarage to call on Mrs Gibson.

13th *(staying with Bertha)* To Whiteley's with Short such an endless shop. However I managed to get through a great deal in a short time.

14th The shops are full of Christmas cards & very beautiful some of them are, but as I had mostly to make my selection by gaslight it was very difficult.

16th Lady Goldsmid & little Jessie at luncheon & Jessy & Carrie at afternoon tea.

23rd *(At home)* Many Christmas arrangements, wrote tickets for the Christmas dinner Gerard gives to the tenants this year.

24th Christmas cards showering in. Christmas carols all day long & the band.

25th Not well enough to go to church. Gerard & Gussie dined here.

27th The 42nd anniversary of our marriage, it is very sad, Mary & I dined with Gerard & Gussie.

28th Took Mary & Gussie to Maidstone to arrange for the school treat, busy in the evening dressing dolls.

29th A solitary evening, for Mary, having with Gussie worked hard & assisted in the school treat, drank tea at The Cottage.

1882 January 6th Mary's first soup day & Kate Gibson at luncheon.

8th An arrival from Canada. Gerard gave him a copy of the will & I gave £50 & he departed. To me a most painful interview. *(Richard's illegitimate son)*

9th Mary departed for Norwich & I am now living alone in this house for the first time. How strange it all seems. Gerard & Gussie came to see me during the morning. Kate Gibson took luncheon with me & a drive to Maidstone.

11th Gerard left early for London to see his doctor & bring home dividend & oriental rugs. Gussie took luncheon with me & Mr & Mrs Nutt & Kate called later.

20th Mrs Harrison (*neé Emily Struth*) came to stay & much pleased I was to see her.

26th The two Miss Savages, Gerard & Gussie took luncheon here, very cheerful.

27th Gerard had a meeting at the Infirmary. Mary & Lolotte have gone to Cheltenham. Kate Gibson came to stay with me.

February 2nd Went to stay for two nights with the Miss Savages at Malling, visited poor Louis, called on Mrs Blunt & Mrs Cheere whilst there. Reached my lonely home. *(Louisa continued to visit Louis about every three months)*

7th Bertha arrived with little Jack & admired the changes & improvements.

15thGerard & Gussie returned from Norwich. Missed church as rheumatic. General Lester at luncheon. A horrid letter from Canada. Mr Gibson called. Bobbie arrived.

March 2nd To Brighton *(via seeing Bertha for the night)* drove at once to Oriental Place & took lodgings at number 5. Then to Lady Abinger's where dined every day till Saturday the 11th. Whilst there saw, Emily Harrison & dined with the Horace Smiths. To mother's grave, saw Ellen Woollett, Ella came to see me twice, first with her daughters, then with son Lewis. Met Jessy & Carrie.

17th *(At home)* House still in confusion from papering & painting. Much business with Gerard.

April 7th Gerard is 34, he saw Dr Hoare yesterday & is to take quinine & cod liver oil. God send him better health than he has had. Did not got to church, rheumatic.

14th To London with Gerard for day, met Bertha & Lolotte at Victoria.

17th Ella's marriage day in 1860. How many who were then present have passed away. My dearest mother & sister, Uncle Go, Mr & Mrs Shaw, & their son Hugh, Mrs Carter Hall, the Rev Charles Shaw & my dear husband.

18th Drove to Maidstone with Gerard in the afternoon to fetch Edward & Julia.

23rd Drove to church, took Edward, Julia & Gussie, the rest struggling. Amply repaid by a most beautiful extempore sermon from Edward.

29th Mary & I started early for London, met Bertha at Charing Cross & then proceeded to Waterloo House. A perfect hurricane for our homeward journey. The wind howling & shrieking over the wild marshes by Rochester & the train groaning & creaking. The carriage waiting at Maidstone & when we reached home found that several trees had been blown down.

May 5th Piles of bricks & timbers by the side of the road a sign of the railway beginning.[182] Dreadful tidings of the assassination of Mr Burke & Lord Fred Cavendish at Dublin. Mr Gibson & his son & Gerard dined here.

12th The Miss Horace Smiths departed. Lolotte purchased a riding horse.

15th Had a lawn tennis ground laid out. To afternoon tea with Mrs Balston, discussed old oak, old china & Chippendale chairs.

20th The lawn tennis ground used for the first time & much approved. The village full of navvies of the noisiest description. Bobbie arrived.

30th The first anniversary of my day of sorrows.

June 2nd *(staying with Bertha)* Mr Rochfort came to see me.

4th To morning service. Mr Rochfort called & we walked in Kensington Gardens.

6th Bertha went to Brighton with her children & Mr Rochfort took luncheon in Roland Gardens.

7th Dined with Bertha & Delmar at the Alexander's, my grandfather's house *(Notting Hill House)*. Such an aesthetic & wonderful banquet. There I sat with all that wealth could give in the way of flowers and viands, & porcelain & I thought of my days of childhood & was more than ever astonished to find myself there. Fleur de Lis of all colours growing in china vases & flower pots decorated the whole length of the centre of the table over which a reflected light cast a dim radiance & most of the ladies were medievally attired.

8th I have forgotten to record that one day Short & I went to the Royal Academy. I did not see half enough. Another day I went to the French Gallery with Mr Rochfort to see the

---

[182]   The railway arrived at last in the village. The Hollingbourne line runs from Ashford to London.

wonderful little picture of Napoleon once bought by Ruskin for £1000 & now sold by him for £6090!! Frederic came in fresh from Egypt & full of the confusion there.[183]

17th Attended a large confirmation at Hollingbourne church, about 120, drank tea at the vicarage & afterwards the bishop called here on his way. Gerard for the first time acted as church warden.

July 2nd Ella arrived to stay. A tennis party here.

16th Roused by a violent ring from Gerard before 4 am. Dr Hoare had been sent for & at 6.45 a daughter was born, a very easy affair & the little maiden entered the world as quietly as possible. I breakfasted with Gerard & Dr Hoare. & retired to bed till one o'clock.

19th Tennis party at the Lester's. Two of Ella's boys arrived to stay a week. Gussie & baby doing well.

21st Robert & Ella & three other children came to lunch & collect the two on their way to move to Norfolk.[184]

24th To the luncheon at Sutton Valance school, called on my old maid Mrs Chittenden & then to Mrs Balston's tennis party.

30th Edward & Julia paid a brief visit to Gussie. Kate went to stay with Louy.

August 2nd Gerard, Mary & I went to the Archaeological Meeting at Maidstone a very dusty affair, & dry too, for there was no one to tell us anything except at the parish church where Mr Scott Robertson discoursed. We visited the Palace, the College, the Priory etc. Dined in the Corn Exchange at 4.30. Sir Edward Filmer more dull than usual in the chair. Lord Amshurst as president said a few words.

3rd Went for the second archaeology day to Leeds. Beginning with the church where Mr Gordon Hills lectured on the building & someone else on the jars found there. We then rushed off to Battle Hall *(a 15th century house on the site of the old abbey)* where Mr Scott Robertson appeared with a candle to illuminate & we all made our hot-pressed way thro' a narrow passage till we were nearly smothered. After this last effort we returned home leaving the archaeologists to their luncheon at Park Gate, & to conclude the day with Leeds Castle.

---

[183]   During 1880 Frederic had became controller of the Crown Lands in Egypt and organised the intelligence department there in the 1882 campaign.

[184]   Robert had been appointed vicar of Wiggenhall in Norfolk.

5th Mary left to stay with Lady Goldsmid, & Lolotte & I did our shopping in Maidstone. *(on this day Edward was in Homburg visiting Milly's grave)*

8th Gerard & I in town for business & on our return a bad accident awaited us. Erin kicked over the pole which she smashed, disfiguring the carriage, injuring the harness & destroying for the future all our confidence in her. In fact, leaving the carriage at Loder's we had to find our way home in a fly.

10th The Baron & Ernst arrived. Mary returned. Tennis here, Nutts & Savages.

17th Bertha & Delmar here, the house so full that we had to put Delmar in the grandchild's room for the night.

21st Leopold & Ernst departed. To a lawn tennis party at Lady Lister-Kaye's <u>everyone there,</u> music. New housemaid Susan Dann came & Sarah Mernall left.

23rd With Mary to the Flower Show. Mr Brassey won no end of prizes but then his gardeners too are endless.

27th To the christening of Gerard's little daughter. Her name Augusta Laura de Visme Thomas. She was gorgeously attired in Embroidery, plush & cashmere, & behaved very well.

September 2nd Gerard up The Hill shooting partridges. Luncheon party here. The railway arch over the road has risen from the ground as by magic. Katie Goldsmid came to stay.

5th Kate Gibson returned from staying with Louy in Scotland bringing Freddie.

11th Mary's departure to meet Leopold & Ernst & accompany them to Homburg.

October 3rd Mr Wilder & his very nice looking daughter Augusta came.

10th Gerard & I started early for London. Wore ourselves out with business, thence to Waterloo House where we met Bertha took luncheon with her & her children.

18th Gerard consulting a London doctor who is optimistic. Lolotte left to stay with Jessy.

19th To London with Short, took through return tickets for Paris tomorrow & then went on to Roland Gardens where Lolotte appeared later.

20th Bertha went with me to the Victoria station at 7 where entered the train for Dover. We dashed down to Dover by the express which planted us on the pier & which we left about 10.30 for Paris reaching the bright city & meeting the Baron

& Mary at the Station du Nord about 6 o'clock, drove to the Hotel du Louvre & entered the brilliant quadrangle where eastern palms were growing beneath electric light. The lift raised us to our rooms on the 4th floor which we found very comfortable & from which we looked on the windowed roofs of the Rue St Honore.

21st Descended the numerous stairs to the dining room with its crimson-bordered carpet & with Leopold & Mary enjoyed a delicious breakfast of café au lait, rolls, eggs, & pale but excellent butter. Then repaired to the salon & looked at the pictures & newspapers. Walked down the Rue de Rivoli with Leopold. Later Mary & I took lunch near the Palais Royale & ended the day by dining at the numerously attended table d'hote in the gilded & painted salle a manger. The mass of people was very amusing in the salon afterwards. English innumerable. At last the room became so hot with the gas & the people that we were compelled to retire.

22nd Went with Leopold to hear mass at the Invalides. The music very fine, we wandered in the quadrangle among all the poor halt & maimed by the battles they had fought.

23rd Mary & I drove to the Rue du Bac where she bought a coat & from thence to the wonderful tomb where rests the Emperor. Leopold dined with us today for the last time to our great sorrow, as he leaves Paris early tomorrow. On Saturday I have omitted to say that we dined with two American lady friends of his in the Champs Elysees, very agreeable & their apartment full of pretty things.

24th Leopold came to our rooms early to wish us good bye. One day we wandered on the Quays & in the Rue des Saints Peres & bought two pictures. Another day walked to my old home in the Rue Laffitte, then the Rue d'Artois. So changed with shops, noise, & traffic, that I could not have recognised it. Another day took Mary to see the old Porte St Martin & St Denys. All that part of the town equally changed, as are also the melancholy Tuileries with their ruined palace, & the Boulevards & the Rue de Rivoli & in fact the whole city. We went to the gallery of the Louvre where we became so tired that we could scarcely stand. On Sunday 29th we went to mass at St Roche & heard beautiful music & in the afternoon to the French Protestant church. Dined for the last time that day at the table d'hote. On Sundays the guests usually number 300.

30th We left the bright & noisy city, reaching Calais & then Dover after a fearfully rough passage. At the Victoria station found Bertha & Lolotte awaiting us & delighted I was & to have a brief talk with them & some tea & rest before leaving for Maidstone. We found ourselves beneath our own roof again about 9.30 & Gerard soon came over to greet us. Edward & Julia are at The Cottage.

31st Edward came over to see us. Mary dined at The Cottage in the evening & Freddie stayed with me. During our absence he had started one morning at 8 & walked to the Nore a distance there & back of over 30 miles without breakfast or dinner, only regaling himself with two apples & a glass of beer.[185] When he reached home at 6.30 his feet were almost without feeling & he could not eat.

November 5th Up at 4 in the morning to see the Comet. Met to my surprise Freddie on the landing with a telescope & the window wide open.

9th The comet was very grand. Mrs Green called & Kate as usual, & General Lester.

December 14th Kate Gibson at tea on her way to a meeting of 'Navvies'. General Lester & Edith at luncheon.

21st Leopold has been accepted by Madame de Hermann which I am very glad of. *(re-marrying)* Sent Ella a cheque for £25.

25th Letters from Ernst, Mr Rochfort, Ella & Lolotte & an abundance of Christmas cards. 'Hymns Ancient & Modern' from Gussie & a beautiful brazen sconce from Gerard. He & Gussie dined with us & in spite of the dull weather & rain I felt very happy as how should I not?

27th To the work sale at the school. Much was sold by auction, much was in lotteries. A full, dirty, close room. A long visit from Mrs Farmer as was Jackson.

28th In the evening to the Village Concert, where some of the singing was very good.

1883 New Year's Day Mary & I dined with Gerard & Gussie on roast turkey & the largest plum pudding my eyes ever beheld.[186]

---

[185]   The Nore is a sandbank in the Thames estuary close to Sheerness where Freddie must have walked.

[186]   It is interesting to note that the family always enjoyed a traditional Christmas dinner on New Years Day.

3rd Went with Gussie & Mary to see 'the wonderful sights' of the village. First the room for the navvies in the Tanyard & secondly the Embankment near Godfrey House & the trucks on the summit.

5th Unfavourable reports of the paper mills.

6th To Maidstone bringing back Frederic & Lisa, he well in spite of his Egyptian life.

8th No whistle from the paper mills & everything still. Frederic & Lisa departed. In the afternoon I played backgammon with General Lester.

11th Started at cock crow with Gerard & Gussie for town. Gussie, Short & I paid Elise a visit where Gussie chose a hat. I went to Roland Gardens & passed the afternoon talking to Bertha & seeing the children.

15th *(At home)* Full of accounts at which Gerard assisted. Mrs Duppa brought a third son into the world last night.

20th Went to see Gibson who is ill, then to The Cottage to see the new panels.

27th Mrs Sellen very poorly, Sellen *(Harriet Sellen the cook)* there last night.

February 7th Lolotte, with Kate Gibson, arrived from Cheltenham. Lewis Shaw here.

12th Went with Lewis to the Ornithological & Cat show. Mary's cat Onyx commended. Screaming & crowing quite distracting & smells worse. It is the last poultry show that I ever intend to see, hear or smell.

15th The paper mills have been bought by a London Stationer. Drove with Gussie to call on Mrs Nutt & Mrs Moore. House painted on outside.

March 9th Again snow & again prisoner in the house. Archie Duppa very ill. The last soup giving of the year & Kate at luncheon.

18th A telegram from Delmar to say that a son was born to Bertha yesterday & on Saturday Edward, Woodbyne & Fraulein Wildenstein arrived here *(two of Bertha's children & governess, to be cared for by Mary)*. On Monday I left for Roland Gardens where I remained a fortnight & returned home on April 2nd. . I went to the Grosvenor Gallery to see the collection of paintings by Alma Tadema, very wonderful. During my absence little Archie Duppa died to the deep sorrow of his father.[187] I left Bertha & her immense son most

---

[187]   Archie died of meningitis aged 9.

flourishing & Delmar's time divided between Russian translations & reviews and his new house at Effingham.

April 19th Mary left for Headcorn on her way to meet Lolotte at Walmer. Called on the Cave Brownes.[188]

23rd With Gerard to London. I went to Waterloo House where I indulged in a Persian Carpet & then to Bertha. She & all the children in high spirits & very well.

26th The papering in the hall concluded. Lolotte's bedroom begun. Pictures hung.

May 3rd New carpets & curtains. Mary's room decorated. Gerard bought the tile & brickfield adjoining Godfrey House.

8th A day of falsehood, confession & repentance on Sellen's part & forgiveness & hope on mine. Gerard to Walmer for three days, Gussie passed the evening with me. Grace Gibson called for a subscription to the drum & fife band.

15th Passed an evening in solitude & thought. Kate will join Lolotte & Mary at Walmer for a few days.

18th Gave a dinner party to Gerard, Gussie, their friend & Mr Kingdom. To Frinsted for the opening of the new organ. Mr Wright having presented it to the parish.

27th *(At Bertha's)* Mr Rochfort came & a great pleasure it was to see him again. During my stay I went to the Royal Academy, to the game of Lacrosse at Stamford Bridge, to the Fisheries Exhibition, to Kensington Gardens, to a garden party with Bertha, to another one at Sir Joseph Hooker's at Kew where we met no end of scientific lions.

June 11th Heard from Mr Rochfort who is full of uncertainty about coming.

13th 'He cometh not'. But about 3 o'clock Lolotte arrived accompanied by Delmar.

14th Gerard & his family left for Norwich quite early.

29th Mrs Rodwell, our late Anne, appeared with her two large boys.

July 5th To London with Gerard, business at the bank, then shopping with Short. Delmar is to accompany Sir Fred to the River Congo on a mission of the Belgian Government.[189]

8th Gussie & baby returned. Called on Duppas. To a cricket match at Harrietsham.

---

[188]   John Cave Browne was vicar of Detling and a keen local historian.

[189]   In 1883 Frederic established an administrative system in the Congo for the Belgians.

30th General Lester called about the presentation to Grace Gibson *(vicar's daughter)* this evening of a gift from the school teachers & children on her marriage, Gerard not being well enough to officiate. Then Grace herself called to wish me goodbye before going to the Institute escorted by Lolotte. The present consisted of dessert knives & forks with a suitable inscription, a Russian leather bag & card case. The ceremony went off very well.

August 2nd Mary & I started at 11 the carriage lamps filled with flowers & coachman decorated with an immense bouquet & horses with roses in their heads for Grace Gibson's marriage. Weather very fine & everything went off beautifully, she, & especially the bridegroom, Mr Charles Malden looking very happy.

4th The parcel post began on the 1st & promises to be a success. With Mary to a large tennis party at Lady Lister-Kaye's. Leopold & Ernst arrived.

6th With Mary to the Hoare's garden party at Iden, Staplehurst. A sale of Indian things going on in the conservatory under the auspices of Miss Hoare who was dressed like a Hindoo in white muslin & sat on a kind of table, the most discordant music going on.

8th Mrs Green made a long call. Mary's treat to her GFS girls at Leeds Castle.

12th To a garden party at Barham Court (the Roger Leigh's), everyone there, the Engineers' Band all scarlet & their tent red & white. The brilliant dresses, bright flowers, & magnificent fruit left nothing to be desired.

September 1st At 9 Lolotte, Gerard, Gussie & baby & nurse left in two flies for Headcorn on their way to Walmer. Mary & I drove to Maidstone & made calls.

6th Went to Sharsted to a party in the woods, to see Punch & Judy, lawn tennis & hear the Toy Symphony by Hayden. The latter was performed by Mrs Erskine's family really well & we were comfortably seated in the hall, but the weather was dismal & cold & the rest of the entertainment under the trees was <u>most dreary.</u>

13th Gerard arrived without his beard & looking much better than he did.

14th Drove into Maidstone early to fetch Bertha who arrived with Woodbyne.

25th Gerard's cottage was attempted last night about one o'clock. First the dining room window & then the drawing room. Fox however heard the thieves, & while they were engaged, opened the nursery window & fired Gerard's gun, when they rushed off. They were evidently practised hands by the way in which paper was pasted on the pane to prevent noise. Gerard & Gussie home from Walmer.

29th A long letter & a very melancholy one from Mr Wilder. He is not at all pleased with the marriage of his daughter Augusta whose bridegroom is 40 years older than herself. Mary & I drove to Barham Court where we were admitted but Miss Leigh too fatigued to see us.

October 3rd Louy arrived to stay, with Mona & Bryan.

12th Henry arrived. Short announced her approaching marriage.

22nd A very small daughter born to Gerard before the doctor could arrive.

November 6th Yesterday Henry left & today Short & I departed for Brighton, deposited ourselves very comfortably at 31 Oriental Place, called on the Horace Smiths & regaled ourselves at Bollen's on veal pie & ginger beer. Dined at Edward's, he & Julia in the highest health.

11th Edward & Julia called for me & we went to hear him preach at St Nicholas, a beautiful sermon. Drove to Preston to my dearest mother's grave in the quiet churchyard. In the evening called on the Horace Smiths.

12th Called on Ellen Scott, still an invalid, & on Mrs Rogers of Hadlow Castle whom it was quite sad to see. She has had a fearful operation for cancer. Four doctors in Paris performed it & received for their fee 400 guineas. This she told me, also that she had been attended by nearly 70 doctors. Dined with Edward, very pleasant.

13th Bertha arrived at breakfast, dined with her at Edward's.

14th Bertha & I left Brighton for Effingham. Got out at Three Bridges & into Bertha's brougham & after four mile drive reached her home. The interior of the house charming, the rooms spacious, but I was disappointed in the exterior & its surroundings. The children all very bright & well as also Bertha.

16th Bertha drove me to Horley, a most dismal dirty station, & there we said adieu & I made my way to Victoria & thence to Maidstone.

22nd Sir Fred is fever-stricken & obliged to return. Delmar, in spite of having three guinea worms cut out of his feet, & the climate, which he describes as loathsome, has decided to

294

remain for the present. Little Short who has been with me four years as maid, departed & is to be married to a Private Vigor.

December 2nd Mary left to stay with Bertha a fortnight. To Maidstone with Mona.

19th Took Gerard & Lolotte to Maidstone on their way to Rochester cathedral to be present at the unveiling of a window put up by the Royal Engineers in memory of those of their number who fell in the South African & Afghan war. Harry was mentioned.[190] Gerard & Lolotte left immediately after the ceremony, it was as much as she could bear, but I am sure that she would not have been absent.

29th Lolotte left to stay with friends & Mary & I took Mona to the pantomime.

1884 New Year's Day Went to the morning service & the christening of my dear little last grandchild Ella Julia de Visme Thomas who behaved beautifully, looked very nice & never uttered a sound. Mary, Mona & I dined with Gerard & Gussie to eat turkey & plum pudding.

3rd To Maidstone to take Gerard to be sworn in a J.P for the county of Kent. Brought back Short, (Mrs Vigor), to try on my dress.

7th Gerard came in from Bearsted Sessions his first appearance there.

9th To Maidstone with Mona, saw a footman by name Cork whom I have promised to take if his character suits. (*it did*)

13th My cold too bad to go to church so stayed at home & enjoyed Lolotte's society she having returned yesterday.

18th Left for London with Springett having taken rooms at 7 Chapel Place, Cavendish Square. They were clean, shabby, convenient & comfortable. Bertha walked in during afternoon looking bright & well.

20th To morning service, a very dull sermon against infidelity. Called on Frederic whom I found looking better than expected & with whom I found Bertha.

22nd To Maples in search of vases for Gerard, found some which I trust that he will like, I saw also their suite of rooms from which people may select furniture & according to which their houses may be arranged & decorated.

23rd Who should appear but Delmar looking thinner but very well without his whiskers & beard, only his moustaches

---

[190]   Harry's name and rank can be read in the list above the great West Door.

remaining. In the morning I went to see the collection of Sir Joshua Reynolds paintings at the Grosvenor Gallery.

25th Left for home after a pleasant stay in town feeling quite independent & a burden to no one. Gerard & Mary awaiting me at Maidstone station.

29th Mrs Lester gave a bad report of Edith who had seen Sir William Jenner.[191]

February 5th Kate Gibson came to read in French. Hip aches, feel a perfect cripple.

March 5th Kate Gibson at luncheon after which we went to the pantomime of Little Red Riding-hood which much pleased the young. The Miss Hampsons called.

7th A man much hurt on the railway works by a truck passing over him.[192]

12th Mona & I took luncheon with Lady Howard de Walden & saw her endless collection of china & the majolica plate for which she has lately given £100.

21st Walked with Gerard to see his renovated cottages & his allotments. Kate came.

Mary returned (*from staying with Edward & Julia*) looking very well.

26th General Lester took luncheon here & we heard no end of Irish ghost stories.

29th Gerard ill with a return of Persian fever, sat with him some time.

April 7th Mary, Bobbie & I started for London where he left & we shopped.

May 5th Gussie & I drove to Maidstone & brought back my two young cousins Jessie & Patricia Goldsmid. (*Frederic's daughters*) Mrs Gibson very ill.

10th Frederic arrived & we had a late dinner, Gerard & Gussie joining us. Lawn tennis in the afternoon with General & Edith Lester.

24th To Maidstone with Gussie & Mona, the latter had her dress tried on which took one hour and five minutes by Mrs Vigor's clock.

---

[191]   Jenner (1815-1898), made the distinction between typhus and typhoid.

[192]   The Ashford to Maidstone railway line through Hollingbourne was at last being built and opened this year. Gerard sued the rail company for severance of his land at Godfrey House. However he profited from developing the tile and brick works in the village which supplied the railway with the millions of bricks required. Hollingbourne station was halfway between Eyhorne Street and the Upper village.

28th *(Staying with Dora Goldsmid)* Lodging hunting, took rooms in Margaret Street, Cavendish Square. A large dinner in Lexham Gardens, Sir Fred & Katie, Jessie & Carrie. A very pleasant & luxurious dinner.

30th Springett & I went out shopping. Mr Rochfort came & sat with me, then Frederic. After dinner we all went to the Health Exhibition.[193] The illuminations very pretty. Countless people walking about the gardens in the dusk & I have no doubt that everything looked better by the electric light than in the glare of day. The noise of machines incessant & the old London street not yet completed.

31st Travelled home. Last night were three explosions of dynamite, one by the Junior Carlton *(Club)* which did much mischief tho' no lives were lost. The other in Scotland Yard & another bag of explosives were found at the foot of the Nelson Monument.[194]

June 2nd *(At home)* Three years ago how sad was today! My dear husband's funeral & the telegram of poor Harry's death. To the great Agricultural Show at Maidstone with Mary, Mona & Kate. The pigs were so fat as to be immovable.

4th Left home again for an apartment in Margaret Street, number18, which proved very comfortable. Mr Rochfort came every day till he was taken ill in the Royal Academy.

15th Mr Rochfort dined with me but was ill & weak.

17th We went to the Health Exhibition together & I dined at Sir Fred's & sat between Mr Greenwood the editor of the St James's Gazette & Mr Severne the artist. That morning too, I met Signor Enrico Belli the copyist at Dora's & arranged with him about my father's portrait. I went to a matinee musicale at Jessy's. Dined with Ellen Scott to meet Sir Sibbald & talked over old times.

18th Mr Rochfort came to say goodbye in the morning as he was engaged on a committee in the House. Went to the Grosvenor Gallery saw the famous 'King Cophetua & the Beggar Maid' by Burne Jones.

19th Left London, Mona met me & I returned home to find Gerard, Gussie & Mary all poorly. With Mona to tennis at Mrs Balston's of Springfield. Saw Mr Balston's collection of 500

---

[193]   At the Horticultural Society's Garden off Exhibition Road.

[194]   This was part of what was known as 'The Dynamite War' being waged by the Irish Home Rule extremists.

humming birds, some wonderfully beautiful with their breasts glowing like fire.

24th Mary & Mona left for Scotland, house very still.

25th With Gussie & Kate to Miss Best's tennis. Dined with Gerard & Gussie. Timetables out for the new railway.

30th Set off for London with Gerard & met Signor Belli to see the portrait of my father. A pleasant morning with Bertha.

July 6th Saw the last train wind round the hills like a comet.

10th Gussie left early with her daughters for Norwich. Mrs Gibson very poorly. Drove to Maidstone, paid Mrs Whatman a long visit, Gerard at tea.

11th Mr Gibson at luncheon & Gerard at tea. The window put up to Mrs Burnett (Emmy Gibson), by her husband.*(in Hollingbourne church)*

12th Early to London with Gerard. We did not travel by the new line as he had to go to Canon Street & I to Charing Cross where met Signor Belli & took the portrait to Lexham Gardens & compared it with the original. We came away satisfied. After eating some very satisfying meat pies we went to the Royal Academy for an hour.

13th *(At home)* To morning service, Mr Gibson preached. Saw the window. The likeness to Emmy Burnett most striking & the view of the distant hill very well managed. *(The window shows the Marriage feast of Cana with Emmy as the bride)* General Lester called to see my father's portrait & Mr Gibson.

14th Gerard left this morning for Margate. Kate came to see me & I wandered & worked in the garden until I saw the express dash by in a streak of light.

15th Mrs Branfill Harrison arrived & I drove to the new station to fetch her. It was a great pleasure to see her again.

21st Gerard returned from his London & Margate stay. Went to a very pleasant tennis party at Mrs Tom Balston's. Mrs Gibson died today.*(the vicar's wife, Elizabeth, was 60)*

24th Gussie & her daughters returned from Norwich. Mr Scott, Canon of Lichfield came to sleep here for his sister's funeral tomorrow. *(Mrs Gibson)*

25th Went to the giving of prizes at Sutton Valence Grammar school. Mrs Harrison left & so now I am alone again. Mrs Gibson was buried today by the side of her daughter Mrs Burnett, & at 10 Mr Scott again appeared to sleep here. He told me that all had passed off most quietly. Gerard was at the funeral in the morning & at the Ophthalmic *(Hospital)* at Maidstone during the afternoon.

The window in Hollingbourne church in memory of Emmy Burnett neé Gibson

August 2nd With Gerard & Gussie to cricket at the Brassey's, Preston Hall. Mary returned with Louis Gipps.

9th Leopold & Ernst arrived. To tennis at the Wynyard's at the Barracks.

16th The Baron & Ernst left, Lolotte arrived. The Wykeham Martins called.

19th Bertha & her boy Edward arrived. To Mr Baxendale's tennis party.

22nd Delmar arrived as we were at dinner having as usual brought nothing.

September 6th The Gibson baby died yesterday. (*Gibson the gardener*) What sorrow for the mother! And the poor absent father.

8th Kate came, Ella & Eleanor arrived. A lawn tennis party at home. Mr Gibson left yesterday for foreign parts. Kate called.

11th Drove to Maidstone with Ella, called on Short. A barrel of saurkraut arrived from Leopold.

16th Gerard, Gussie, Mary, Freddie & I drove up to Yew Tree Farm *(owned by Gerard)* & very nice & neat & prosperous everything looked. All in first rate order. I should fancy that Wormshill had never yet seen the like. Couchman the bailiff & his wife are living in a most comfortable & rustic farmhouse. The old rugged yew is the only thing not improved. It seems to have dwindled since I saw it last.

20th Lolotte & I drove to Maidstone & heard that Mrs Vigor & her baby were very flourishing & took her some flowers.

23rd Major Trevor (*Lolotte's friend*) took luncheon here & was very calm & pleasant.

24th Gerard still suffering neuralgia. Mary & I drove to Malling & took luncheon at St Leonards where met my old friend Mrs H. Duppa. Saw Louis who was more than usually out of sorts. Louy & son Bryan arrived.

October 3rd Left for Horley, met Bertha & arrived at Effingham, house very nice & children blooming but I like the grounds as little as ever. Dinner party there. Delmar received a personal letter from the King of Belgium in recognition of services in the Congo & is awarded the Golden Order of Leopold. Left on 7th.

8th Sellen's father has been drinking & fighting & is in prison for a month.

25th A very cheerful dinner party at home, the first for years. Mr & Mrs Duppa, General Lester, Gussie & Gerard, etc.

28th Jessy & Carrie arrived for the day. Julia arrived at The Cottage.

30th Louy packing to go & little Louis crying so much at his mother's departure it was decided he should go with her, so on 31st they left for Scotland.

November 1st Kate came down to say that Mr Sedgwick considered the fever in the Upper village, of which Mrs Fuller has died, to be smallpox.

3rd Four of the sick moved to the fever ward at the Union.

4th The sick which had been conveyed to the Union have the smallpox which some of the Fullers had imported to Hollingbourne from Brompton.

6th Left for Brighton, Edward & the Horace Smiths had been to my lodgings, 31 Oriental Place to enquire for me, & the next morning they all appeared. Dined with Edward & Julia. Another day dined with Edward & larger party. Dined too at the Horace Smith's. Took luncheon with Lady Abinger. Twice went with Edward to the charming loan exhibition. An afternoon drive to Rottingdean. Twice I went to Preston churchyard to my dearest mother's grave. The stone cleaned & the letters painted. Bertha has scarlet fever but is doing well. At the Horace Smith's met Herman Merivale the dramatic writer & his wife. He is the American who writes under the nom de plume of Hans Britmann & has visited the wild tribes of North America & lived among the gypsies. Also met Mr Leland, he & Mr Merivale made more noise than I ever heard made by two people in any room public or private.[195]

I also had a visit from Mr Henry Wagner the genealogist who is full of the de Visme pedigree which he says must be concluded soon as next year is the bi-centenary of the revocation of the Edict of Nantes. After a very delightful fortnight at my old haunt Brighton, took leave of my old friends on the 20th, & my once home. Found Mary awaiting me at the station & Gerard & Kate came in the afternoon.

23rd Mary & I to church where Mr Gibson preached. After the service went to look at the window erected to the memory of Harry which I much admired. Gerard & Gussie at luncheon.

24th Robert came in unexpectedly in the evening & brought the most painful intelligence. We could scarcely realize it. He slept here. *(Bobbie is in serious trouble, he has disappeared. Possibly he has stolen money from the bank where he works.)*

29th Lewis Shaw came in the evening. No further news of Bobbie.

1885 January 3rd Drove with Lolotte to call at the vicarage where found Kate & her father looking most comfortable, & then to the Lester's who soon leave for Italy.

---

[195]   This was Herman Charles Merivale 1839-1906, dramatist & poet.

7th Sir Fred & Patricia arrived & we dined at The Cottage, very pleasant, but it would have been pleasanter if Frederic & Canon Scott had not kept all their talk about Egypt to their two selves.

8th Patricia much with Gussie practising for the concert this evening at the board school. Gerard was unfortunately too ill to go. Gussie sang very well.

9th Frederic & Patricia departed. Marys first day of soup distribution.

17th Went to see Gerard's new road, a deep cutting through heavy clay.

21st My cold so bad could not get up, & from this day to February 1st passed in my bed and room. During my retirement two fearful battles have been fought in Egypt. Attempts have been made to blow up by Dynamite the Tower, Westminster Hall & the House of Commons. *(by the Irish Fenians)*

February 2nd A visit from Dr Hoare & a letter from Bertha who had been guided & lighted to the scene of dynamite devastation in the House of Commons by Palgrave where a policeman keeps guard day & night by a dark hole.

5th News in the evening that Khartoum had fallen into the hands of the Mahdi & nothing was known of the fate of Gordon.

10th Left for 18 Margaret St, Cavendish Square. Bertha came to see me in the evening kindly to persuade me to dine with her but did not feel strong enough. Managed to call on Ellen Scott & Mrs Thomas Thomas. On 12th had a very pleasant day with Mary & Lolotte who came up to town to shop. Had visits from Mrs Palgrave, Frederic, Edward, etc, till the day I was seized with such violent bleeding in the nose that I had to call for Dr Wood, to lie in bed two days, with ice on my head. Another weakening attack again kept me in bed & it was not till Tuesday 24th escorted by Gerard, that I returned home to my intense joy. The Sunday following I had two shivering fits, like ague which sent me to bed again. Bertha has been down with Woodbyne to pay us a visit.

March 9th Sir Fred came for the Conservative meeting at the Manor House.

13th Have been round to The Cottage to see Gerard's excavations & improvements.

16th Got up to breakfast which I had not done for nearly a month, & most thankful I felt to be so well again. Mary & I drove to Maidstone to enquire after Miss Best who has undergone a most fearful operation.

April 5th A letter to Gerard from Bertha telling of Bartle's (*Goldsmid*) dreadful doings. Wrote to Frederic to learn more than the newspapers tell.[196] Gerard rheumatic but crawled round three times during the day. To church for first time for two months.

7th Mary left for Maidenhead & Kate came to stay. Gerard at Quarter Sessions. A letter from Ella saying she had heard from Bobbie who had been at Suakim, Berber as translator but finding the climate too hot had made his way to Australia & America having been taken as a traveller for a large trading house at Ceylon.

15th Edward & Julia arrived bright & well, I went to dinner party at The Cottage.

17th Dinner party at home. Edward preached in Hollingbourne church, very fine.

May 9th Freddie Gipps came to stay here & Lewis Shaw at The Cottage.

13th Mary at Maidstone attending the meeting for the Prevention of Cruelty to Animals of which she was appointed secretary. General & Edith Lester called.

15th Mrs Green called looking very youthful, also Kate. Gerard very busy at the Conservative cause.

20th With Hughes to hunt for lodgings in London, saw seven before I could find one to suit. Ended by taking rooms at 9 Margaret Street, took luncheon with Bertha & her children, all in high health.

26th Hughes & I left for Margaret Street where I am most comfortable. Called on Jessy & Carrie & found them looking most gloomy seated in their dining room.

27th Mr Rochfort came in late, quite unexpectedly, just off his journey. I went three times to the Royal Academy; with Mary, with Mr Rochfort & with Hughes. Lolotte came to see me twice, & Mary passed a day & night in town. One day I dined with Frederic to meet Malkhom Khan the Persian Minister. Khan has a great admiration for the English & brings up his children as such.

---

[196]   Bartle Goldsmid worked as a stockbroker in the City. He went bankrupt and absconded leaving liabilities of £250,000 and assets estimated at £15,000.

June 7th Walked in the park with Mr Rochfort. Saw the immense procession against the Beer Tax, seventeen bands of music & countless banners. Drank tea with Bertha & Delmar.

9th With Mr Rochfort to the Grosvenor Gallery.

10th An adieu visit, left my pleasant lodgings. Mary met me at the station.

15th Mary left for Norwich. Kate, Freddie & I drove to Maidstone.

17th Began Italian with Freddie who also busied himself looking over my coins.

July 2nd In the paper the death of Sir Sibbald Scott, very sudden. He is an old friend & I am much grieved for it. Gussie & Gerard to Norwich. (*For a lengthy stay*)

5th To the school treat at the vicarage. With Freddie to tennis at Mrs Balston's. Sellen, Gibson & Hughes went by a Gardeners Excursion train to Margate & Ramsgate.

20th Had tea with Mrs W. Martin & with the two elderly maiden grand-daughters of Southey the poet who have rented Godfrey House for two months.

25th Hollingbourne & Leeds Flower Show, to which had given prizes. To a tennis party at the Balston's at Springfield, everyone there.

August 3rd Gerard at the Bearsted Sessions. Freddie went with him. Leopold & Ernst arrived.

September 14th With Gussie to a musical party at Mrs Balston's. Ella & Eleanor arrived.

24th Left for 'The Firs' Maidenhead Thicket with Hughes to stay with Lolotte. Drawing room long & low & filled with oriental treasures & art & too dark for my old fashioned taste. My bedroom was immense & there dearest Lolotte had thought of all that I could like. Left there for Brighton & my old lodgings, 31 Oriental Place.

My time here divided between dining with Edward & Julia & with the Horace Smiths. Visited Mother's grave. Lolotte & Sybil Laurie came for the last week & inhabited the dining room floor while I was in the drawing rooms & a delightful time I passed, also brightened by a day's visit from Bertha. After a fortnight at Brighton I returned home on 12th October to find all damp & dreary in the extreme.

October 31st Gibson & Sellen married by Mr Gibson at 8.15 a.m.

November 3rd Felt too rheumatic to go to church. A Conservative meeting at Leeds where Gerard & Mr Duppa spoke. Read aloud to Mary & played backgammon.

7th To GFS meeting at Maidstone with Mary, Kate & Gussie. Tried to paint Freddie but without light or eyesight what can be done?

10th Walked in the road with Gussie & my little grand-daughters in their new & very pretty crimson dresses trimmed with grey astrakhan. Gerard meeting near the viaduct Mr Day etc for the purchase of land for an Infectious Hospital.

15th To Maidstone on polling day the town full of purple & orange & pale blue flags. Major Ross elected & drawn about the town at Midnight in triumph. The majority about 300. Mary & Gussie driving about canvassing.

30th The manager's house at the Turkey Mills is burned & part of the stable. This is supposed to have originated in revenge. Mr John Hollingworth the owner is very ill, as well as his brother & is quite in ignorance of the fire.[197]

December 1st Called on Mr Betts to present him with a purple & orange rosette which he declined to wear, saying that he could not show his colours, tho' he meant to vote for the Conservatives.

2nd Polling at the board school here & the committee sitting at the Manor House. The village very bright with the purple & orange rosettes which I gave to the joint committees of Holllingbourne & Leeds & to many of the voters. In the afternoon drove to the Manor House here & also to Leeds to see all that was going on. Much cheered by the 'break-loads' of Conservatives in our progress.

3rd Gathorne-Hardy elected by a majority of 1094 over Sir Sidney Waterlow.[198]

7th Left with Mary for London, Bertha met us at the Victoria station & Lolotte at Gorringes. Passed a most pleasant day with them both. Took luncheon with Bertha & saw all her charming children except Edward. Delmar much altered.

7th Major Murphy was killed out hunting on Saturday. The horse caught in some wire netting threw the Major & it is supposed trod on his head, as his head was quite crushed.

---

[197]   The wealthy Hollingworths were the owners of the famous Turkey Mill where paper was made.

[198]   Gathorne-Hardy (1814-1896) president of the Poor Law Board, later Earl of Cranbrook.

8th Gerard off to town as delegate of the Poor Law Board.

24th My very grand diploma came as being one of the first founders or fellows of the Huguenot Society of London.

30th Through snow & cold went to the amateur theatricals at the Board school when were acted 'The Chimney Corner' & 'Who's to win?'

1886 January 1st Heard the bells last night all around us. At 8.41 this morning Willie arrived from Whitehaven having travelled all night. Dined Mary, Willie, Freddie & I at The Cottage.

5th Willie sat for me for his portrait & left for Whitehaven.

8th The first day of the soup. Kate Gibson at luncheon.

16th Mary came home, very glad to see her again.

25th *(in lodgings in London)* Bertha came early & we went out shopping, purchased Mary's dress at Marshall & Snelgrove, went in the evening to the collection of Millais' pictures in the Grosvenor Gallery. They looked lovely beneath the electric light.

28th In the afternoon called on Dora & Lady Goldsmid, both out, & on Mrs Thomas Thomas, looking, for her, very well, & on poor Jessy who was only just up & had been seriously ill with interior inflammation. Frederic paid me a long visit.

February 10th *(At home)* Lolotte arrived with Sybil Laurie, Gerard & Freddie in Maidstone making plans for Freddie's journey to Australia. *(Freddie is 20 and had inherited his parents' restless adventurousness)*

22nd A letter from Lewis saying that Bobbie has not been heard of for eight months.

March 11th A luncheon here. Gerard as usual was a good boy & came to see me in the evening. Mrs Waller the mistress of the Union died yesterday. She is much lamented & will be much missed. Mary has gone to Norwich.

15th Gerard went to Malling & thought Louis better than usual.

18th Gussie & I paid visits including Mrs Bland who enrolled me as a Dame of the Primrose League. *(a Conservative association)*

22nd Walked over to The Cottage & saw my nice little grand-daughters, the first time for quite two months. Wrote a cheque for Freddie's passage.

25th Gerard so poorly that he had sent for Mr Sedgwick. He was in great pain. Went over to see him again in the afternoon. Louy, Freddie, Ella & Leo arrived. Mary returned.

27th Packing & tumult consequent on Freddie's departure. His mother & he went up to town by the 11.20 train to see the 'Orient' & his quarters there.

29th Much shopping with Louy for Freddie.

30th Gerard in bed still & suffering much pain. Painted Freddie's portrait.

31st Gerard very poorly & Freddie going & I feel all sorrow. Met Louy & him in Maidstone & brought her home after the sad parting.

April 1st A card from Freddie to say that the 'Orient' was only to leave London this morning at 10. So Louy & little Ella started for Gravesend in the hope of seeing him once more, but they only saw the large vessel on her way.

3rd A letter from Freddie to his mother, a great comfort to all of us as it was written happily. Dear Gerard decidedly better, thank God. Mr Sedgwick called to talk to me of him.

6th Much troubled about Gerard but Mr Sedgwick does not think him worse & he has less pain.

7th Dr Hoare came to meet Mr Sedgwick & considers Gerard very ill. He is to remain entirely in bed & to take nourishment every hour, but nothing solid.

9th Lolotte arrived, I think Gerard a shade better, Dr Hoare came.

10th Gerard slightly better, he was prayed for in church, & preparations for the Archbishop & the Confirmation.

13th The Archbishop came at nearly 2, we sent the carriage for him to the station. Then after sitting here for a time he disappeared with his chaplain. Back after the ceremony to take tea & coffee. There were about 80 confirmed & Mary & Kate superintended a tea in the evening to the confirmees. The Archbishop is very agreeable & courteous & invited me to Lambeth.

15th Gerard much better, Lolotte left for Maidenhead. Mr Duppa paid me a long visit to enquire about Gerard & to talk about his New Zealand life.

25th Easter Sunday, took the early communion, Gussie & I went together. Gerard certainly better though weak. The church beautifully decorated with primroses. & Mary's cross over the altar of white alyssum & hyacinths. Mrs Duppa's baby daughter was christened.

27th Louy departed with Leo, little Ella remaining behind in great grief for the loss of her mother.

May 7th Gerard came out of his room for the first time & sat ¾ hour in the nursery. Julia came for the day.

15th To London, Margaret Street, Mr Rochfort called every day. Saw Bertha a number of times, made other visits every day for a fortnight including to Lambeth Palace under the guidance of the Archbishop. Called on the Palgraves to congratulate on his success in becoming Clerk to the House of Commons. To the 'Colonies' exhibition & three times to the Royal Academy. Mary & Lolotte came one day shopping. Home on 31st, much painting of house done in absence.

June 1st Gerard strolling with me in the garden. Kate Gibson appeared.

The back of Eyhorne House and garden

4th To Maidstone with little Ella shopping. *(Ella Gipps is 16)* Mr Gibson called.

14th The Eyhorne cricket club played against Lenham in the front meadow.

15th To the Barracks for lawn tennis invited by the 40th Regiment Queens Own.

16th A telegram from Delmar to announce the birth of a son & Bertha doing well.

22nd Our old coachman George Brenchley appeared with his second wife, he is looking very large & portly & very prosperous.

July 4th To London with Mary shopping, met Bertha & Datie Clayton, saw Bertha's giant son, a very nice looking baby. Freddie is in Sidney.

13th Gerard left for Margate. Tennis party here with Nutts, Lesters, Mrs Green etc.

16th Gussie & girls left for Margate. Willie came. To flower show at Boughton Malherbe with little Ella.

20th Did nothing but talk to Kate on a most painful subject. *(Her father Rev. Gibson is to remarry to a woman who is 40 years younger than he. Mary had hoped to marry him.)*

August 1st We all think of nothing but the wretched marriage.

2nd It is decided that Mary go abroad with Kate Gibson.

3rd Mary left for Sir Fred's & Lolotte is most kindly going to stay with me.

7th Lolotte heard that Sybil Laurie has had a bad fall from her horse, so she set off for Maidenhead & *little* Ella & I have the house to ourselves. Kate Gibson took luncheon with me.

9th Little Ella has measles. I made calls but no one home. Kate Gibson at luncheon in very low spirits. *(does not want to live with her new step-mother)*

11th Jack Shaw came in on his bicycle. I drove up The Hill in the pony carriage & called on Mr Duppa & saw his leg which is in a fearful state, crimson from the knee to the ankle. Went all round the gardens with him.

13th Kate is kindly coming to stay with me. To a large tennis party at Lady Lister- Kaye's.

14th Gerard I grieve to say again has a nurse & doctors, Lolotte is with him. Mrs Green passed the afternoon here. *(On this day Edward noted that Gussie had written to say Gerard's inflammation of the colon has broken out again at Margate & he was unable to move. Lolotte telegraphed to say he was better & dozing due to the opiates.)*

15th Mr Gibson did the service well but feebly, Mrs Gibson looked bright & nice.

17th A much happier report of Gerard. Kate Gibson left with Edith Lester, I feel relieved at her departure for I am sure that the change will be of benefit to her. Called on Mrs Gibson. It was all so strange that I could not believe my senses. Then on to Mrs Wykeham Martin at the Castle.*(Edward's diary for this day notes 'Gerard's complaint is now peritonitis, Pom returned early to be with her mother')'*

19th Mr & Mrs Gibson called, she bright & pretty. He looking much better.

23rd Mary drove up to see the farm. Everything looking well & shipshape & Couchman grieving that Gerard could not be there to see it.

24th *Little* Ella & I went to the flower show a very good one. Met many there whom I knew & all most anxious in their enquiries for Gerard.

27th A letter from Lolotte, Gerard I grieve to say has had a relapse & Dr Rowe came at 5 am.[199] Sir Fred & Katie came by the 5.47 train.

29th Gerard prayed for by our united wish in church. Mr Duppa drove me home & sat here afterwards till 4, or rather laid, for he could not move from the sofa.

September 2nd Gerard still ill at Margate in bed, on liquids, but improving. Lolotte still with him as well as Gussie & the children. To a tennis party at the Forster's.

5th Tennis party here. Mary drove up The Hill to look at Gerard's farm again.

24th Gussie *(who is heavily pregnant)* & children returned leaving Gerard better.

25th I left for Margate. (*to look after Gerard*)

October 26th *(At home)* To The Cottage & saw my new grandchild & mother, both as well & flourishing as possible & their nice Welsh nurse, Evans. Wrote to Gerard.

28th A day of incessant business. A long visit to Gussie & the baby after which wrote to Margate. Kate is kindly giving *little* Ella lessons in music.

30th Mary left early for Margate. A good account of Gerard.

31st Sat for a long time with Gussie.

November 1st Kate & *little* Ella at church & I sitting with Gussie. Sellen was sentenced to a month's imprisonment with hard labour for ill treating his wife, poor wretched being! To the first of the subscription concerts with Kate & *little* Ella, room crowded.

---

[199]   Dr Arthur Rowe (1858-1926), was a Margate surgeon, physician, palaeontologist & archaeologist. It was as a palaeontologist that he became famous as the greatest chalk fossil expert. He was a kindly man, much loved by his patients & gave the same care to rich and poor alike.

2nd Letter from Ella with the news that she had heard from B (*Bobbie*) & that he was married with two children.

5th Sat With Gussie in the morning & saw my two nice little grand-daughters in their blue stockings.

17th Gerard is to get up today, the first time for 14 weeks.

19th Started early for Margate driving to Sittingbourne, & by train. Found Mary awaiting me. Gerard looking <u>wonderfully</u> better in his Magdalen black & white shirt. Saw Dr Rowe who thinks very well of him. Lolotte was not looking her best.

22nd *(At home)* Drove up The Hill & sat with Mr Duppa who is better, he says, & drank some tea made in his own peculiar way.

24th Mrs Lester brought me an Italian letter to correct, that is not the word, it must be re-written. Poor Kate departed to stay with the Moores at Boughton Malherbe.

December 3rd Mary returned from Margate.

4th Gussie left for Margate without the children.

6th Gerard has used his chair & gone into the next room. He had not left his bedroom for nearly five months. I called on the grandchildren.

8th Went with Mary & *little* Ella to see Maskeleyne & Cooke & very wonderful & incomprehensible we found it. The musical part played from all parts of the room by electricity was charming & quite magical. Then the dancing plates & the automaton.[200]

18th Gussie returned, she thinks no chance of Gerard's return before mid January.

22nd Gussie returned to Margate. Hughes, Katherine, George, Couchman & Tom all went to the Primrose League Concert.

24th Kate came to stay. *(she has not lived in the vicarage since the marriage)*

25th Cards & presents pouring in from family & friends. A vase from Gerard & Lolotte, Tennyson's new book from Gussie, a pretty preserving jar from Ella Gipps.

1887 January 1st Willic arrived from Whitehaven. *(later taking his sister Ella back with him)*

6th Bertha & son Edward arrived. *(to stay)*

24th Gerard arrived at his own home accompanied by Lolotte, Dr Rowe & Nurse Miriam. The carriage left the house for Margate this morning before 6 & brought him here without

---

[200]   John Maskelyne successful stage magician & inventor & George Cooke cabinet maker & magician.

hitch or hindrance about 1.30 after an absence of 6 months. Thank God that he is once more among us! Lolotte & Dr Rowe came to stay here. Gussie arrived by an earlier train than the rest.

25th Went over to Gerard & found him looking most happy & comfortable. It was quite delightful to see him.

27th Gerard in his chair for his afternoon airing & I drove out to call on Lady Howard de Walden, returning sadly rheumatic & to bed early.

30th A walk in the road with Gerard in his chair.

February 17th Baby christened 'Ethel Lilian Mary de Visme Thomas,' & behaved.

March 1st Wilson passed the day here & went to The Cottage. She is engaged to the Duchess of Leinster as nurse to her first born & is going to Ireland.

8th Saw Gerard <u>walk</u> from his room to his Bath chair after eight months that he has been quite unable to do so.

14th Lolotte came in the evening, an immense pleasure. Lewis Shaw left. He is a very nice boy & much improved.

21st Do not feel happy about Louy who is far from well. Kate arrived to stay.

22nd Constant letters & telegrams passing between Blackstone & ourselves on the subject of Louy. Ella wrote to say she had heard from Bobbie.

26th Isaac Bolton who lived with the Carter Halls in days long past as a boy of all work came to ask for assistance for emigration. He is now a very respectable, well spoken, middle aged man with nine children.

April 4th To Maidstone with Lolotte & to London where met Bertha & had lunch with her, Wilson called there to say goodbye. Edith Lester called to ask Lolotte & Mary to tea on the departure of the emigrants from the village on the 6th.

14th Edward & Julia arrived so a dinner party here with Nutts. Edward & Mr Nutt told ghost stories.

16th Frederic arrived in the middle of our tea party which included Mrs Duppa. Edward preached beautifully in Hollingbourne church.

18th Edward & Julia left. *(Edward's diary notes how interesting Gussie's children are 'Gerard looks pulled but in excellent spirits', also that he & Ju travelled with Sir Fred when they left.)*

20th Gussie has a few flint weapon heads from the Coxheath excavation, *(by Maidstone museum, in Gerard's wood)* it will take many days to reach the centre of the mound. Mary & Gussie watched the excavations.

30th There proved to be no buried warrior, it is a fiasco.

May 21st A begging letter from Mrs Minter, I wrote to her, I pity her much.

31st With Hughes to 9 Margaret Street & found myself very comfortable in my clean but small lodgings, & now, June 16th, I am at home again.

June 18th Mary left for Norwich. Gerard & I drove to Maidstone & saw the humble preparations for the Jubilee which is to be kept there tomorrow.[201]

21st Drank tea at The Cottage with Mrs Balston there. Gussie & I started to view the Beacons on all the hills which were really grand & 'roused in many an ancient hall the gallant squires of Kent. Boxley was by far the most conspicuous & sent its glow far & wide, costing £30 & burning larches innumerable, three tons of coals & no end of tar barrels. Mr Duppa lighted up four. There is I think an old beacon on Bearsted church which was also lighted & the Union was brilliant with coloured lamps & Chinese lanterns. The night tho' cold was lovely & we much enjoyed our drive.

22nd The ceremony of yesterday appears to have been faultless & so very grand in feeling as well as expression.

27th I drove in the afternoon to make calls at Bearsted. In Maidstone after a little banking I visited poor Mrs Farmer, much out of spirits as her husband is almost out of work & her child quite out of health.

29th The Institute cricket match in the Front Meadow & tonight Gerard gives his Jubilee Supper at the Institute. The mowers began yesterday with the orchard, & today the Lawn Meadow was mown.

July 1st Lampard came round to say how successful had been my Jubilee Fete to the choir & how much they had enjoyed their day at the American Exhibition & the sight of Buffalo Bill.[202] They went by the 9 train to Victoria & left town by the 8 pm train singing all the way home & reaching here about 10.

6th Sent a cheque for £20 to Anne Rodwell as a loan for a month or 6 weeks. Mrs Wykeham Martin called. Gerard & I went to the school treat at the vicarage. A band, Punch &

---

201   Queen Victoria's Golden Jubilee

202   Bill Cody's cowboy shows, 1883 onwards.

Judy & no end of children, but no animation. Indeed I missed so many long accustomed faces that it was to me very sad.

9th Gussie & I left for Lambeth Palace. At Victoria Bertha met us looking very well, then on to the Archbishop's Garden Party which was very grand. On the old lawn by the old Palace, in great contrast the multitude of gaily & fashionably dressed people, the successor of Thomas a Becket stood on a Persian carpet with Mrs Benson receiving their various guests. I wonder what the two Chinese dashing up the massive time-worn stairs outside the building thought of it, & the turbaned Indian, with his tawny, white-veiled wife. Home again at 10.

12th To a tennis party at the Barracks invited by Colonel Manners, took Gerard & Gussie, we all found it very agreeable & everyone seemed so much delighted to see Gerard again after his long illness.

13th Sent Mrs Rodwell a dress for her child. Gerard & Gussie came to dine with me, a great delight to see him here again.

16th Gerard came over for the 3rd time today in the evening when Mary arrived laden with souvenirs.

17th Gerard was to have dined with us today but felt too ill to come. He thinks & we all dread, that it is his old attack coming on, as he is in much pain. Sent for Dr Hoare who did not consider it so.

18th Gerard not worse but still doctor is convinced now that is is really the old complaint peritonitis.

19th Gerard much the same. Mrs Duppa brought her very nice little baby daughter to see me.

20th Mary slept last night at The Cottage or rather did not sleep for Gerard had a most painful night. She came round here between 4 & 5 in the morning & at 5 Dr Hoare was sent for. He could say but little, only that his pulse was good & there was scarcely any fever. He is coming again tonight & Nurse Miriam is sent for.

23rd Dr Hoare very pleased with Gerard. Mary with a bad headache so I went alone to Mrs Nutt's tennis party, refreshments served on the lawn & very cheerful.

26th Julia came down for a few hours to see Gerard & Gussie. Gerard went into the next room today.

August 8th Took the Miss *(Horace)* Smiths *(who are staying)* to the Balston's.

12th Ella arrived to stay looking very well, with Eleanor & Jack. Took them to tennis at the Knatchbull Hugesson's.

19th Nurse Miriam left. Mary is now staying with the Dean of Durham, having met Edward & Julia at Harrogate. Took Ella to a tennis party.

September 2nd Mary wrote to ask for an extension of leave to stay with Bertha.

6th Gerard, Gussie & I to a tennis party. Mary arrived after her long absence, laden with presents for everyone, & looking very well.

15th To Malling to take luncheon with the Miss Savages & see Louis. He was very quiet, having just dined, but still he referred to past times & people in a way that showed he still remembered them well. Lewis Shaw arrived.

21st Freddie has obtained some surveying work. Gussie & Mary went to a ladies' cricket match at Torry Hill.

22nd Reports of Mrs Duppa's serious illness. Mary & I drove to Maidstone to Mrs Manner's at the Depot, Thursday being her day of reception.

24th Henry, Louy, Willie, Richard & Bryan here after their night's travelling & Lolotte arrived. Willie sleeps at The Cottage but our house seems full to overflowing.

25th Such a stir in the air after the calm of so many weeks. Lolotte wonderfully bright & well. Mr Gibson preached on the trials & uncertainty of life.

29th Drove to Maidstone with Louy, did some shopping & then went to the reception of Mrs Manners. Everyone talking of the Duppa affair though no one knows what it is.[203]

October 2nd Went to see Gerard in the morning about the clock. Willie left for Crewe. *(The family gave many gifts to the church over the years including the clock in memory of Richard.)*

18th Yesterday Henry & Richard departed, Louy accompanying them as far as London, returning here in the evening.

19th Mrs Green called full of the Duppa affair.

25th Frederic arrived about 5 & soon after Mr Gathane Hardy, Mr George Marsham & Mr Hoare. We dined at 6, & at 7 Louy, Mary, Gussie & Lolotte drove up to the Manor House for the Conservative Meeting. They were followed by our guests, Mr

---

[203]   On the same day Mary wrote in her diary:'Poor Mrs Duppa went to London by train with luggage, saying she never meant to return.' Alice Duppa had been turned out of the house as her husband had found out about her lover. For a full account of her life see 'Every Girl's Duty,' M. Parsons, 1992.

Hardy making a good but not a brilliant speech. Frederic very bright & looking well & on his return amusing himself with the Acrostic.[204]

27th Louy & Bryan departed, heavily laden. These leave-takings are most sorrowful as one advances in life.

28th As often as I woke in the night I thought of Louy & her little boy rattling along all the long hours through in the train, while I lay in my peaceful bed. Gerard & I walked down to the Corner Field to see the changes.

November 5th Boys with masks & the old verses. Gerard came over & Mr Gibson.

11th Gloomy but not raining, so drove to Harrietsham & called on Mrs Nutt who accompanied me to call at Leeds Castle but Mrs Wykeham Martin was at Brighton.

12th Mr & Mrs Nutt took luncheon & Gerard & Gussie came in afterwards. Mr Nutt has just succeeded to the living of Chelsfield about 15 miles from London.

16th The two sequoia were planted in the corner field by Gerard, Mary, Gussie, Willie, Lolotte, Laura & little Ella. Gibson & Ashenden officiating. The second event of the day was that the stag took refuge in the house & made his way into the smoking room. The dogs were just shut out in time or I can scarcely fancy the scene. At last, after tearing down a shelf of books, leaving his footprints high up on the wall, & his foam on the chairs he was induced to find his way to the wash house where he passed the afternoon among the saucepans till the little cart came to take him away. Mary & Willie were in the yard with other spectators when he turned round & rushed upon Mary & threw her down, & had not Willie seized hold of his leg & Tom Longly assisted, matters would have been worse. Willie left for Whitehaven, he had come up to town to see the managers of his railway.

19th Mr Sedgwick came about Hughes's foot as she cannot stand yet. Gussie & I went to a meeting of the Primrose League at Chilston called by Mrs Akers Douglas. Such a lovely house! The drawing room all gold, Japanese gold walls & the curtains of old gold coloured satin. The whole bright with electric light.[205]

---

[204]   An acrostic is a short poem in which the initial letters of the lines spell a word, or sometimes the last or middle letters.

[205]   The Akers Douglas of Chilston Manor were very wealthy, Mr Akers Douglas M.P. was a barrister.

22nd Drove up The Hill to call on Mr Duppa. Found him in a most melancholy state complaining much of shortness of breath & sleeplessness. A most gloomy afternoon & the wind howling among the trees of the dark avenue & the sad circumstances of the owner of all rendered it more so than ever.

29th A great crash in the house at 6.45 am which startled us much, & the consolation was not great when we found that it was caused by the fall of *(Philip)* De Loutherbourg's 'Siege of Valenciennes', grazing the picture & much damaging the frame besides taking the corner off the tea-chest.

30th An early visit from Gerard & his tall friend Mr Sidney Pelham.[206]

December 6th Delmar & Bertha arrived about 11, both well & in good spirits. We talked of everything under the sun.

7th Delmar left for town, he seems full of affairs & Bertha & I drove in the afternoon to Leeds Castle but Mrs Wykeham Martin too ill to see us. Hughes much the same & can't stand yet. Mr Sedgwick called & said that Mr Duppa was very ill.

9th The Lesters arrived for luncheon & took tea at The Cottage, dining here afterwards, full of the anxieties of a 'demagement' after living here eleven years.

13th Wrote to the chaplain of the Hollingbourne Union with our contribution to the Christmas treat.

14th Such a brilliant morning that I wandered in the garden for a short time & saw Mary's new chicken house & the partly demolished hedge. Mr Gibson came, looking ill & depressed. Hughes went to the Infirmary & was told to try & walk.

23rd Called on Mr Duppa & found him worse. Recommended him to have a nurse & begged Edith Duppa to arrange it. Kate here.

24th Heard from Sophy Riddell on Wednesday that she & Mrs Riddell were to start for Egypt on the 3rd & she, (Mrs R), wished to ascend the Great Pyramid, & today came news of her death. Another of the solemn warnings we have lately had!

25th A pair of cloisonné vases from Gerard, Gussie & Mary & one of Langley china from Lolotte, all most charming. Many cards. Also two little pen-wipers from my dear little grand-daughters at The Cottage.

29th Bad report of George Duppa.

---

206   Rev Sidney Pelham (1849-1926) became Canon of Norwich in 1896.

1888 January 1st A visit from Gerard. Mary & Kate full of school arrangements.

2nd Mr Duppa sent for Mr Gibson, he is very ill indeed.

3rd We went to the Primrose Fete at Lenham, a large gathering, a good speech, music, and very good acting. General Lester arrived during our absence.

5th Mr Duppa passed away this morning at one a.m. So now life's fitful fever has ended for him! Such a life of struggle & success & disappointment & misery.[207]

6th To Maidstone early with Lolotte, much shopping & mud. General Lester departed. Mr Gibson called, Mr Duppa is to be buried on Monday.

9th General Carnegie came about 4. A very nice elderly soldier & a great friend of Lolotte. Dined late.

10th Yesterday, we sent, Gerard & I, our respective carriages to Mr Duppa's funeral. He was buried as he wished, by the side of his boy Archie. The church crowded. Drove Lolotte & General Carnegie to Maidstone & to call on the Bests. He had never seen this part of the world. A late dinner & General Carnegie sad but pleasant. He has had much sorrow & disappointment.

17th Lolotte & I departed for town & took up our quarters at number 11 Margaret Street where we were very comfortable. Bertha rushed in to see us.

19th A morning at Marshall & Snelgrove & an afternoon at the delightful Grosvenor Galleries among pictures by Hogarth, Romney etc. I should like to go there many times. Bertha went with us & General Carnegie.

20th Drank tea in Roland Gardens & saw Kate Gibson with her pupils. The children very nice. *(Kate is being employed by Bertha as governess)*

21st Had a brougham & made a round of Kensington visits. Dora out. Frederic at home & looking ill, so was Jessy. Mrs Thomas in cap with mauve ribbons was sitting at her window as she has done for the last thirty years.

26th *(At home)* Gerard walked in the morning to see how the church clock was advancing. The erection is to take a fortnight.

27th To see the clock which is very massive & just as it ought to be.

---

[207] George Duppa died before his petition for divorce could be heard thus saving his wife from ruin.

28th Sir Fred & Lisa came to stay & we dined late.

A sketch of Gerard by Louisa

February 2nd Heard the church clock strike slowly & clearly, a most pleasant sound. Felt rheumatic.

5th Called on the Nutts, the Wykcham Martins, & the Manners at the Barracks. Gerard attended the petty sessions for the first time for two years & was rather better for the exertion.

13th To Brighton accompanied by Hughes to stay at 22 Oriental Place. Dined with the Horace Smiths several times. To the old St Nicholas church where so much has happened to me & mine. To see Mother's grave. Left Brighton on 24th.

25th Mr Gibson called looking not quite so dejected & wretched. Sent £92-10 to Messrs Gillett of Croydon for the church clock.

March 17th The Electric Belt arrived from Harness. A Primrose League meeting in our dining room. Much business was transacted after which came tea.

18th A blizzard. Wore my Electric Belt.

20th We were startled from our calm as Mary was summoned to Gussie, the son nearly born. All went on very well. Old Mrs Sage was summoned to the rescue & officiated most satisfactorily. The baby has a great deal of black hair.

23rd Lolotte arrived in the evening from Cheltenham.

26th Went to see Gerard, & saw Gussie looking fairly well, & the little round plump son very flourishing, & I think, with others, like his grandfather.

31st Gerard full of parish matters & came to see me twice.

April 7th Sir Fred & Jessie *(his daughter)* come to stay. Mary went to church in the snow, she always manages to get there when no one else can.

10th Mr & Mrs Nutt to tea. Sir Fred left, Jessie remained. Lolotte acting nurse to Gerard as usual. Tidings of death of Mr Wright of Frinsted one of our oldest neighbours & friends. Sent the carriage to his funeral.

20th Jessie left on her way to Brighton. To luncheon with Mrs Whatman at Vinters. Bertha's daughter Woodbyne is very unwell & has a nurse & Kate to look after her.

30th Kate arrived with much better report of Woodbyne whom Bertha has taken to Brighton.

May 2nd Edith & Maud Duppa came in & Julia arrived, we had a cheerful dinner. Maud played the banjo.

3rd Julia went round to The Cottage & left early to meet Edward.

8th Mary left for London & Lolotte returned with her in the evening.

22nd My grandson behaved very well & did not utter a sound. Like his father he bears the name of Richard Gerard de Visme. Mr Gibson & General Lester dined here afterwards & Mrs Green came in during the afternoon looking much harassed & worn. Mr Green is still very ill & incapable.

24th A letter telling that *(cousin)* Jessy died early yesterday morning. I was much pained, but not surprised. Poor thing! She had suffered much, mind & body, & now it is all over, but in this world we shall never meet again & it is sad to think how small our little circle is becoming.

28th Mary & Lolotte left early for London. Mr Pryce Jones the new vicar for Wormshill took luncheon here, a rotund, homely little man.

31st Mr Rochfort is compelled to give up his London stay this year.

June 5th To London *(for two weeks)* saw Bertha & Frederic & Lisa, went twice to the Royal Academy. Went to Maples & saw a charming collection of watercolours with Bertha. Saw Mrs Treherne & Ellen Scott. Bertha took Sir Fred & myself to a garden party where met Lord & Lady Chetwynd, Woodbyne accompanied us & was much admired.

23rd Willie arrived looking very ill & weak.

July 8th A day of Bertha here, very pleasant. Gerard, poor boy, a martyr to toothache!

12th Lolotte & I drove to West Malling & saw Louis in his own room.

23rd Ella arrived & Jack an hour earlier & Lolotte. The house is now brimming full.

26th The school treat went off with great éclat. Abundance of cake & flags. The Bearsted Band & games & dancing in the Front Meadow. We had the teachers at tea in the dining room & they seemed to be enjoying themselves much.

August 1st Village flower show like the Slough of Despond due to pouring rain.

11th Frederic arrived to stay, called with him at Wormshill vicarage. Mr & Mrs Pryce Jones a most comfortable little elderly couple, who are delighted with their dreary home, also on Mr & Mrs Knatchbull Hugesson at Lynsted. Heneage & Dering Harrison came & stayed the night.*(sons of Mrs Branfill Harrison)*

20th Dering is in search of a poultry farm which he seems to have found. To Linton with Gerard for cricket & the Engineers Band. Gerard's house is delightful. Sent a P.O. for 10/ to Mrs Minter.

23rd Mary returned *(from Norwich)* in great spirits. To tennis at Lady Lister-Kaye's.

September 3rd *(The Miss Horace Smiths have come to stay)* Rosa Smith & I passed the afternoon at the Barracks with Colonel & Mrs Manners.

24th Edward has resigned the Deanery of Norwich partly owing to his age & health & more particularly that of Julia.

26th Went to an afternoon dance, Mary, Frederic & I. Plenty of room & pleasant.

27th Mr Gibson called & says that a Captain Rickett has bought the Manor House, he has nine children. Ecarte as usual with Gerard in the evening.

October 3rd Henry & Louy arrived. Mrs Forster & Mrs Southey called.

10th To London with Henry & Louy & did much shopping.

16th Frederic & Dora arrived for the day. Mr Pryce Jones called. Mary poorly.

18th Henry & Louy left to stay at Effingham with Bertha, they are undecided as to where to go.[208] Dering Harrison called after looking at more sites for poultry farm. Gerard & Gussie moved out after staying here five months. *(while work done on their house)* Mrs Branfill Harrison came for day to see Frogs Hole *(a Hollingbourne farm)* for Dering.

November 1st Started from Hollingbourne station for Brighton. In the evening sat with Edward & Julia in Lansdowne Place.

6th Bertha arrived with May, a dinner at Edward's.

7th Went to have my coat tried on, much shopping with Hughes. Drove out with Bertha. In the evening to Landsdowne Place.

10th To Landsowne Place in the evening, walked with Edward in the morning & drove with him in the afternoon over the wild Downs & to Stanmer.

11th To St Peters where Edward preached a beautiful sermon, after lunch went to Preston & stood by my dearest Mother's grave & thought of all she had done & all she had suffered in life, & was very miserable at not having done more for her. Mrs Balston called late & she & I went to see the Horace Smiths in their bright little room & with their kind & warm welcome to all their friends.

17th *(At home)* A letter from Henry & Louy saying that they had been much pleased with the farm & now we are hoping that it may not be beyond their means.

24th Dering Harrison came in quite early. He is not in the highest spirits over his domain of Frogs Hole & his new life.

---

[208]   Henry had retired from the army, he & Louy still had six children to educate so he needed to work.

29th Went to the bazaar at Elsfield for the old women at the Union to provide them with armchairs instead of hard benches.

December 2nd Lolotte & Sybil arrived. Carried on with my painting of grapes.

18th Wrote to Freddie in New South Wales. He is now an assistant mining surveyor. Little Edward Morgan, Bertha's son, passed his exams as Naval cadet.

21st Henry & Louy have bought a farm, Bowmans at Etchingham near Hastings. [209]

23rd Wrote Christmas dinner tickets & Henry arrived to stay.

26th Henry took Mary to see the farm & Batemans Farm which has been offered to him as a dwelling house but Mary found the latter too dreary & unwholesome & damp to inhabit though very picturesque.[210]

27th Dined with Mary, Kate, Henry, Gerard & Gussie on Norfolk turkey, Gussie sang beautifully.

1889 January 1st Lolotte arrived. A concert at the Board School for the Sunday schools to which Mary, Lolotte & Kate went. Very bad.

4th Lolotte, Gussie & I went to the Amateur Theatricals of the Primrose League at Lenham.

9th Captain & Mrs Ricketts called. They seem very nice.[211] Did not see Gerard the whole day.

10th Louy is now, I trust, in Hastings. Went to the school in the evening to distribute the prizes to the Sunday school children.

12th Bertha, Edward, Woodbyne & Jack arrived quite early. Bertha & Jack returned to town in the evening. Edward & Woodbyne remaining till morning, a day of pleasure & bustle.

14th Mary & Lolotte left by early train for Brighton, Edward & Woodbyne accompanying them to Victoria. Gerard & Gussie came in during the afternoon.

15th Gerard dined with me, & Mary returned. Lolotte to The Cottage as Gussie has gone to Norwich for a week.

21st Lolotte came here for her last day of packing before starting for London early tomorrow en route to Brighton & was full of busy-ness.

---

209   The farm had no house & Louisa lent them money to have one built.

210   Nevertheless Louy & Henry did rent Batemans for a while. Later it became Rudyard Kipling's home & now belongs to the National Trust.

211   Captain Ricketts had purchased Hollingbourne Manor.

25th Mrs Manners, Mr Larking, Gerard & Gussie took luncheon here & afterwards came in Mrs Ricketts & Dering Harrison. Mrs Manners whistled & Mr Larking sang & did the castanets with his hands. A very cheerful afternoon.

26th Gerard & I went in the afternoon to call on Captain & Mrs Ricketts when we saw the Manor House under quite a new aspect. So charmingly full of lovely old furniture & looking so delightfully comfortable. I could hardly recognise its bare old walls & chilling passages.

February 2nd Took Mrs Ricketts to see Mrs Balston's house & treasures. Arranged my autographs. Captain Ricketts very pleasant & much pleased with the Manor House.

16th Mary left for Norwich. Lewis Shaw came & stayed the night. Poor Louis taken ill & a telegram from Dr Adam there advised me not to go. Louy arrived looking very well & a great pleasure it is to have her here.

22nd A telegram telling that my dear brother had passed away quietly. Dr Adam came & gave a full report to us of Dear Louis's end & said how much he was liked by all the inmates & how thoughtful he was of others.

31st Louis was buried at Malling & all anxiety is over on his account. I had become so entirely accustomed to the painful thought of him that I can scarcely believe it at an end.

March 3rd A letter from Dr Adam telling of the funeral of my dearest Brother, the snow falling fast the whole time. Gerard came twice to see me in spite of the snow showers, & Thurlow & Dering Harrison took luncheon here.

8th A dreary day ending in torrents of rain & about 6 o'clock the front door opens & in walks Bertha. Such a pleasure to see her brightness.

9th Mrs Balston at luncheon & Mr Gibson & Gerard afterwards. We drove up to see Captain & Mrs Ricketts & the Manor House. Bertha much pleased with it.

11th Mr Rochfort is doing all he can to make Dublin pleasant to Lolotte & Sybil.

15th Saw my Grandson who is so fine & fat that he is quite a prize child.

16th Mary arrived full of regrets for having left Norwich & Edward & Julia.

29th To Maidstone to an S.P.G. (*Society for Propagating the Gospel*) meeting at the Town Hall. The Archbishop was very eloquent & told us it was not so much ambition or wealth or power that swayed us, but 'Pleasant Ease' & he asked was this the life of our Saviour? Ought it to be our life? The hall was crammed.

April 2nd Gerard was at the Petty Sessions & the better for seeing his friends.

3rd To a Primrose League meeting with Gerard. Gussie & Mary at Chilston.

6th With Mary to the Manor House & looked at drawings & treasures without end.

10th Gerard to London for the day, over three years since he has been there. George Corke our manservant having lived here five years, left & Alfred Mitchell came. Edith & Maud Duppa's father Charles died. Poor Charles Duppa, how many memories rise up at his very name!

15th Maud & Edith Duppa came to stay. The Miss Savages to luncheon & I sent by them to Dr Adam & Mrs Adam at the asylum a cheque for £100 & a silver cream jug.

May 3rd Mr Rochfort again prevented from coming to town this year.

8th Louy & Co to move to Batemans, the farmhouse at Burwash today.

16th To London with Hughes, reached 5B Sloane Street, the staircase steep & narrow as that of the Eiffel Tower but the drawing room cheerful & the bedroom most spacious & altogether far less gloomy than Margaret Street. Bertha came in looking as bright as possible during the afternoon & I went to Roland Gardens later & drew with the children. Many days of shopping, two evenings at the Royal Academy. Almost every evening with Bertha & her children. Two Sundays at St Margaret's Westminster, a visit to Ellen Scott, two visits to Mrs Thomas Thomas, an afternoon with Dora, visits from Frederic. One day Sybil Laurie & Lolotte took luncheon with me. Lolotte is now in Brighton. I occupied a fortnight very agreeably in London. Returned home on the 30th

June 10th Much flower gathering to decorate the house for Bishop Marsden. He came here before the church where he did confirmations. An afternoon tea here followed. Gerard exerted himself much as churchwarden, Gussie with the quire & Mary universally as usual. I inherit poor Louis' money.

15th Bought Mr Crooke's two cows as a present to Henry & Louy & they went with the pigs from Gerard. Dering Harrison to luncheon.

16th A startling letter from Lolotte who then appeared suddenly to discuss this imminent change. *(thinking of remarrying)* Gerard & Mary at a cricket match at Wormshill. New dining room chimney piece up.

22nd With Mary to the Archbishop's garden party at Lambeth Palace. No end of people & most agreeable it was. Bertha met us at the station. Met many friends.

25th Dr & Mrs Arthur Rowe stayed with Gerard & came & see us. Dr Rowe sings charmingly. Took the Rowes to Leeds Castle & Mrs Martin took them round, then went with them to the Manor House for tea & wandered in the bare & barren garden.

29th With Hughes to London, met Bertha & saw the copy of Lionel Goldsmid's head made by Miss McKay from the large picture by Devis. I think Frederic will like it.

July 1st Mary left for Brighton to stay with Lolotte.

3rd Occupied in arranging books & hanging pictures with Gerard in the dining room. Jack Shaw is having trouble with his eyes.

6th Edward & Julia arrived at The Cottage. Went in the evening to see them.

7th Took Edward & Julia to morning service in the carriage. Edward preached a most excellent sermon written by him in the early morning. He came over here after dinner & we talked much on Lolotte.

17th Lolotte arrived in the evening, a great pleasure to see her.

19th Lolotte & I drove to Maidstone to fetch Mary on her return from Louy.

25th Ella, Eleanor & Jack arrived. We have had a tennis party & passed an afternoon at the Manor House. Our school treat has taken place at the vicarage.

August 1st Ella departed with Eleanor leaving poor Jack behind who is still under the charge of the oculist. Dering at luncheon & he, Mary, Jack & I to a cricket match at the Brassey's.

2nd A little daughter was born to Gussie. Ethel & Flora Ricketts to tennis.

12th The Miss Smiths arrived to stay for a week in high spirits. A tennis party here.

13th To the Manor House with Rosey & Tizey Smith & Jack. Willie arrived for the night looking much better than last year.

26th Frederic & Lisa arrived, took them to Leeds Castle & to the Manor House.

326

September 3rd Mary returned from Switzerland & Lolotte & I, accompanied by Major Ricketts, went to a tennis at Major & Mrs Best's at Boxley. The Engineers Band & a very pleasant afternoon.

5th Miss McKay arrived & went to the Cottage to see les petites before beginning her sketches tomorrow.

6th Went to The Cottage with Miss McKay to arrange the room & children for their portraits. In the afternoon to Maidstone with Lolotte shopping.

14th To The Cottage to watch the progress of Miss McKay. Sat for a little time with Gussie who is going on well.

24th Miss McKay's pictures very successful, she leaves tomorrow.

25th Lisa & Lolotte arrived & then Kate. Kate & Lisa are to be godmothers to Gerard's daughter Bertha, tomorrow.

October 3rd Jessie, Katie & Patricia Goldsmid came to see Godfrey House & pass the day. They were all in a state of rapture on their future home. May it last!

11th Lolotte left for Brighton. Major & Mrs Best called. Sent Ella her quarterly cheque. General Lester came & Gerard gave an afternoon tea in his honour.

15th Mary & I went to West Malling & stood by the grave of poor Louis next to that of a captain who was, it seems, a friend of his. Poor Louis! The cause to all of us of such deep anxiety & sorrow. We passed the afternoon with the Miss Savages. Mary & I arranged for the stonemason to make a cross for Louis' grave.

November 1st Left for Brighton with Hughes & found Lolotte awaiting us in her comfortable little home at 5 Oriental Place. Edward & Julia came, then Kate, then we called on the Horace Smiths. During my stay there dined with Edward in his new house. Met many friends & heard Edward preach twice. One afternoon Lolotte gave a tea to about 20 people, & I should have enjoyed myself thoroughly but for my miserable rheumatism. And yet I feel very thankful that I have no worse ill. On the 20th I took leave of my dear child who had made all so pleasant & reached my own old home. I had also the pleasure of seeing Bertha.

23rd A letter from Louy. Batemans is sold & they will be obliged to leave in May.

26th Called on Mrs Ricketts, sat in the old hall over a delightful fire of logs & saw the settle. Went also over to Godfrey House to see the changes & improvements.

December 2ⁿᵈ Dering Harrison came to luncheon. Went to the music practice at The Cottage, Cave Brownes, & Ricketts there. Lewis Shaw came for the night.

21ˢᵗ Kate Gibson arrived, she & Mary decorated the church. No end of cards.

26ᵗʰ Went over on Christmas Day & saw the dear little girls laden with dolls. Another pamphlet from Dr Barnardo. He showers them everywhere! *(Barnardo homes were set up first in 1867)*

1890-1899: Old age

Louisa received a great blessing in 1890 when her cousin Sir Frederic Goldsmid and his family came to live a short walk away in Hollingbourne. They rented Godfrey House from Gerard. Frederic then visited Louisa daily for they were very fond of each other, each appreciating the other's intellect and outlook. Frederic and his wife had four daughters and they too now figured largely in Louisa's daily round. Lisa, Patricia, Jessie, and Katie were all good company, intelligent and lively.[212] Their mother is mentioned very little in the journals for Lady Goldsmid was an invalid.

During his long life Frederic had excelled as soldier, administrator, scholar, and linguist. In retirement he had been appointed Vice-President of the Royal Asiatic Society and the Royal Geographical Society. In Hollingbourne he served as churchwarden and was never too grand to visit the village children at school and indeed went weekly and helped several of the scholars to find jobs.

Louisa's life was also much enhanced by the fact that Gerard called daily or more frequently when at home. Then in 1894 new friends were made when Colonel and Mrs Knatchbull moved into the village, and they too saw Louisa every week. She was virtually never left in the house with only servants for company. If Mary was away another daughter, or Kate Gibson, or one of Frederic's daughters would come to stay.

Louisa continued to feel useful too since her linguistic and artistic skills were still in demand. Various of her numerous grandchildren came to stay to have their French, German or perspective skills improved by Nonna. Louisa's interest in current affairs endured helped by having Gerard and Frederic to mull things over with. All in all hers was an enviable old age.

Anyone in their eighties with a large circle of friends loses one to death now and then, and in 1891 there came the painful loss of Mr Rochfort. The saddest worry of the decade was that of the prolonged serious illnesses of Lolotte and Gerard. There are occasional gaps of several months in the journals when

---

[212]   Lisa Goldsmid's real name was Eliza & earlier in the journals Louisa called her this. Later she changed to calling her Lisa. For clarity I have used Lisa throughout.

Louisa herself was ill in bed. This decade of her eighties saw her final visits to London and Brighton.

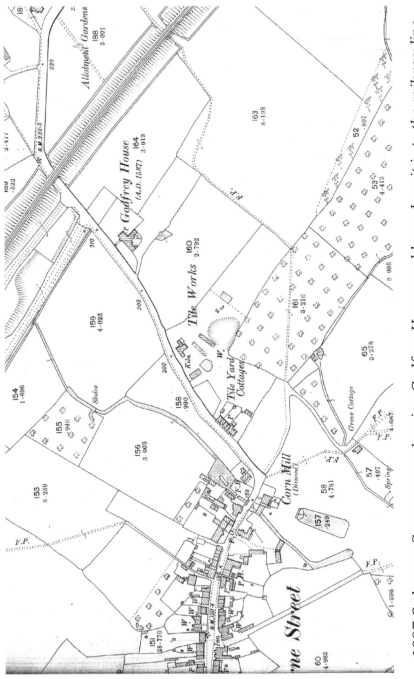

1897 Ordnance Survey map showing Godfrey House and how close it is to the railway line

1890 January 1st Gave Sam Lampard a list of poor people for coals. Each receive two cwt.

4th Bertha, Delmar, Edward & May arrived.

6th Took Bertha & Delmar to the Manor House in the afternoon where we had tea & viewed the oaken carving & the great changes.

7th Delmar & Bertha left. Mary's evening for giving prizes at the school.

8th Kate, accompanied by Edward & May left.

9th Wrote to Anne Rodwell with a cheque. Poor Gerard still very weak & in bed with the influenza, & Gussie poorly.

12th Felt too poorly to get up. Not real influenza but a very bad cold. Dr Whitestone called & said that I was not to leave either room or bed, but I could not have done either.

20th Gibson & Tom both taken ill with influenza & obliged to give up work.

22nd Servants gone to the Primrose *League* entertainment at Lenham.

23rd Lolotte arrived quite unexpectedly, going first to The Cottage.

February 3nd Gerard much better. Lolotte went to stay at The Cottage. Jack Shaw arrived & planned his poultry farm with Mary. The Ricketts & Gibsons called.

9th Lolotte left for Brighton, Dering took luncheon.

20th Mona arrived to stay. An unexpected visit from Mrs Branfill Harrison. Mary & Mona at the Soup Kitchen.

24th Mary left for Brighton. Began a portrait of Mona.

27th Went with Gussie to the music practice at the Manor House, a large gathering.

March 10th Started early in pouring rain for London with Mona & Hughes, drove straight to Marshall & Snelgrove. Bought dresses for Mona & Ella & one for myself, on to Elise where purchased a bonnet. Took luncheon at a baker's in Vere Strcct.

14th Ethel Ricketts at luncheon & a drive to Maidstone & Detling afterwards. Called on the Cave Brownes & had coffee with them.

15th Mary came home laden with presents from Edward & herself.

17th Went with Gerard to Godfrey House which is very charming. Then in the afternoon with Mona to Maidstone returning in time to fetch Lolotte & Katie Goldsmid from the station. The latter in ecstasies as she passed their future home.

18th Katie & Lolotte at Godfrey House in the morning.

22nd Furniture arriving at Godfrey House, also trucks of furniture arriving for the new inhabitants of Cotuams. *(an old Hollingbourne house close to the Thomas home)*

24th Lolotte at breakfast & then with Katie at Godfrey House as usual.

25th Katie departed & took up her residence in Godfrey House. Patricia is to arrive in the evening. I went to see it during the morning & very nice it all is. Dering Harrison had another accident & Ida & he were both thrown out of the dog cart. Lewis Shaw writes he has decided to go to Brazil, Lolotte having kindly interested Jack Pierson on his behalf.

27th Yesterday Gussie left for Brighton to stay with Edward & Julia & today Mona went home. I went over to see Gerard who is suffering pain in his side.

April 1st Sir Fred & Lady Goldsmid arrived at Godfrey House & were quite delighted with their new home. Took them a drive to Leeds & Harrietsham.

3rd Lolotte left & Gussie returned.

8th Kate arrived to stay. Grandson Richard Gipps visited, a very nice boy.

15th With Kate to visit the Brasseys. Lewis Shaw visited.

17th Louy arrived. Drank tea at the Manor House, Louy, Mary, Kate & I.

May 14th Mr Cave Browne who is writing the history of Hollingbourne, called to discuss matters & borrowed the 'History of Bath Abbey'.

19th A letter from Willie containing a long one from Freddie who had just received all his Christmas presents.

22nd Great excitement & preparation for the concert at the Board school. Mary as busy as possible arranging the flowers sent by Mr d'Uphaugh for the platform & the concert itself proved a great success. The much practised Glees & Cantata, Gussies 'Goodbye', Mr McNaughton in his gorgeous Scottish attire & with his bagpipes, & the operetta of 'Two Blind Men' by Mr Hughes & Dr Whitestone gained immense applause.

23rd To the cricket match at The Mote, Grace,(*W.G. Grace*), such an immense man, distinguished himself greatly as usual.

27th Visits from Frederic, Patricia, Katie, Mr Gibson & Mrs Green. Mary at tennis.

29th Left for town, went to my old haunt, 9 Margaret Street, but to pleasanter rooms, Bertha came to see me in the afternoon & before she left, enter Lolotte. Many were the sights I saw, the Panorama of Niagara, beautiful, the Royal Academy where Sybil & Colonel Laurie met us. Another day went to see 'The visit of the Queen of Sheba to Soloman'. Went to see Sir Frederick Leighton's house, 2 Holland Park Road, filled with treasures, tiles, tapestry, & porcelain of all kinds & ages, part of it Moorish with a fountain of black marble.[213] From there we went to Mr Athelstan Riley's house in Kensington Court, saw the chapel he is building, very small but beautifully decorated. Called on Mrs Thomas Thomas.

June 10th *(At home)* In the afternoon a party at the Manor House, took Lisa. The betrothed *(Ethel Ricketts & Mr d'Uphaugh)*[214] seemed very happy.

11th Dined at Gerard's to see Mrs Lester & Edith very pleasant to see them again.

14th Drawing room dismantling prior to painting & re carpeting. Went to a tennis & croquet party at Mr d'Uphaugh's.

19th Called on Lady Lister-Kaye. Went to The Cottage to see Gerard & his pictures.

22nd <u>To our surprise</u> in church this morning Mr Gibson published the banns of Hughes & Mitchell, which proved to be a hoax. Wrote to Mr Gibson to inform him & also to beg him to enquire into the matter. Dering at luncheon. Frederic, Major & Mrs Ricketts & Ethel, Mr d'Uphaugh, Gerard, Gussie & Dering at tea, much sauntering on the lawn afterwards.

26th Lisa came to luncheon & brought me a novel she with a friend is translating from the Russian.

July 5th With Lisa to the bazaar at Leeds Park. Mary very poorly with her old attack, a sort of indigestion. Dr Whitestone came, at times she has a pain in her side.

7th Attended the marriage of Mr d'Uphaugh & Ethel Ricketts. She looked very nice & pretty with her large bouquet & little bridesmaids in their Kate Greenaway dresses & mob caps. There were six, Flora & Audrey her sisters, & my two grandchildren Laura & Ella from The Cottage included. We

---

[213]   Leighton House is now open to the public.

[214]   George Duppa had left his estate not to his son Bryan but to his nephew, on condition he took the ancient family name De Uphaugh (pronounced Duppa). So Richard Turbott became Mr d'Uphaugh, known in the village as Dicky Duppa.

took Frederic & Lisa. Roses decorated the altar rails & an archway was thrown over the gate to the church. Mary, by means of starving, contrived to be present at the ceremony. Smith left after being our cook 4 ¾ years, her place is to be taken by Elizabeth Featherstone. Mr Gibson called.

10th Lolotte arrived, Sir Frederic, Lisa, Katie & Jessie called. Mary better.

12th Major & Mrs Ricketts called & arranged with Mary their treat to the village children to celebrate the wedding of Ethel. Frederic gave me a number of autographs for my book. Drove with him to Maidstone.

22nd Mrs Rickett's party to celebrate the wedding. Dances, swings, a grand tea for the children in the coach house, a dance for all the villagers in the field, all sorts of games. Major & Mrs Ricketts exerted themselves in every possible way to make everyone happy & it is long, if ever, that such a bright fete had been given in Hollingbourne. Dancing was kept up in the meadow (lighted with coloured lamps), till 11. Mary's procession of children with teachers, band, garlands & flags was very pretty.

25th Took Goldsmids to Hollingbourne Flower show, the Yeomanry Band, cricket & a tennis tournament.

27th Took Jessie & Patricia to a lawn tennis. A letter from Ella, Robert has written to the bishop to ask leave to retire & has taken a house at Bungay in Suffolk.

August 5th Major & Mrs Rickett's party, a beautiful day & Morris dance. All most successful, most numerously attended. Sir Roger de Coverley was also danced. It was quite a revival of the 'olden times'.

6th Mary & Lolotte left by early train, Mary to stay with Edward at Malvern, Lolotte for a day in town. Katie & I drove to Maidstone.

11th Called on Mrs Gardner-Waterman in her very nice vicarage at Bicknor, on Ricketts & on Lady Goldsmid.

22nd A garden party at Lady Lister-Kaye's. Frederic & Lisa went with us. Very pleasant met many old friends.

23rd Old Knott came to tell us histories of the village. He told us that he remembered 'the wet harvest' which occurred in 1816 when the corn was not carried at Christmas & when the bread 'drew out' in long strings & had to be re-baked on the grid iron before it could be eaten.[215] *(John Knott was 10 in 1816)*

27th A letter from Lewis Shaw saying that the doctor will not pass him for a tropical climate on account of his heart.

September 13th To a tennis party at the d'Uphaugh's taking Lisa & Patricia, croquet too. I thought much of the first day I saw the house *(Hollingbourne House)* & how my fate was decided by coming to that house *(where she met Richard)* & how all those blooming healthy bright girls, (save Lady Marjoribanks), & those strong, active, energetic men had all passed away.

16th To a tennis party at Mrs Hampson's, Thurnham Court, with Frederic & Lisa.

22nd Heard from Mona that Henry is very ill. To Manor House for tea.

25th Edward & Julia arrived to stay at The Cottage. Edward preached the harvest sermon. Sent Willie a cheque of £200 *(to help Louy & Henry)*. A big afternoon tea.

October 1st Edward & Julia left, & Lisa who is to stay away for some months.

4th A letter from Mona, Henry much the same, they talk of getting into their house next week. Major Ricketts came to show me his drawings, then Sir Frederic & Patricia at tea & to play the letter game.

9th Sammy Lampard left early with a van full of things for Louy, Gipsy ridden by a very small boy, & the chickens in the front of the van. Old Knott is very ill not expected to recover. Mary went to see him with Jessie.

11th Dined on the goose Gerard had given us which was excellent. All the rest of the party went to Godfrey House in the afternoon & I stayed at home. Frederic at tea & we played the letter game.

13th Lolotte went up to town with Frederic for the day. Mrs Green paid me a long visit & Lady Goldsmid, Jessie & George *(Frederic's son)* also came.

14th Bertha & Stewart left this morning to my great regret. A long letter from Mona, they have moved into the house & a restful feeling pervades them all after so many years of uncertainty & change.

---

[215]   1816 was known as 'the year there was no summer' & there were major food shortages across the northern hemisphere.

16th Willie surprised us by appearing this morning. The report of his father not encouraging. A telegram came summoning Willie back to Whitehaven which I much regret as they need his assistance in their new house.

21st Mary, Lolotte, Hughes & I drove to Headcorn en route to Walmer. Parted from Mary at the station as she went to look at a horse. Very nice rooms, 3 Cambridge Terrace. Mrs Branfill Harrison arrived to see us in the afternoon, as she did almost every day that we were there, sometimes with Ianthe & once with Mr Harrison. On Wednesday we went to the beach but found no amber. Went To Dover & very charming it was, made some purchases. On Sunday we went to the garrison church. On Monday a vessel was wrecked on the Goodwin Sands, the crew escaping to Dover. On Wednesday as we drove to Walmer Castle we saw the ship still on the sands, her sails idly flapping in the wind. Lolotte & I parted at Headcorn on 30th she for Heatherland (*Louy's new home*) & Hughes & I for our old home. Gerard arrived. Found Mary much as usual.

November 7th Frederic gave a lecture in the school room which was full.

14th Frederic came as usual to discuss the Acrostic.

26th The furniture & much of the machinery at the paper mills is sold. Heavy snow.

December 1st Dr Whitestone called on his way from skating at the Castle moat.

8th Ella Gipps returned home. Dering appeared about his sheep & took coffee here.

9th Gerard came in, not well while Dr Whitestone was here & consulted him. I walked out & looked round the garden & brought in a very pale primrose, a frozen chrysanthemum & a little rosemary.

11th Gerard very poorly from chill & toothache, went over to see him, Frederic came in to discuss the lecture on Peru he is giving this evening.

16th Lisa came in this morning nearly frozen & fresh from London & the black fogs & bright theatres.

24th Wrote dinner tickets as I have done for over 50 years. How wonderful it all seems. 'I have been young & now am old'.

25th Mary & I had a quiet day broken by visits from Frederic, Gerard & Gussie.

1891 January 1st I had a feverish attack of rheumatism & could only remain in bed, but the dreariness was brightened by the arrival of Bertha & Edward. He had just been appointed to the 'Rodney', to sail very soon for the north of Spain. It was a great pleasure.

19th Lisa & Katie & Ethel d'Uphaugh drank tea here before the Sunday school prize-giving. Mary & Kate had been busy all week in counting up marks & arranging the prizes which were given by Mrs d'Uphaugh.

21st Kate departed for Brighton accompanied by Bertie Ricketts. Our two cows Pearl & Jubilee departed for their Sussex home. *(Louy's)*

28th Mr Pierson is very ill & Lolotte has been summoned to Norwood. *(her father in law)* Couchman gave notice. Alas!

29th Mary busy with the Soup. Went to The Cottage when Gerard informed me that Streeter wished to take Couchman's place. Frederic came in for a long sit.

30th Mary drove to Detling & brought back Cave Browne's work on Hollingbourne. Not very interesting except for Major Rickett's illustrations. Took Streeter for our coachman.

February 10th Tried a mustard leaf on my hip. Intend to try it again though it drove me nearly wild.

12th Made a number of calls with Frederic. Gerard poorly. Went over & saw his translation of Heine which is very good.

19th Lolotte arrived to stay at The Cottage, she has been ill. Drew hieroglyphs for Frederic's lecture on Egypt.

22nd With Lolotte to the Manor House. Lady Goldsmid & Patricia called.

March 1st Drove to the second service with Mary, a great pleasure to me, I had unfortunately been entirely prevented going to church so long. The cross & the vases on the altar I had never seen, & the church itself so clean & nice under the care of Katie Goldsmid.

5th Lolotte left for Brighton. Mary & I to Malling. Went to the churchyard to see the cross & grave *(of poor Louis)*. Laid there some snowdrops. Perhaps he will know it. I like to think that he will. Then passed two hours with the Miss Savages.

7th Frederic came in after his week of work & committees in London.

10th Snow & wind the whole night, a perfect blizzard & by the morning-light the whole country deeply veiled in white. They say that such a night has not been known for 60 years. All the roads blocked & letters came very late by train.

13th A path cut through the snow & sanded, & I went to see Gerard.

337

April 1st Kate came to stay, Frederic & Lisa to luncheon, Gerard looking very ill.

5th To the Manor House with Gerard. He asked Dr Whitestone to go & give a second opinion on Henry in Sussex.

9th Left for Brighton. Lolotte awaiting me there & the Miss Smiths to see me. Dr Whitestone confirms poor Henry can never be much better, the nerves of the brain are affected & there is a tendency to paralysis. It is most sad God only knows.

20th Said goodbye to dearest Lolotte & Brighton, had an hour with Bertha.

22nd Took to my bed rheumatic.

25th Got up today. Gussie went to visit Edward & Julia at Tunbridge Wells. Lolotte has gone to stay with Louy instead of Cheltenham as Henry is so bad.

May 1st Children with garlands & very pretty they were with their abundance of primroses. Mary went to Tunbridge Wells to see Edward & Julia.

5th Mrs Ricketts came to see me, Mary is looking for a servant for Louy.

7th Hudson the painter recommended an elderly, homely Mrs Hollands, so she is to go to Heatherland tomorrow. Frederic came & assisted us in the Acrostic.

10th Mrs Hollands is giving great satisfaction.

11th Lolotte arrived, Henry is rather better.

12th Mrs Ricketts & Mrs d'Uphaugh came to call on Lolotte & then she, Gerard & I drove through herds of cows & flocks of sheep from the fair to Maidstone crowded with farmers & all the people they bring together.

13th Katie came, Gerard too poorly to come out. Lolotte left for Heatherland.

19th Frederic & Lisa came in in the morning & Gerard & Gussie in the afternoon. Mr Rochfort died on the 16th, the oldest of all my friends!

22nd Wrote to Mrs Farmer, neé Jackson, about a servant for Louy as Mrs Hollands cannot stay much longer. A long letter from Freddie who is busy collecting opals.

25th The Thomas Thomas money is settled *(Mrs Thomas Thomas has died)* & Gerard has paid it into Lolotte & Louy's accounts & to Mary her share. The new carpet laid down in my room.

26th Katie came for perspective. Mary has worn herself out in the search for a servant for Louy but in vain. Gerard came in, & Dr Whitestone, Katie & Patricia.

28th Sent off a wash hand-stand to Heatherland, and rhubarb & spinach. Gerard has now paid to all their respective share of the T.T. money.

June 2nd Dering came for my grandfather's suit of flowered velvet which I lent him for the theatrical. Gerard's three little daughters went to Brighton to stay with Edward & Julia.

4th The theatricals arranged by Major Ricketts. Bertha arrived for two nights with Vera, a very nice little child, & in the evening we watched the carriages on their way to the play. The acting of the Goldsmid family was considered first rate. A very depressing letter from Lolotte who has been told she has a weak heart & must not go to Heatherland.

5th A further letter from Lolotte, she must not walk, she must lie down, must be pushed out in a chair. Mary left for Brighton to be with her. The Ricketts called.

10th Gerard & his three little girls looking so well & bright called.

12th Young George Goldsmid *(Frederic's son)* is to go to India.

20th Went to the Primrose meeting at Chilston with Gerard. Lolotte improves.

July 5th Young Edward came in from Sheerness, looking very bright & rosy. He is a charming boy. Dering at luncheon, Frederic later.

6th Frederic, with Lisa, is invited to the Prince of Wales' garden party at Buckingham Palace to meet the Emperor & Empress of Germany.

14th Gerard's machine did not come to mow the hay as Dering had promised, it not being in order. A bad report of Henry.

20th Mary to Heatherland. Mrs Green came, & then Frederic & Gerard.

21st Gerard & I went to the Manor House in the afternoon, everything looking lovely, the garden very brilliant, filled with roses.

August 5th Louis Gipps came to stay. He is a very good looking dark-eyed, tall boy & silent, bringing honey & rabbits *(Louis was 17)*. Mr Gibson has been here 25 years.

10th Tizey & Rosey Smith came to stay & I gave an afternoon tea.

15th This morning a boy was born to Gussie! We all rejoice.

20th Mary to Brighton to stay with Lolotte. To an afternoon dance given by the officers of the West Kent to which I took Ida Harrison, Frederic & Jessie.

September 1st To a tennis party at Hollingbourne House taking Lisa with me. Mary returned with rather better report of Lolotte.

3rd Ella & young Henry arrived. He is a nice, bright looking boy.

9th A tennis & tea here. One day we went to Maidstone, another was devoted to photography. On Tuesday they went to Tunbridge Wells to meet Jack, & on Wednesday they returned to their Norfolk home.

10th Mrs Ricketts called to ask Mary to bring her bow in the afternoon & shoot. Gerard also went. I felt too poorly. Frederic came in for the new Acrostic.

13th A letter from Dr Scott about Lolotte, he thinks it absolutely necessary that she should see another doctor. He considers that her illness will be a very long one.

December 18th More than three months have passed & most of my time has been passed in bed, & dearest Lolotte, although confined to her couch, is better & dear Henry after much suffering, passed away last Monday. *(aged 54)* All the children are with their mother except Freddie in his far off home. I cannot realise that Henry with all his brightness is gone, & he was buried at Burwash yesterday. Delmar & Bertha were present.

21st Willie came to stay at The Cottage looking very pale & ill but giving a fair report of his mother.

24th Gerard came in as usual, full of business. Mary overwhelmed with church decorations. Wrote tickets for the Christmas dinner.

26th This evening arrived Louy & Mona, Louy looking very ill & worn, naturally.

29th Wrote to Dr Rowe & sent him a Christmas souvenir from Mappins in silver, six teaspoons & pair of sugar tongs.

1892 January 2nd Dr Whitestone came. Gerard & I did 'The Kentish Child' together. He is kindly improving my lines.[216] Frederic came later & Louy, Mona & Kate paid me visits.

3rd All my usual visitors. Frederic did duty at the Union (*helped with their chapel service*).

---

[216]   Louisa's poem 'Lines to a Kentish child by a Kentish Mother' was first printed in 1875.

6th Felt better than usual. I worked & pasted (*scrapbook*) & read.

7th Letter from Edward, Lolotte has the influenza. *(Edward & Julia were still in Brighton & Edward often wrote about Lolotte in his diary, they saw a lot of her)*

8th An accident on the S.E. Railway near London, General Lester had his leg broken & his hand injured. We are all deeply grieved for the kind little man.

10th A long solitary time. Mary & Kate all day at church & schools.

13th A letter from Mrs Lester, the poor General is in the Charing Cross hospital & suffers much with his broken leg & various other injuries but bears them most cheerfully. Gerard very poorly, Dr Whitestone thinks it influenza.

16th Gerard is decidedly better though still very wretched & weak. At Leeds Castle all but Mrs W. Martin & one housemaid ill. Our gardener Gibson is attacked & quite disabled & many in the village are stricken.

17th Mary not well & by Dr Whitestone's orders to remain in bed. Frederic is off to town tomorrow for nearly a week to superintend the Gordon Boys' Home.[217]

18th Mr Gibson came in & we droned together a little.

22nd Mary was allowed to come downstairs today though to me she must remain invisible. (*in case gives her mother flu*) The Cressolene Lamp burning & scenting the whole house with carbolic odours.[218]

23rd A letter from Edward who writes there is a slight lull in the influenza at Brighton but two of the principal undertakers have put out notices that they can take no more orders. It is most sad. Frederic came & seemed pleased with the success of his lecture on Persian poets at Kings College. Mrs Vigor (*Short*) came to see me, quite the Nora Short of old days but thinner. Finished yesterday 'A week's stroll in Dickens Land' which interested me much.

24th Dr Whitestone came & still forbids that Mary & I should meet.

---

[217]   The Gordon Boys Home in Surrey was established by public subscription as a memorial to Gordon of Khartoum. Initially a home for underprivileged boys it soon became a boarding school.

[218]   Cressolene was liquid made from coal tar & was used as a disinfectant. The lamp heated it so it could be inhaled.

26th Mary & I talked for a short time & a great pleasure it was to see her better. Frederic came & we guessed nearly the whole Acrostic.

February 2nd Dr Whitestone called *(several times a week).* Gerard is back to his daily visits.

5th Mrs Gibson is more outrageous than ever, Mr Gibson very poorly. Read the first of Edward's little 'Postals' or Discourses which he sends to Lolotte each Sunday now that he cannot go to her.

10th Frederic at the Union officiating again on Sunday. Dined downstairs for the first time for months. Sent Lolotte violets. Louy writes of Willie's engagement to a Miss Yorke. Wilson writes that she has left Ireland & means to go in for nursing in this neighbourhood.

March 4th Louy's son Leo came, a very fine tall boy, & very pleasant, not at all shy. Frederic came as usual, fresh from London sights & sounds.

17th Gerard came in for the first time in weeks. Leo returned home. Lolotte is to have a nurse, she is very poorly. Louy arrived looking better but very sad.

21st Yesterday Mannie, *(Gerard's son)* was 4 years old & he & his sisters came in to see me looking bright & blooming & very charming.

24th An adieu visit from Major Ricketts & very glad I was to see him. Also from him a present of a pretty little etching, pens, Indian ink, & paper to begin to etch. I feel too old & stupid. *(82)*

April 2nd Mary came home a great pleasure to receive her improved report of Lolotte. Gerard too has begun his <u>crawl</u> round to see me. Mr & Mrs Cave Browne & Mrs Balston called.

6th The dear little Cottage children came to sing to me. Sent my 'Lines to Kentish Children' to be printed.

20th Mary to Brighton again. Mona arrived to stay.

May 1st Mr Gibson made a most unwise address to the afternoon congregation & said that the religious teaching in the parish was abominable.

2nd The Misses Phillips have sent in their resignation as teachers. Garland children came I dispensed my little bounties for the sight of very pretty wild flower garlands.

5th Saw Dr Whitestone who wishes me to stay upstairs as am feeling very poorly.

6th Katie came full of domestic worries. Wrote to Wilson as Lolotte has some thought of taking her. Mary returned & Mona left for home.

Mona was 22 in 1892 (painted by Louisa)

13th Wilson came & is leaving tomorrow for Brighton to stay with Lolotte as nurse.
20th Mrs d'Uphaugh, Edith & Maud Duppa here. Began a sketch of the view from my window.

21st Edward & Julia came early from Tunbridge Wells, a great delight to see them both. Frederic also came full of the Assyrian mission at Lambeth Palace. *(The archbishop's mission to Assyrian Christians)*

24th Our own confirmation. Sent the carriage to Sutton Valence to fetch the Bishop who took luncheon with Gerard, then went to the church. On his return the young Bishop came to see me with Gerard & then returned to The Cottage for tea.

28th Mrs Branfill Harrison passed the day with me, I was delighted to see her.

30th The celebration of the Club, one garland, a band & the meeting at our door. How long has this celebration lasted, which was founded before I came by my husband.

31st Drove out for the first time for nearly eight months. Everything so fresh & lovely.

June 6th Mary to Tunbridge Wells house-hunting for Lolotte, then to Brighton. Took my solitary walks about the house & liked the new paper on the back staircase much.

18th Mary returned leaving Lolotte in most comfortable rooms & as well as could be expected. Drove to Maidstone for the first time for nine months.

July 4th Minnie Greathed arrived to stay, my old friend of so many years, which of course have changed her much and all of us who are left, but it was very pleasant to see her again.

6th We donned purple & orange ribbons & drove off to Maidstone the day of nomination for mid-Kent. Gerard full of election matters.

7th The report of Lolotte discouraging. Dr Rankin says that he gives her hope of feeling better in a year's time but to Louy he says it will be two years. Took Minnie Greathed out driving by the Castle & through the village, & at The Cottage for tea.

13th Our polling day. A flag painted on the parapet of our house & everyone but Frederic at the very summit of excitement. Drove about in purple & orange colours. Gerard busy from morning till night.

14th The poll declared when Major Warde was ahead. Gerard & Gussie took luncheon with him in The Star to celebrate the declaration.

16th Mary went to a tennis at the Manor House & Gerard & Gussie had a pic-nic on The Hill at his farm to celebrate little Laura's birthday. Frederic sat with me.

21st In the afternoon to a tennis tournament at Mrs Best's, about 100 guests.

August 3rd Mary & I made calls. Gussie & Gerard went to Tunbridge Wells to see dear Lolotte whom they thought rather better. Bertha's children Woodbyne & Jack arrived to stay.

13th To Lady Lister Kaye's Boughton Place, with Frederic & Jessie.

14th Due to rain Mary compelled to have her Sunday school treat in the paper mills. An immense room, no end of children & noise.

18th Ella & Eleanor arrived to stay, took them to Mrs Sage's enticing Oriental shop.

20th To Mrs Whatman's garden party with Ella, Eleanor & Mary. Garden delightful.

25th Ella & Eleanor left, Kate Gibson arrived. Called on Mrs Balston the new house is a perfect palace, the work of the architect Waterhouse.[219]

September 9th Bryan *(Gipps)* walked up the hill to see Gerard's farm & his new reaping & binding machine.

13th Edward & Julia arrived, he looking blooming, she thin & worn. It was delightful to see them again.

14th Frederic at dinner. Edward & he delighted with one another.

16th Lady Lister-Kaye, Frederic & Gussie etc at afternoon tea, poor Gerard suffering too much toothache to come. Edward & Julia departed.

19th Edith Lester took luncheon here. The Railway Company gave General Lester 600 guineas for injuries received from his accident.

23rd Taught Bryan perspective & heard him read the Iliad.

29th Drove to Preston Hall & called on Mr & Mrs Brassey.

October 1st Bryan helping Mary with church decorations. Read French with him. Gerard had four teeth out.

4th Mary went to the Church Congress & stayed. Called on Mrs W. Martin at the Castle. Tennyson died. A great man has passed from the earth. Bryan went home.

12th Gerard had four more teeth extracted. Mrs Green called. Richard Gipps stayed overnight. Called on Mrs Farmer.

18th Mary returned with a sad report of Lolotte, Dr Rankin considers her no worse & that her last attack was due to hysteria.

---

[219]   Springfield House.

November 4th Lewis Shaw arrived looking delicate as usual, he give an unsatisfactory report of his father.

6th Lewis acknowledged to being a Socialist but far more in theory than in practice.

18th With Mary early to Maidstone. To Mrs Sage's Eastern shop full of treasures for Christmas from all parts of the globe.

19th A visit from Lisa in the morning & in the afternoon as usual from Frederic. Began to read Besant's 'London'.

21st Frederic, Mary & I went to the service at All Saints Maidstone to hear Canon Mason's instruction. It was the beginning of the mission. He walked down the church during his discourse, speaking the whole time & looked a thorough monk.

23rd Louy arrived. Mary's first village working party for the 'waifs & strays'.

December 1st Louy departed to see Lolotte on her way home.

18th Mary returned from Lolotte. The Walsh family have rented the Manor House. Gerard & family left for Brighton possibly for two months.

26th Willie & his bride Nancy arrived for the night, she sang nervously. Skating on Castle moat for the last week.

1893 January 5th Sam Sage who was in Barming Asylum last week was buried here yesterday & a muffled peel rung last night as he belonged to the Quire.

6th Kate arrived to stay, as pleasant & plump as ever.

9th Mary & Kate busy preparing for the prize-giving. She saw her father in the vestry yesterday.

10th Tea at Godfrey House, after which Frederic gave the prizes.

23rd Mr Pryce Jones *(vicar of Wormshill)* at luncheon, his interview with Mr Gibson on Sunday (not <u>alone</u>). Mrs Gibson told a greater untruth if possible than ever.

26th Mary returned with a better report of Lolotte, on the whole.

31st Sent the carriage to follow on Mrs Wykeham Martin's funeral, quite one of gone by days. A hearse of plumes, mutes, & six mourning coaches.

February 2nd Gerard is feeling better in Brighton & enjoying the company.

5th Called on Mrs Balston. Jessie at luncheon. Mary still busy with RSPCA & GFS. A dreadful affair with Mitchell, gave him his warning to go on Monday.

March 2nd I am glad to say that Gerard has arrived with Gussie & the rest.

3rd Today I have been inundated with visitors beginning with dear Gerard, then Jessie, then Lady Goldsmid & Patricia, then Frederic. Went to The Cottage & saw them all.

13th Mary left early for Tunbridge Wells. Wilson came to pass the day with me & tell all details of Lolotte who really is fatter & she thinks rather better.

Four of Gerard and Gussie's children: Lillian, Laura, Dick and Ella. This was taken around this time when they were 7, 11, 5 and 9. Dick would have been about to go into trousers

14th Bertha writes that Edward (*her son*) has returned from Japan on sick leave in the 'Tamar', laden with curios. Gerard & Gussie called.

20th Little Dick's birthday, a visit from him & his three sisters who sang to me. He is five years old today.

21st Mary & I left early to take luncheon with the Miss Savages & then she went to see Malling Abbey which has just been sold by Mr Akers Douglas to a Benedictine Sisterhood for £10,000. His grandfather gave £3,700 for it.

24th Hughes and I went to town, went to Waterloo House, (Swan & Edgar now), then to Elise & wound up with Gorringes.

27th Louy came to fetch _her_ Ella who has been here for the last week & is very nice & pretty. Dering Harrison at luncheon.

April 2nd Arthur Hewitt, the footman, departed. He was so eccentric that I did not feel happy till he left. Mrs Hampson called. Went to Mary's sale for Waifs & Strays.

15h To morning service a great pleasure after a long gap. Mary has given up the Sunday school, in fact all church work & the rest of the teachers & workers have followed her example. _(further trouble with the vicar's wife)_

May 1st Only two garlands! Gave an afternoon tea.

7th Mr & Mrs d'Uphaugh, Gerard, Gussie & Frederic at afternoon tea. Gussie sang beautifully. Mrs d'Uphaugh like one of the ladies of Burne Jones.

12th We left for Tunbridge Wells in the carriage to stay with Lolotte. Hughes went by train from Maidstone. We drove the whole way halting for 1½ hours at Hadlow & on 24th we started on our homeward way.

25th Gerard is now the owner of Cotuams _(a house very close by in the village)_ & in immense spirits.

26th Louy arrived for the day & consulted Gerard about the horrid income tax paper. Mona was with her & blooming.

27th Gerard came about my income tax paper & I am most grateful to him for settling these incomprehensible matters.

31st Lisa called to announce Jessie's engagement to Dr Whitestone.

June 3rd Called at The Cottage & on Mrs Walsh. Lisa went to visit Lolotte.

6th Grandson Richard Gipps arrived to take leave before sailing for Australia, probably the last time I shall see him in this world. He sails on 'The Orient' by which Freddie went. May he have better fortune than Freddie. It will be an intense pleasure for the brothers to meet.

348

12th Frederic came tired out with his London dinners & parties. Mrs Green to tea.

15th To church, Mr Gibson dull & feeble. To a lawn tennis.

18th Mary to stay with Louy & then Edward & Julia.

21st Ella Gipps to stay here. Called at the Castle.

July 6th Mona & Louis Gipps arrived.

8th The day of our fete champetre *(rural)* in celebration of the royal wedding, beginning with afternoon tea to the school children & a procession of bands & banners to the lawn meadow where they were to be joined by the elders of the village whom Gerard & Gussie had kindly entertained to tea in their dining room. But soon a violent storm came on & all had to crowd into the house, passages, den, kitchen etc being completely crammed, the teachers & some of the guests being in the dining room & others in the drawing room. However at last the evening cleared & all rushed out into the air & 'God Save the Queen' & 'Rule Britannia' were sung & medals given & then games were played & races run & dances danced, till past 9 when the revels closed as the light waned. All the helpers, Mary, Mona & Louis exerted themselves to the utmost & everything seemed to give satisfaction.[220]

27th Started for Tunbridge Wells, railway as far as Tonbridge then fly, to find dear Lolotte on her couch awaiting us. She was again better than I had expected. Then Edward came in looking well, though Julia is more than ever restless.

31st Took Ella & her children to Maidstone on their way to meet Louy & her Ella & to see Lolotte for day.

August 3rd To Mrs Bosanquet's tennis party took Eleanor & Henry.

7th Bertha & her little boy Stephen arrived & also Ernst. A great pleasure to see them again. An afternoon tea, Mrs Balston, Cave-Brownes etc, Ernst played & Gussie sang.

15th Mr & Mrs Kingdom to lunch. Ella Gipps arrived to stay.

22nd Frederic & Gerard had an interview with Mr Gibson. They describe him as in a most enfeebled state of mind. Tennis at Mrs Best's met no end of friends

September 13th I drove early to Maidstone with Ella taking her to the station on her homeward way, & bringing back Mary from Tunbridge Wells.

---

[220]   The wedding of the future George V to Princess Mary of Teck.

Ella and her daughter Ella Florence, known as Florence. This photograph would have been taken about this time when Ella was 53 and Florence 21

21st To a large & pleasant party at Barham Court. There were bell ringers & glee singers & the Yeomanry Band. Saw almost all our friends.

October 12th A day in London with Mary shopping.

19th I went to stay with Lolotte, she came into the sitting room for her tea. Edward & Julia called each day. Louy came for the day. Dr Rankin considers Lolotte much better. Left her in good spirits.

November 6th Many Guy Fawkes's about the village. Dismissed them all summarily.

7th Louy & Willie arrived both looking worn & wan.

8th Edward Morgan (*grandson*) appeared looking very blooming & well & went over to sleep at The Cottage.

9th Louy, Gerard, Gussie & I went to Maidstone taking Gerard on his way to Tunbridge Wells. Edward left at five for Sheerness & 'The Howe'. He sails for the Mediterranean on Saturday. Mrs Whatman called.

17th Heard from Willie that his wife had had a very bad confinement & that the baby, a boy, was dead. Wrote to him.

20th A letter from Willie. Nancy & her baby both dead after a fearful confinement. The funeral takes place tomorrow. Louy did not reach St Bees till 12 at night & poor Nancy died in the morning.

21st General Lester came, it was very pleasant to see his kind cheerful face again.

25th Frederic came in early to see General Lester. Lolotte has written a book, 'Short stories for long journeys' and published it. Gerard brought over a copy. I hope that it will prove a success.

(This year Louisa began to occasionally repeat facts in the journal)

27th Gerard, Gussie, Mary & I went to the vicarage Maidstone, to hear a lecture to a crowded room on the Christian church in Assyria, Frederic too spoke a few words.

December 5th A letter from Ella telling that Lewis has given up his post in the London bank from ill health. Leo Gipps, came to stay.

1894 January 19th Colonel & Mrs Knatchbull came again to see Cotuams & ended by taking it for three years.

20th A visit from Gerard much pleased with the prospect of his future tenants.

24th Frederic told us of the happiness of Katie whom he saw, & who becomes a novice very soon.

26th *(Louy & son Leo are staying)* Louy & Mary went to see Lady Howard's stock which was to be sold today & Leo bought for his mother a Jersey cow & a very handsome carthorse by name Elspeth MacGregor of illustrious lineage. Frederic came in & gave an account of the reception of Katie yesterday as a novice of Clewer & her putting on the white veil.[221]

29th Mary, Lisa & Leo went to 'Cinderella' the entertainment given at Maidstone for the Soup Kitchen.

30th Mary went to Tunbridge Wells to stay & Leo left for home. Frederic came in quite tired with all he is doing for the Archbishop & the Assyrians.

February 2nd Louy left & Mary returned. Flora Ricketts called.

5th Mr Gibson too unwell to visit a dying woman, the police sergeant's wife, so Mr Pryce Jones went from the Union. She died the same day having had twins three weeks earlier, one living.

8th Kate arrived to stay & to see her father. Jessie & Mrs d'Uphaugh called.

March 8th Bertha arrived unexpectedly for the day & a great pleasure it was to see her, she is looking very bright & well. Then Gerard came in & later Frederic.

15th Went with Gerard & Mary to see Cotuams, full of workmen & much improved. Sent the carriage to follow at Mr Sedgwick's funeral. He & poor old Sage the baker were buried today.

16th Our new neighbours at Cotuams, Colonel & Mrs Knatchbull took luncheon, they seem very nice & pleasant.

20th Letter from Lolotte who dreads the isolation to which Dr Rankin dooms her & yet feels it better for herself. Colonel Knatchbull, Flo Ricketts & Jessie Goldmid at afternoon tea. Wrote to Lolotte to tell her that Harry's name will be in the Dictionary of Universal Biography with a short notice.

22nd Poor Lolotte is forbidden to see anyone even Mary who is going to Tunbridge Wells.

28th Mary went to Edward & Julia for the day but was not allowed to see Lolotte. Wilson does not think her better.

April 2nd Katie came to luncheon with her father much encumbered with the amplitude of her dress & her very long white veil, but still it was becoming to her.

28th Mary returned having seen Lolotte. Tea at Cotuams. Leo came for the night.

---

[221]   In 1853 architect Henry Woodyear designed the chapel and offices that became the Convent of St. John the Baptist at Clewer, Windsor. A place of help and shelter for outcast women, the Convent was the home of the Clewer Sisters who, by 1860, were caring for and educating a community of around 80 people.

May 1st The garlands for May Day which are now far fewer in number. We reached our very nice lodgings at 15 Robertson Terrace. Mary & I after a little tea sat out on the esplanade.(*Hastings for a week)*

2nd So many memories crowd round me today. The birthday of poor Louis & its celebration by going to Brook Green Fair & seeing Richardson's theatre & Gingeli's conjuring. Then also the marriage of our Uncle Gerard de Visme with Miss Toriani (our dear Aunt Ella), in Kensington church when we, Louis, Milly & I sat in a near pew with our nurses & saw the ceremony. Now I alone remain of all who saw it!

4th Louy, Mona & Bryan came in to pass the day. Mona off in the evening for Wiesbaden with Miss Josephine Gipps.

7th Louis Gipps appeared having bicycled here. Mary & he went to see the St Clements Caves beneath the castle.

11th *(At home)* Mary & I shopping in the rain in Maidstone & very miserable we found it. On afterwards to the station to fetch Ella, Florence & Henry. Florence is a pretty dark haired girl with a very good complexion.

13th Paid for Lolotte's chair *(new wheelchair)*, Mary, Florence, Henry & I drove to Lenham to call on Mrs Akers & then to Boughton Malherbe vicarage.

25th Ella departed with Florence leaving Henry with us. *(he is 17)* In the afternoon came Colonel Knatchbull, Major Wedderburn, Frederic & Gussie to afternoon tea.

23rd Mary, Henry, Miss Knatchbull & I went to the loan exhibition in the museum. Afterwards we drank tea at the Barracks with Colonel Sufford. He produced no end of cats for our inspection & Mary is to have a little angora kitten.

June 2nd Taught Henry as usual. Willie is to manage the Didcot Branch railway at an income of £300 a year.

6th Mary went to stay with Lolotte for a week. To a party at Gerard's with music.

15th A tennis party here, five Knatchbulls, Gerard & Gussie, Goldsmids etc.

July 1st Went to the second service. Frederic came in during the afternoon.

2nd Hay-making. Weather lovely & warm. The two Miss Hampsons paid a long, late visit, wandered in the garden & were very agreeable.

5th A musical matinee at Godfrey House. Mr Pryce Jones came in to ask for two copies of my lines on Hollingbourne which he purchased.

9th Featherstone left & Annie Ellis came as cook.

10th Much housekeeping with the new cook & explaining.

11th Mary hurried to see the fall of the high chimney of the Paper Mill at which all Hollingbourne was (or wished to be) present. It was very wonderful & well managed without failure or accident & at 4.45 tottered & fell. Everyone rejoicing in the fall.

12th Mary departed. Ellis fell in the wash house & fainted.

14th Last night we were all disturbed by a most dreadful event. Ellis roused everyone by describing she was suffering immense pain from indigestion & walked up & down the room in agony, when all at once the cry of a child was heard & a little girl arrived in the world. I sent instantly for Dr Whitestone & Mrs Gibson (*wife of the gardener*) & after some time all was quiet. Smith came to give aid as cook, it was very kind of her & a great pleasure to see her. Mr & Mrs Goodwin, Ellis's relations, came to see me & were in the greatest trouble about her.

19th Letters from Ellis's relations to say that they could do nothing for her.

21st Sent Ellis & her baby to the Union in Lampard's fly. Saw her before her departure. Poor woman! She looked more miserable than I can describe. I could not bear to see her. Gerard came later, then Frederic, then Mrs Knatchbull.

25th Yesterday saw a nice little cook by name Rose Seal. She is to come on Monday.

26th Matilda Tennyson at luncheon, she is much what she was before so many years had passed. Mary & Henry at the Manor House.

29th Mr Pryce Jones came to see me about Ellis, she leaves the Union tomorrow.

30th Our new cook Rose Seal came & Smith, I am sorry to say, departed.

August 3rd The Hollingbourne flower show, George Lampard won my best prize. The Balstons of Springfield called.

9th Bought a tortoise in Maidstone. Looked at the motionless emotionless tortoise in the rose garden. Richard Gipps has found a magnificent piece of opal. Called with Mrs Knatchbull on Mrs Hampson & Mrs Scarth.

10th Woodbyne & May arrived to stay. Mrs Gardner-Waterman came to tea.

23rd Kate came to stay. Mary took her teachers & pupils to the number of 23 to the Crystal Palace.

September 6th Mary left for Tunbridge Wells. Mrs Knatchbull & Frederic came in.

13th Today Minnie Greathed arrived looking well, she & I talked over old times.

14th To a delightful musical & tennis party at Mrs Hampson's.

17th Minnie departed. The marriage gifts on view this afternoon at Godfrey House. (*wedding of Dr Whitestone & Jessie Goldsmid*)

18th Mrs Walsh had kindly lent the Manor House Hall for the reception of the guests who repaired thither for refreshment. The bridesmaids were Patricia & Miss Whitestone & Little Laura. (*Gerard's daughter*) Dr Whitestone gave them gold brooches in the form of a shamrock. Saw the marriage gifts en route home which were very pretty & numerous. Called on Lady Goldsmid.

October 1st Taught Eleanor French & English. Gerard & Gussie to Tunbridge Wells. Gerard gave a very poor report of Lolotte. Ella Gipps came to stay.

14th Mary ran a bazaar helped by Ella *(Gipps)* & Eleanor. Katie is now at the House of Mercy, Bovey Tracey.

17th Dering Harrison is engaged to Miss Whitestone. Lolotte has chosen a house at Tunbridge Wells. A Colonel Vibert of the Royal Engineers called with Frederic. He had known Harry & said he was the most remarkable man he had ever known for his universal talents & greatness of character. Read in The Times of the death of my dear old friend Mrs Treherne, my first English friend after leaving Paris.

22nd Ella arrived from Norfolk to collect her very nice daughter Eleanor. A book from Edward with a dedication to myself! 'Thoughts on some passages of Holy Scripture.' The thoughts were originally written for Lolotte in her long & trying illness & so I value them the more. Dr & Mrs Whitestone took luncheon here.

November 2nd Left home for Brighton. Reached my rooms in Oriental Place & almost immediately appeared Bertha, very nice & bright & Vera grown quite tall. Edward is improving & between seeing a few friends & shopping, time passed very happily & quickly & our home saw us again on 12th.

13th Mary off to Tunbridge Wells & Louy arrived from thence. Sent off a few things to Lolotte for her house.

22nd Lady Goldsmid, Patricia & Frederic came in & last of all Mary just fresh from Tunbridge Wells where Lolotte's move had been managed most happily.

December 2nd Gerard is very busy with the Parish Council. My rheumatism severe.

4th Gerard & Gussie to Tunbridge Wells for a few days. Sent Woodbyne, for her coming out, some antique jewellery set with emeralds. General Lester came.

12th I gave prizes & testimonials at the school to an infinite number of children.

17th Gerard accompanied me to vote for the Parish Council which event took place at the board school and for which we had to disappear within a little canvas erection.

23rd Wrote tickets for Christmas dinners.

24th Carol singing by village children all day.

26th The village young men sang outside as Christie Minstrels.

31st The first parish council, which passed off very well thanks to Gerard.

1895 January 1st A servants' ball at the Castle to which John, Emily & Priscilla went & were not home till nearly 6.

12th Willie arrived looking very pale & ill as usual & full of his railway & his great wish to make it a success.

16th A meeting for Church Defence at the Institute which had a most troublous course & ended in nothing. Gerard did his very best but nothing would appease Frederic. Mrs Knatchbull came to see me & said what a fiasco it had been & that our vicar was an utter 'dumby'.

March 1st Mary left at 11 to meet Frederic at the Church Defence meeting in the Queens Hall Langham Place.[222]

2nd Mary home at 8 having had a day she much liked as well as the speeches of the Archbishop of Canterbury, Frederic was also pleased.

4th Bertha tells that Edward has passed his exam & is now a Lieutenant R.N. & full of excitement.

11th A letter from Louis Gipps who leaves in April for Queensland. He is to be with a Mr Braddon at the Copper Mines. Drove to Maidstone which was more noisy than ever with organs & the steam roller.

21st Took Frederic & Lisa to call at Leeds Castle.

25th Drove into Maidstone to fetch Louy & Louis who has come to say goodbye before leaving for Brisbane. He & I played chess in the evening.

---

[222] The Church Defence League had just been formed to guard against the disestablishment of the Anglican church because the church in Wales had just been disestablished.

26th Day passed by Louy & her son in rushing backwards & forwards to The Cottage.

30th The death in The Times of my dearest old friend Emily Harrison neé Struth. I never expected to see her again in this world but I could hear from her & think of her in her Welsh home, & the sad void she has left will never be filled.

Bertha painted by her daughter Woodbyne

April 12th To Maidstone to sign my will. Mary to stay with Lolotte.

20th To a Primrose League Concert, Frederic was chairman. Bryan Gipps came to stay a few days. Freddie has had great success & found gold.

24th To London with Hughes, met by Bertha, Delmar & Edward at Victoria. Shopping with Bertha, the greatest pleasure to see her.

May 1st Only two garlands. The glories of May Day are fast fading here.

6th Drove up the Hill to call on Mrs d'Uphaugh & the new baby, who is very large, & looks very strong & is I think a perfect d'Uphaugh.

10th Went to the Confirmation where the Bishop of Dover gave a very good & most impressive address to all the boys & girls of whom there were about 50 from the various parishes. The Bishop returned here to drink tea, very bright & pleasant.

29th Mrs Knatchbull came to look over some seeds sent by Major Ricketts from the Riviera. So many that we were quite exhausted. Selected a few. The club day & the village all in commotion & noise. Also the first day of cricket.

June 23rd Returned home leaving dear Lolotte rather better.

24th Mona arrived having seen Lolotte. To the cricket match at The Mote between Oxford & Kent with Mona & Gussie.

July 29th Mona departed. Felt very sorry for the departure of my bright, cheerful grand-daughter.

August 2nd Ella & Florence came to stay. Gerard in bed with lumbago.

7th Streeter & John to Hastings on a Band of Hope expedition. Had opal found by Freddie set into a brooch with brilliants. Mrs Knatchbull called. Mary went to stay at Tunbridge Wells. Jessie Whitestone neé Goldsmid has a baby.

10th Gerard is dreadfully crippled with rheumatism & can hardly stand or sit. Dr Whitestone injects him with morphia which helps. Am giving drawing lessons to the three grand-daughters from The Cottage.

15th To the Primrose Fete at Chilston. Gerard better.

20th To Malling for lunch with the Miss Savages. Bertha writes that old Perfect *(their footman during the 1840s)* is in the Guildford Union & encloses a note.

September 1st To morning service. Miss Roper's barn at Penn Court caught fire about 9.30, the village all in a commotion. The fire engine dashed along the road about 11.30, having been sent for too late.

2nd The Miss Savages at luncheon, then Frederic came in. We all went over to a party at Gerard's. The afternoon gave the greatest satisfaction.

9th Gerard came & in the afternoon appeared Lisa again & Frederic, then Gerard again & later Heneage & Dering Harrison.

10th Bertha arrived in the afternoon while Frederic was here, & as usual announced her arrival by looking in at the window. Woodbyne & she in great spirits.

14th Gave our own tennis party. The morning passed in preparation, filling glasses with flowers & Hughes arranging the fruit. The weather was lovely & so were the peaches & all went off very well.

19th Mary gone to Tunbridge Wells to see Lolotte in her new home & assist in her garden. Lolotte <u>decidedly</u> better I rejoice to think.

20th Gerard took luncheon with me most kindly in spite of lumbago. Took Frederic, Gerard & Patricia to Mrs Balston's, Mary going with Gussie.

23rd Drove to Chilston to Mrs Akers Douglas, she spoke of Mr Douglas' constant engagement in London with 'the works' & he is just now arranging a lift for the Queen at Windsor.

24th Mary up The Hill giving 'her children' a blackberry party & tea at Yew Tree Farm. Poor little Laura very ill & attacked with a sort of fit. Dr Hoare was sent for as well as Dr Whitestone & a nurse.

25th Little Laura better.

October 8th To the Theatricals at the Manor House. Ate Louy's goose.

November 6th Through London where met Bertha, Woodbyne, Edward & May for an hour. To Brighton returning home on 16th.

21st To Maidstone to fetch Louy & Bryan, they had seen Lolotte en route.

December 9th Mary left to stay with Bertha. Leo Gipps is staying as well as Louy. Sent Edward & Julia a silver gilt dish for their golden wedding anniversary from Gerard, Gussie, Mary & myself. Called on Mrs Best who has had a fearful operation.

10th Gussie went to Tunbridge Wells & passed the anniversary day with Edward & Julia.

25th Dear Gerard came to see me in spite of lumbago & other ills. Mary went to church through mist & mud & quite in the dark. Lisa appeared full of good wishes.

1896 January 4th Frederic & Gerard came in during the afternoon & discussed politics till they were quite wild.

7th The whole world in confusion with the Transvaal, with the German Emperor's telegram & Captain Jameson's 'fight' the cause of all. No one knows what to think but all are full of surmises.[223]

16th Mary & I went to Maidstone & met Colonel Urmston who said that everything was quieting down & that there would be no war.

February 10th In the evening Dora *(Feakins, housemaid)*, who had been unwell during the day produced a baby! All the house in commotion of course & Dr Whitestone & old Mrs Sage summoned.

April 26th *(long gap in journal)* Now I am up & about again tho' reheumatic. My illness proved to be the shingles. The second time I have had them, pain & weakness extreme. Could only lie in bed & eat jelly of the strongest kind sent by Bertha & Lolotte. I had a very good nurse from Malling, Nurse Warren, for three weeks & visits from all my dear children with the exception of Lolotte who is always in bed. Edith Lampard is now our housemaid & Alfred Coleman footman.

May 4th Teaching Gerard's children drawing as usual. Mary to Tunbridge Wells for day. Frederic continues busy in London & Lambeth as well as in the village.

7th An afternoon tea including the good looking American; one-armed General Warner. Delmar set off for the capitals of northern Europe with Woodbyne & Vera to end with St Petersburg.

9th An autograph merchant came from London to see the Johnsonian autographs. I had no wish to part with them. Frederic & Mary busy with Church Defence.

11th To Maidstone for the Church Defence meeting, a crowded room, Frederic spoke well, magic lantern, a great success. Poor George Lampard died he will be much missed & regretted.

15th Mary at Canterbury for the annual GFS. Bertha & son Edward came to stay.

---

[223]   The Jameson Raid, when Dr Jameson led 470 men into the Transvaal intending to overthrow Kruger's government.

21st To London to stay with Bertha, was met by Edward & Jack. Shopping with Bertha. To Maples & bought curtains & pictures.

25th Minnie Greathed to luncheon & Dora, & Sophy Riddell. To the new Portrait Gallery, admittance 6d. Saw Edward in full Naval dress & very well he looked. I had spent a delightful four days with Bertha

June 1st Streeter's little boy *(William)* is very ill & his death hourly expected.

8th Streeter's poor little baby buried.

13th Frederic came in laden with meetings & invitations, two to the Archbishop's garden parties at Lambeth & one to the concert at Buckingham Palace.

22nd Drove to Maidstone with Mary & called on Miss Tennyson & Miss Lushington.

26th Mrs Green passed the morning here looking very well & plump. Gerard thinks Lolotte stronger.

27th Jack Shaw came to stay.

July 4th Mary superintending the church cleaning. To tennis at Langley vicarage.

10th We all left for London, Jack for Holborn & Mary & I for Victoria where Bertha met us with a carriage & we accomplished our shopping at Gorringes. Took luncheon with Delmar, Bertha & the blooming Woodbyne. Home.

14th General & Mrs Lester came to stay & we gave a tea.

20th To Tunbridge Wells & found Lolotte in a most comfortable little house & Wilson at the garden gate to welcome us. Lolotte is decidedly better, thank God. She is more natural. A most delightful day I had with her, Mary taking luncheon with Edward. Lolotte got up for dinner, then came Edward, Julia & Mary. We left at 5 leaving my dear child, I do think, really making progress at last.

24th To Preston Hall to Lady Violet Brassey's At Home with the Blue Hungarian Band, refreshments in a tent. Met many old friends.

26th Mrs Green called with Edith & Maud Duppa, Maud is now painting in oils. Mary went on an Archaeological Expedition. Gerard came twice to see me in my solitude. Later Frederic appeared, & later still Lisa.

August 6th Ella & Eleanor came at 6 having travelled all day, very bright & well.

13th A garden party at East Sutton Park, many people there & the fruit & the garden lovely.

17th Colonel Fred Pierson *(Harry's brother)* & his wife came to take luncheon at The Cottage, then went to see the memorial window to Harry in the church after which they returned here for tea.

20th Took Frederic & Patricia to Mrs Forster's At Home where little comedies were enacted. It was very agreeable & very full. We met all our friends.

27th To a large garden party at Barham Court, Lisa & Patricia accompanied us.

28th Frederic came in full of a meeting he had had with the Turkish Ambassador on the subject of these horrible massacres a few days ago.[224]

31st Poor little Mrs Farmer came. She had grieved much the death of her child.

September 5th Mary to Tunbridge Wells to see Lolotte. Edith & Maud Duppa came to stay.

8th Mrs d'Uphaugh, Mary, Edith & Maud went into Maidstone in the pony carriage & on bicycles. Acrostic with Frederic.

12th Gerard brought little Laura & Ella in with their violins & they play surprisingly well. Seal, *(the cook)*, is stealing, gave her notice.

20th Did not feel happy till Seal was out of the house. Fanny Buttons came to assist. To a garden party at Lady Lister-Kaye's, saw many old friends.

24th Mona arrived bright & well. Went with her to Thurnham Court to call on Lady Hampson.

25th Jack Shaw arrived on his bicycle, he came 115 miles & was not tired. Mary's bazaar, the room was crowded & she cleared £32. One side of the room consisted almost entirely of poors' clothes. New cook came on trial & little Fanny Buttons departed.

October 7th For the last four days have not seen Gerard who has a cold. I seem to do nothing & yet my days seem fully occupied.

14th The Amateur Theatricals at the Manor House. Dering acted far better than was expected. Dr Whitestone was, as ever, Dr Whitestone.

16th The bells tolling around for the sad ceremony of the dear Archbishop's funeral at Canterbury. *(Edward Benson)* Less than a week ago he was alive and apparently well.

17th I went to see Gerard who was very poorly.

---

[224]   Massacre of Armenians by the Ottomans.

18th Frederic came to take leave as he goes tomorrow to London for a fortnight principally to give Persian lessons.

November 2nd Sent Streeter to Ashford to look out for a horse. To Lady Lister K's & we all went into the servants' hall to see her Annual Tea. A gorgeous spread given to 20 old women of the parish. The hall looked very comfortable with its fire & rose coloured lamps & large amount of plate. Gerard in bed with pain in his hip.

17th Mona left, & very still the house is without her. To a meeting for Waifs & Strays at Mrs Balston's. Gerard improved but in bed.

19th A tea here, Knatchbulls, Gussie, Goldsmid girls etc. Streeter sold poor old Derby, we now need two horses, have hired one so far. Dering came to talk over horses with Mary. Leo Gipps arrived on his bicycle for night.

21st Called on Mrs Wykeham Martin. Mary to London with Dering to Tattersalls to see about a horse.

December 15th Frederic came in a little less deaf than usual.

25th Cards & presents no end. A clock from Mary, a flower vase from Gerard, a lamp from Mona. Visits from Gerard, Gussie & the children, from Mr Pryce Jones, Knatchbulls, & Goldsmids.

1897 January 1st Mr Pryce Jones took luncheon here. Mrs Knatchbull came to wish us a Happy New Year. Removed all my Christmas cards.

4th Mary to Tunbridge Wells where she found Edward & Julia very weak & poorly but the nurse had arrived. Lolotte very anxious but better.

5th Mary's first day of Soup for the year.

6th Went to see Gerard who is better. Woodbyne arrived.

7th Mary, Gussie, & Woodbyne went to the ball at Chilston. Kate Gibson arrived looking very well.

11th Woodbyne left. Edward has now a night as well as a day nurse.

14th Kate went see her father who mends slowly. Went to Leeds Castle, a mixed party of babies & children & young & old.

April 18th (*a gap since January*) All this long time since I last wrote has been almost passed in my room & six weeks in bed & seven under the care of Nurse Dinne from the West Malling home. I have had two visits from Dr Rankin of Tunbridge Wells, a month's visit from Louy & one of a few days from Bertha & every care & thought from Mary & Gerard. I feel quite overwhelmed with all the thought & care that my dear children have showered upon poor <u>worthless</u> me. Well! Now I am again crawling about & Frederic has been to see me & Mary & Lolotte & Gerard have sent me little presents & cards & my dear grandchildren too. Kate passed last Friday here & saw Mr Gibson who is very ailing & quite unable to exert himself in any way.

21st There were Amateur Theatricals & music at Bearsted. The performance 'got up' by Mrs d'Uphaugh to procure a nurse for the Hollingbourne sick. Frederic gave a recitation of Hotspur's speech from Henry IV.

25th Maude Knatchbull came to see me looking very pretty & smart in her new violet-covered red tocque, two visits from Gerard.

29th Mary is with Lolotte. Edward better & Julia full of plans for everyone as usual. Drank tea downstairs on Thursday for the first time.

May 3rd Edward suddenly passed away without any suffering. What a loss! Now I alone of the seven, whose early lives were together, am left. I cannot realise the world without him. Gerard & Gussie went off at once to Tunbridge Wells & found all most sad & that Lolotte assisted by Dr Rankin had been to take a last look at dear Edward.[225]

4th Mary left for Tunbridge Wells & Gussie returned late & came to see me in the evening. Edward had been to church with Julia on Sunday morning & received the Holy Sacrament, had gone to see Lolotte in the afternoon & read with her the usual little service &, (what struck her much), had asked on leaving to promise to take every care of Julia 'when he was gone'. On his return he read aloud a sermon of Liddell & after he was in bed said he felt a slight heart-burn upon which Julia gave him the sal-volatile mixture he always took, when he just sank back & never spoke again. It was so sudden that she could not believe he was gone.

5th Mary returned giving much the same account & preparing to go tomorrow with Gussie to Aynho for the funeral on Friday. Gerard also returned having assisted in all the sad arrangements. Julia too has decided to go. So they will all be at the rectory with Mr Frederick Cartwright. Gerard is not strong enough to go.

---

[225]   Gerard wrote in his diary of 'dear kind, loving Uncle Edward'.

6th Mary left this morning with Gussie. They will not reach Aynho till nearly 7. Gerard kindly came three times to see me.

7th A most sad letter from dearest Lolotte, wrote to her. This is the day of the funeral at Aynho. I cannot realise that I shall never see Edward again in this world & in the next I <u>dare</u> not hope for it. Gerard was with me often during the day & Frederic came in. He went on Wednesday to see Katie take the veil at Clewer. Dr Whitestone also paid me a visit. A stroll in the garden, my <u>first</u> since my illness, with Gerard.

8th Gerard again came in three times to see me. It is so very good of him. Mary & Gussie returned about 5. There was an immense gathering of relations & friends. Two younger Cartwright cousins read the service. Wreaths & flowers in profusion, Delmar went.

15th Went in Gerard's chair as far as the distant firs in Lawn Meadows, everything so lovely & bright that I felt quite revived. All was so beautiful around me that I cannot describe my feelings.

19th Frederic came in & is going to the dinner to meet the Duke of York at the Gordon Boys' Home. Lolotte is still sadly ill & dejected. Yesterday I went to The Cottage to hear Mr Morfill give his violin lesson to my dear little grandchildren Laura & Ella & very well they played.

25th Mary left early for Tunbridge Wells & Gerard kindly dined with me.

26th A tour each day in my chair in the garden. Mary returned giving a better report.

28th Mr Tindell was here yesterday full of boring for coal on The Hill & wishing to be allowed to make trial of Gerard's land.

31st Wrote to Louy touching a cheque for Bryan who is going to Neufchatel to learn to speak French before entering a Bank at Buenos Ayres.

June 10th Mrs Knatchbull came to talk over Cotuams & letting it to Lolotte.

16th Gerard, Gussie & the children all left for Tunbridge Wells. Mary very busy with the parish council & the Diamond Jubilee celebration plans.

20th A new dinner service from Maples, sent the old one to Ella.

July 21st A gap in my journal until today. The day before the Great Jubilee, had a terrible fall backwards on the front steps when I dislocated & fractured my wrist. Dr Whitestone was fortunately at home & came in at once & set it. All my hope of driving out to see the Beacons quite at an end.

August 3rd Dearest Lolotte, after more than six years appeared at Hollingbourne. She has taken Cotuams from Colonel Knatchbull for a month & has borne the journey from Tunbridge Wells wonderfully well.

5th Ella & Eleanor came from Norfolk to pay us their yearly visit. Ella very well & much fatter.

September 2nd Ernst arrived looking very delicate & stayed a week. He is much regretted now that he is staying with Bertha.

8th Kate came to stay. Mr Southey our future curate came in at supper.[226] He is very musical & pleasant. I go to Lolotte or she comes to me most days & lies on the sofa.

15th Lolotte left for Tunbridge Wells, I felt very sad, but thankful for the change in her. I dined downstairs for first time since my fall. Took my daily drive round the garden in my wheel chair. Can now use my arm a little.

20th Mrs Harrison came for the day, a great pleasure. Typhoid fever spreading rapidly in Maidstone. Old Mrs Sage, the strong-hold of the parish, very ill, she was the nurse & one of the few old relics of the village. Her place will not easily be filled.

October 1st Major Ricketts called & most kindly brought me 'The Time Spell' a little book beautifully illustrated by himself.[227]

6th Mr Southey at luncheon very bright & pleasant.

7th The typhoid fever in Maidstone is as bad as ever. We are having a supply of clothing made for the sick.

8th Mr Southey took luncheon here, quite overwhelmed with the arrival of all his furniture.

11th Went to Elnothington to see Mr Southey's countless treasures.

22nd A concert at The Cottage for the celebration of young Ella's birthday. It gave great satisfaction. Mary & three of our maids there.

24th Mr Southey at luncheon. Frederic & Katie in the afternoon, she looking very well & bright in her conventual attire & he all the better for London.

---

[226]   Rev. William Southey came as curate to assist the elderly Rev. Gibson. Southey later became the next vicar of Hollingbourne.

[227]   'The Time Spell of the Chateau d'Arpon' by Mary Sturge, published 1897.

It is now Mary who takes Mrs Knatchbull out, Louisa no longer makes calls. Her handwriting is variable and shaky at times. Now she only writes one or two letters a day and receives fewer than she did. She frequently sends money to her daughters.

31st Mr Southey came & administered to Mary, Katie & me the Holy Sacrament.

November 4th Dering Harrison married Miss Whitestone the Doctor's sister. Mrs Knatchbull called. Frederic & Gerard as usual.

8th A clock bought by the family for Tilman for his long service. He & his wife so much overcome that they wept over it, so a public presentation would have been impossible.

20th Mary to Tunbridge Wells for the day. Mr Southey explained to a parish meeting at the Institute all he would need for the church. £300 is collected.

25th An architect came to see the church. Mr Southey at luncheon. Louy came to stay. A chair drive in the road.

December 3rd A parish meeting at The Cottage in the morning & service at the Institute in the evening.

5th Mr Southey at luncheon & going immediately afterwards to superintend his afternoon meeting of boys. Read some of Tennyson's 'Life' which always does me good.

7th Mary off before 9 to Tunbridge Wells. Gussie came to see me, then Colonel Knatchbull & he was followed by Frederic.

8th Mary returned from Tunbridge Wells leaving Lolotte fairly well. Julia too, as well as could be expected. Stoves are being put in the church & the organ pulled down.

13th Everyone seems occupied at the church every day, did not see Gerard all yesterday.

17th I went out in my chair drawn by Gibson, air like spring. Gussie went to Tunbridge Wells yesterday to Julia. Gerard was to have dined here today but was too poorly to come. Mrs Knatchbull called.

18th Drove in my chair to see Gerard who is not well, though better.

21st Edward Morgan came looking very bright & well & while here received his appointment to one of the new battle ships – 'The Jupiter'.

23rd Gussie gave the prizes at the Board school, Frederic & Mr Southey spoke. I was at home occupied in sending & receiving Christmas cards till quite tired out.

25th The post of course very late & postman loaded. Visits from all the dear children in their new purple dresses, from Gerard, from Gussie, from Lisa & Patricia & from Mrs Knatchbull & Maude. Tidings that Katie is going to India for five years with two other Clewer sisters.

26th Mr Southey played the new organ in church which gave great satisfaction. The new stoves were lighted last Sunday & seem also to have been a great success. On Christmas Day Mr Southey gave the Holy Communion at 7.45 at the Mission Room & at 8.30 at church. It was again given by Mr Gibson after the later service. The like has never been known here during my time.

28th Gerard brought a photo of dear Edward's tomb at Aynho.

30th Frederic came in & then we had quite a musical evening, Mr Southey & his nieces & nephew, Mr S sang most of the evening.

1898 January 1st Last night was Old Year & New Year service at which 130 were present. Bells ringing all round. Mr Southey played the organ & also preached.

3rd Mrs & Miss Walsh called full of good wishes for the New Year & Colonel Knatchbull. Mary to Maidstone & there Alfred *(footman)* saw his father who told him that dear Lady Lister-Kaye had died the Sunday night.

5th Yesterday was Mary's first Soup Day of the year.

7th I went out in my chair & saw poor Gerard very ill & with influenza.

10th Saw two housemaids, one very nice but she had varicose veins in her leg so could not engage her.

15th A musical afternoon here, Kate played beautifully. The party a great success.

25th Mr Southey had a supper at the Institute for the ringers and the choir, very successful.

27th Mary off to London. Ella writes that Henry is anxious to start for Winnipeg.

February 1st Bertha has cheered us & seen her old friends. We had a tea with Mrs Dering Harrison & Mrs Whitestone & music.

9th The new organ was dedicated at a special service by Dean Farrar.[228] We had a gathering here for the occasion with Mr & Mrs Dering, Gerard, Frederic, the Dean & others. The Dean is

---

[228]   Dean Farrar, Dean of Canterbury wrote a number of books including the popular 'Eric, or little by little' for children.

a very thin, quiet man. Gerard & Mr d'Uphaugh had both been pupils of his at Harrow. Sent a cheque for £10 to Lolotte for Mr Avison Scott for the windows he is arranging to put up in his church at Tunbridge Wells to the memory of dearest Edward.

14th A chair drive in the road. Wrote to Ella with a £50 cheque for Henry for Winnipeg. Mr Southey was thrown from his bicycle on his way from Maidstone & brought home in a fly. His knee injured, one of his ribs broken & suffering from concussion of the brain. Gerard went to him & found him insensible in his study. By degrees he regained his senses but is quite unfit for any duties. Bryan Gipps is thinking of taking up music as a profession. Colonel Knatchbull called.

March 3rd Fredric is ill & Dr Hoare was called in & ordered him to have a nurse. Willie is engaged to Miss Grace Money.

10th The death of my old friend Minnie Greathed. We became acquainted in, I think, 1826 in Paris when she with all her family began an intimacy which has lasted all our lives. Though our meetings have been rare of late I cannot say how great the blank will be to me.

20th Dear little Dick's birthday. Gave to his father for him the gold pencil-case given to me by dear Aunt Ella & which had belonged to my grandfather Philip Nathaniel de Visme who died at Notting Hill, now Aubrey House, & is buried in the church yard at Kensington.

24th Yesterday the cheque arrived from dearest Edward's executors which has enabled me to give £278 to each of my children.

31st Mr Southey & Henry *(Ella's son)* at luncheon. He is a very nice & good looking boy. He leaves for Winnipeg in April. It was very sad to me as I shall probably never see him again.

April 4th Mr & Mrs d'Uphaugh took tea & I felt very stupid among the young. Mary at Maidstone so I had no one to help me not even with the tea kettle!

May 4th I was occupied with Alfred hanging the prints in my newly papered room.

16th A chair drive in the garden. Gerard at luncheon, afterwards Gussie.

17th Mona came, she looks very blooming.

20th Mr Gladstone died this morning at five. Bells tolling.

21st Mary left for Tunbridge Wells to stay with Julia. Frederic came.

25th Mona departed. She is so bright that we were much grieved to lose her. Mrs Balston of Springfield called, Gerard & Frederic as usual.

30th Whit Monday, everyone en fete. The road full of bicycles & the neighbouring fields with cricket.

June 7th The new dining room carpet put down. My first drive since February 1897, Gerard accompanying me. It was quite delightful. A red roof on the Tile Yard, all the paper mill buildings quite abolished, & all along the road by Greenway Court, Mr Fremlin the new owner *(and brewer)* has made endless plantations. Home by Elnothington where stopped to see the new stable.

8th Mrs Balston came en route with Mary to a tennis party at Hollingbourne House. Dreadful difficulties at the vicarage.

9th Letter from Ella enclosing one from Henry full of disappointment in his new life at Stonewall. Only salt pork to eat & his life passed in a tent with a dirty old Canadian.

10th Bertha & Edward R.N. came to pass the day & of course the house was never still & Frederic arrived to see her & Gerard & Gussie.

11th Mrs Branfill Harrison came here. An immense pleasure to see her again, then appeared Mrs Green & her sister in law, these last I think came to hear all about the events at the vicarage.

12th About 1 who should arrive on his bicycle but Bryan Gipps? Having ridden over from Burwash chiefly to hear the organ which delighted him.

16th Julia arrived by fly, soon after 3 & delighted I was to see her. She tells me it is six years since she last came. She is wonderfully active but so very very thin.

17th Mr Southey at luncheon to meet Julia who went to church to hear the organ which I also accomplished. It is very fine & Mr Southey plays it beautifully.

18th Mrs Nutt came in unexpectedly here & took luncheon at The Cottage. I was delighted to see her again & she was as bright & talkative as ever. After luncheon drove Julia to Maidstone & paid the dentist a flying visit. Not tired with my drive.

19th Julia intends to give a paten & chalice for the use of the Holy Sacrament at the Mission Room in memory of Edward & wished Mary to consult Mr Southey on the subject.[229]

---

[229]   The Mission Room was the old charity school room in Eyhorne Street where soup

21st William gave warning alas, as he wishes to take Mr Southey's place.

22nd Mary & I have taken a successor to William by name John Cornford, an orphan now working on the road.

28th Three children & Gussie came to wish me Goodbye ere leaving for Margate today. Mary & I went to a large party at Miss Lushington's Park House, 117 present. We met on the lovely lawn described in Tennyson's 'Princess'. It was very pleasant meeting so many old friends after my two years of illness. There was a band on the lawn beneath the fine old elms. Tried to talk to Mrs Lushington but she is sadly deaf. She is still handsome with the refined features of the Tennysons.

July 5th Sent Louy the old drawing room carpet which is in very good condition. Went to a party at the Knatchbull's, tennis, tea & talk.

6th A scene of excitement between Mrs Gibson & Mr Southey beginning in front of our house. To a party at Mrs Balston's Springfield with the band of the Engineers. Gerard suffering neuralgia in Margate & seeing much of Dr Rowe.

10th Frederic full of the Gordon Boys Home. Gerard is better in the sea air. Mr Southey has chosen the chalice for the mission room.

13th To a large tennis & garden party. Gerard & family returned after 3 weeks.

15th Held a tea, Lord Theobald who had been at Harrow with Gerard came.

20th Lolotte arrived to take Cotuams. Went in my chair to see her & thought her less feeble than last year. Leo Gipps arrived on his bicycle to stay.

22nd To a party at The Mote. Sir Marcus Samuel the owner now, a very kind host. Leo stopped Weston's runaway horse in the village. To see Lolotte every morning.

August 6th I felt quite ill & had to see Dr Whitestone & stay in bed.

October 9th *(gap in diary)* Much has occurred since I last wrote. Much time by me has been passed in my room & in bed. Lolotte has left for Hastings & has now returned to her own home. Little Dick has begun his school life at Windersham House Brighton, very happily. Ella has been & gone leaving Eleanor here. Mona has come. Mary's Waif &

was given out.

Stray bazaar has proved a <u>great</u> success. Colonel & Mrs Knatchbull have departed I am sorry to say. Mr & Mrs Gibson & Violet have disappeared & it is not known where. Henry Shaw has been, returned from Manitoba, all having been misrepresented. The Harvest Celebration took place today, all the four services well attended. Mr Southey at luncheon. Major George Goldsmid (*Frederic's son*) & Patricia called here in the afternoon. Gerard too much disabled by neuralgia to come over today.

11th A letter from Lolotte who is by degrees recovering. The vicarage now is quite empty with the exception of Mrs Cheesman *(housekeeper)* & her daughter.

12th Mr Southey came to see me & talked over his most wearing & endless affairs.

14th A visit from Gerard with a very charming article on Hollingbourne which he has written for the new magazine.[230] A long visit from Mrs Green.

17th Mr Southey came early full of parish matters, the new magazine etc. Mona I grieve to say departed.[231]

30th Mr Southey at luncheon positively shouting with lumbago & afterwards Alfred had to iron his back.

31st Lady Goldsmid & Patricia came & Lady G had unfortunately one of her attacks, became quite insensible & ended by walking upstairs.

November 7th Woodbyne & May are attending the Slade School in London. Gerard to Brighton via Tunbridge Wells. Discussed politics with Frederic.

1899 February 27th After all this long time, most of it passed in bed, attended by two nurses & visited by all my dear children & Dr Rankin & Dr Whitestone, I am now thank God, able to remain up for a few hours & am feeling daily stronger.

March 11th The Queen passed through Hollingbourne today en route to Cannes about 12.10 in a gorgeous carriage with a gorgeous engine. No one was allowed to enter the station. So Her Majesty was almost unseen though all the Parish was there to catch a glimpse of her.

12th Gerard came to see me morning & afternoon, still very languid from the effects of the whooping cough.

---

[230]   It is a poetic, historic description showing Gerard's love for the landscape & in particular the brook.

[231]   Rev William Southey was capable, enthusiastic & dedicated to his parishioners. The congregation swelled during his time in the village.

April 5th Emily Knell, May's maid left after living here nearly 6 years & her sister Florence came in her place. Kate came to stay. Went downstairs for the first time since my illness. Everything looked so bright, lovely & spacious, carried down in a chair by Streeter & Alfred. Gerard & Frederic daily as usual.

10th Dined downstairs for first time for about four months. My very nice nurse Janet Fleetwood departed after two months stay. As usual Kate & Mary at church Sunday morning & evening, Mary teaching in the village school in the morning & having her own school of girls in the Den in the afternoon. Went to bed at my usual time about 7 very tired.

12th Leo came on his bike. Mr Southey to lunch. Kate took Dick to Brighton. Gerard went to see Lolotte.

May 1st The garlands came as usual but I did not see them. A parish meeting about church affairs in the Mission Room, Mary the only woman. Mr Pryce Jones wrote asking for help in restoring his ruinous Wormshill church, sent a cheque.

9th Mary to Tunbridge Wells & found Julia very feeble I am sorry to say & Lolotte rheumatic. Streeter spoke of leaving as he wants higher wages.

18th Dr Whitestone is as averse as ever to my going up or downstairs.

24th Alfred at church between 4 & 5 to ring for the Queen's birthday.

31st Mary off to Canterbury for GFS. Frederic visited me in my solitude.

June 2nd Mr Southey promised me the Culpeper altar cloth. The church roof repaired. In the garden in my chair. Frederic full of the Dreyfus affair. A man thrown from his bicycle almost through the window of the Kings Head died at the hospital in Maidstone.

6th Mr Southey came to give me communion. Shall I ever receive it in church again? Major Ricketts visited & told me of his seven years wandering, to the Holy Land, to Egypt etc. New cook Elizabeth Bonny arrived.

11th Mrs George Thomas came to see me & very pleasant to see her after so long. Her little grand-daughter *(Edie Ramage)* was 'Cherry Ripe' of Millais & has now married a very wealthy Spaniard.

14th Woodbyne & Edward arrived & went to Lady Samuel's ball at The Mote with Mary, then they went to the cattle show which was opened by the Prince of Wales.

18th Leo & Mona came to stay a few days.

20th Ella & Robert are to move to Suffolk. Went to a garden party at Park House arranged by Cecilia Lushington.

July 8th Lolotte is coming & we are all on the tiptoe of expectation. About 4 she arrived looking much better. The pleasure that it is to see her cannot be described.

11th Lolotte went to see Frederic & he came to see her. She went in her chair.

15th Lolotte went up in her chair to the church where she had not been for 14 years & was delighted with the changes, the new organ, the uncovered roof etc & the road leading to the Upper Village which Mr Duppa had planted where the trees are now grown & flourishing & was formerly so bare & exposed.

16th Little Laura's birthday. She is now, wonderful to say, 17. She & Gerard & Gussie came in & later Major Ricketts full of art & heraldry & engraving. I have had a slight attack of erysipelas & have been confined to the house & my room.

18th Willie was married to Miss Grace Money of Newbury.

20th Dearest Lolotte left for Walmer, she is wonderfully better than last year.

26th A letter from Willie in Paris, such a happy one! God grant that the happiness may continue as it has begun.

28th Wrote to old Perfect & sent to him 5/- in answer to his begging letter. *(he is in a distant workhouse)* Frederic came to see me. He had not been here for weeks owing to his accident & he looks older & more infirm.

29th Mona arrived looking very blooming & giving a glowing description of the marriage which went off very well & Willie was laden with gifts.

31st A starving 'owlet' on the lawn which was fed on raw meat by Mary & Mona. A letter from Perfect telling of his discomfort at 24 men in his bedroom etc.

August 5th Gerard went to Dover to stay a few days with Lolotte.

10th Mary & Lisa off on a tour to Germany with her brother Major Goldsmid, Miss Rowsell & Mr Southey. Mona, Frederic & Jessie went to see them off at Dover.

12th Frederic reported that the Hollingbourne boys were all good & all prospering at the Gordon Boys Home. Discussed Dreyfus & also church reform with him. Dr Whitestone called.

15th Mary wrote from Homburg & from Frankfurt delighted with everything. Mrs Green visited looking feeble. Bryan arrived growing a most disfiguring beard.

17th Bryan cut off his beard I rejoice to say. I drove out in the carriage with Gerard. Everything sadly brown & parched, however felt truly thankful to be driving with Gerard again in the open air.

September 4th Alfred & Streeter both out in the hop gardens so I am doomed to pass the day in my room. I can go downstairs but who is to bring me up?

6th Mary returned looking very bright & well & delighted with her tour & time.

10th Lisa, George & Miss Rowsell came to afternoon tea & talked & laughed over their German adventures & Mr Southey did the same at luncheon.

16th Jack *Shaw* departed. Many motor cars about. A visit from Mrs Ricketts.

19th Sent Mr Southey £25 for the side aisles of the church. Frederic came & Gerard & he discussed the Transvaal.

21st Mary went to Tunbridge Wells. Sent off the carpet to Ella at Darsham. (S*he & Robert have just moved from Lodden)*

28th The children & teachers met at Mr Southey's for tea & afterwards for games & fireworks in *our* Lawn Meadow.

October 11th War declared.[232] Mr Southey & his nieces came to drink tea. Frederic & Gerard as usual. Dora came to see me.

13th Mary & Mona busy with church matters. Willie & his wife arrived, she very tall & nice looking & pleasant. Repairs of the church complete.

15th Willie left & Grace, his wife, stayed another day & left with Gussie who was going to see Julia. Chair ride in road. Julia's donkey arrived.

17th Julia's donkey vehicle arrived & was much approved. Gerard not well. Alfred Colman left after living here 3 ½ years.

23rd Such sad news from the Cape. A grand victory but many officers killed & today another victory but terrible slaughter. Mrs Branfill Harrison visited. Dentist came. Gerard better & came twice as usual. Gussie at Tunbridge Wells.

November 7th Last evening Mr Anderson came & put in my teeth. A great success.

---

[232]   The Boer War

10th Mr Southey took the members of the quire to London to the Lord Mayor's Show, the Tower, St Pauls & the theatre.

21st Frederic came & told of little Major George's decided engagement to Miss Rowsell, then came Leo & stayed the night.

December 3rd Mary & Mona went to the concert at Major Best's for the sailors & soldiers in the Transvaal.

4th Mary went to see Lolotte. Louy summoned Mona home as her Ella is ill. She will be much missed she is so bright & helpful in every way.

8th Gerard too ill to come. Sad news from the war. Bertha's Jack is to report himself on the reserve. Frederic & Patricia to see me.

28th Bertha's Jack is now appointed to the African Corps. He is 21, & in the Yeomanry. Kate came to stay.

1900-1905: The last years of the journal

The new century began for Louisa with the greatest sorrow of her long life, the death of Gerard. Other blows followed with the deaths of two grandsons. Yet Louisa's resilient nature still enabled her to take some pleasure in life. She never lost her great interest in people and enjoyed the company of her children and grandchildren.

1900 January 4th Miss Rowsell came & was <u>very</u> nice. She & Major Goldsmid are to be married in April. A parish <u>ladies meeting</u> yesterday. Sent a cheque for £5 to Mrs Rule & wrote to her.

13th Mrs Jackson & her little boy called. Kate & I had our backgammon.

17th Kate departed I am sorry to say for Brighton & no end of care, & Dick under her charge.

20th My <u>very</u> old friend Sir Montagu Scott has died suddenly & quietly in his chair.

February 5th Took a neat looking footman by name Henry Fowler. Wrote letters to each of my children to send them a little remembrance as I shall be 90. Mary found Lolotte unwell.

22nd Gerard came to me for some time & looking better than he had done for many days & made me so happy.

23rd Mary heard that Gerard had had a very bad night & that Dr Whitestone had been with him. Not feeling better, Dr Hoare was sent for. He did not think well of him & came again at 6. Before that however Dr Rankin had been telegraphed for but nothing could have done any good & my dearest Gerard had passed beyond all earthly care or skill & a second telegram was sent to Tunbridge Wells to arrest his coming. I can scarcely realise my life without Gerard. *(He was 52)*

24th Such a day of sorrow & gloom. But dearest Louy & Bertha came at different times & Mr Southey full of kindness.

25th Such a sad Sunday! How much I missed my dearest Gerard & his cheering visit! But <u>that</u> may never be again.

26th Bertha left & dear Ella came. Mr Southey came today & yesterday. Poor Gussie came.

27th All days alike & only one more sad than the other.

Louisa aged 90

March 1st Dearest Gerard's funeral. Willie came last evening & today Delmar, Bertha, Woodbyne & Leo & Ella Gipps & at 12.30 my dearest Gerard was borne to his last home on earth & buried in our old churchyard near the chancel. They say the service was all that could be wished, that the anthems were beautifully chanted & the Dead March beautifully played

& that the church was crowded. And now all is over & in this world I shall never see nor hear him again.[233]

2nd Mr Southey came to see me. Mary exerting herself but very miserable & ill with lumbago. Louy & Mona remain here for the present.

3rd Frederic came & poor Miss Buck (*governess of Gerard's children*) at tea. She feels our sad loss as much as anyone.

4th Mary very poorly & in bed with lumbago.

5th Laura, Ella, Lillian & Dick came to see me. (*Gerard's children*) Gussie a long time with Mary talking over business matters.[234]

6th Poor little Bee & Stephen came to see me. (*Gerard's six children were aged from Laura the eldest who was 18 to the youngest Stephen who was 9.*) All seemed so sad. Frederic too came. Mary is better today.

10th Heard that Major Ricketts had sold the Manor House to a Mr Arbuthnot.

11th Mr Southey kindly took Dick to school. (*Brighton*)

14th Dear Lisa came full of grief.

17th Visits from Lillian & Stephen.

24th Gussie & two daughters went to Tunbridge Wells & found both Julia & Lolotte better than she expected.

27th Louy left I am sorry to say. She goes to Tunbridge Wells.

May 6th A long month in bed, poor Mary very miserable with rheumatic pains.

7th Gussie called on her way to Tunbridge Wells.

9th Mary went to Tunbridge Wells, she is far from well, to see Dr Rankin & stay a day with Lolotte. My nurse, Bailey, who has been here a month departed.

11th Mary returned, she has seen Dr Rankin & is to return to stay with Lolotte & to try galvanism. Her illness seems to be a form of sciatica. A visit from Frederic.

15th Louy arrived. Mrs Green came to see me, also the children.

---

[233] All the village tradesmen closed for the funeral and blinds were drawn throughout the village. The coffin was wheeled on a bier by ten of Gerard's tenants from Eyhorne House to the church.

[234] Mary & Gussie were executors of Gerard's will. There were no financial worries since his estate was valued at £30,330 which is the equivalent of a spending value of £1,730,629 today. Mary was left an annuity of £30 a year, there were legacies for godchildren. Gussie was to receive the income from the estate for life & then all would be divided between the children.

19th Mafeking relieved yesterday. In London bells ringing & flags flying everywhere & today the same here.

21st Mary returned, certainly better, but not as well as I should like to see her. I wrote on Friday to Dr Rowe who did not know of the death of dearest Gerard. He wrote a very nice letter, full of affection & appreciation for him who is gone. Mary brought back the enlarged photo of Gerard which is <u>most</u> real & charming like himself speaking to one.

Gerard in his later years

23rd A letter from Louy to say that she & the calf arrived safely. Gave to Mona & Hughes each a photo of Gerard.

26th The Hollingbourne Club came & gave us the usual serenade & greeting, Mary decidedly better but, I grieve to say, very lame. Mr Southey came at 12 to talk of the lychgate which we propose to put up at the church gate in memory of dearest Gerard. Later Frederic came. The new housemaid Alice Thomson arrived.

30th Mary went to Harley Street to consult the specialist in nervous pains from which she suffers so much. His opinion favourable on the whole.

June 5th Bertha & daughter Vera arrived & stayed nearly a week which was a great pleasure. In the garden in the chair.

20th Lolotte arrived & sat or lay by me in my room, I returning her visit later in the day in the Red Room. Lisa called.

July 1st Saw much of Lolotte, a great enjoyment I have every day. She is certainly better.

2nd The children & Gussie came as they leave for Tunbridge Wells tomorrow. Mrs d'Uphaugh & Mrs Wykeham Martin called.

11th Lolotte departed with her maid Shepherd.

15th Last week poor Mr Gibson died & on Friday he was buried here beside his first wife. By the desire of the present one no bell was tolled or hymn was sung.

16th Mary in Maidstone to fetch Bryan & Ella Gipps & in the evening they went up to the station to meet Vera who also came laden with little wares, to give her services at the sale. No end of packing & preparing, practising the piano & violin.

17th Mona in Maidstone all day with Bryan & Ella at the Howard de Walden rooms. Mary joined the party. Mr Southey & Frederic called here. The pony carriage sold.

18th Everyone gone to the sale. Mary & Vera home in the evening. Mona & Ella slept there to superintend all the arrangements for tomorrow.

19th The theatrical, musical & other performances most successful, the debt on the church was more than paid. Frederic came to see me, all came home much satisfied & quite worn out.

21st Mr Southey brought the plans for the lychgate. Vera had gone to Godfrey House but came home saying that Lady Goldsmid had been taken suddenly ill. That was all she knew but it seems on going up to see if she would take another cup of tea Jessie found her dead. It is a great mercy that she passed away so quietly & suddenly.

25th The funeral at 2.30 which Mary & Mona attended. Lady Goldsmid now lies in our quiet churchyard near dearest Gerard. The funeral was, I hear, beautifully solemnised. George & his three sisters, Dr Whitestone & Mr Pryce Jones there.

29th Donned my black satin dress which has been made two years & remained unworn with one exception.

30th Mary went to Godfrey House & found them all fairly well.

31st The assassination of the King of Italy *(Umberto)*, one so popular & doing so much good.

August 3rd Mr Southey at tea. Cottage grandchildren called.

6th Frederic called, Mary to Tunbridge Wells. Gussie called & sat.

12th Bertha's son Edward has died on the 'Majestic' in falling from the mast. He seems to have been wandering in mind. His father & mother are gone to Portland. It is all so sad. *(Edward was 24)*

20th Dear Edward was laid to rest on the 18th in Copthorne church yard *(Copthorne Sussex where Effingham House, Bertha & Delmar's country home was)*. Admiral Rawson & all the officers who could be spared were there. The Union Jack was laid on his coffin, an anchor of flowers & wreaths innumerable. He was most popular, always kind & thoughtful of everyone & they added that 'he had not a vice'. Captain Scott who commands the Antarctic expedition remained the night at Effingham.

23rd General Lester came, accompanied by Kate Gibson, to see the church. He came up in my little room to see me & I went down to tea, Kate remaining.

26th Notice on the church door to say that Mr Southey is vicar of Hollingbourne which, with very few exceptions, gives universal satisfaction.

29th Alfred Colman our former servant is applying to be postman here & in the meantime is acting as our footman. Lisa came to see me & later Frederic.

September 3rd Dear Bertha with her sons Stuart & Stephen came & told all dearest Edward's end history. For him there seems nothing to grieve for, he was so thoroughly good & so much beloved and valued. It is for those who remain that the loss is great & poor Woodbyne has felt the blow fearfully. She is still obliged to go about in a Bath chair. Bertha & her boys left about 8.

6th My chair drive in the road. To see the fence to the Jubilee tree & Elnothington.

7th Woodbyne is much better. Leo arrived on his bike & I saw much of him.

14th Enclosed to Willie a cheque for £50 to assist Freddie in a speculation.

15th Mona as usual arranging the church. Mary calling on Mrs Arbuthnot. The Manor House quite changed from Ancient to Modern Life so that she scarcely knew where she was. Frederic came.

17th Drove in the large carriage with Mary to church. Such a grand ceiling & not a vestige of the old plaster & all so nice & clean. Then Mary's <u>beautiful</u> gift of the communion table the litany desk & the alms box. All was new to me & yet brought back to my mind 62 years ago when Richard & I met for the first time.

20th Mrs Green, Edith & Maude at tea, they all came up to see me & were very bright & pleasant.

21st Mr & Mrs Arbuthnot at tea, very bright & young.

October 3rd Laura & Ella from The Cottage departed for Effingham. Gussie called.

5th Bee & Stephen came from The Cottage. Out in my chair.

8th Ella & Eleanor arrived to stay looking well. Major Goldsmid & his wife called.

10th Dering has resigned his care of Gerard's farm as agent & Leo is to take it at which I much rejoice.

15th Ella left, leaving Eleanor behind. Mona went home. Mr Southey to lunch.

November 2nd Leo at the farm on The Hill. Gussie called & the children.

8th Mary to London to meet Bertha & settle their wedding present for Ernst.

22nd Arrangements for the arrival of Archdeacon Spooner & other clergy on the admission of Mr Southey to the cure of Hollingbourne. Mr Spooner dined here while the remainder of the party consisting of Frederic, Mrs Connop, Mr Pryce Jones etc, took tea in the book-room. All the party to the church. I was very glad to see the Archdeacon again. He was a friend of Gerard's at Magdalen College & I had known him at Maidstone when he had Trinity Church there.

24th Gussie & the bairns returned from Brighton & Leo came.

26th Leo with Eleanor bicycled to Chatham. The cow sent to Louy in the morning, she sent us the Persian cat in the evening.

27th Bertha wrote that Jack had been wounded <u>slightly</u>. *(he is in South Africa)*

December 2nd Mr Southey brought the sketch of his future vicarage.

4th Mr Southey gave me the Holy Communion, Gussie, Mary & Eleanor being present. Miss Wykeham Martin came to see me.

6th Frederic brought a very sad report of Dora. *(Dora Goldsmid the widow of Louisa's cousin Yeats)*

15th Lisa came to say that they had had a telegram that Dora had passed away from this world. How much Dora will be missed & lamented. *(She was 67)*

17th Ella arrived looking very well & plump, & in the evening Mary gave her tea party to the village girls. It took place in the den.

19th Gussie brought Dick to see me. Wrote to Mrs Rule with a cheque.

20th Ella & Eleanor departed & Kate arrived. Frederic came to tell me of Dora's funeral, many there.

22nd A long letter from dear Jack in South Africa giving a history of terrible fighting & his wounds.

29th Mary & Kate in Maidstone buying New Year & New Century cards.

1901 January 3rd General & Mrs Lester came early & passed the day. Frederic & Lisa met them at luncheon. Lewis Shaw wrote to announce his engagement to Miss Edith Nelson.

8th Louy arrived. A letter from Bertha telling of the poor Napiers & their sorrow for their son. *(Jack's friend Lieutenant Basil Napier died of his wounds in South Africa)*

10th Frederic came & talked much of Dora. He told me too, to my great sorrow, of the death of Edith Duppa. Lilian & Dick at backgammon.

11th Frederic came bringing the lawyer's letter telling him he is to have the Goldsmid pictures for his life to go afterwards to Colonel Albert Goldsmid his nephew.

12th Gussie came about letting cottages. A letter from Lewis asking me to write to Miss Nelson.

15th Wrote to Lewis & his fiancée. Bertha & May to go to Southampton tomorrow to meet Jack who is sent home wounded from South Africa.

17th Stephen came to take leave, as the dear little boy is off to school tomorrow.

18th A letter from Bertha. Jack is well but his shoulder is still stiff & his right eye dim. Great preparations are being made for his welcome home. Laura came in.

22nd A letter from Bertha full of the reception of Jack on his return & the procession, the wreaths, the banners etc. Lisa came.

23rd Our dearest Queen died! All the Empire plunged in the deepest grief. I can scarcely believe that this long, long, reign is over! And all her children & grandchildren gathered round her. It is all too sad & I can scarcely believe it.

27th The Union Jack was hoisted on the church & a muffled peel rung.

February 2nd Our dear Queen's funeral, our church was hung with purple. I remained at home in quiet & solitude during the whole day thinking of the stir all over every quarter of the Globe & how wonderful it all was.

3rd Our church was really crowded yesterday. Some present who had not entered it for years. Laura & Ella came to read 'The Lady of the Lake.'

6th Leo came today. A long visit from Mrs Arbuthnot who was very pleasant.

9th Dr Whitestone came to see Mary's maid & advises her going home as she is still very hysterical, so under the care of Hughes she departed.

15th Vera, *(Bertha's daughter)* Laura & Ella came to read & later Vera to exhibit her 'drawings from the nude' at the Slade School.

20th Last evening Mr Southey's quire supper which was a great success, Leo spoke. Streeter & Sammy Lampard are also said to have spoken well & briefly. This evening Mr Southey came to see me & unfolded the wish of the parish to erect somewhat in memory of dearest Gerard & that a vestry room is proposed.

27th Leo departed after a long stay, concluding most of his legal & agricultural business with Gussie & Mary.

28th Looking over old journals. My Father died December 1st 1853 at Waterloo Town in America. It is all too sad to think of, & more than 23 years since we had seen him.

March 4th Mr Southey to luncheon. Mary did a round of calls, myself doing nothing but intending much.

12th Mona arrived. Began to read 'Marmion' with Laura & Lilian.

17th Kate arrived having brought back the two Cottage boys from school.

29th Mrs Gibson appeared on the scene again with three dogs, her brother in law Smith, & her poor little dead baby in its coffin intending to bury it here. Of course she could do nothing without Mr Southey who would not, as they wished, allow it to be buried in Mr Gibson's grave but he allowed her to have a grave dug in another part of the churchyard & read the service himself. After which they all retired. Frederic &

Lisa left to stay in London. A telegram that a son was born to Willie Gipps. All going on well. So I am now a great-grandmother.

30th Mr Southey came in to tell the Gibson history & to talk over our lychgate.

April 10th Bertha came with May & Jack for the consecration of dearest Gerard's lychgate tomorrow. Jack still feels discomfort from his wounds but thank God is better than could have been expected.

11th Mr Southey most kind & indefatigable, indeed all are so. The Bishop of Dover performed the service & he & all the clergy & other & numerous friends met here afterwards for tea. I saw & knew many whom I had not met for a very long time & many whom I did not know. They said that all was beautifully done, quire & all & I think if dear Gerard had been present he would really have liked it. Many too of the poorer parishioners were there. He was so much liked & valued by all. Our large table in the dining room looked very nice & bright with jonquils etc. I hear that the lychgate is beautiful & Gussie has also erected a cross of white marble to his memory. Leo & Ella Gipps came for the ceremony, Bertha, May & Jack departed too in the evening. Mr Southey had arranged all so well that there was not a hitch in any way & dearest Mary & Mona looked quite worn out.

12th All The Cottage children at tea & feasting on the fragments of the cakes that were left.

23rd Mary went to Tunbridge Wells & Julia's two maids Eliza & Rose came from thence to see the lychgate to our dearest Gerard's memory which I drove to see yesterday. It is very beautiful & what he would have liked himself, but I agree with Mary in thinking that the green oak tiles (considering our old & venerable church) would look better of a darker & less conspicuous hue. It is long since I have driven out & the last time was with him. The two maids came to see me & spoke much of their devotion to him & how great was our loss. Later in the day came Frederic very feeble & deaf I grieve to say, but he & Lisa have made the pleasant arrangement to live ultimately with Miss Stewart *(Frederic's sister in law)* in Lexham Gardens.

24th Mary found Lolotte yesterday very poorly & suffering much from her back.

26th Leo departed & Kate came looking very well & plump.

The lychgate today

May 1st Garland children, a chair drive round the garden. Frederic came.

2nd A day of memories. The birth day in 1811 of my dear brother Louis. The marriage day of dear Uncle Gerard & Aunt Ella 1818 or 1817. The death day of dearest Edward. All these memories crowd upon me.

3rd Mrs Wykeham Martin came to see me. Photos & cake from Lewis Shaw & his bride. Gussie & children left for Tunbridge Wells. Dick & Stephen came to wish goodbye on going to school.

6th Dined downstairs. Mr Southey & Mrs Arbuthnot & later Lisa called. I grieve to find how very deaf Frederic has become. Gibson had been turfing Gerard's grave.

15th Mary & Mona started for London in view of a little shopping & the Royal Academy. Gussie kindly passed nearly the whole day with me.

17th Mr Southey at tea. Frederic came but was so deaf that he would not remain.

21st Mary's visit with Mona to the Union which occasioned much pleasure to givers & receivers.

23rd Mary in Maidstone & brought Hughes a very pretty little clock as this year she has lived with us 20 years.

27th Bank Holiday Monday, much noise & rushing of holiday folk. Mary & Mona went to see Harrietsham church.

28th Lisa paid me a visit. Frederic & she are off to London tomorrow to consult about his sad deafness.

June 12th Dearest Lolotte arrived to stay, better but easily tired. Leo here full of Gussie's business. Poor Frederic is deafer then ever. Gussie & little Bee called. Mrs Branfill Harrison died suddenly without pain. She was one of my oldest friends. Alas now they are almost all gone.

20th The children came to read. Mrs Arbuthnot at afternoon tea.

24th Mary, Mona & Hughes to the GFS fete at Boxley. Leo & Mona at Sittingbourne about a tricycle for Mary. Patricia came in with Frederic & Mrs Green.

July 4th Two days in bed with sharp rheumatism. Lolotte went yesterday to see the lychgate with which she is much pleased.

8th Lolotte is still here & we visit one another daily in our rooms & a great happiness it is.

10th The Hollingbourne school treat. Every one there. Frederic came with his ear trumpet, a great relief.

14th Lolotte as usual at tea in my room. It is delightful to see her better.

18th Mona all day at the Wormshill school treat for which she had a summons at 6.30 am & which went off very well & did not end till the shades of night. She enjoyed it much. Mary also went but for a short time.

19th Dearest Lolotte departed after a stay of five weeks & I rejoice to say much better. Mr Southey had kindly last Friday a short service for her in the church of her childhood & marriage. A few of the old & feeble of the village were also present.

20th In the dining room much of the afternoon & looking out with melancholy pleasure on the view & the trees which I had known for more than 60 years, changed & improved by time.

22nd Frederic came but no trumpet, so no talk.

23rd Mrs Hockin *(wife of the rector of Hucking)* came for Mona's singing lesson & stayed for luncheon. She talks much & is clever & original & finds the solitude of Hucking almost too great for her.

25th The rats have been very destructive of late to the chickens so a ferret was borrowed & Leo & Streeter went out with a gun but in vain. Ten chickens had disappeared

30th Gussie & Co returned home. Frederic came to see me & brought his trumpet I am glad to say. Mary & Bryan went to the Archaeological Society meeting at Leeds.

August 12th Lisa paid me a long visit to talk over their plans. Ella & Eleanor arrived to stay a few days.

26th Mrs Rowe at tea. Dr Rowe cannot leave Margate as he seems quite overwhelmed with his professional career & geological work. I gave her for him a photo of dearest Gerard.

28th Matilda Tennyson & Mr Southey at afternoon tea when he & Mona sang & Matilda was as bright & happy as age will allow. Sent her home to Park House, Mary escorting her with her maid. Poor old Lady! She is like myself very feeble.

September 2nd Mary left for St Leonards to stay with Lolotte.

3rd Mr Southey kindly drank tea in my little room & Gussie later for backgammon.

7th Mona at church & school all day except at dinner when I dined downstairs with her & Mr Southey. Patricia came in at 3 & Gussie at 6.30.

12th Mary returned from Heatherland I rejoice to say. A party of children from The Cottage for backgammon.

13th Mary & I had no end of talk together & I heard all her histories of everyone.

20th Mary & Mona took luncheon with the Miss Savages at Malling. I read & wrote & worked as usual & passed my day in my room. Children at backgammon in the evening.

26th Jack's (*Morgan*) marriage with Miss Locker Lampson announced, very satisfactory. Children here in morning for drawing yesterday. Leo & Mona left.

30th Frederic & Lisa came. A chair drive round the garden. Mrs Farmer came back with Hughes from Maidstone & left at 9. I was quite glad to see the poor little woman who was more cheerful than usual. Vera came to say goodbye.

October 1st Frederic came at 11 to say really 'Goodbye' & now he finally leaves Hollingbourne. I was truly grieved for his departure & I think he has been here 11 years! He has gone to his son Major G at Canterbury.

2nd The sale *(of some of Frederic's things)* at Godfrey House which seems to have been successful. Leo arrived & was there with Mary to bid. She bought several things, among others the old French clock which had a great interest for me.

9th Leo departed. Mary making visits. Mona returned looking very bright.

13th The church crowded all day at all the services (*harvest)* Mr Southey a victim to Neuralgia & 'the Rheumatics'. Leo came owing to the pressing needs of Gussie's Hill Farm.

17th Mary off early to Tunbridge Wells & Leo on his bicycle for Heatherland. A begging letter from poor 'hopeless & hapless' Mrs Minter. The children for drawing.

18th Mary returned last evening about 8, seeing little of Julia but much of Lolotte whom she found wonderfully better & brighter. She also saw Dr Rankin.

27th Mr Southey as usual at luncheon, full of the parish including Mrs Gibson.

30th A chair drive as far as Elnothington, a lovely day & a most refreshing excursion.

November 2nd Kate left & Leo too. Mrs Gibson has re-appeared on the scene. Laura & Ella came for drawing.

4th Lisa called. She is staying with Mrs d'Uphaugh. She says Frederic is well.

6th The sale at the farm on The Hill went well. It is now let to a new tenant. Gussie & the children to Brighton for a few days. Mona to assist at Mrs Hockin's Penny Reading at Hucking.

10th Mary went to stay night with Julia, a great void in the house. Children for drawing, Gussie for backgammon.

29th Bertha arrived, a joy to see her after a long time. No end of talking.

December 3rd Much of Bertha's society & talk over old times. Mrs Maxwell Spooner kindly came to talk on the opening of the <u>new</u> hall & for the Mothers meeting, which I hear she did with great success & so very well. She drank tea here afterwards as did Mr Southey & Gussie. It was a <u>very</u> great pleasure to me to see her again. It is so long since we have met.[235]

5th A village concert in Mr Southey's new hall. It was a great success I hear.

6th Dorothy Locker Lampson, Jacks fiancée came to take luncheon here & I am most pleased with my future grand-daughter. She is <u>very</u> nice & sensible & agreeable & has lovely eyes. The whole party departed at 3.30 after looking at

---

[235]   Rev Southey had paid for a hall to be erected close to the church in what is now the garden of Six Bells Cottage. It was demolished during the 1970s.

autographs & other treasures, & the house seems quite still & void.

7th Mona at the Union where she received as usual a warm welcome.

9th Magic Lantern 'A Record Reign' at Board School for which took tickets. Much approved by Mona, Miss Buck & the children. Mrs Hockin gave her music lesson.

11th Major & Mrs Goldsmid came. She is very nice & he much improved in every way. They do not give a very favourable report of Frederic who is still with them at Canterbury but meditating a change to London.

23rd Wrote the village dinner tickets for the 62nd time. Christmas cards sending & receiving, also letters, till I felt quite bewildered.

24th Most of the servants asking to go out tomorrow.

25th Mr Southey at luncheon. Visits from all the children & Gussie. Little home presents & cards given & received. Innumerable cards from all my grandchildren.

1902 January 1st Letters from Freddie in his distant home where he is subject to all sorts of inconvenience in his tent life. Mary found Julia very feeble.

6th I thought of my early Twelfth Days at Notting Hill when Uncle Gerard sat with the large cake before him distributing that & the wine to all the servants who stood round in a circle while Louis & I carried it to each. They also drew for their various characters. Now all so still & myself an old woman of nearly 92.

8th Mona gave a children's party at tea & later a game of 'Ping Pong'. It went off very well. Mr Southey was also present. Gussie played backgammon with me.

11th The children planning Christie Minstrels but without success, as Streeter, their factotum, objected to blacken his face. A parish meeting today on the subject of a (parish) nurse. Mary present of course.

13th Dick & Stephen disguised & singing as Ethiopian serenaders & taking round the mission box. The Ethiopians came to my room in the evening. Mona more busy if possible than ever.

14th Leo came to Mr Southey to be present at the school treat this evening & assist with the Magic Lantern. Dick & Stephen again disguised as Ethiopians & appeared at the school treat. Some of the children much frightened at them.

21st Ella (*Gipps*) arrived looking very bright & blooming. Mary & Mona at a Mothers Meeting.

23rd A meeting on the subject of a village nurse, Mary & Mona present. Mrs d'Uphaugh the great promoter.

24th Wrote to Jack to congratulate on his approaching marriage & enclosing a cheque for £20, my gift on the occasion.

February 6th Mrs & Miss Locker Lampson at lunch, I like them so very much. They are such good people that I think there is every prospect of happiness.

10th I am 92 today, & I am receiving no end of kind letters & little souvenirs.

12th Mona sang at Mrs Hockin's village party in Hucking. Stuart Morgan, Bertha's son, writes of going to Oriel. Backgammon with Leo. Just two years since my great sorrow. I can scarcely believe it & my usual life still going on.

March 10th Louy arrived at 6. Read & worked as usual during the day which was one of monotony. How can it be otherwise at 92?

12th Louy & I had much talk together. A card from Lewis Shaw to tell of the birth of a daughter.

17th Mary to Tunbridge Wells where she saw Lolotte & discussed much, also Julia.

25th Louy I grieve to say departed. The boys home from school. I took my first chair ride.

27th Kate came to stay looking very plump & well.

April 3rd Mary & Mona at the Mother's Meeting. A good chair drive, much pleasant gossip with Kate discussing old times & friends.

5th Mr Southey to Sunday luncheon & gave me sacrament. Backgammon with Kate. The dear Cottage children came to play their violins & sing. I much rejoice that they have such good ears & voices.

11th A tea party here, a very cheerful one. Kate left. Lolotte has found a comfortable lodging in Tunbridge Wells for Frederic & Lisa. Dick came to say goodbye before leaving for Harrow. I can only say God bless & keep him.

15th Out in my chair. Mary to London to meet Bertha. Mrs Green to tea.

May 2nd The repairs of the house & stable & painting & papering the Red Room in progress. Mrs Whatman called, I was very glad to see her after so many years.

13th Mary left at 11 for Effingham & Jack's marriage tomorrow with Miss Locker Lampson. Mona & I dined early together.

16th Mary returned home about 5 full of wedding news & details. What a good sermon was given by the Bishop of Kensington & how pleasant he was. How happy the bridegroom looked, how badly the bride's mother was dressed, how handsome Bertha looked in dark green satin & how the American envoy asked to be introduced to her in consequence. How abundant & beautiful were the presents & how numerous were the guests, 117 from London alone. Nine bridesmaids.

21st A concert when our children performed on the violin & were encored. There was also a wonderfully gifted little girl by name Nora Cordwell, nine years old who astonished everyone by her talent & precocity, the niece of Mr Arbuthnot's butler.

23rd Nora Cordwell came to see us with her mother, she played with wonderful talent & sang comic songs as well. Her eyes dark & fine & her manner most pleasant. Some day I think she will make a name.

25th A delightful chair drive & saw all the changes in the scullery & stable & also the new coach house.

June 2nd Peace declared, bells ringing wildly.[236] A lovely chair drive.

3rd Rejoicings everywhere. Mrs Green came. Mr Southey better & at tea, tho' doomed to Bovril & dry toast.

7th Matilda Tennyson to tea. Woodbyne thinks of becoming a professional artist. Sent a peace & coronation souvenir of money, to my children & grandchildren.

22nd Dearest Lolotte arrived. Terrible news about the King & his fearful operation![237]

25th Mary & Mona in London with Bertha to see all the wonders of preparation *(for the coronation)* all in the process of demolition.

July 5th The King continues to improve. The dentist came to see me. The 180 coronation mugs I had provided were given to the children at the board school, I had intended them for coronation day. Mrs Green called.

---

[236]   The end of the Boer War.

[237]   Edward had been diagnosed with appendicitis two days before his coronation. He was operated on, a procedure which then had a high mortality rate.

8th Lolotte & I visit each other on our sofas. Mr Southey came. Finished my cushion for Mary.

16th A tennis here, Gussie, Laura & Ella, May & Vera Morgan now staying at The Cottage. We had a tea party & then I retired to my room.

24th A concert arranged by Mrs Hockin for funds for a bier for Wormshill at which our children assisted.

August 1st Lolotte & I passed much time together as usual. Gave all the autographs to Mary.

3rd Lolotte in bed the greater part of the day & feeling very tired with her visit to the church & the Manor House yesterday. Gave Lolotte on Friday, for her life, my dearest Mother's French ear rings. They are of the finest French paste. I was with my Father when he bought them in Paris in 1827 or 1828.

5th Mary & Mona in London for the Soldiers & Sailors meeting in Langham Place opened by the Queen. Frederic & Lisa at tea. He sadly infirm & deaf.

8th Mona slept at Elnothington as Mrs Connop dreaded to be alone & her children & governess had gone to see the sights & wonders of the Coronation.

9th Almost everyone but ourselves in town. We stayed at home & 'illuminated' instead. Really the house was a sight with its lamps & banners & was seen for miles around. The village in a crowd gathered in the front meadow & sang & shouted for at least two hours.

13th Gave Hughes warning yesterday a great pain to me after 21 years. Today was our village celebration of The Coronation, sat with Lolotte at the front window on the landing to see the assembling of the village & the arrival of the band which took place about 2.30. The fete went off, dinner, tea & games as well as possible.

15th Lolotte with her handmaid Shepherd departed at 11, a great sorrow to me. And now everything, public & private seems so still.

18th The Shah passed through Hollingbourne, very slowly.

September 2nd Settled to take Streeter's sister in Hughes place. Everyone in Hollingbourne came to see the passing of 100 motor cars.[238] Very dull!

---

[238]   This was an Automobile Club trial of reliability. For several days over 100 cars left Crystal Palace & drove about 100 miles on set circular routes, not exceeding the legal speed limit of 12mph.

10th Leo & Richard *(Gipps)* came for day, had not seen Richard for nine years. He has become quite colonial & dark, is very tall & large & his voice seems to have changed. Ella & Eleanor arrived for a week's stay, delighted to see them looking so well & happy. Frederic & Lisa at luncheon. Ella saw all the progress of the parish, the changes in the church, the parish room & the vicarage.

19th Richard & Louis came to stay a few days. Backgammon with Richard. Mary to Tunbridge Wells. It is very sad to me to part with Hughes but was necessary. My new maid Streeter's sister, Wright, promises well.

October 21st A chair drive to see the greenhouse, a great success. A lovely day, the sun shining & the autumnal tints of earth & sky beautiful. A visit from Mrs Green.

26th Richard & Louis Gipps bicycled from Heatherland & slept here.

November 4th On Sunday Mona was as usual busy teaching & services all day. Mary to R.S.P.C.A. Meeting. Mr Southey to luncheon.

8th A visit from Gussie. Mrs Minter wrote that her husband has died & she is in great distress, sent her a sovereign.

15th Leo came on Gussie's affairs, played backgammon with him. Frederic is happy in his far-away flat in Hammersmith.

20th Mary to Tunbridge Wells. Cecil Maunsell came, an intense pleasure to see him after I should think 40 years. The son of my dearest old friend Dodo whom I knew & loved first as Theodosia Palmer. He is unfortunately ill-formed & small but very clever & agreeable & with a charming voice & reminding me much of his mother.

25th Bertha arrived after almost a year. Lots of talk. Fanny Riddell called she has become quite elderly, hair quite white but looks very well. She has taken a place with a lady in Wales as head gardener![239]

December 15th Richard & Louis arrived looking very well. A little dinner party was given by Mary consisting of Mr Southey, his nephew, Mona, Richard & Louis while I retired to bed.

19th Mona off to Maidstone with Richard & Louis, their last goodbye I should think before they leave for South Africa.

---

[239] Female gardeners were just starting to be socially acceptable. The first women gardeners were employed at Kew Gardens in 1896.

21st Hughes came to see me looking very bright & blooming. Lolotte arrived <u>unattended</u> from Tunbridge Wells to stay with us for a week. She is much better & indeed quite a different person. Mona is departing for her home.

25th Lolotte wonderfully well. Two brace of pheasants, two of partridges & lilies of the valley from Leeds Castle.

29th Dear Lolotte left at 12 for the train at Maidstone, Mary seeing her safe so far. She has I am thankful to say recovered wonderfully. Mona returned later & Mr Southey came before departing for Rome tomorrow. Then I had many visits from The Cottage children.

1903 January 1st No end of cards given & received. Kate has arrived. Mona has returned from Heatherland, Richard & Louis have sent me a pretty book stand. Poor Boys! I trust they will succeed. They are in great spirits.

3rd Yesterday a meeting of all The Cottage children in the afternoon in the drawing room. A very unusual gathering as they generally drop in separately.

5th Bertha gave a party by invitation to Mona & The Cottage children to Roland Gardens when she & Delmar took them to the Wild West. A great delight! Beginning at 9 from here & ending in about 12 hours later.

9th Stuart *(Bertha's son)* came to accompany Mona & Laura & Ella to a Ball.

10th Stephen *(Bertha's son)* came, Kate departed I am sorry to say. Stephen came with me in the drawing room & I showed him many of my old treasures.

12th The two Morgan boys sat with me in the morning & left in the afternoon.

27th I have tried to do the genealogy for Lewis Shaw but progress is <u>very</u> slow. I feel lame & rheumatic & more than stupid. Mary I grieve to say not quite herself.

28th Looked over my 'maternity box' for poor women & the clothes having been so long unneeded & unused, decided to give the contents between Mrs Hales & Mrs Baker neé Streeter.

February 10th My birthday. 93 today! What an age! How sad to think of the years I have lived, the time lost & misused & the little done! Mary poorly & unable to leave her bed as was her maid Annie. When a sudden & most unexpected tumult & all at once enter Bertha & her daughter Vera who, too, suddenly became so ill that she had to remain in bed all day. They both left in the evening.

15th Hughes appeared with a shawl to sell for a poor woman in need & her husband without work. I bought it for £2. Mary will find it a comfort when lying on the sofa.

March 5th More than a week has passed since I wrote my journal & I scarcely know how. Mary is I rejoice to say really better but she cannot yet leave the house & I am feeling very stupid. Richard & Louis have arrived in South Africa.

April 4th Louy, Mona, Laura & Ella to a concert in London & lunch with Bertha & Delmar. It is sad to think how fast the days go by & how little I do or remember.

May 26th A gap in my journal. Mary is in Tunbridge Wells. Ella Gipps is staying here as well as Mona & brightening the house & myself.

31st Yesterday was the day of the Club founded by my Husband before I came. They met as usual with their Band at our gate & I saw many old grey beards & heads that I had remembered in youth & strength so many years ago.

June 15th Mary returned from her stay with Lolotte & a great delight it was to see her again & so much better. She came last Thursday leaving Lolotte in good spirits & fairly well. But Willie is I grieve to say <u>very</u> ill with peritonitis & we are all in great trouble. Two doctors are attending him & he seems a shade better.

July 2nd Gussie came from Aynho last evening. Julia still in very uncertain state. Willie having undergone the operation seems, tho very weak, to be going on hopefully. Gussie, most unsettled & anxious came in to see me.

3rd A telegram from Southampton. All hope of dear Willie seems fading. At least the doctors give but little. Mona has gone to Southampton.

4th A telegram from Mona, his own doctor & a specialist give slightly more hope. Gussie off to Aynho early in consequence of another telegram.

6th Hopeless tidings of dearest Willie from Mona.

7th Yesterday Mrs George Goldsmid's baby was brought to see me by his nurse. A nice bright little boy with a look, I think, of Frederic. Dear Willie alive & sensible but <u>very</u> weak. He feels himself that he cannot live.

8th Willie as before & the doctors say hopeless.

12th Today the saddest of all as we scarcely think he will be alive tomorrow.

14th A letter from Mona telling that our dearest Willie has passed away most quietly. I cannot write more except how sad it all seems to us all. *(He was 39)*

15th Dearest Willie is to be buried quietly at Burwash.

16th Mona & The Cottagers made wreaths of white lilies & roses for the funeral.

17th Mona returned to my great joy.

18th Julia too is gone after gradually fading. The telegram came today.

23rd Leo came a few days ago & is just leaving & Ella *(Gipps)* came yesterday bringing little Henry, Willie's dear little boy. She & Leo have just left, leaving little Henry here. Julia's funeral is at Aynho today & Cottage Laura & Ella went there yesterday. Tizey Smith died a few days ago. Her mind was sadly failing. She is about the same age as myself.

29th Gussie & the children returned last Saturday from Aynho after attending their dear Aunt Julia's funeral. Dick & Stephen are home. Dear Willie's little boy is with us & gives much pleasure to the whole house.

August 3rd Mrs Green came full of discomfort in her own parish of Hucking where Mr Brown is a drinking vicar. It is difficult to say how he attained the living. Looked over old letters which made me sad, mostly from friends of my dear brother. Lewis Shaw has another daughter.

6th Mary to Tunbridge Wells & passed the day with Lolotte. Gussie went to the now empty desolate house at Tunbridge Wells, much of it to be her own.

11th Gussie returned. The school treat went off very well. Our manservant Austin gave notice to leave. He seems to have a promising opening as a builder.

14th Ella writes that Robert *(her husband)* can take nothing but liquids. Leo departed after seeing the house on The Hill bought by Mary & being built by Tong which seems to give great satisfaction. Mr Southey came, his engagement to Miss Wykeham Martin publicly announced.

20th The Cottage children in & out. Mary to see Lolotte. Jack Shaw came. A chair ride in the garden, delightful.

September 1st Jack seems dull & dispirited, he gives a bad report of his father who has paralysis of the throat & of his sister Florence.

3rd Frederic came to Hollingbourne for the day with Katie looking very well in her Clewer *(convent)* attire, it was a <u>great</u> pleasure to see him again.

4th A wagon load of things, books & furniture from Tunbridge Wells to The Cottage. Jack sitting & talking with me.

5th Leo & his fiancée *(& cousin)* Eleanor *(Shaw)* came & Jack Shaw left to 'try his fortune'. Letters from Richard & Louis in South Africa, Richard on a diamond mine.

8th Mary went with Leo & Eleanor to see <u>her</u> cottage at Broad Street now building & <u>their</u> future home. *(Mary is having the cottage built for her nephew and niece in the hamlet of Broad Street, Hollingbourne which lies on the Pilgrims Way)*

9th Kate came to stay looking very plump & well. Mary called at the Castle to congratulate but congratulations were decidedly not welcome.

13th Looked over many of the books from Julia. Saw Kate & heard her many little histories of old friends. A footman not to be heard of.

17th A letter from Ella, Robert has finally allowed himself to see a doctor.

18th Kate departed for Brighton & Windisham House with Stephen, the holidays being at an end.

21st My old friend Mrs Dolling died at Christ's Hospital Gravesend & her daughter Fanny hopes to succeed her there.

26th Mrs Green brought poor Fanny Dolling, very much aged & worn, & anxious about her mother's recent death & her own election. Leo is here & is naturally much pleased with all Mary's arrangements. Mr Southey brought his fiancée who is very nice & cheerful.

October 1st A poor man by name Day, killed yesterday. He was employed in moving luggage from the Manor House & was crushed by the wagon.

2nd Hughes came looking very blooming & told me of her engagement which seems a <u>very promising</u> one. Her fiancee is a widower, what she called a 'decorator' at Faversham.

12th Robert a shade better. Leo came; 'for good' & has a lodging in the village. Our new footman Albert, came. Dark, small & very well mannered.

30th Dearest Mary returned in the afternoon having had a very pleasant though quiet time with Lolotte. *(in Deal)*

31st A telegram telling of poor Robert Shaw who has passed away very quietly.

November 3rd Robert is to be buried at Cuxton in the Shaw vault, Leo is going to the funeral. Dearest Lolotte came looking well, & delightful it was to see her.

6th Matilda Tennyson called & I went downstairs to see her.

8th Mr & Mrs Deakin the new owners of the Manor House came to drink tea. He is American & very handsome & tall.

11th The Archbishop came for the confirmation & the dedication of the Vestry, organ chamber, organ & reredos after which he came here & met the neighbourhood. Our two rooms were brilliantly lighted & quite filled with many neighbours & old friends, among others General & Mrs Lester. It was most pleasant to me to see them especially the Primate who was at Harrow with dear Gerard & who ended by giving me his blessing. He had also known Edward well.

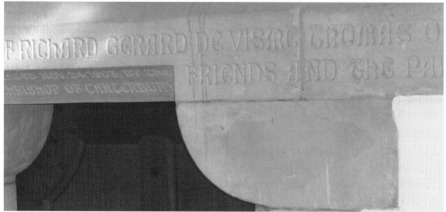

The vestry entrance with inscription in memory of Gerard

18th The engagement of Mr Southey & Miss Wykeham Martin at an end. Fraulein Engel the new German governess at The Cottage came to see me, very nice & agreeable.

December 7th A week almost gone since writing & I can scarcely believe it. A large quantity of game came from Leeds Castle, sent Frederic & Bertha each a pheasant.

19th All this blank in my journal & in my life for I seem to forget everything & all the days pass on & I seem fully occupied. Leo comes & goes & his cottage occupies him & makes progress. Bertha & her son Stephen have been here for a few days & a great delight it was to see them. He was fresh from America & is intent on becoming an engineer. Stuart has unfortunately failed at Oxford but has one more chance. I have written tickets for the Christmas dinners. This has been done annually since 1838 but they have latterly much diminished in number.

25th A very long blank in my journal. I feel so utterly dull & incapable, hopelessly so! But I will try to do better. Everyone but myself at church in turn. Cards & letters innumerable. Mr Southey is off to Rome on Tuesday.

1904 January 5th Leo came & has I believe taken up his abode at the 'Pilgrims Way', & last evening too the upper housemaid appeared, nice looking but tired with her journey, by name Florence.

6th Last evening Anderson the dentist appeared to see my teeth & after many discomforts & <u>little</u> operations but very disagreeable, departed. Today Mary, Mona & Leo full of business. Ella Gipps is to arrive today. The ladies came to see Cotuams & found it fuller of Gussie's furniture than they expected.

8th Mary gave warning to our boy footman Albert. He is constantly at the Sugar Loaves.*(pub)*

9th Leo & Ella full of business at the 'Pilgrims Way'. Mary at the 'Pilgrims Way' with Dick. She went to supervise the planting.

14th The dentist measured my mouth for some new teeth. I think I shall scarcely have one left of my old friends that have served me so many long years.

16th My teeth were taken to Maidstone & returned so that I am rather better.

19th Kate departed with little Stephen for Brighton & their school duties. Louy at the 'Pilgrims Way' & passed the day here. Mr Anderson came in the evening & brought me some wonderful teeth & they seem unusually comfortable & real.

23rd A visit from Lisa who seems well. Gussie also came for a longer visit than usual & next appeared Leo to say goodbye as a 'bachelor', Louy too came before leaving the 'Pilgrims Way'.

24th A flying visit from Mr Southey who took his early dinner here as usual, delighted with his Italian tour & all the better for it.

26th Mary off very early to Tunbridge Wells to pass the day with Lolotte who is fairly well. Mona kindly spent much time with me in the Red Room where I had taken refuge during the chimney sweeping & cleansing of my own. Mr Anderson here on the subject of my teeth. Mary returned about 6 thoroughly worn out.

27th A telegram from 'Mr & Mrs Leo Gipps', so the deed is done. Dick came to say goodbye before leaving for Harrow again. Church bells ringing almost all day.

28th Mary gave a dinner to Gussie & The Cottage children & Mr Southey to celebrate the wedding & I received visits at various times from the party.

February 2nd Our beautiful cat missing for two days. Gave 5/- to the Glee Club to begin under Mona's management.

10th The pleasure of Bertha's unexpected arrival on my birthday, I am 94. What an immense age! How much have I to be thankful for even with all my deep sorrows! The church bells rang this morning at 5.30. Letters from many of those dear to me.

11th Leo & Eleanor have arrived at the 'Pilgrims Way' & are delighted with their future home for which they have to thank dearest Mary.

12th The school treat at which Mary & Mona were present, Gussie kindly came to see me twice. Incessant & hard rain, most unfavourable to the school treat.

13th A visit from Leo & Eleanor on the summit of human happiness.

15th Wrote also to Stephen my little grandson at Windlesham House who had sent me a little Tunbridge Ware needle case as a birthday gift.[240]

19th Hughes came, she is to be married in June.

23rd Mr Southey brought the outlines of the figures for Mary's window & very beautiful they are. They are the figures she copied from those in the cathedral at Norwich; the Virgin, St Catherine & St Margaret. Wrote to Hughes with a cheque.

24th Mr Southey came & we discussed the window that Mary is giving to the church & which we both much approved & admired. Backgammon with Mary.

March 10th Mr Southey brought back his motor car from town.

15th A letter from Lolotte delighted with her house which is nearly finished & thanking for a little aid I had been able to give her. Leo & Eleanor dined here.

24th Edith the wife of my grandson Lewis Shaw came. She seems most gentle & unassuming.

30th Edith has departed. She is very nice, gentle, sensible & very long suffering.

April 4th The anniversary of dearest Gerard's birth. How many many years have passed since then! How many dearly

---

[240]   Windlesham House is still an eminent prep school in a an attractive mansion & spacious grounds in West Sussex.

loved have passed away! I, one of the oldest, am still left to tread the old rooms & look upon the old cedar, quite a small shrub when I came.

10th Mrs Young & Mrs Poore, the new inhabitants of Cotuams came to see me. Mrs Poore is a young widow. In the evening Hughes appeared looking blooming.

17th Mary's window is completed & I hear immensely admired.

19th The parish & this house full of stir & movement of all kinds on account of the dedication of the church window but in my little den I saw & heard but little of the commotion except that Laura & Bee from The Cottage took up their quarters here. Yesterday Dick & Stephen came to see the relics & minerals which I have given them. Mrs Green came as nice as ever & looking quite blooming.

Mary's window in Hollingbourne church in memory of Edward and Julia

20th The Canon & Mrs Medley at luncheon here & came up to see me afterwards. Mona went early to stay with Lolotte & returns tomorrow.

21st Mary took the Canon & Mrs Medley to Maidstone to see the fine old church of All Saints & their drive terminated with a visit & tea with Leo & Eleanor at the 'Pilgrims Way' where lately the skull & bones of a skeleton have been exhumed.

26th Ella Gipps & Kate Gibson arrived in the morning from Burwash to pass the day & later Ella came from Norfolk & our party was increased by Leo & Eleanor.

May 9th I have, sad to say, missed writing my journal for many a day & my memory I am fast losing. During the last week Mary was for two days at Tunbridge Wells with Lolotte & saw some horses one of which I have since bought. She found Lolotte rather better & her house really charming. She has built & arranged it all so sensibly & tastefully. Yesterday, Sunday, I had a visit from Gussie & all the children in turn & also from Mr Southey.

17th A delightful turn in the garden with Mona & yesterday with Mary.

24th Woodbyne has come & gone full of life, spirits & projects. She & her sisters as usual in London & their Father & Mother in their country home. Richard & Louis Gipps have left the Cape & returned to Australia.

27th In the morning I was in the garden escorted by my charioteer Gibson. All so very lovely & the more so to me who have been so long ontro le Quattro mura. Mary at the parish meeting & in Mr Southey's motor car.

28th The club as usual visiting in the road with band & banners, as they have done for more than 60 years on their return from church. Hadlow said that he had never missed dining with them during that time. I went to see them from the window.

June 2nd I feel 'good for nothing' but not ill. I write & read & play backgammon.

15th Today Gussie & the children leave for Eastbourne, all in high spirits except Gussie. Mary & Mona off with the Girls Friendly Society for their day holiday. So I have the house to myself & my ink & my ideas are so thick I can scarcely write.

25th Nearly a week & nothing alas written or done! A sad blank mind & body! I have however been twice in the garden

& enjoyed the flowers & the air & I have played backgammon with Mona in the evenings as usual.

July 4th My own little room here underwent its half yearly cleansing. Chimney swept & I was forced to take refuge in the Red Room. I have just purchased Lady Granville's letters, to me most interesting, for I made my debut at the embassy in Paris when she presided there & Lord Granville was our Ambassador.

8th Yesterday Milgate, the former servant at The Cottage came to see me, we talked much of old times & of 'the children', now no longer so, to whom she is much attached. The new horse much approved. A visit from Laura.

9th Gussie came but not looking well, having much liked her stay at Eastbourne.

12th Backgammon as usual in the evening. I felt as usual intensely stupid which need not have been recorded.

13th Fox, The Cottage nurse came to see me & very kindly brought me a little souvenir from Eastbourne, an oyster shell with a little <u>daub</u> of Beachy Head, all blue.

23rd Frederic appeared, he has swapped houses with Mrs Connop for a few days & later Lisa appeared. A great pleasure to see them.

August 2nd Mrs Rule neé Edmed, our earliest governess who lived here nine years, came to stay but was forced to leave after a day or two on account of her sister's illness. It was a great pleasure to see her after all these years.

6th In the evening came Miss Poore & brought some charming home views in water colour by herself, principally of her garden at Cotuams. We showed her my dearest Mother's drawings which she much admired.

8th Mary left for Tunbridge Wells in the dog cart driven by Streeter. Lillian came in.

13th I had the great pleasure of a visit from my old friend Mrs Balston & <u>very</u> well she was looking, tho' her hair had become quite <u>grey</u>, & as bright as ever.

15th A visit from Katie looking so very bright & well but I grieve to write, not giving much hope that Frederic will again come to Hollingbourne. He is so very feeble. *(Frederic died in 1908 and was buried in Hollingbourne churchyard. His memorial on the chancel wall draws attention to his "self-denying devotion to duty...his gentle courtesy and his charity to all men." Throughout his life he had put his great energy and talents to excellent use.)*

16th Accompanied & assisted by Mary & Mona, in the large carriage, I at last made my way to the church & saw all the many & wonderful changes. Indeed I cannot believe it, the bare & colourless & 'high-pewed' building I once knew, when walls & roof & windows were all one white. The windows interested me more than all, especially that copied & given by dearest Mary from the old frescos at Norwich Cathedral. There is also another window given by Mr Southey with the three saints, St George, St Michael & St Patrick, & a third in memory of her husband Major Pierson given by Lolotte. The reredos too given by Gussie to the memory of dearest Edward &, one of the greatest improvements, the new vestry room in memory of our dearest Gerard. I was quite bewildered & at the same time delighted with the many many changes. Then I drove to my old haunts in the Upper Village.

18th Mr Southey called to hear all I thought of the church & its changes which I found it <u>impossible</u> to express! I find myself becoming each day <u>more stupid</u> & my friends more kind.

19th Yesterday our former cook, Smith & her <u>nice</u> little baby girl came to see me she is now living in Hollingbourne. I was very glad, we have not met for many years.

22nd Mary had a tea party. Frederick, the hopelessly untidy & dirty manservant left on Saturday. A letter from dear Freddie Gipps announcing his appointment as manager of the stannery company which gives him £600 a year to be raised to £1000 later. I trust that all will go well but he does not come to England this year as we all expected. Wrote to him with congratulations.

September 6th Much has happened since I last wrote. Lolotte has arrived. She came unattended but two days ago her maid Shepherd arrived. Last evening Mr & Mrs Deakin drank tea here & today he took Mona out in his spacious motor car. Lolotte has been to see the changes & additions in the church, & 'the children' have been indulging in croquet & cricket.

10th Mary early in Maidstone & bought me some black wool as I mean to begin working again. Lolotte & I made return visits to & from the Red Room.

22nd Much has happened since I last wrote. Louy has been staying at the 'Pilgrims Way' & has twice been to see us. She departed yesterday.

23rd Lolotte & her maid departed for Deal. We shall miss her very much. Her presence is so cheering. I must be more regular in writing my uneventful biography for my memory, sad to say, diminishes daily.

25th A delightful long letter from Bertha in Scotland where she is staying with Jack & his wife, both so happy & arranging all so nicely at home & in their neighbourhood. The baby too is most nice & flourishing & all is couleur de rose & I trust is likely to remain so as they are doing so much good.

28th Smith our former cook, came to see me & brought her dear little baby girl. Gave her a doll & her brother a book.

29th Mary left early to join Lolotte. It will be most pleasant for both & I trust will do them good.

31st Drove with Mona 'over the hills & far away'. Saw the Pilgrims Way, the abode of Leo & Eleanor built by Mary on the ancient & famous road & though so near yet never seen by me. The air from the surrounding hills was delightful. Stopped at the vicarage on our way home. No one at home, but since I have seen it the increase of building & trees is wonderful & more wonderful still since the days of Mr Hasted.

October 18th My former maid Hughes came. She looked quite blooming. Wrote letters & sent cheques to my children & grandchildren.

November 2nd Mona left for her own home, & Leo came to talk business with Mary.

21st Bertha came looking very well & bright. She has been seeing all the villagers & all the changes in the village & cheering us all. There has been, as usual, not much going on but some of our neighbours have come in at tea & there was much in the church that she had not seen & yesterday, tho' Leo & Eleanor are absent, she visited 'Pilgrims Way'.

25th Bertha, I grieve to say departed, taking with her Bee to stay the night. It has been a more than usually pleasant week to me seeing my child & talking over her children & her life & friends & long past times. Now Jack is settled in Scotland & prospering with his wife & little boy as a civil engineer, & the daughters are as full of painting as ever.

December 17th I felt very dull & wrote the tickets for the Christmas dinner.

1905 February 9th Still my journal is sadly interrupted. I will endeavour to do better for the future. Today dearest Lolotte arrived, she has much improved in looks since we met, brighter & stronger.

10th My birthday & the church bells ringing at 5 this morning. From Louy a letter & flowers & from Gussie a very pretty letter rack. The church bells ringing again this evening.

11th This is the anniversary of dearest Edward's birthday. 'We were seven' like the children in Wordsworth's poem & now all gone from this earth but myself the eldest. Much pleasant time with Lolotte. Wrote to Ella.

March 2nd Our man servant Alfred who went out having he said the toothache & has not yet returned.

3rd A day of domestic disturbance. Our manservant who had been absent <u>without</u> leave & <u>with</u> the excuse of toothache, dismissed. A 'fair maiden' awaiting himself & his boxes on the style smoking a cigarette. Backgammon as usual.

5th Alfred Colman our former footman who is assisting in the house came to see me. He is now the village postman & his wife a dressmaker.

12th A whole week passed & my journal unwritten & my memory alas shorter & shorter day by day. Mrs Colman, Alfred's wife, came to see me. A nice pleasant woman & very well dressed of course as she is a dress maker.

13th A visit from Leo in trouble for his sheep have the rot & one of the maid servants has failed to keep her engagement & come.

14th Last evening Mr Southey came in, full of re-painting & papering his house for his near approaching marriage.

18th Mona returned from Bexhill & seems much refreshed with the change, she has sent & brought most picturesque postcards for my book.

28th How the time has passed I know not but between reading, writing & backgammon I find that it has flowed rapidly away. I have been twice breathing the delightful air & inhaling the delightful odours of the garden. I have written to Bertha on the subject of a wedding gift to Mr Southey, nothing very grand for his house is already full.

30th Delmar was thrown from his dog cart & brought home insensible.

April 3rd Telegrams yesterday & today to say that he remains still in the same state. Bertha has sent for Woodbyne & the others but the doctors still not hopeless.

27th *(Next entry)* There was a very successful village concert on Monday at which all our children including Mona were the successful performers. Major George Goldsmid also sang. Yesterday Louy passed the day here coming from the Pilgrims

Way where she is awaiting Eleanor's lingering event. We hear that Delmar is gradually improving though vcry slowly.

28th A much better report of Delmar who has been out. Tidings that a son is born to Leo & Eleanor. Doctors Hoare & Ground both in attendance.

May 21st Days & weeks have passed & not a word written. Instead of the London specialist Mary went to Dr Rankin & he says that her hand is not to be cut nor is she to have the discomfort of a stay in town but that she is to try the rubbing it with a remedy which he desired that she would persevere in using. The hand is, I rejoice to say, much better already. Without all the dreaded discomfort.

June 5th (*Next entry*) Mr Southey & his bride are home again after their wedding excursion. Leo's son christened, his name Leopold Henry. Bertha & Delmar have left Brighton & are at their country home. He is much better but still feels much the effects of his accident.

10th Mary & Mona in Maidstone. The former for shopping the latter for a music lesson. Mr & Mrs Southey have just called, but I did not see them, 'Madame n'est pas visible' & no one but myself at home. There has been almost constant rain lately, but now the sun is shining & the King of Spain, (who is just going), has scarcely had a bright day, though his reception has been brilliant.

This is the last journal entry Louisa ever wrote. So there we leave her sitting upstairs in her comfortable sitting room looking out over the sunny garden & still at the age of 95 taking an interest in the affairs of the world and of her family.

1910-1911: Reaching a century

On Louisa's hundredth birthday in February 1910, the flag was hoisted on the church tower and the bells peeled out at mid day and in the evening. A dinner was given for all the tenants and in the afternoon some 200 village school children and their mothers were entertained to tea in the Vicar's Hall, supervised by Mary and Mona. The children received sweets and oranges and the mothers a framed photo of Louisa each. The oldest and poorest villagers were given parcels of groceries and also coals. Meanwhile Louisa was enjoying a happy family gathering.

The photograph of Louisa aged 100 which was given to the villagers

Journalists from the 'Evening News' and 'Morning Post' arrived to interview Louisa, it being a rare thing then to reach a hundred. The 'Evening News' reporter found Louisa 'very gentle-mannered, refined and courteous with an old world air of dignity. She still enjoys life, thanks God for good health, eats well, and has no ailments. She is able to read and write without spectacles.'

Louisa wished to show the journalists her especial treasures so Mary then produced a beautiful fan said to have been painted by Watteau and to have belonged to Marie Antoinette, a gold and enamel watch studded with diamonds which once belonged to Madame Elizabeth sister of Louis XVII, as well as a beautifully illuminated Koran picked up in a Sikh camp during the battle of Gujerat by Louisa's old friend, Colonel Crawley.

The local reporter from the 'Kent Messenger' noted that Louisa was 'still able to charm her listener with interesting anecdotes and takes a lively interest in the news of the day.' He dwelt upon her interest in the history and antiquities of the county and was shown many sketches which preserve scenes now gone.

The article in the 'Kentish Express & Ashford News' dwelt upon Louisa's intellectual curiosity. 'All her life she has been a student, even now she likes to study dictionaries and is an expert on derivation of words. She is a linguist, a lover of art, a painter.'

In addition to Louisa's journals Bryan Gipps inherited a large bound volume of cuttings made by Mary on the occasion of Louisa's 100th birthday. It includes the telegram from the King sent by his private secretary Knollys, alongside ten other telegrams.

There are many, many letters of congratulations and press cuttings all carefully pasted into this album by Mary. A letter of congratulations from the Archbishop of Canterbury and one from the Huguenot Society of London. Letters came from children of old friends such as Mrs Treherne, Mrs Maunsell, and Mrs Riddell.

Her old friend Mrs Nutt the wife of the vicar of Harrietsham wrote – 'In our day at Harrietsham in the 1880s you were very much the best conversationalist in the neighbourhood, and a visit to you was a treat for our guests. Besides this you greatly brightened our lives by your kind attentions. What pleasant drives I have taken with you! I am afraid that a gulf has opened for you, between those bright days and now, since the loss of your gifted son, a worthy inheritor of your abilities and charm, and so good..'

An aged member of the Duppa family sent a rather barbed comment which Mary may have kept to herself: 'I remember your dear mother before her marriage – always a fascinating personality which could by no means be ignored.'

It rings true, for Louisa with all her talents and energy into her eighties must at times have left her companions tired out, if charmed.

Then there were several letters from ex-servants which movingly show the devotion which Louisa could inspire in those close to her. Her long-serving lady's maid Emily Hughes wrote:

'Dear Madam

I think of you often and can picture you in your comfortable little room with spring nosegay, where I have passed so many pleasant & profitable hours. You taught me so much and I shall always remember with gratitude your kindness and forbearance to me all through the years I was with you.'

Another came from from far off Winnipeg where lady's maid Short heard of the celebrations:

'Will you allow me as one of your former servants who spent a few happy years in your service to add my earnest congratulations? How often I have talked of you & those happy years.'

A third was written to Mary from Frances Parks a former housemaid.

'Dear Miss Thomas

Will you please excuse the great liberty I have taken in writing to you but in a Maidstone paper I had sent to me I read of a remarkable centenarian and found it to be my Dear Kind Mistress of long ago. Dear Miss Thomas I do not know which of the young ladies I used to know that I am addressing, but perhaps you will remember me Parks was my name then. Dear Miss Thomas will you give my duty to your dear Ma & my heartfelt congratulations. It seems so many years ago I lived at Eyhorne House the happiest 14 Years of my life was spent there. Dear Miss Thomas I was pleased to hear you have all your sisters living but sorry to hear of their great bereavements.'

She wrote a second letter:
'Dear Miss Thomas

Louisa's tombstone when new.

I am writing to thank you very much for your kind letter & for the photograph of Dear Mrs Thomas it is beautiful. I shall prize and value it as long as I live. I have already had it hung up where I can see her as I sit and think of them happy days

413

gone by..God bless you Miss Mary for your life of love and devotion..it is 46 years since I left Mrs Thomas.'

Louisa died a year later in 1911 at the age of 101. The vicar of Hollingbourne was then the Rev. Herbert Jones and he wrote her obituary in the parish magazine.

'On Saturday February 18th Mrs Thomas passed peacefully away. She appeared well and as bright as usual to within a few hours of her death. There was no illness... "It was just that her day was ended & so she went to sleep". She will be very much missed in Hollingbourne for tho for some years she was unable to get about yet her interest never ceased in the people amongst whom she dwelt and nothing gave her greater pleasure than to help those who needed help and to endeavour to make the lives of all a little brighter. She loved Hollingbourne and Hollingbourne was proud of her and loved her too. May her soul rest in peace with Christ in Paradise'.

Louisa's will made Mary and grandson Leo Gipps her executors. Everything was to be divided equally between her daughters. Lisa Goldsmid was to have £100, Gibson the gardener £50 and William Streeter the coachman £30. There was £5 each for all the other servants.

Mary lived out her days at Eyhorne House looked after by Mona who never married either. Eyhorne House itself, remained with the family until 1945 when it was sold. Sadly it was then allowed to become derelict and was condemned for demolition in 1976. Its grounds have disappeared under the workings for the Channel Tunnel rail link.

When people die all living memory of them eventually ceases. But the words Louisa wrote are here and through them we rediscover the person, we hear her voice. Louisa was born with good health, charm, intellect and the privilege of wealth. She was much loved. It has been a joy and a privilege to read her journals. There was a sadness at finishing and no longer turning the pages of the volumes which she had handled and in which she had so assiduously recorded the events of her life. A sadness in no longer hearing her voice in my ear.

Timeline

Some national events mentioned in the journals are included in bold

1810 Louisa born Louisa Goldsmid
1829 Papa left the family
1837 Queen Victoria crowned
1838 Louisa married Richard Thomas
1840 Ella born
1840 start of Penny Post throughout Britain
1843 Louy born
1844 Bertha born
1846 Mary born
1848 Gerard born
1849 Lolotte born
1850 Death of Sir Robert Peel
1851 Opening of the Crystal Palace
1853 Papa died in Waterloo town America
1863 Mama died
1864 Aunt Ella died
1866 Atlantic telegraph laid
1868 Uncle Go died
1869 Lolotte married Harry Pierson
1870 Franco-Prussian war
1873 Louisa visited Ostend to see Milly
1873 Bertha married Delmar Morgan
1876 Gerard travelled to Sweden, Russia & Germany
1876 Lolotte & Harry set off for Aden & India
1877 Gerard appointed Sir Frederick's private secretary in Paris
1878 Mary & Gerard to Paris
1880 Gerard married Gussie Cartwright
1881 Milly, Richard, and Harry Pierson died
1882 Assasination of Lord Frederick Cavendish in Dublin
1882 Opening of the railway station in Hollingbourne
1882 Louisa visited Paris
1883 Parcel post began
1885 Fall of Khartoum
1889 Louis died
1893 Nancy Gipps, wife of grandson Willie died in childbirth
1897 Cousin Edward Goulburn died

1898 Death of Gladstone
1899 Willie Gipps married Grace Money
1899 Boer War begins
1900 Gerard & Louisa's grandson Edward Morgan died
1901 Queen Victoria died
1903 Willie Gipps & Louisa's son in law Robert Shaw died
1904 Grandson Leo Gipps married his cousin Eleanor Shaw
1910 Louisa celebrated her 100th birthday
1911 Louisa died aged 101